cht n ankh

"tree of life"

Sema Institute/Cruzian Mystic Books

P.O.Box 570459
Miami, Florida, 33257
(305) 378-6253 Fax: (305) 378-6253

First U.S. edition © 2007 By Reginald Muata Ashby

The author is available for group lectures and individual counseling. For further information contact the publisher.

Ashby, Muata
The Kemetic Tree of Life
ISBN: 1-884564-74-7

Library of Congress Cataloging in Publication Data

Other books by Muata Ashby

See catalog in the back section for more listings

Biography of Dr. Muata Ashby

Mr. Ashby began studies in the area of religion and philosophy and achieved a doctorate degree in these areas while at the same time he began to collect his research into what would later become several books on the subject of the African History, religion and ethics, world mythology, origins of Yoga Philosophy and practice in ancient Africa (Ancient Egypt/Nubia) and also the origins of Christianity in Ancient Egypt. This was the catalyst for a successful book series on the subject called "Egyptian Yoga" begun in 1994. He has extensively studied mystical religious traditions from around the world and is an accomplished lecturer, musician, artist, poet, painter, screenwriter, playwright and author of over 40 books on yoga philosophy, religious philosophy and social philosophy based on ancient African principles. A leading advocate of the concept of the existence of advanced social and religious philosophy in ancient Africa comparable to the Eastern traditions such as Vedanta, Buddhism, Confucianism and Taoism, he has lectured and written extensively on the correlations of these with ancient African religion and philosophy.

Muata Abhaya Ashby holds a Doctor of Divinity Degree and a Masters degree in Liberal Arts and Religious Studies. He is also a Teacher of Yoga Philosophy and Discipline. Dr. Ashby is an adjunct professor at the American Institute of Holistic Theology and worked as an adjunct professor at the Florida International University.

Dr. Ashby has been an independent researcher and practitioner of Egyptian Yoga, Indian Yoga, Chinese Yoga, Buddhism and mystical psychology as well as Christian Mysticism. Dr. Ashby has engaged in Post Graduate research in advanced Jnana, Bhakti and Kundalini Yogas at the Yoga Research Foundation.

Since 1999 he has researched Ancient Egyptian musical theory and created a series of musical compositions which explore this unique area of music from ancient Africa and its connection to world music. Dr. Ashby has lectured around the United States of America, Europe and Africa.

Through his studies of the teachings of the great philosophers of the world and meeting with and studying under spiritual masters and having practiced advanced meditative disciplines, Dr. Ashby began to function in the capacity of Sebai or Spiritual Preceptor of Shetaut Neter, Ancient Egyptian Religion and also as Ethics Philosopher and Religious Studies instructor. Thus his title is Sebai and the acronym of his Kemetic and western names is MAA. He believes that it is important to understand all religious teachings in the context of human historical, cultural and social development in order to promote greater understanding and the advancement of humanity.

Table of Contents

Table of Figures

Table of Diagrams

Table of Tables

Table of Plates

 Companion Volume: The following book is recommended as a companion volume for the study of the Tree of Life of Anunian Theurgy.

African Religion VOL. 1- ANUNIAN THEOLOGY THE MYSTERIES OF RA, by Muata Ashby, ISBN: 1-884564-38-0

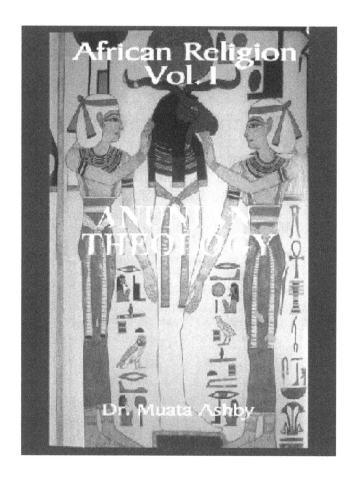

African Religion VOL. 1- ANUNIAN THEOLOGY THE MYSTERIES OF RA The Philosophy of Anu and The Mystical Teachings of The Ancient Egyptian Creation Myth Discover the mystical teachings contained in the Creation Myth and the gods and goddesses who brought creation and human beings into existence. The Creation myth of Anu is the source of Anunian Theology but also of the other main theological systems of Ancient Egypt that also influenced other world religions including Christianity, Hinduism and Buddhism. The Creation Myth holds the key to understanding the universe and for attaining spiritual Enlightenment. ISBN: 1-884564-38-0 $19.95

Preface: The Ancient Egyptian Origin and Mystery of the Spiritual Tree

The concept and iconography of the tree as a spiritual symbol and or metaphor has been used from time immemorial throughout human history. Most people, in modern times, have become familiar with the concept of the "Tree of Life" through a system of spirituality called Kabbalah. However, the idea of having direct access to God through special knowledge, in Kabbalism, was already evident in the teachings of the Ancient Egyptians, the Christian Mystics (Gnostics), the Hindus and the Buddhists who all came long before the Kabbalists. In Ancient Egypt, however, the teaching of the Tree of Life took on a special meaning. In its earliest form, originated in Ancient Egypt, it was related to theurgical religious system developed in the Ancient Egyptian city of Anu and the tree was seen as the source of life, and it was the Goddess, as the divinity being worshipped, who extended the nectar of life itself through the tree (see below). This idea, of a nectar of life, is also evident in the special Bodhi tree of Buddha and the Tree of Life in the Garden of Eden, which is also, according to some Christian traditions, known as the tree upon which Jesus was crucified. Also, the cross of Jesus is often referred to as a Tree of Life. In present day practice, the Christmas tree was originally supposed to be a manifestation of the same idea. The star at the top of the Christmas tree was supposed to symbolize the attainment of Cosmic (Christ) Consciousness.

In Ancient Egyptian Spirituality there is a concept called [hieroglyphs] *chet-n-ankh* – "Chet-n-ankh" means "staff of life" – "foodstuff from wood" –"vegetation," "sustenance from the tree," etc. It relates to the physical sustenance that is derived from plants and trees and the mysteries of the tree goddess who provides astral sustenance. It is also related to the Djed pillar of Asar[1] which is symbolized by a tree trunk. The Djed pillar is made out of wood and contains Asar's body, which when planted in the ground, brings forth food crops but which also represents the spiritual and mystical essence of a human being and of God.

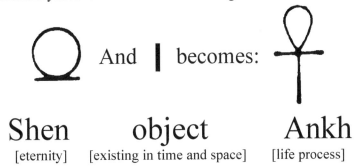

Shen	object	Ankh
[eternity]	[existing in time and space]	[life process]

The Ancient Egyptian Ankh ♀ is composed of two hieroglyphic symbols. The top of the ankh hieroglyph is called ◡ *Shen* and it means eternity. It is composed of a rope that has been formed into a circle and knotted at the bottom. The other glyph is a vertical line ❙ which is a determinative glyph that means object, as in the objects that exist in time and space. So this combination of eternity, which is derived from the Spirit, and the objects of time and space, which are finite, ephemeral and limited, produces a "life process" which we know as mortal existence on earth.

---

[1] For more on the mysticism of the Djed see the books *The Ancient Egyptian Book of the Dead* and *Serpent Power* by Muata Ashby.

Worship of the Tree Goddess in Ancient Egypt. The Tree Goddess Motif is Fundamental in the Art of the Ancient Egyptians.

Figure 1: right: Worship of the life sustaining tree goddess, Papyrus of Ani, Ancient Egypt, Africa.

In Kamitan (Ancient Egyptian) myth, the tree is a life sustaining and enlightening source, and the tree goddess is the divinity (Goddess) of wisdom who lives in the tree and extends its bounty to the spiritual aspirant. Thus, the tree goddess motif is fundamental in Ancient Egyptian iconography. It symbolizes the Goddess in general, but the goddesses Nut and Hetheru in particular, as the compassionate, life-giving female Divine Essence. The goddess sustains as a mother looking after her children, nurturing them with physical and spiritual sustenance, and when their time is up on earth she reaches down and lifts them up to the heavens.

In Kamitan myth the tree goddess in the form of goddess Nut treats all human beings as she did her son Asar in ancient times. As she lifted him up following his resurrection, so too she treats all human beings as though all human beings are Asar, incarnated souls who will one day return to the source from whence they came, in the sky, the heavens.

Figure 2: A- The Ancient Egyptian Tree of Life of the Goddess, B- Christian Tree of Life. C-Buddhist Tree of Life, D- Christian Christmas tree. E- The Caduceus of Djehuti (Hermes), F- The Psycho-spiritual Energy Centers of Serpent Power Yoga in Ancient Egypt and India.

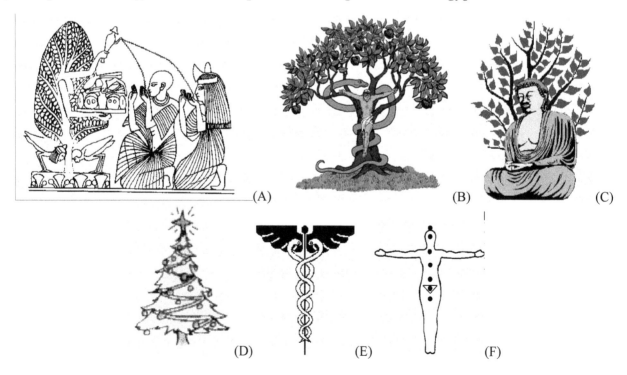

The Ancient Egyptian Mystical Tree and the Implications of the Pillar of Asar

The *Djed* pillar[2], is associated with the Ancient Egyptian Gods Asar, as well as Ptah. It is part of a profound mystical teaching that encompasses the mystical Life Force energy that engenders the universe. It is the driving force that sustains all life and impels human beings to action. In the Asarian Resurrection myth[3], it is written that when Asar was killed by his brother Set, his body was thrown into the Nile and it came ashore on the banks of Syria. There it grew into a tree with such a wonderful fragrant aroma that the king of Syria had it cut into a pillar for his palace. The pillar of Asar-Ptah, made from an Acasia tree, is a mystical reference to the human vertebrae and the Serpent Power or Life Force energy which exists in the subtle spine of every human being. It refers to the four highest states of mystical psycho-spiritual consciousness in a human being, with the uppermost tier symbolizing ultimate spiritual enlightenment wherein one discovers one's higher identity as one with the Supreme Being (the Mystical spiritual movement). Also, the Djed refers to the special realm of the Duat (astral Plane) wherein Asar, symbolizing the spiritual resurrection, can be discovered.

Figure 3: Below- The Divine Tree grows from the coffin of Asar (A), The tree is cut down to make a pillar (B), Examples of the Asarian Djed (C), the Tree of Life which is the body of Asar Himself (D).

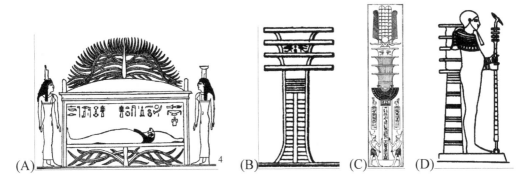

(A)   4   (B)   (C)   (D)

The Duat or Ancient Egyptian concept of the *Netherworld* is a special place of existence. This is the abode of Asar-Ptah as well as the ultimate destination of those who become spiritually enlightened. It is the realm of Supreme Peace. It is known as *Sekhet-Aaru* or in other times *AmenDjed*. AmenDjed is a reference which unites the symbolism of the Ancient Egyptian deities Asar and Ptah with the diety Amun, thus relating these three deities of Ancient Egypt into a singular essence (and dispelling the notion of polytheism). This underlying non-dualist monotheism is an important tantric theme. The Djed symbolizes the awakened human soul that is well "established" or "steadfast" or "stable" in the knowledge of the Self, that is, enlightened. The Ancient Egyptian word *Djeddu*, refers to the abode of Asar within the Duat, "steadfastness" or "stability," as well as to the pillar of *Asar*. In mystical terms it refers to being firmly established in the Netherworld. The idea is to become steadfast and upright as a tree (vertical), as opposed to unstable and falling over horizontally as the dead, in order to reach up to unite the earth and the sky, thus destroying (in the form of transcending) duality. Djeddu thus means having the knowledge of what is below and above and transcending both, thereby attaining the goal of Mysticism, to transcend duality and become one with all. This concept of "steadfastness" as the essence of a human being is being referred to in the following line from the *Egyptian Ru Pert Em Heru*, Rau (Chapter) I:

---

[2] For more on the mysticism of the Djed see the books *The Ancient Egyptian Book of the Dead* and *Serpent Power* by the author of this book.

[3] See the book *African Religion Vol. 4 Asarian Theology* by Dr. Muata Ashby

[4] See the book *African Religion Vol. 4 Asarian Theology* by Dr. Muata Ashby

nuk Djedi, se Djedi au am-a em Djeddu Mesi - a em Djeddu
"I am Djedy (steadfast), child of Djedy (steadfast),
conceived and born in the region of *Djeddu* (steadfastness)."

The Ancient Egyptian concept of creation includes three realms. These are the TA, ⚊⚊ 𝕀𝕀 (Earth), Pet, ⬠□◠ (Heaven), and the Duat ★🐍□ ⤳⌐ (the Netherworld). Ta is the gross physical plane. Pet is The Duat is the abode of the gods, goddesses, spirits and souls. It is the plane of thoughts, the subtle nature devoid of gross physicality. It is the realm where those who are evil or unrighteous are punished (Hell), but it is also where the righteous live in happiness (Heaven). It is the "other world," the spirit realm. The Duat is also known as Amenta since it is the realm of Amen (Amun, The Hidden Supreme Being). The Duat is the realm where Ra, as symbolized by the sun, traverses after reaching the western horizon, in other words, the movement of Ra between sunset and sunrise, that is, at night. Some people thought that the Duat was under the earth since they saw Ra traverse downward and around the earth and emerged in the east; however, this interpretation is the understanding of the uninitiated masses. The esoteric wisdom about the Duat is that it is the realm of the unconscious human mind and the astral plane.

Foreword

This book is about the Ancient Egyptian concept of the Tree divinity and the unique philosophy of a Tree of Life spiritual system for promoting spiritual evolution to enable human beings to attain spiritual enlightenment. We need to clarify that the Tree of Life that is the subject of this book is from the Ancient Egyptian Religion, and is not associated with Judaism or the Kabbalah. Rather, there is some evidence that these religious systems may have taken some elements from the Ancient Egyptian tradition of Anunian [from the city Anu] Theurgy in order to develop their religious systems. Theurgy as used here refers to the practices of Ancient Egyptian religion, including its *Sebait* (Philosophy), priestly disciplines, rituals, wisdom teachings, metaphysics, hieroglyphic texts, and architecture related to the process of Shetaut Neter (Hidden Mysteries {Ancient Egyptian Religion}). Anunian Theurgy emerged at least 4,000 years before the supposed date of the existence of Abraham, the reputed founder of Judaism, and at least 4,500 years prior to the earliest evidence of the earliest known texts of the Jewish Bible. Therefore, the Tree of Life of Anunian Theurgy is a far more ancient teaching and offers insights into the nature of Tree of Life mythology for all mythologists, metaphysicians, and religious studies proponents.

Due to the factor of the greater notoriety about the Kabbalistic Tree of life it has been thought useful to add a further section discussing the concepts of the Kabbalistic tradition based on the Jewish teachings and a brief comparative look at it and the Ancient Egyptian teaching for those who have some familiarity with the Jewish system. In this way the rest of this book, which details the Kemetic tradition of a Tree of Life spiritual system exclusively, will be more delineated and the special unique insights in it will be clearer to distinguish and easier to understand.

Kabbalism, Ancient Egypt and the Mysticism of the Tree of Life

The *Kabbala* (also *Cabalah*) is regarded as a form of Jewish mysticism which is officially said to have originated in the 12th century (C.E.). This date closely followed the crusades and it is possible that the opening up of European society, due to the foreign wars, allowed the stagnant living conditions of the Dark and Middle Ages in Europe to give way to a more mystical interpretation of the Jewish scriptures. Kabbalism is considered a way of approaching God directly as opposed to through the Temple. The concept was that through the acquisition of special hidden and secret knowledge of divine revelation, an aspirant can achieve divine communion. The major text on Kabbalism of the time was the "Book of Brightness," which came out in the 12th century C.E. This book contained ideas about the transmigration of souls and other ideas that were alien to orthodox Judaism. Echoing the Ancient Egyptian mystics, the Kabbalists expressed a great interest in mysticism and cosmology. Kabbalists believe that the Jewish scripture, the Torah, contains the knowledge of all Creation if every word is interpreted according to precise fixed principles, and that meditation upon these would lead to a state of mind wherein the meditator would attain cosmic vision of the Divine Self. Kabbalism also contained elements of messianism and was later influenced by *Hasidism*.

Hasidism is a partly mystical movement within Judaism. It first appeared sometime during the 18th century A.C.E. in Poland. Partly revivalistic and partly reformist, it is considered as a reaction against the rigid and legalistic Jewish orthodoxy. It was founded by Israel ben Eliezer. Like the philosophy of the Kabbalist, he emphasized direct communion with God and awareness of His presence in all creation. In Hasidism, worship is a part of all the ordinary activities of a person's daily life. In Hasidism, the tzaddikim, leaders of Hasidic communities, are viewed as intermediaries between the people and God.

The Mysticism of the Ancient Egyptian Pautti and Its Relation to the Sefirotic Tree of Life of the Kabbalah

The exposition of the *Anunian Tree of Life* in the Shetaut Neter (Ancient Egyptian Religion) expresses the understanding of Creation as an emanation from that which is subtle (the spirit) to that which is gross (the earth). A brief overview of the Ancient Egyptian Pautti or Company of Gods and Goddesses of Creation provides insights into deeper teachings that may be intimated in the Kabbalistic tree mysticism. The Kabbalistic text, the Sefer Yezirah, is a scripture of cosmology and cosmogony that attempts to explain the nature, structure and substance of Creation. The Ancient Egyptian Creation myth explains the nature of Creation as a scripture of cosmology and cosmogony. The extraordinary feature about the Ancient Egyptian Creation myth is that it achieves the teaching, not through the use of abstract spheres as in Cabbalism, but through abstract and anthropomorphic, as well as composite anthropomorphic-zoomorphic, realms governed by the *Neteru,* Cosmic Forces symbolized as god and goddess principles. These Neteru represent the natural forces, but also the energies that go to compose the human personality, thus allowing a practitioner to connect from the human to the divine and beyond. In addition to the Neterian realms, the system includes the Spheres of the Psycho-spiritual consciousness centers of the Serpent Power (known as chakras and Kundalini, respectively, in Indian mysticism).

Neterian (Shetaut Neter, Ancient Egyptian spirituality related to the gods and goddesses) Religion expressed the tree concept of the creation of the universe and the human personality through a Creation Myth. Neterianism puts forth three important Creation myths. One creation myth was developed in the Ancient Egyptian city of Anu, the other in the Ancient Egyptian city of Menefer and the other in the Ancient Egyptian city of Waset. The Mysteries of the Ancient Egyptian city of Anu from around 5,000 B.C.E. are considered to be the oldest exposition of the Ancient Egyptian teachings of Creation. They formed a foundation for the unfoldment of the teachings of mystical spirituality which followed in the mysteries of the city of *Men-nefer* through the god Ptah, and the Mysteries of *Newt (Waset or Thebes)*, through the god Amun.

The process of creation is explained in the form of a cosmological system for better understanding. Cosmology is a branch of philosophy dealing with the origin, processes, and structure of the universe. Cosmogony is the astrophysical study of the creation and evolution of the universe. Both of these disciplines are inherent facets of Ancient Egyptian philosophy through the main religious systems or *Pautti*– Companies of the gods and goddesses. A *Pautti* or Company of gods and goddesses is a group of deities, each of whom symbolizes a particular cosmic force or principle which emanates from the all-encompassing Supreme Being, from which they have emerged. They also represent cosmic laws of nature. The Self or Supreme Being manifests creation through the properties and principles represented by the *Pautti*. The system or Company of gods and goddesses of Anu is regarded as the oldest, and forms the basis of the Asarian (Greek term: Osirian) Trinity (Asar {Osiris}, Aset {Isis}, Heru {Horus}).

Since the Jewish Bible states that its patriarch, Moses, was knowledgeable in the teachings of the priesthood of Ancient Egypt, it is plausible that the relations between the early Jews and the Priests of Anu influenced the development of Judaism in the time period of the first millennium B.C.E. [the years 800 B.C.E. to 300 B.C.E.]. Thus, it would be no surprise if there were several fundamental principles in Judaism, and consequently Kabbalism, that would correlate to the Anunian doctrines of religious practice. But we may note here that the period of the early interaction during the formative years of Judaism is more than 1,500 years before the formation of the first Kabbalistic texts. However, Ancient Egyptian religion was still in practice until the Orthodox Christian religion, under the direction of the Catholic emperor Flavius Theodosius (347 C.E.–395 C.E.), decreed that all non-Christian religions should be stopped by force and proceeded to carry out that decree. One example of a correlation of the practices of Ancient Egypt that Judaism also adheres to is the practice of the daily worship routine. Anunian Theurgy prescribes that there should be a three-fold worship performed daily (dawn, noon and dusk) by the initiates. This is a metaphysical discipline related to Ra, (symbolized by the sun) in his three phases: Creator (morning sun), Sustainer (noonday sun) and Dissolver of the world (setting sun). So too the Jewish worshiper is admonished to perform a daily three-fold worship program.

The Kabbalistic Mysticism of the Tree

As in the Ancient Egyptian Mysticism related to the Pillar of Asar (see pictures below), the discovery of the *Sefirotic Tree of Life* (see picture below) in the Kabbala is seen as the ultimate goal of life. The symbolism of the Kabbalistic Tree of Life is to be understood as a mystic but complicated code, requiring advanced intellectual capacities in order to be understood, which holds the symbolism for the understanding of God and Creation, as well as a mystic map showing the path to spiritual enlightenment. There are many who have approached the study of the Kabbalah who have found the highly intellectual emphasis of its teaching to be arduous or even perplexing, convoluted, and even abstruse. The Sefirotic Tree of Life consists of ten spiritual centers or Sefirofs which emanate from the Divine Self, God. These centers represent spiritual as well as psychological principles that need to be understood and mastered by the Kabbalistic aspirant in order to attain spiritual enlightenment (at the top of the tree). It relates to the mystic symbolism of climbing up to heaven.

In the Zohar text of Kabbalism, it reads: "The Tree of Life extends from above downwards, and is the sun, which illuminates all." Similarly, in the Bhagavad-Gita of India (c.500 B.C.E.), the tree is used as a metaphor symbolizing that the world is not the source of its own existence, but that indeed the Spirit is the source of Creation.

1. The Blessed Lord said: The scriptures speak of the imperishable Ashwattha tree (of the world-process) with its roots above and branches below; the Vedic verses constitute its leaves.
He who knows this Tree is the knower of the essence of the Vedas.

Gita: Chapter 15
Purushottam Yogah-The Yoga of the Supreme Spirit

The philosophy of Kabbalism holds that the right side of the tree represents light and good and that the left side represents darkness or evil. This understanding is reminiscent of the Zoroastrian philosophy, which influenced early Judaism. Like Neberdjer of Ancient Egypt and Brahman of India, Kabbalism views God as Absolute and transcendental, *En-sof* (the infinite). Yet some have judged the Neterian conception of the Tree of Life teaching as no less intellectual and advanced but more humanistic and more accessible. Being grounded in a more personal, human psychology and feeling, combined with abstract cosmic anthropomorphic symbolisms, its wisdom teaching offers lucid erudite philosophy without complicated, burdensome, overly fastidious, eruditeness in which every teaching is seen as a hypercritical point requiring over-scrupulous, painstaking, and rigorous memorization.

The Sefirot (spheres) of Kabbalh are seen as attributes of God. As a human being develops these attributes they become Godlike and therefore, Divine. The spheres have been compared to Ancient Egyptian Serpent Power mysticism (Sefech Ba Ra) and the Chakras of Indian Kundalini Yoga. The meditations on these centers produce a similar mystical movement of energy (light and heat) in the subtle body of a human being, which leads to greater experience of the Divine. When this form of ecstasy occurs, it is called *shefa (divine influx)*. In contrast to the Serpent Power-system of Ancient Egypt, it is seen as an energy that comes into the body rather than lying dormant within it. As a human being masters the psycho-spiritual principle of the center, he or she is able to move closer to the infinite. *Malkuth* represents the physical body, *Yesod* represents the *heart*, *Hod* represents the *Glory*, *Netzach* represents the *Victory*, *Tipthereth* represents the *Intellect*, *Geburah* represents the *Force*, *Chesed* represents the *Mercy*, *Binah* represents the *Wisdom*, *Chokmah* represents the *Light*, and Kether represents the *spirit* and *humility*. The lower seven spheres have, by some Kabbalistic philosophers, been related to the seven psycho-spiritual consciousness energy of the subtle spine (Serpent Power, Kundalini Yoga). The three upper spheres are explained as mystical steps towards unity with God. Thus, through meditation and contemplation on the tree, an aspirant climbs up through the principles of life and Creation.

The *Sefer Yezirah* or Kabbalistic "Book of Creation" says that God created the universe through thirty-two paths of wisdom. These are represented by the ten Sephirot and the twenty-two letters of the Hebrew alphabet.

The Sephirot originally represented numbers and later came to be interpreted as emanations from which all existence originates and has its basis.

Kamitan Mysticism of the Tree: The Psycho-spiritual Journey Through The Principles of Creation.

First, we will begin with an introduction to Ancient Egyptian culture, history and religion. Then we will proceed to discuss the Tree of Life aspect of Anunian Theurgy, which is the earliest aspect (tradition) of Ancient Egyptian religion. This aspect of the teaching of Anunian Theurgy is treated in detail in this current lecture series on the Tree of Life of Ancient Egypt. According to the teachings of Kamitan Mysticism, every human being is on a psycho-spiritual journey. They are in various ways trying to discover happiness, peace and fulfillment. Most people search in the world for these coveted goals. However, invariably they can only find limited fulfillment at best, and in the end, all of a person's achievements, no matter how grand, are relinquished by them at the time of death. Mystic philosophy shows that people are really searching for a deeper happiness and that if they were to understand how to pursue it, their worldly desires, actions and experiences would be directed towards an inner spiritual discovery. The fruit of this inner journey is the discovery that one has infinite peace and bliss within; this is the true goal of life.

In order to successfully complete the journey of life, everyone needs to evolve spiritually. Therefore, the characters of the Ancient Egyptian myth of Creation and their various forms of interaction with each other are in reality an elaborate mystic code relating to the areas of human consciousness that need to be developed for spiritual growth to occur. The first thing that is noticed when the deities of the Ancient Egyptian Creation, based on the teachings of Anu, are placed in a hierarchical fashion according to the order of their Creation (see below), is that they arise in accordance with their level of density. Density here refers to their order of subtlety of the elements in Creation. Ra is the first principle to emerge out of the Primeval Waters. He is the subtle, singular principle of Creation, the focus of oneness in time and space. The Primeval Ocean itself transcends time and space and is beyond existence and non-existence. Ra is the first principle to emerge out of the Absolute (as Ra-Tem). His emergence signifies the beginning of existence (Creation).

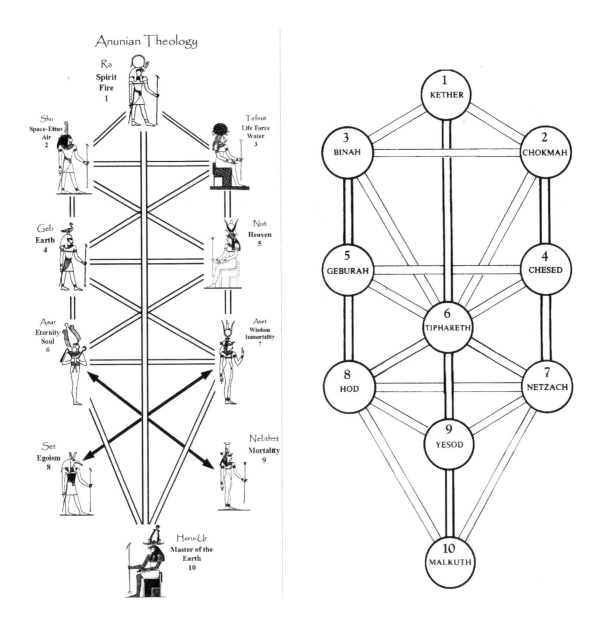

Figure 4: Above left: The Tree of Gods and Goddesses of Anunian Theology. Above right: The Tree of Life of the Cabbala (Kabbalah).

In Anunian Theology, as in the teachings of Bhagavad-Gita and the Kabbalistic Tree of Life, there is a spiritual journey of self-discovery that every human being must undertake. The journey of self-discovery refers to a coming into awareness of one's own Divine Essence. As such the mystic understanding is that the Spirit and the physical world are not separate entities. They are indeed related. Creation is rooted in the Spirit, and so too is every human being. When a human being comes into this knowledge, it is said that heaven has been discovered on earth. Indeed, this teaching is directly given by the Ancient Egyptian God Djehuti in the injunction "As Above, So Below." This is similar to the statement in the Christian Bibile that is attributed to Jesus, "Thy will be done on earth as it is in heaven." In Anunian Theurgy Tree of Life, the journey of spiritual evolution begins at the principle denoted by the number 10, and leads to the number 1, the Supreme Spirit. Each principle relates to an aspect of the personality and a cosmic aspect of Creation that must be discovered and mastered. When this occurs, the spiritual evolution of the aspirant is promoted until the ultimate destination of spiritual Enlightenment (Nesast) is reached.

Figure 5: Above-The Boat of Ra with nine divinities (Neteru) and Ra in the form of a Ra-Harakti (From Pert M Hru {Papyrus} Nu)

The diagram of the Anunian Theology above shows that the *Pautti* (Company of Gods and Goddesses), or the creative principles which are embodied in the primordial gods and goddesses of creation, emanated from the Supreme Being. Ra or Ra-Tem arose out of the *"Nu,"* the Primeval waters, the hidden essence, and began sailing the *"Boat of Millions of Years"* which included the Company of gods and goddesses. (see below) On his boat emerged the "Neteru" or cosmic principles of creation. "Sailing" signifies the beginning of motion in creation. Motion implies that events occur in the realm of time and space, thus, the phenomenal universe comes into existence as a mass of moving essence we call the elements. Prior to this motion, there was the primeval state of being without any form and without existence in time or space. The neteru (gods and goddesses) of the Pautti are Ra-Atum (Ra-Tem), Shu, Tefnut, Geb, Nut, Asar, Aset, Set, and Nebthet. Shu, Tefnut, Geb, Nut, Asar (Asar), Aset (Isis), Set, and Nebthet (Nephthys) represent the principles upon which creation manifests.

In the Kemetic Tree of Life each sphere and its divinity represent a particular human and/or a transcendental philosophical issues (lower five spheres) and cosmic issues (upper five spheres) that must be experienced and mastered in order to progress. Once the aspirant progresses to mastery of the ten spheres they can transcend all and enter into the realm of cosmic consciousness, in other words the mystical awakening, oneness with the absolute, the transcendental. So along with the ten spheres or realms there is another, a transcendental realm that may be referred to with the number infinity (∞).

Figure 6: Lord Nun pushing the boat of Khepri out of the ocean to engender and sustain Creation.

INSTRUCTION: How to use this book

This book has been laid out in the form of lessons that disseminate the metaphysical wisdom of the Anunian Theurgy Tree of Life philosophy and disciplines.

1. Proceed by first reading the book once completely all the way through.

2. When you get to the last lesson you will receive specific instructions for meditations, visualizations, chants and breathwork to activate the Tree of Life in your personality.

3. Once you have read the intere book once and have studied the final lesson then go back and begin again with lesson #1 and proceed in accordance with the instructions given at the end of each lesson.

HTP
Sebai Muata Ashby

Introduction: Ancient Egyptian Culture, Religion and the Kemetic Tree of Life

This volume is related to the Creation Myth of Anunian Theurgy. Anunian Theurgy is the first major theological system of Ancient Egyptian culture and the earliest known developed religion in human history. It is based on the Tree of Life (T.O.L.) of Anunian Theurgy; the conception of the gods and goddesses of Anunian Theurgy. Anunian Theurgy is the mythological description of how Creation came into being based on the teachings of the Ancient Egyptian priesthood of the city of Anu (called Heliopolis by the ancient Greeks). The hieroglyphs for the namce of the city are:

The city's Ancient Egyptian name (shown in hieroglyphs, (above) may be transliterated into *iwnw* or *anu*), it can mean literally "place of pillars" or place of the first beginning {the mound of Creation}. The name was usually written in Greek as Ὤν *On*, and written as אן *'Ôn* and און *'Āwen* in biblical Hebrew. The divine hierarchy of Anunian Theurgy is headed by the God Ra. Ra emerged from a primeval ocean and brought forth certain gods and goddesses. These compose Creation itself as well as the nature of human existence. This aspect of the teaching of Anunian Theurgy is treated in detail in this current lecture series on the Tree of Life of Ancient Egypt. First we will begin with an introduction to Ancient Egyptian culture, history and religion and then we will proceed to discuss the Tree of Life aspect of Anunian Theurgy which is the earliest aspect (tradition) of Ancient Egyptian religion.

Who were the Ancient Egyptians and Where is the land of Egypt?

Figure 7: A map of Africa showing the location of the land of *Ta-Meri* or *Kamut,* also known as Ancient Egypt.

The Ancient Egyptians were descendants of the Nubians, who had themselves originated from farther south into the heart of Africa at the Great Lakes region, the sources of the Nile River. These ancient African people called their land Kemet (Kemet), and soon after developing a well-ordered society based on the concept of cosmic ethics and spiritual conscience (Maat Philosophy). The Ancient Egyptians lived for thousands of years in the northeastern corner of the African continent in the area known as the Nile Valley. The Nile River was a source of dependable enrichment for the land and allowed them to prosper for a very long time without the harsh struggles experienced by people in other geographic locations such as the desert regions of Asia Minor, and the temperate zones of East Asia and Western Asia (Europe). Their prosperity was so great that they created art, culture, religion, philosophy and a civilization which surpassed everything that had come before, and has not been duplicated ever since. The Ancient Kemetians (Egyptians) based their government and business concerns on spiritual values and therefore, enjoyed an orderly society which included equality between the sexes, and a legal system based on universal spiritual laws (Maat Philosophy). The *Egyptian Mystery System* is a tribute to their history, culture and legacy. As historical insights unfold, it becomes clearer that modern culture has derived its basis from Ancient Egypt, though the credit is not often given, nor the integrity of the practices maintained in the new religions. This is another important reason to study Ancient Egyptian Philosophy, to discover the principles which allowed their civilization to prosper over a period of thousands of years in order to bring our systems of government, religion and social structures to a harmony with ourselves, humanity and with nature.

The flow of the Nile brought annual floods to the Nile Valley and this provided irrigation and new soil nutrients every year that allowed for regular crops when worked on time. This regularity and balance of nature inspired the population to adopt a culture of order and duty based on cosmic order: Maat {Ma'at}. This idea extends to the understanding of Divine justice and reciprocity. So if work is performed on time and in cooperation with nature, there will be order, balance and peace as well as prosperity in life (for the individual, family, and community).

Kemet (Kemet, Egypt) is located in the north-eastern corner of the continent of Africa. It is composed of towns along the banks of the Hapi (Nile River). In the north there is the Nile Delta region where the river contacts the Mediterranean Sea. This part is referred to as the North or Lower Egypt, "lower," because that is the lowest elevation and the river flows from south to north. The middle of the country is referred to as Middle Egypt. The south is referred to as Upper Egypt because it is the higher elevation and the river flows from there to the north. The south is the older region of the dynastic civilization and the middle and north are later.

A Brief History

The history of Egypt begins in the far reaches of time. It includes The Dynastic Period, when it was populated and controlled by its original African inhabitance, and later by those Asiatic peoples that conquered it, including the Greeks (The Hellenistic Period), Romans (The Roman Period) and The Christian Byzantine Rule (30 B.C.E.- 638 A.C.E.), the Caliphate and the Mamalukes (642-1517 A.C.E.), Ottoman Domination (1082-1882 A.C.E.), British colonialism (1882-1952 A.C.E.), as well as modern, Arab-Islamic Egypt (1952- present).

Ancient Egypt or Kemet, was a civilization that flourished in Northeast Africa along the Nile River from before 5,500 B.C.E. until 30 B.C.E. In 30 B.C.E., Octavian, who was later known as the Roman Emperor, Augustus, put the last Egyptian King, Ptolemy XIV, a Greek ruler, to death. After this Egypt was formally annexed to Rome. Though in the late 20th century evidence was uncovered that proved Ancient Egyptian civilization existed at least as far back as 7,000 B.C.E. to 10,000 B.C.E. mainstream Egyptologists normally divide Ancient Egyptian history into the following approximate periods: The Early Dynastic Period (3,200-2,575 B.C.E.); The Old Kingdom or Old Empire (2,575-2,134 B.C.E.); The First Intermediate Period (2,134-2,040 B.C.E.); The Middle Kingdom or Middle Empire (2,040-1,640 B.C.E.); The Second Intermediate Period (1,640-1,532 B.C.E.); The New Kingdom or New Empire (1,532-1,070 B.C.E.); The third Intermediate Period (1,070-712 B.C.E.); The Late Period (712-332 B.C.E.).

In the Late Period the following groups controlled Egypt. The Nubian Dynasty (712-657 B.C.E.); The Persian Dynasty (525-404 B.C.E.); The Native Revolt and re-establishment of Egyptian rule by Egyptians (404-343 B.C.E.); The Second Persian Period (343-332 B.C.E.); The Ptolemaic or Greek Period (332 B.C.E.- c. 30 B.C.E.);

Roman Period (c.30 B.C.E.-395 A.C.E.); The Byzantine Period (395-640 A.C.E) and The Arab Conquest Period (640 A.C.E.-present). The individual dynasties are numbered, generally in Roman numerals, from I through XXX.

The period after the New Kingdom saw greatness in culture and architecture under the rulership of Ramses II. However, after his rule, Egypt saw a decline from which it would never recover. This is the period of the downfall of Ancient Egyptian culture in which the Libyans ruled after the Tanite (XXI) Dynasty. This was followed by the Nubian conquerors who founded the XXII Dynasty and tried to restore Egypt to her past glory. However, having been weakened by the social and political turmoil of wars, Ancient Egypt fell to the Persians once more. The Persians conquered the country until the Greeks, under Alexander, conquered them. One of Alexander's generals, Ptolemy, became the ruler of Egypt and started a Greek Pharaonic dynasty. The Romans followed the Greeks, and finally the Arabs conquered the land of Egypt in 640 A.C.E to the present.

However, the history which has been classified above is only the history of the "Dynastic Period." It reflects the view of traditional Egyptologists who have refused to accept the evidence of a Predynastic period in Ancient Egyptian history contained in Ancient Egyptian documents such as the *Palermo Stone, Royal Tablets at Abydos, Royal Papyrus of Turin,* the *Dynastic List* of *Manetho,* and the eye-witness accounts of Greek historians Herodotus (c. 484-425 B.C.E.) and Diodorus. These sources speak clearly of a Pre-dynastic society which stretches far into antiquity. The Dynastic Period is what most people think of whenever Ancient Egypt is mentioned. This period is when the famous pharaohs (kings & queens) ruled. The latter part of the Dynastic Period is when the Biblical story of Moses, Joseph, Abraham, etc., is supposed to have occurred (c. 1,100? B.C.E); yet there is no evidence of their historical existence of such personalities in Egypt, only the statements in the Judeo-Christian tradition. Therefore, those with a Christian background generally only have an idea about Ancient Egypt as it is related in the Bible. Due to evidences uncovered in the late 20th century, it is now widely accepted, even by mainstream Egyptologists, that he tradition based on the old Jewish bible recounting about how the Jews were used for forced labor and the construction of the great monuments of Egypt such as the Great Pyramids is impossible since these were created in the predynastic age, thousands of years before Abraham, the supposed first Jew, ever existed. Also, archeological evidence has been discovered of the Ancient Egyptian workers who did the construction and who were not slaves, but ordinary Ancient Egyptians and not Jews. Although this such biblical statements and accounts are impossible as they do not coincide with the verifiable history of Ancient Egypt, the significant impact of Ancient Egypt on Hebrew and Christian culture is evident even from the biblical scriptures, as an example of religious myth and philosophy and also as a rival for the hearts and minds of all peoples, including those of Asia Minor, Europe (especially Greece) and the Far East, especially India.[5] Actually, Egypt existed much earlier than most traditional Egyptologists are prepared to admit. The new archeological evidence related to the great Sphinx[6] monument on the Giza Plateau and the ancient writings by Manetho, one of the last High Priests of Ancient Egypt, show that Ancient Egyptian history begins earlier than 10,000 B.C.E. and may date back to as early as 30,000-50,000 B.C.E.

It is known that the Pharaonic (royal) calendar based on the Sothic system (star Sirius) was in use by 4,240 B.C.E. This certainly required extensive astronomical skills and time for observation in order to develop the theory and then extrapolate mathematically and prove it correct by observing it again. Therefore, the history of Kemet (Egypt) must be reckoned to be extremely ancient. Thus, in order to grasp the antiquity of Ancient Egyptian culture, religion and philosophy, we will briefly review the history presented by the Ancient Egyptian Priest Manetho and some Greek Historians.

The calendar based on the Great Year was also used by the Ancient Egyptians. The Great Year is based on the movement of the earth through the constellations known today as the zodiac, through a movement cycle referred to as the *Precession of the Equinoxes* and confirmed by the history given by the Ancient Egyptian Priest Manetho in the year 241 B.C.E. Each Great Year has 25,860 to 25,920 years and 12 arcs or constellations, and each passage through a constellation takes 2,155 – 2,160 years. These are the "Great Months." The current cycle or year began around the year 10,858 B.C.E. At around the year 36,766 B.C.E., according to Manetho, the Creator, Ra, ruled the earth in person from his throne in the Ancient Egyptian city of Anu. By this reckoning, at the time of this writing, our current year (2,008 A.C.E.) is actually the year 38774 based on the Great Year System of Ancient Egyptian history.

---

[5] see the book *THE AFRICAN ORIGINS OF CIVILIZATION, RELIGION AND YOGA SPIRITUALITY AND ETHICS PHILOSOPHY* by Dr. Muata Ashby
[6] ibid

Introduction to Shetaut Neter

The Ancient Egyptians created a vast civilization and culture earlier than any other society in known history and organized a nation that was based on the concepts of balance and order (Maat) as a foundation for the practice of religion and the pursuit of spiritual enlightenment (Nehast). The Ancient Egyptians began to realize that the world is full of wonders, but also that life is fleeting, and that there must be something more to human existence. The spiritual leaders of Kemet, the priests and priestesses, realized a deeper aspect of human existence and the existence of higher dimensions of reality as well as an intelligent underlying transcendental consciousness as the essence of Creation. They developed spiritual systems that were designed to allow human beings to understand the nature of this secret being who is the essence of all Creation. They called this spiritual system "Shtaut[7] Ntr (Shetaut Neter)."

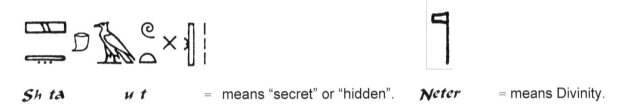

Sh ta   u t   = means "secret" or "hidden".   *Neter*   = means Divinity.

Who is Neter in Kemetic (Ancient Egyptian) Religion?

"**Ntr**

The symbol of Neter was described by an Ancient Kemetic priest as:
"That which is placed in the coffin"

The term *Ntr* ⌇, or *Ntjr* ⌇, comes from the Ancient Egyptian hieroglyphic language which did not record most of its vowels. However, the term survives in the Coptic language as *"Nutar."* The same Coptic meaning (divine force or sustaining power) applies in the present as it did in ancient times. It is a symbol composed of a wooden staff that was wrapped with strips of fabric, like a mummy. The strips alternate in color with yellow, green and blue. The mummy, in Kemetic spirituality, is understood to be the dead but resurrected Divinity, Asar, and every human being is a potential resurrected being, an Asar. So the Ntr is actually every human being who does not really die, but goes to live on in a different form. Further, the resurrected spirit of every human being is that same Divinity. Phonetically, the term Nutar is related to other terms having the same meaning as Nutar in its mundane aspect relating to the forces of nature, such as the Latin "Natura," the Spanish Naturalesa, the English "Nature" and "Nutriment", etc. In general usage, the term "Ntr" (Neter or Netjer) means Divinity; in this context meaning: androgynous, incorporating the male and female, or refering to neither, in other words genderless divinity. In a real sense, as we will see, Natur means power manifesting as Neteru and the Neteru are the objects of creation, in other words "nature."

---

[7] May also be pronounced "Shetau-tu Neter"

Neter and the Neteru

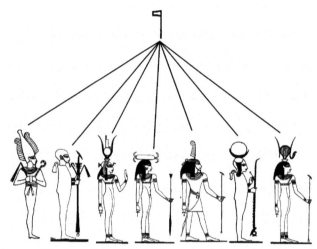

Figure 8: The Neteru (Gods and Goddesses) proceed from the Neter (Supreme Being)

The concept of Neter and Neteru binds and ties all of the varied forms of Kemetic spirituality into one vision of the gods and goddesses all emerging from the same Supreme Being (Neter). This concept has been referred to as "henotheism". The Supreme Being is an all-encompassing Absolute Divinity while expressing as lesser divinities that operate in time and space. So in Kemetic (North-Eastern African Traditional Religion) spirituality, the divinity is both transcendental and absolute as well as temporal and local, sustaining and affecting the world directly in the form of Gods and Goddesses (Neteru).[8]

The Neteru

"Neteru"

The term "Neteru" means "gods and goddesses." This means that from the ultimate and transcendental Supreme Being, "Neter," come the Neteru. There are countless Neteru. So from the one come the many. These Neteru are cosmic forces that pervade the universe. They are the means by which Neter sustains Creation and manifests through it. So Neterianism may be thought of as a form of "monotheistic polytheism" though a more technical religious studies term to describe it would be henotheistic religion. The one Supreme Being expresses as many gods and goddesses. At the end of time, after their work of sustaining Creation is finished, these gods and goddesses are again absorbed back into the Supreme Being.

Among a myriad of elements of commonality, all of the spiritual systems of Ancient Egypt (Kemet) have one essential aspect that is common to all; they all hold that there is a Supreme Being (Neter) who manifests in a multiplicity of ways through nature, the Neteru. Like sunrays, the Neteru emanate from the Divine; they are its manifestations. So just as one can study the sunlight that hits the earth and learn about the Sun, their source, so too by studying the Neteru we learn about and are led to discover their source, the Neter, and with this discovery we are enlightened. The Neteru may be depicted anthropomorphically or zoomorphically (or as a

---

[8] For more details see the book *Egyptian Mysteries Vol. 2 Dictionary of Ancient Egyptian Gods and Goddesses* by Dr. Muata Ashby

composite/combination of the two) in accordance with the teaching about Neter that is being conveyed through them.

The Neteru and Their Interrelationships

The image below (diagram) demonstrates how the divinities of the three major theurgies (religious sciences and their related temples and priests and priestesses) of Ancient Egypt are related and originate from Anunian Theurgy. The study of the interrelationships of the neterian neteru, the practice of their teaching and the experience of the elevation that comes from that study and practice constitutes the practice of the Theurgy as well as the practice of theology of Neterian religion. Theurgy and religion are not the same thing. Religion is the organized practice of worship directed at a divinity, based on dogmas and traditions of worship for promoting a spiritual goal, an eschatology, such as ending up in heaven with God, however that may be conceived in accordance with the form of *theism* of the religion (monotheism, pantheism, polytheism, henotheism, etc.). Theurgy is a science of religion, a prescribed program for promoting higher consciousness through a philosophy and disciplines carried out by priests and priestesses in accordance with a prescribed and precise program of religion and metaphysics designed to lead an aspirant to experience higher consciousness. In the case of Ancient Egyptian religion the program is dedicated towards the attainment of *Nehast* or Spiritual Awakening {Enlightenment}, a mystic experience of oneness with the divine and the discovery of one's immortality. Religion and Theurgy may also be studied through the discipline of theology. Theology is the study (ology) of religion (Theo). Therefore, Memphite Theurgy is studied as Memphite Theology; Anunian Theurgy is studied as Anunian Theology, and Theban Theurgy as Theban Theology. However, the Theurgy of Ancient Egypt, as well as any other mystical tradition, is best studied under the rubric or within the context of Mysticism as opposed to within a purely theological context. The same Supreme Being, Neter, is the winged all-encompassing transcendental Divinity, the Spirit who, in the early history, is called "Heru." The physical universe in which the Heru lives is called "Hetheru" or the "house of Heru." This divinity Heru (in the aspect as Nefertem), is also the Nun or primeval substratum from which all matter is composed. The various divinities and the material universe are composed from this primeval substratum. Neter is actually androgynous and Heru, the Spirit, is related as a male aspect of that androgyny. However, the androgynous aspect (Nun), gives rise to the solar principle and both the male (Heru) and female (Hetheru) divinities. The Neterian traditions are composed of companies or groups of gods and goddesses. Their actions, teachings and interactions with each other and with human beings provide insight into their nature as well as that of human existence and Creation itself.

The Neteru and Their Temples

The line connections between the main temples of ancient Egypt (below) indicate direct scriptural relationships and the labels also indicate that some divinities from one system are the same in others, with only a name change. Again, this is attested to by the scriptures themselves in direct statements, like those found in the ***Prt m Hru*** text Chapter 4 (17).[9]

Diagram 1: The Ancient Egyptian Temple Network

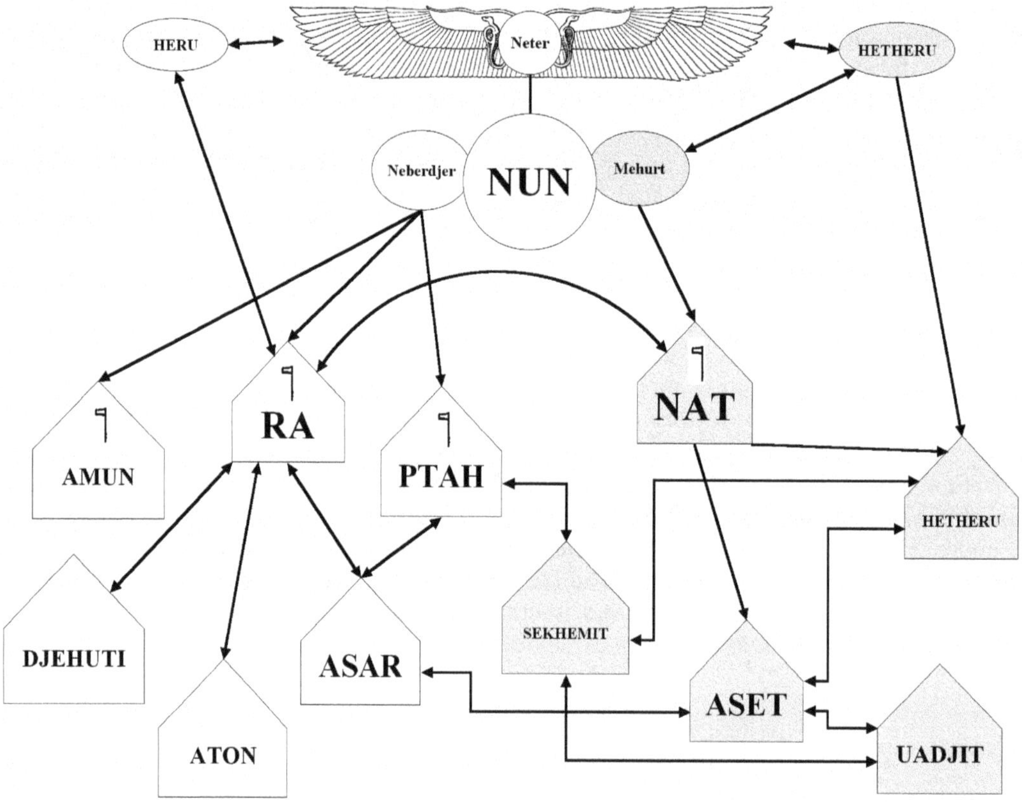

The sages of Kemet instituted a system by which the teachings of spirituality were espoused through a Temple organization. The major divinities were assigned to a particular city. That divinity or group of divinities became the "patron" divinity or divinities of that city. Also, the Priests and Priestesses of that Temple were in charge of seeing to the welfare of the people in that district as well as maintaining the traditions and disciplines of the traditions based on the particular divinity being worshipped. So the original concept of "Neter" became elaborated through the "theologies" of the various traditions. A dynamic expression of the teachings emerged, which though maintaining the integrity of the teachings, expressed nuances of variation in perspective on the teachings to suit the needs of varying kinds of personalities of the people of different locales.

In the diagram above, the primary or main divinities are denoted by the Neter symbol (). The house structure represents the Temple for that particular divinity. The interconnections with the other Temples are based on original scriptural statements espoused by the Temples that linked the divinities of their Temple with the other divinities. So this means that the divinities should be viewed not as separate entities operating independently, but

---

[9] See the book *THE EGYPTIAN BOOK OF THE DEAD MYSTICISM OF THE PERT EM HERU* " by Dr. Muata Ashby, ISBN# 1-884564-28-3

rather as family members who are in the same "enterprise" together, in other words the enlightenment of society, albeit through variations in form of worship, name, form (expression of the Divinity), etc. Ultimately, all the divinities are referred to as Neteru and they are all said to be emanations from the ultimate and Supreme Being. Thus, the teaching from any of the Temples leads to an understanding of the others, and these all lead back to the source, the highest Divinity. Thus, the teaching within any of the Temple systems would lead to the attainment of spiritual enlightenment, the Great Awakening.

The Scriptures and Symbols of Shetaut Neter

The most important elements of the myths, wisdom teachings and rituals associated with the Shetaut Neter can be found in the Pyramid Texts, Coffin Texts, Papyrus Texts, Temple Reliefs, Steles, Obelisks and other monuments of Ancient Egypt. All of these put together constitute what is referred to as the sacred texts of Ancient Egypt or the teachings of Egyptian mystical spirituality. The writings are referred to as "Khu" or "Hekau," meaning utterances or words of power, and collectively they are known as "Medtu Neter" (Words of The Divine) or "Neter Medtu" (Divine Speech). Modern Egyptology, the scholarly study of Ancient Egyptian civilization from the early nineteenth century to the present has labeled these utterances as spells or incantations. In a way this assessment is correct because these utterances are to be understood as incantations or words which, when understood, can have the effect of transforming the mind, allowing an expansion of consciousness and spiritual enlightenment. However, they are not to be understood in the context of Western magic, witch's spells or chicanery, nonsense, etc. To do so would be a grievous error of either ignorance, in the case of the uneducated masses, or intellectualism and conceit, in the case of highly educated but uninitiated scholars. These faulty interpretations would yield the conclusion that Ancient Egyptian spirituality as well as other myths from around the world are a conglomerate of a myriad of conflicting stories and baseless ritualism devoted to idol worshipping, imagination and primitive occult nonsense. In reality, the Shetaut Neter is an extremely sophisticated philosophy and educational process for understanding and realizing the transcendental reality of life which is the basis of all existence.

The following scriptures represent the foundational scriptures of Kemetic culture. They may be divided into three categories: *Mythic/Mystical Scriptures*, *Mystical Philosophy/Ritual Scriptures*, and *Wisdom Scriptures* (Didactic Literature).

MYTHIC SCRIPTURES Literature	Mystical (Ritual) Philosophy Literature	Wisdom Texts Literature
Shetaut Asar-Aset-Heru The Myth of Asar, Aset and Heru (Asarian Resurrection Theology) - Predynastic Shetaut Atum-Ra Anunian Theology Predynastic Shetaut Net/Aset/Hetheru Saitian Theology – Goddess Spirituality Predynastic Shetaut Ptah Memphite Theology Predynastic Shetaut Amun Theban Theology Predynastic	Coffin Texts (c. 2040 B.C.E.-1786 B.C.E.) Papyrus Texts (c. 1580 B.C.E.-Roman Period)[10] Books of Coming Forth By Day Example of famous papyri: Papyrus of Any Papyrus of Hunefer Papyrus of Kenna Greenfield Papyrus, Etc.	Wisdom Texts (c. 3,000 B.C.E. – Ptolemaic Period) Precepts of Ptahotep Instructions of Any Instructions of Amenemope Etc. Maat Declarations Literature (All Periods) Harper's Songs

Medu Neter

"Medu Neter"

The teachings of the Neterian Traditions are conveyed in the scriptures of the Neterian Traditions. These are recorded in the Medu Neter script.

---

[10] After 1570 B.C.E they would evolve into a more unified text, the Egyptian Book of the Dead.

Example of Hieroglyphic Script

Above: A section from the pyramid of *Teti* in Sakkara Egypt, known as the "Pyramid Texts" (Early Dynastic Period) showing the cross, a symbol that was later adopted by the practitioners of Christianity

The Medtu Neter was used through all periods by Priests and priestesses – mostly used in monumental inscriptions such as the Pyramid texts, Obelisks, temple inscriptions, etc. – since Pre-Dynastic times. It is the earliest form of writing in known history.

Hekau, Medu Neter and Shetitu

"hekau"

The concept of the divine word or *Hekau,* is an extremely important part of Ancient Egyptian religion and is instructive in the study of all African religion. The main difference between Ancient Egyptian religion and other African religions in this area was the extensive development of the "written word." The word religion is translated as Shetaut Neter in the Ancient African language of Kemet.

Shetitu

This Shetaut (mysteries- rituals, wisdom, philosophy) about the Neter (Supreme Being) are related in the *Shetitu* or writings related to the hidden teaching. And those writings are referred to as *Medtu Neter* or "Divine Speech," the writings of the god Djehuti (Ancient Egyptian god of the divine word) – also refers to any hieroglyphic texts or inscriptions generally.

The Cities in Ancient Egypt Where the Three Main Theurgies were developed, Anu, Menefer and Waset

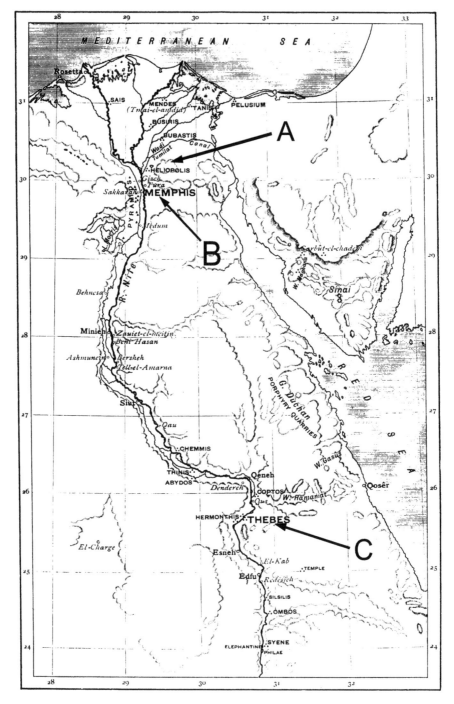

Egypt is located in the north-eastern corner of the African Continent. The cities wherein the theology of the Trinity of Amun-Ra-Ptah was developed were: A- Anu (Heliopolis), B-Hetkaptah (Memphis), and C-Waset (Thebes).

The Anunian Tradition

 Shetaut Anu

Diagram 2: Anunian Theurgy Divinities and Their Interrelationships

Below: The Heliopolitan Cosmogony.

The city of Anu (Amun-Ra)

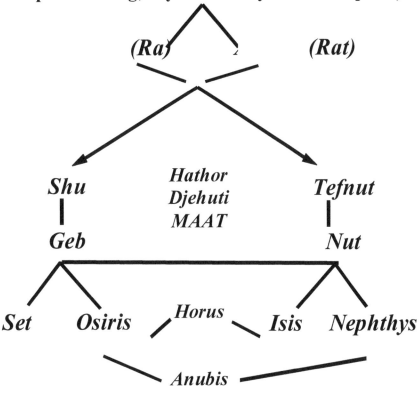

The Neters of Creation -
The Company of the Gods and Goddesses.
Neter Neteru
Nebertcher - Amun (unseen, hidden, ever present,
Supreme Being, beyond duality and description)

(Ra) *(Rat)*

Shu *Tefnut*

Hathor
Djehuti
MAAT

Geb *Nut*

Set *Osiris* *Horus* *Isis* *Nephthys*

Anubis

The Mystery Teachings of the Anunian Tradition are related to the Divinity Ra and his company of Gods and Goddesses.[11] This Temple and its related Temples espouse the teachings of Creation, human origins and the path to spiritual enlightenment by means of the Supreme Being in the form of the god Ra. It tells of how Ra emerged from a primeval ocean and how human beings were created from his

[11] See the Book *African Religion VOL. 1- ANUNIAN THEOLOGY THE MYSTERIES OF RA,* by Dr. Muata Ashby, ISBN: 1-884564-38-0

tears. The gods and goddesses, who are his children, go to form the elements of nature and the cosmic forces that maintain nature.

Figure 9: Gods and Goddesses of Anunian Theurgy

Top: Ra. From left to right, starting at the bottom level- The Gods and Goddesses of Anunian Theurgy: Shu, Tefnut, Nut, Geb, Aset, Asar, Set, Nebthet and Heru-Ur

The teachings of the Tree of Life have been laid out in this volume in such a way to disseminate the philosophical teaching related to the principles of the Tree of Life system of spiritual evolution from the bottom up, that is to say, from the existence on earth, as an earthly conscious being to becoming a being of higher consciousness. It should be treated as a manual for a journey and the map is the Anunian Theurgy Tree of Life Cosmiconomythograph.

The reader should go through the entire text once and then spend extended time working with each lesson separately, keeping a journal of their reflections and meditations. The time frame is indeterminate; some individuals may require more time than others to assimilate, process and integrate the teaching and apply it in life. In Lesson 14 the main parameters for the disciplinary practice related to the T.O.L. evolutionary teaching have been discussed in detail. That discipline is to be applied to the principles learned in each lesson. The best way to progress effectively with the T.O.L. evolutionary teaching is to work with a competent spiritual preceptor, someone who can explain the teaching and provide competent guidance on its application.

Lesson 1: The Mythical and Metaphysical Origins of the Anunian Company of Gods and Goddesses

The Tree of Life is a conception based on Anunian Theurgy. Anunian Theurgy is the earliest extensively developed and codified religious teaching of ancient Kemet, which makes it the oldest developed religion of the world, and of Africa. It entails a system of Neteru (gods and goddesses) who are related to the teaching of the city of Anu; therefore, from the word "Anu" we get the term "Anunian."

From a mythical perspective the teaching of the Anunian Theurgy is based upon the Anunian Creation Myth. The myth is recorded in parts in different Ancient Egyptian writings, inscriptions and steles and papyri, including the Creation Papyrus. (see below)

Figure 10: Above-Papyrus of the Creation

At the head of the company of gods and goddesses of Anu is the god Ra. The Kemetic word for a company of gods and goddesses is *Paut* or *Pautti*. Ra can be considered as the head of the family of gods and goddesses, for example, as the patriarch or king of the gods and goddesses. All the other gods and goddesses emanate from him. However, remember what we had discussed in the Anunian Theurgy lectures[12], that Ra is merely the image of the Supreme and Transcendental Being in time and space. In other words, he and all the other gods/goddesses that come after him, that compose the physical creation, are all but transient aspects of a Transcendental Supreme Being that is beyond time and space, and beyond the Ra manifestation itself; but we will elaborate on the transcendental aspect later on.

---

[12] The Anunian Creation Myth: Series dates: 8/4/02 10015-10020, by Dr. Muata Ashby, See the Book *African Religion VOL. 1- ANUNIAN THEOLOGY THE MYSTERIES OF RA,* by Dr. Muata Ashby, ISBN: 1-884564-38-0

Therefore, from that one Supreme and Absolute comes the one divinity in time and space, Ra, and from that one divinity comes all the multiplicity that you see in the world of time and space. And Anunian Theurgy explains that this multiplicity arises because Ra gives rise to nine other gods and goddesses (Neteru); they emanate from him a hierarchal manner and manifest as the different principles of creation. The higher divinities are the more subtle ones, whereas the lower divinities are grosser. In addition, each god and goddess has a specific principle that he/she presides over, that he/she controls. So, for all the elements and the principles that govern the elements, there is a cosmic force that emanates from Ra that controls all of these physical aspects of creation.

Shu is Ra's firstborn son. He controls the principle of space, ether and air. Tefnut, his firstborn daughter, controls the principle of water. According to the teaching, these divinities emanate from the Ra, who is the highest and subtlest being in time and space. Next comes the divinity Shu, follwed by the divinity Tefnut. They are a little grosser than Ra. Shu and Tefnut come together, and they produce Geb and Nut... earth and heaven, respectively, and they are even grosser. Geb is the physical earth and Nut is the sky with the stars and planets; thus, they form the physical world (solar systems, galaxy, and universe.). Then Geb and Nut come together and they produce five more divinities: Asr and Aset, Set and Nebthet, and Heru Ur. These lower divinities are the grossest ones; they compose human existence, and are the ones that make up the aggregate of the human psyche. Thus, you have these main aspects of your personality that are composed of these five divinities, and the cosmos, the physical (gross and subtle) universe, is composed of the other five (Ra, Shu, Tefnut, Geb, Nut). In a broad sense, actually, your personality is composed of all of these because you are a microcosm of the entire creation. You have Shu in you, space, air, ether, and you have the waters, the power of moisture. Within you, you have a little bit of you that is up in the sky, and a little of you that is down on the earth. In this lesson we will start to focus on the lower divinities, and how to understand this conception of Anunian Theurgy as a tree which has its roots in the sky, in Ra, and its branches coming down to the earth.

The obelisk (see Plate 13) is one of the main symbols of Anunian Theurgy; others include the sundisk, the divine eye, and the serpent, etc. And as you can see on the Anunian Cosmiconomythograph of the Tree of Life (Plate 2), the obelisk is the central image. The image is a 2-D representation of a 3-D object....an obelisk, which you can understand as an elongated pyramid. At the top of the pyramid, you have the uppermost point of the obelisk. It is called the "Ben Ben" point. This is the point where it all begins. This is the point where the Transcendental Being, Nun, touches a special spot on the waters [which is also a part of Himself]. The Ben Ben point is the first place where coagulation occurs, and from that coagulation comes all the rest of the physical creation, the physical universe, like a stone falling into a vast ocean and its ripples cause waves expanding throughout the ocean, changing it from flat to wavy shapes. That beginning point of Creation began at *Anu*, and Anu is also the place where Ra established his court and from where he directed the Creation.

In the introduction we started to discuss the interconnection of these divinities, which are to be understood as pathways...if you will, to understanding the spiritual journey expressed as psycho-spiritual cosmic forces. In order to understand the philosophy of the Kemetic Tree of Life and practice it properly, it is important to understand the two forms of worship. One form of worship is for the divinities that are in Time and Space, and the other for the Divinity that transcends time and space. In the Anunian Cosmiconomythograph, time and space is everything from the physical universe up into the heavens, up until the *Ben Ben* point...everything at all levels of creation, the netherworld, the physical world, the transcendental Duat... these are still in the realm of time and space. So we have three aspects of Creation: *Ta, Pet,* and *Duat.* Thus, the beginning point of Creation began at *Anu*, and Anu is also the place where Ra established his royal court, composed of the gods and goddesses of the Creation, and from where he directed the Creation.

Diagram 3: The Supreme Being and The Three Realms of Time and Space

There are three realms of existence, the Ta or physical, the Pet or heavenly realm, and the Duat or netherworld. Beyond the Duat is the Transcendental, Neberdjer, the all-encompassing Divinity.

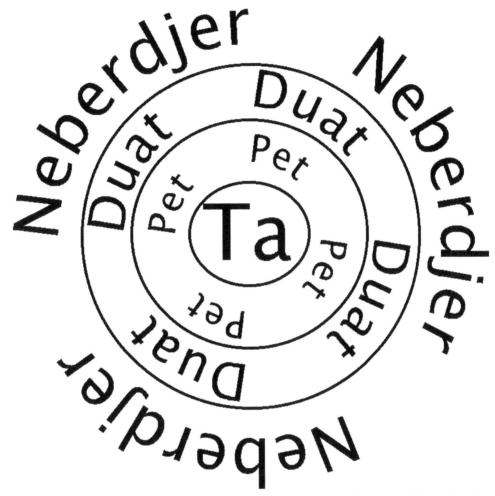

In order to climb the ladder of The Tree of Life, you must master various principles. Climbing the ladder means learning about these divinities and cultivating the cosmic energies they manifest, in order to master the principles and levels of existence they preside over, within yourself. If you do not master the principle, the opposite (egoistic) force of the principle will master you. It will control you, and will lead you into worldly existence, into a generative existence. It is also important to understand that this realm of time and space is a realm of generation, while the realm that transcends time and space, the realm of the Nun or Primeval Waters (also called Nunu), is formless, nameless, and undifferentiated; it is also called the realm of *Yanrutef*. Yanrutef is described in the *Pert em Heru* (*Book of the Dead, Book of Coming Forth By Day*) as "the place where nothing grows," meaning, where nothing is generated, where nothing is changed, nothing is desired, nothing is wanted, nothing is created and nothing is missing. And in reality, even though they may not realize it, this is the level of consciousness, of divine experience of fulfillment and contentment, that all human beings are trying to reach through all the religions of the world and actions in daily life. However, most people end up searching for fulfillment in the world of time and space. This searching can manifest as looking for a spouse, looking to have children, looking to have a car, looking to go to the mall to buy something, going to a party to be with others and have fun together, etc. In doing those things, people are really trying to find completeness, fulfillment, and truth. Since the realm of time and space is limited and changeable, there can never be abiding contentment there. The realm of time and space may be a manifest reality, but it is not an absolute truth because it is not abiding. Anything that is not abiding is only a relative reality and not a truth.

So in the realm of generation, the realm of time and space, you can never find that abading contentment because everything changes and nothing is abiding. All you are going to find is something that is going to appease you temporarily, until another desire arises. Then you are going to have to go on pursuing that…and you will never be happy in that way, for there will be renewing stress about searching and then securing happiness, which, again, can never happen. The only way you will be truly happy and fulfilled is when you attain transcendental consciousness…the Nunu level. And so, the Anunian Theurgy explains that a human being is to become *Heru Ur* or *Master of the Earth*. Heru Ur is the lower most divinity on the cosmiconomythograph, but Heru Ur represents the perfection of enlightened consciousness. He is human and knowledgeable about the physical creation, but he also knows Ra and the higher realms of existence, even while living as a human being on earth, the grossest realm (Ta). He is not the lowest neteru on the diagram of the Kemetic Tree because he is the lowliest being; he is the lowest because he is the master of the lower, master of the earth realm, the Ta. Heru represents the potential of every human being, who, living on earth, can also attain the heights of spiritual evolution and self-discovery. And that is what you are supposed to be striving for. All those who are not enlightened beings are ordinary human beings, slaves to the world of time and space, and desires, which is symbolized by Heru, the child, before he becomes Heru Ur.

Heru Ur, from the perspective of human existence, is the goal of a spiritual aspirant. But how does Heru Ur come about? As we proceed further on in our discussion, we will discuss about the different aspects of Heru: Heru as the blind one, Heru as the child, Heru as the fighter, etc. We will talk about the struggle that has to go on for Heru Ur to be developed within you from Heru. Heru symbolizes spiritual aspiration…the kind of aspiration that allows you to have the determination and fighting character to forge ahead despite the formidable obstacles in the way of attaining higher consciousness. Egoism is the most powerful foe {obstacle} of a spiritual aspirant to attaining enlightenment; Set is that foe, the rival of Heru. And what does attaining enlightenment mean…from a nuts and bolts aspect? It means that you must control the lower forces that are operating through you, that are generating through you, that are leading you astray, that are controlling your life, and then you are to come into the knowledge of the Higher Self, the transcendental aspect of "you."

And here, now after our brief recap, we begin with today's lecture. In order to take your first steps in transforming yourself into Heru Ur, your Heru Ur Self, your master of the earth Self, you must make the journey to discover Ra within yourself. But you have all of this layering between you and Ra, you on the lower end, walking around on the earth, and all these layers of cosmic forces, which are symbolized by the divinities, the Neteru. What are you to do? How are you to begin the journey? How long will the journey last, and how will you know when you have reached the destination? Let us firstly discuss the purpose of the Anunian Theurgy and the Tree of Life. Then you will also have insight into the purpose of life and the proper course that life should be directed towards.

What is the Purpose of Anunian Theurgy and the Anunian Tree of Life?

Know Thyself:

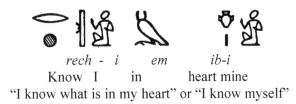

rech - i   em   ib-i
Know   I   in   heart mine
"I know what is in my heart" or "I know myself"

The *iab* or heart is the mind of a person, the ego thoughts aspect of the personality. It is the essence which contains the desires, feelings and unconscious thoughts which emanate from the soul (Ba) of a person. Thus to know one's heart is the great injunction of spirituality, for to know this heart is indeed synonymous with knowing the innermost Self.

Like the 42 injunctions of Maat{Ma'at}, the teachings contained in the writings of the *Pert em Heru* (*Book of the Dead, Book of Coming Forth By Day*)[13] are given from the first person singular perspective, but are indeed meant as universal injunctions, and therefore may be read:

"Do not Lie" instead of "I have not lied" and likewise "Know thyself" instead of "I know myself."

In the text of Chapter 26 of the *Pert em Heru*, the initiate *Ani* says he has gained control of his body and his soul will not be imprisoned. This clearly means that he has gained knowledge of his true, deeper, powerful Self. He no longer knows himself as Ani, but as the Higher Self. This gives him the power over his ego personality in the physical world as well as the Netherworld. There are other passages in Chapter 17, Chapter 64 and elsewhere in the *Pert em Heru* as well as temple inscriptions with the same teaching (know thyself) that later was popularized by the Greek Temple of Apollo at Delphi.

Sheta (Mystery), *Sheta* (Hidden)

In our study, the first and most important teaching, to be understood by a spiritual aspirant who wants to practice the teaching of Ancient Egyptian religion surrounds the Ancient Egyptian word "Sheti or Shedy" [**Shedy** {Spiritual disciplines}.] Sheti comes from the root *Sheta*. The Ancient Egyptian word *Sheta* means something which is *hidden, secret, unknown*, or *cannot be seen or understood, a secret, a mystery*. Rituals, Words of Power (Khu-Hekau, Mantras), religious texts and pictures are S*hetaut Neter* or *Divine Mysteries*. *Sheti* (spiritual discipline) is to go deeply into the mysteries, to study the mystery teachings and literature profoundly, to penetrate the mysteries. Thus, Sheti is the spiritual discipline or program to promote spiritual evolution, which was used in Ancient Egypt. Now we can begin to expand on the teachings of that spiritual program. These all fall under the broad term *Smai Tawi* or "Egyptian Yoga." The hieroglyphic texts related to the terms that explain the mysteries provide insight into the vast philosophy of Kemitic (Ancient Egyptian) Spirituality. The essential aspects of the teaching of Ancient Egyptian religion outlined in the Kemitic Mystery System hieroglyphs are explained below.

The first term is *Sheta,* meaning a mystery, and *Sheta* means something hidden. This leads us to **or** *Sheta* **or** *Shetau* – something hidden and difficult to understand – a

---

[13] see the book *THE EGYPTIAN BOOK OF THE DEAD MYSTICISM OF THE PERT EM HERU* " by Dr. Muata Ashby, ISBN# 1-884564-28-3

mystery, something hard to get through. This term relates specifically to the mystery teaching and its secret nature, implying that it is difficult to understand and assimilate the mystery teachings, and for this reason a guide is needed. Sheta is derived from the term ⟨hieroglyphs⟩ **or** ⟨hieroglyphs⟩ ***Shetai*** which means hidden or secret being, in other words, God-the Divine essential nature. The Divine is also ⟨hieroglyphs⟩ ***Shetaiu*** - hidden of forms as well as ⟨hieroglyphs⟩ ***Sheta Kheperu*** - hidden creator of forms that will come into being. Therefore, the Divine is also ⟨hieroglyphs⟩ ***Shetau Akhet*** – the hidden essence behind the properties which sustain matter. The Divine Self is not only hidden in the present and future forms but also ⟨hieroglyphs⟩ ***Sheta Ba Neter*** - The Divinity of the hidden souls, meaning that the Divine manifests as the souls of human beings. Just as the land of Kemit (Egypt) is ⟨hieroglyphs⟩ ***Shet - Ta*** – hidden when covered by the Nile flood and then reemerges resurrected with vibrant new life, so too the ⟨hieroglyphs⟩ ***Shety*** or person hidden, covered in the coffin - the mummy, resurrects into a new life. The aspirant may wear a ⟨hieroglyphs⟩ ***Sheta Hobesh***- Shroud or covering garment and the best such garment is ⟨hieroglyphs⟩ ***Shetita Heru***- the Shroud or covering garment of Heru, that is, taking on the protection as well as identity of the Divine Self. Heru is the Divine king incarnate and as such he is the ⟨hieroglyphs⟩ ***Shetau Aset*** - Divinity in the hidden abode, the throne. These mysteries are contained in the ⟨hieroglyphs⟩ ***Shetit*** - writings related to the hidden teaching, a philosophical treatise. And those writings are referred to as ⟨hieroglyphs⟩ ***Medtu Neter***- "Divine Speech," the writings of the god Djehuti – also refers to any hieroglyphic texts or inscriptions. The term Medtu Neter makes use of a special hieroglyph, ⟨hieroglyph⟩, which means "***medtu***" or "staff - walking stick-speech." This means that speech is the support for the Divine, ⟨hieroglyph⟩. Thus, the hieroglyphic writing is a prop which sustains the Divine in time and space. That is, the Divine writings contain the wisdom which enlightens us about the Divine, ⟨hieroglyphs⟩ ***Shetaut Neter***.

The purpose of Shetaut Neter is to attain ⟨hieroglyphs⟩ *Nehast* {spiritual awakening and emancipation, resurrection}. The body or *Shet-t* (mummy) is where a human being focuses attention to practice spiritual disciplines. When spiritual discipline is perfected, the true Self or *Shti* (he who is hidden in the coffin) is revealed.

⟨hieroglyphs⟩

Shetaut Neter
(Secrets about the Divine Self)

Shetaut Neter means "the way or wisdom of the hidden Divinity which is behind all Creation." Religion has three levels of practice. The first is the myth, which includes the traditions, stories and everything related to it. The next stage is the "ritualization" of the myth. The final stage is the metaphysical philosophy behind the teachings given in the myth. In our book series on the Shetaut Neter Religion of Ancient Egypt, the book *African Religion Vol. 4, Asarian Theology,* presents the complete myth of Asar (Ausar or Osiris), Aset (Auset or Isis) and Heru (Horus), representing a first level of religions practice. The *Book of Coming Forth By Day* represents stage two, the ritualization of the myth of Asar, Aset and Heru, and through the practice of the rituals contained in the book it is possible to feel, think, act and ultimately experience the same fate as did Heru, spiritual enlightenment, stage three. Thus, a spiritual aspirant is to understand that {he/she} has incarnated on earth and has been dismembered by egoistic thoughts and actions. However, by gaining an understanding of the hidden mysteries, it is possible to reach a state of reintegration, beatitude and resurrection, just as Heru.[12]

Therefore, a serious spiritual aspirant should see every aspect of {his/her} life as a ritual in which the soul within him/her (Asar) is struggling to be reborn again (as Heru). This spiritual rebirth is accomplished by the practices of listening to the teachings, practicing them and meditating upon them. With the understanding of the hidden knowledge, you can see that all of nature around you is Divine. This includes plants, animals, planets and stars, food, other people, etc. So, through your understanding of the myth and how it relates to your life, and by living your life according to this understanding (ritual), you can lead yourself to discover and realize (mystical experience) the deeper truth behind your own being. This is the true practice of religion. If you only understand the superficial teachings of a religious myth, and you practice its rituals blindly without understanding the deeper implications, you will not obtain the higher realization. Your practice will be at the level of dogma. This is why there is so much religious conflict in the world today. Most orthodox religions practice only the first two levels of religion, myth and ritual…the level of dogma. At the level of dogma, each religion has different myths and rituals and therefore, little if any common ground upon which to come together. And even when there are common principles, those principles are founded upon, couched in and transmitted through parochial ideas based on local folklore, histories and geographical variations.[14] The results of this misunderstanding and ignorance have been personal disillusionment and wars. Yet, at the mystical or metaphysical level, all religions are actually pointing towards the same goal, that of spiritual realization.

If Medtu Neter is mastered then the spiritual aspirant becomes 〔hieroglyphs〕 Maakheru or true of thought, word and deed, that is, purified in body, mind and soul. The symbol medtu 〔glyph〕, is static, relating to support to help prop up, while the symbol of kheru is dynamic, relating to constant movement.

This term (Maakheru) uses the glyph 〔glyph〕 *kheru*, which is an oar (rowing), and is also a symbol of voice, meaning that purification occurs through the righteous movement (rowing-movement) of the word, that is, when it is used to promote virtue, order, peace, harmony and truth. So Medtu Neter is the potential word and Maakheru is the word in action, moving towards perfected word.

The hieroglyphic texts (Medtu Neter) become (Maakheru), useful in the process of religion, when they are used as 〔hieroglyphs〕 *hekau* - the Ancient Egyptian "Words of Power," when the word is 〔hieroglyphs〕 *Hesi*, chanted and 〔hieroglyphs〕 *Shmai*- sung, and thereby one performs 〔hieroglyphs〕 **or** 〔hieroglyphs〕 *Dua* or worship of the Divine. The divine word allows the speaker to control the gods and goddesses, in other words the cosmic forces. This concept is really based on the idea that human beings are higher order beings if they learn about the nature of the universe and elevate themselves through virtue and wisdom.

The word is perfected through 〔hieroglyphs〕 ***Shedy***, *which* means to study profoundly-penetrate the mysteries. Shedy is a matter of 〔hieroglyphs〕 **or** 〔hieroglyphs〕 ***Shedd*** "digging" or "excavating" the depths of the teaching, the heart and unconscious mind. It is a 〔hieroglyphs〕 ***Shedt*** – "suckling" process whereby as a child, the aspirant receives nourishment from the teacher, and so the teacher and the student become like 〔glyph〕 **Aset and Heru**, respectively, the wisdom (Aset) being imparted to the qualified aspirant (Heru). Thus the process of 〔hieroglyphs〕 ***Shedu*** to "educate" – "train" - rear a child occurs. So the path to 〔hieroglyphs〕 ***Sheta*** - the "secret" – "hidden Divinity" is 〔hieroglyphs〕 ***Shedy***.

---

[14] see the book *Comparative Mythology* by Dr. Muata Ashby

Shedy involves the disciplines of 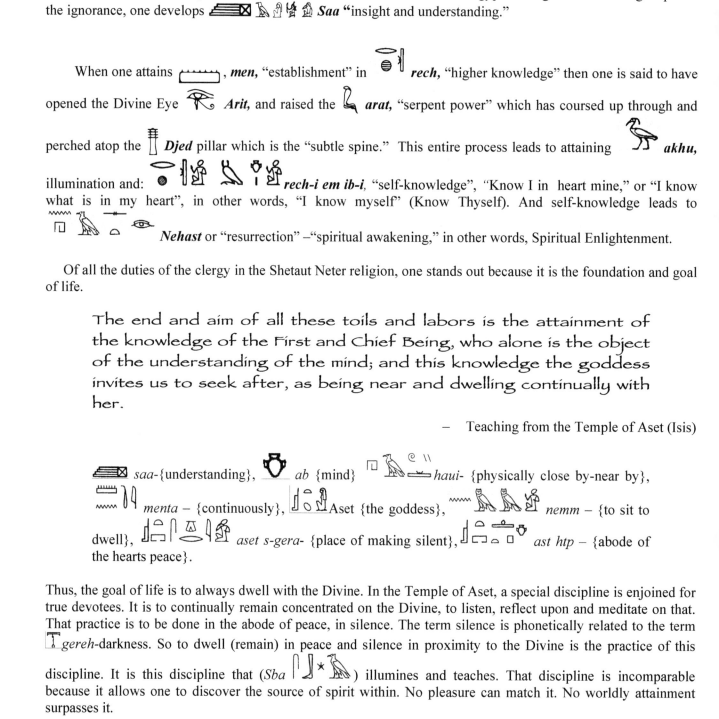*Smai Tawi* or "Egyptian Yoga." After having dispelled the ignorance, one develops *Saa* "insight and understanding."

When one attains , *men,* "establishment" in *rech,* "higher knowledge" then one is said to have opened the Divine Eye *Arit,* and raised the *arat,* "serpent power" which has coursed up through and perched atop the *Djed* pillar which is the "subtle spine." This entire process leads to attaining *akhu,* illumination and: *rech-i em ib-i,* "self-knowledge", "Know I in heart mine," or "I know what is in my heart", in other words, "I know myself" (Know Thyself). And self-knowledge leads to *Nehast* or "resurrection" –"spiritual awakening," in other words, Spiritual Enlightenment.

Of all the duties of the clergy in the Shetaut Neter religion, one stands out because it is the foundation and goal of life.

> The end and aim of all these toils and labors is the attainment of the knowledge of the First and Chief Being, who alone is the object of the understanding of the mind; and this knowledge the goddess invites us to seek after, as being near and dwelling continually with her.

> – Teaching from the Temple of Aset (Isis)

saa-{understanding}, *ab* {mind} *haui*- {physically close by-near by}, *menta* – {continuously}, Aset {the goddess}, *nemm* – {to sit to dwell}, *aset s-gera*- {place of making silent}, *ast htp* – {abode of the hearts peace}.

Thus, the goal of life is to always dwell with the Divine. In the Temple of Aset, a special discipline is enjoined for true devotees. It is to continually remain concentrated on the Divine, to listen, reflect upon and meditate on that. That practice is to be done in the abode of peace, in silence. The term silence is phonetically related to the term *gereh*-darkness. So to dwell (remain) in peace and silence in proximity to the Divine is the practice of this discipline. It is this discipline that (*Sba*) illumines and teaches. That discipline is incomparable because it allows one to discover the source of spirit within. No pleasure can match it. No worldly attainment surpasses it.

When the personality finds peace in silence and contemplation, there is a special peace that emerges, a peace that transcends problems, faults and misgivings. It is a peace wherein the opposites are cancelled out. That is what

"Hetep" means, the appeasement of the gods and goddesses. From this perspective, those gods and goddesses are the opposing energies, the desires, the ideas, imaginations and delusions of the mind. To appease them there must be understanding of the teaching of life and death. Then there must be constant reflection upon it, and then there emerges a meditative absorption…this is the divine act of *dwelling*. Even while working, talking, sleeping, studying, eating, bathing, breathing, and doing anything, dwelling always in the glory of Self is indescribable, and yet all encompassing, wholistic and most satisfying. It is a different way of relating to the world in which there is a realization that silence is the only answer to everything because everything is in reality no-thing. The sense of the mind that relates to the world gives way to the mind of thoughtless form and that world of the thinking mind falls apart and the rationale of the things that must be done or should have been done or are hated or loved or imagined show their true nature as demons and tricksters of senseless grief. And that mind that dwells with that wisdom of timeless nature that is sought after by all who pursue "the aim of all toils" discovers the first and the chief being, and there is a realization of "that is I." And this is why the priests and priestesses say:

tf pu nuk tjsy wdjb – "he is me tied to each other"- *He is I and I am He.*

The Great Awakening of Neterian Religion

The ultimate purpose of all the traditions of Shetaut Neter, including the Anunian Tradition, is to attain "Spiritual Awakening" (Enlightenment).

"Nehast"

Nehast means to "wake up," to Awaken to the higher existence. This is a mystical movement of self-discovery and union with the Supreme Divine framed as a "hidden" deeper existence of life discussed in various sections of the Prt em Hru (Ancient Egyptian Book of the Dead) text, for example, where it is said:[15]

Nuk pa Neter aah Neter Ziah asha ren[16]
"I am that same God, the Supreme One, who has myriad of mysterious names."

The goal of all the Neterian disciplines is to discover the meaning of "Who am I?," to unravel the mysteries of life and to fathom the depths of eternity and infinity. This is the task of all human beings and it is to be accomplished in this very lifetime.

This can be done by learning the ways of the Neteru, emulating them and finally becoming like them, Akhus, (enlightened beings), walking the earth as giants and accomplishing great deeds such as the creation of the universe!

---

[15] see the book *THE EGYPTIAN BOOK OF THE DEAD MYSTICISM OF THE PERT EM HERU* " by Dr. Muata Ashby, ISBN# 1-884564-28-3
[16] (Prt M Hru (Ancient Egyptian Book of the Dead) 9:4)

udjat

The Eye of Heru
The Eye of Heru is a quintessential symbol of awakening to
Divine Consciousness, representing the concept of Nehast.

What is the Philosophy of Shems?

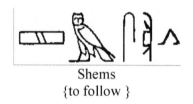

Shems
{to follow }

This purpose, awakening to Divine Consciousness, representing the concept of Nehast, is fulfilled through the process of "Shems." What does it mean to follow something? Why should some things be followed and others not? What should be followed in life and why? These are certainly some of the most important questions in life because if serious thought is put to them, they involve the crucial questions of life, who am I? Why am I here? What is my purpose? etc., which are or should be the most important concerns in life. This treatise (on Anunian Theurgy) suggests some answers.[17] They are offered from the perspective of an Ancient Egyptian concept and its attendant teachings as developed by the sages of Shetaut Neter-African religion in ancient times.

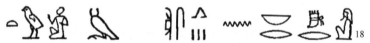

tu-a m shems n Neberdjer
"I am a follower of Neberdjer[19]

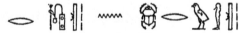

er sesh n Kheperu
in accordance with the writings of Lord Kheperu"

The answers to the important questions of life were given by the sages of ancient times following the spiritual path. In ancient times that path was known as *Shetaut Neter.*

See Plate 19

The term *Shetitu* means "teachings of spiritual philosophy" of Ancient Egypt, "The Mysteries," in other words "Shetaut Neter." The teachings of Shetaut Neter were given by the Supreme Being, Neberdjer, and written by the Creator, *Kheperu* (A) in the form of a philosophy *Shetitu. Lord Djehuti* (B) codified those into the hieroglyphic texts and these teachings were passed on to goddess Hetheru (C), the god Asar (D) and goddess Aset (E), who

---

[17] also see the book *CONVERSATION WITH GOD: Mystical Answers to the Important Questions of Life,* by Dr. Muata Ashby (2007)
[18] "I am follower of Neberdjer…" *Pert M Heru* Chap 4 (commonly 17)
[19] The Supreme Being, all-encompassing Divinity

taught it to Heru (F) and through history to succeeding generations of sages, priests and priestesses(G) of Neterian Religion. What does it mean to be a follower of the Shetaut Neter spiritual teaching? If you are reading this, it is because at one time or another you have come to the recognition of the need for the betterment of humanity, but also to promote your own 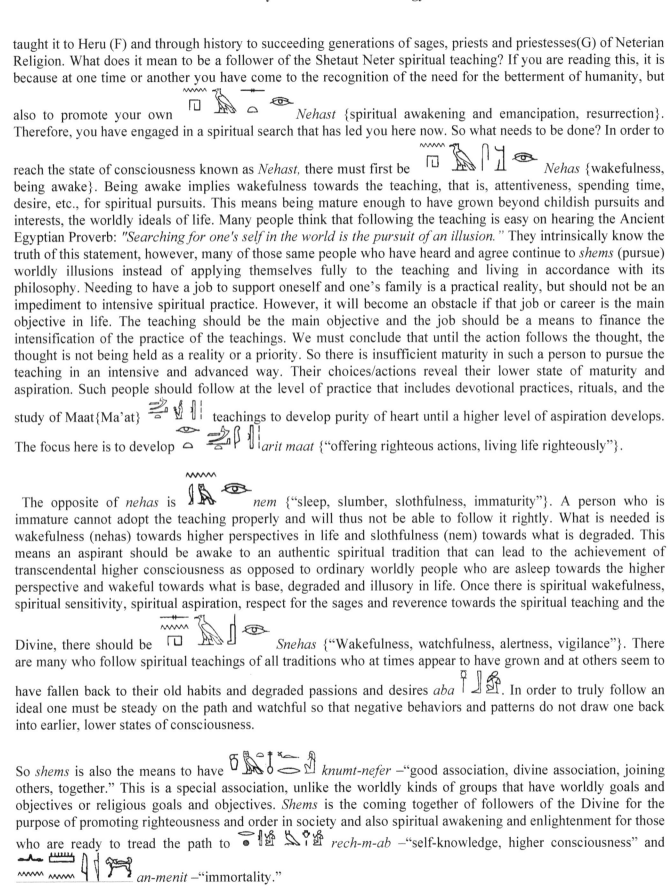 *Nehast* {spiritual awakening and emancipation, resurrection}. Therefore, you have engaged in a spiritual search that has led you here now. So what needs to be done? In order to reach the state of consciousness known as *Nehast,* there must first be *Nehas* {wakefulness, being awake}. Being awake implies wakefulness towards the teaching, that is, attentiveness, spending time, desire, etc., for spiritual pursuits. This means being mature enough to have grown beyond childish pursuits and interests, the worldly ideals of life. Many people think that following the teaching is easy on hearing the Ancient Egyptian Proverb: *"Searching for one's self in the world is the pursuit of an illusion."* They intrinsically know the truth of this statement, however, many of those same people who have heard and agree continue to *shems* (pursue) worldly illusions instead of applying themselves fully to the teaching and living in accordance with its philosophy. Needing to have a job to support oneself and one's family is a practical reality, but should not be an impediment to intensive spiritual practice. However, it will become an obstacle if that job or career is the main objective in life. The teaching should be the main objective and the job should be a means to finance the intensification of the practice of the teachings. We must conclude that until the action follows the thought, the thought is not being held as a reality or a priority. So there is insufficient maturity in such a person to pursue the teaching in an intensive and advanced way. Their choices/actions reveal their lower state of maturity and aspiration. Such people should follow at the level of practice that includes devotional practices, rituals, and the study of Maat{Ma'at} teachings to develop purity of heart until a higher level of aspiration develops. The focus here is to develop *arit maat* {"offering righteous actions, living life righteously"}.

The opposite of *nehas* is *nem* {"sleep, slumber, slothfulness, immaturity"}. A person who is immature cannot adopt the teaching properly and will thus not be able to follow it rightly. What is needed is wakefulness (nehas) towards higher perspectives in life and slothfulness (nem) towards what is degraded. This means an aspirant should be awake to an authentic spiritual tradition that can lead to the achievement of transcendental higher consciousness as opposed to ordinary worldly people who are asleep towards the higher perspective and wakeful towards what is base, degraded and illusory in life. Once there is spiritual wakefulness, spiritual sensitivity, spiritual aspiration, respect for the sages and reverence towards the spiritual teaching and the Divine, there should be *Snehas* {"Wakefulness, watchfulness, alertness, vigilance"}. There are many who follow spiritual teachings of all traditions who at times appear to have grown and at others seem to have fallen back to their old habits and degraded passions and desires *aba*. In order to truly follow an ideal one must be steady on the path and watchful so that negative behaviors and patterns do not draw one back into earlier, lower states of consciousness.

So *shems* is also the means to have *knumt-nefer* –"good association, divine association, joining others, together." This is a special association, unlike the worldly kinds of groups that have worldly goals and objectives or religious goals and objectives. *Shems* is the coming together of followers of the Divine for the purpose of promoting righteousness and order in society and also spiritual awakening and enlightenment for those who are ready to tread the path to *rech-m-ab* –"self-knowledge, higher consciousness" and *an-menit* –"immortality."

Plate 1: The Interrelationships of the Gods and Goddesses of Ancient Egypt

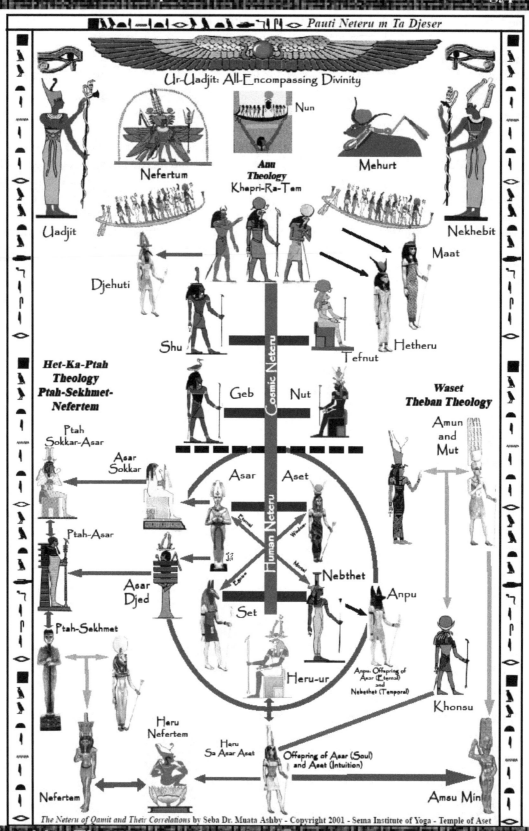

Pauti Neteru m Ta Djeser

Ur-Uadjit: All-Encompassing Divinity

Nun

Nefertum

Mehurt

Uadjit

Anu
Theology
Khepri-Ra-Tem

Nekhebit

Djehuti

Maat

Shu

Hetheru

Tefnut

Het-Ka-Ptah
Theology
Ptah-Sekhmet-
Nefertem

Geb   Nut

Cosmic Neteru

Waset
Theban Theology

Ptah
Sokkar-Asar

Amun
and
Mut

Asar
Sokkar

Asar   Aset

Human Neteru

Ptah-Asar

Eternal

Wisdom

Mekat

Love

Asar
Djed

Nebthet

Anpu

Set

Ptah-Sekhmet

Heru-ur

Anpu: Offspring of
Asar (Eternal)
and
Nebthet (Temporal)

Khonsu

Heru
Nefertem

Heru
Sa Asar Aset

Offspring of Asar (Soul)
and Aset (Intuition)

Nefertem

Amsu Min

The Neteru of Qamit and Their Correlations by Seba Dr. Muata Ashby - Copyright 2001 - Sema Institute of Yoga - Temple of Aset

Memphite Theurgy ⇔ Anunian Theurgy ⇔ Theban Theurgy

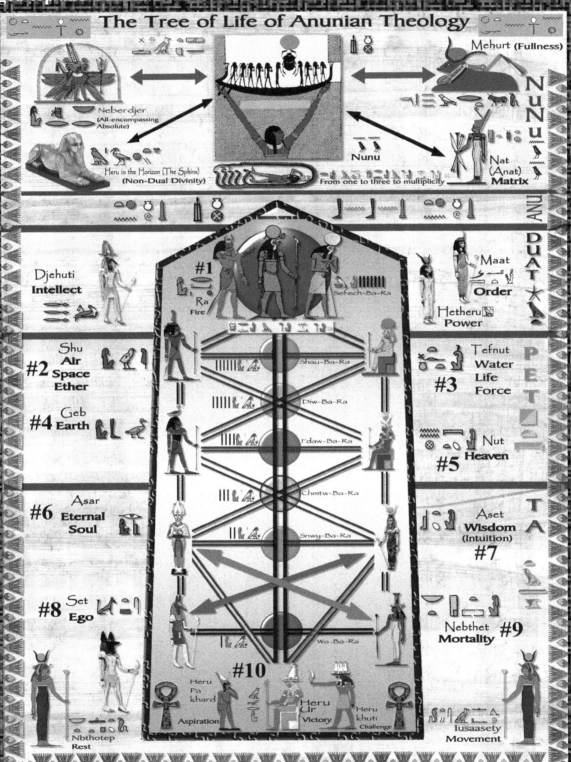

The Tree of Life of Anunian Theology (5,000 B.C.E.). From the book "Anunian Theology" by Muata Ashby ©2002-8 Sema Institue (305) 378-6253, www.Egyptianyoga.com

The Tree of Life of Anunian Theology

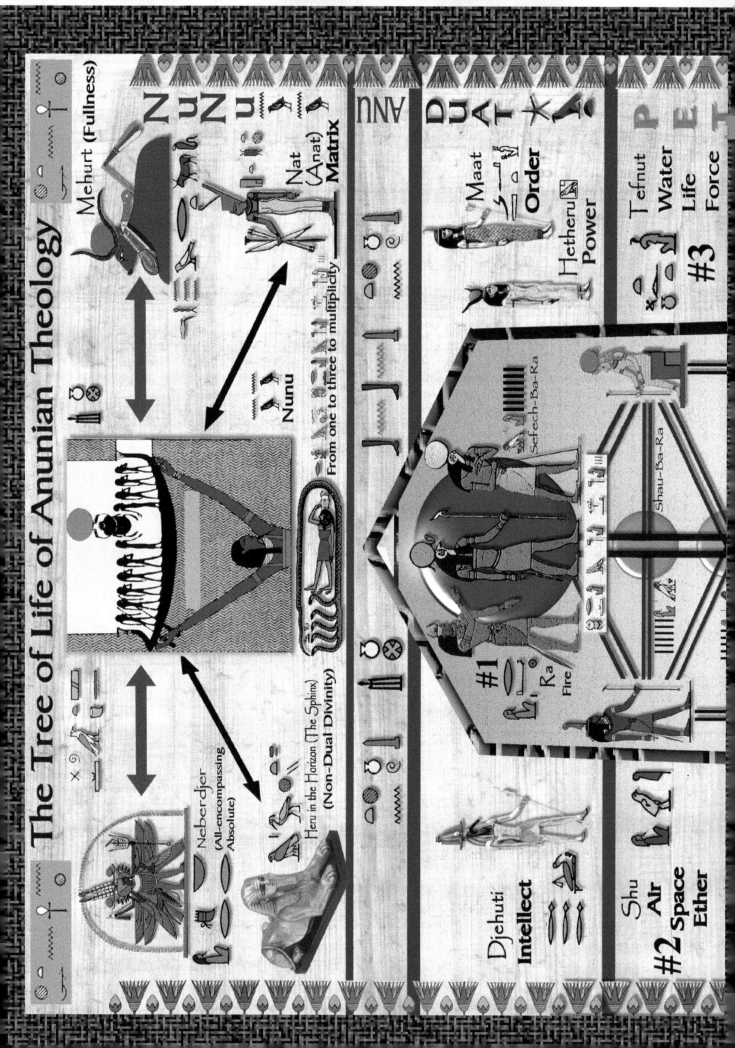

Mehurt (Fullness)

NUNU

Nat (Anat) **Matrix**

Nunu

From one to three to multiplicity

ANU

Neberdjer (All-encompassing Absolute)

Heru in the Horizon (The Sphinx) (Non-Dual Divinity)

DUAT

Maat **Order**

Hetheru **Power**

Tefnut **Water** **Life** **Force** **#3**

Sefech-Ba-Ra

Shau-Ba-Ra

#1 Ra **Fire**

Djehuti **Intellect**

Shu **Air** **Space** **Ether** **#2**

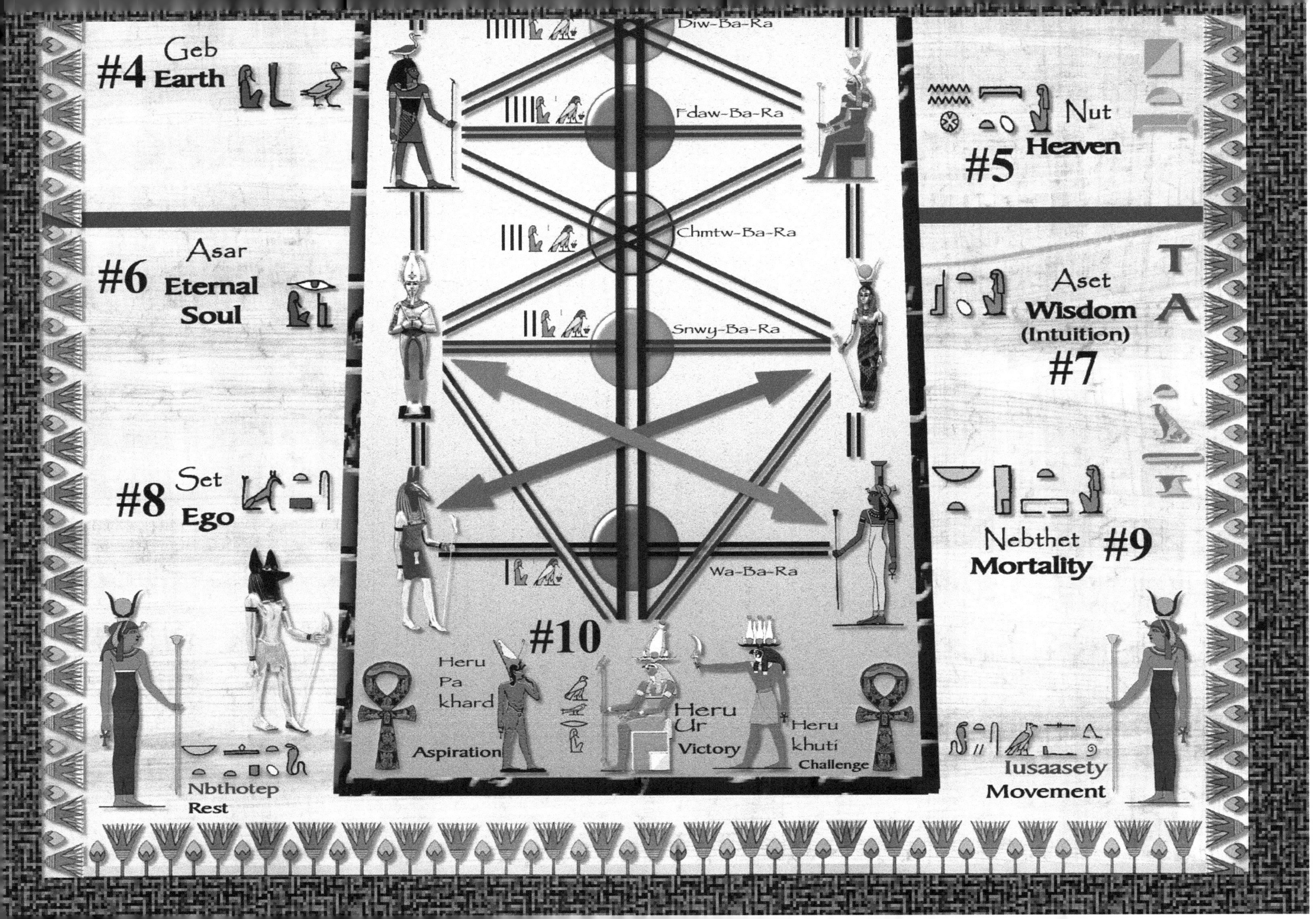

#4 Geb Earth

#5 Nut Heaven

#6 Asar Eternal Soul

#7 Aset Wisdom (Intuition)

#8 Set Ego

#9 Nebthet Mortality

#10

Diw-Ba-Ra

Fdaw-Ba-Ra

Chmtw-Ba-Ra

Snwy-Ba-Ra

Wa-Ba-Ra

Iusaasety Movement

Nbthotep Rest

Heru Pa khard Aspiration

Heru Ur Victory

*Heru khuti Challenge

Plate 3: The Trinity of Ra- Khepri-Ra-Tem

Plate 4: The God Shu

Plate 5: The Goddess Tefnut

Plate 6: The God Geb

Plate 7: Goddess Nut

Plate 8: The God Asar

Plate 9: The Goddess Aset

Plate 10: The God Set

Plate 11: The Goddess Nebethet

Plate 12: The God Heru Ur

Plate 13: Obelisk at Temple of Karnak

Plate 14: Limestone Pyramidion Dynasty 25-26 Ancient Egypt

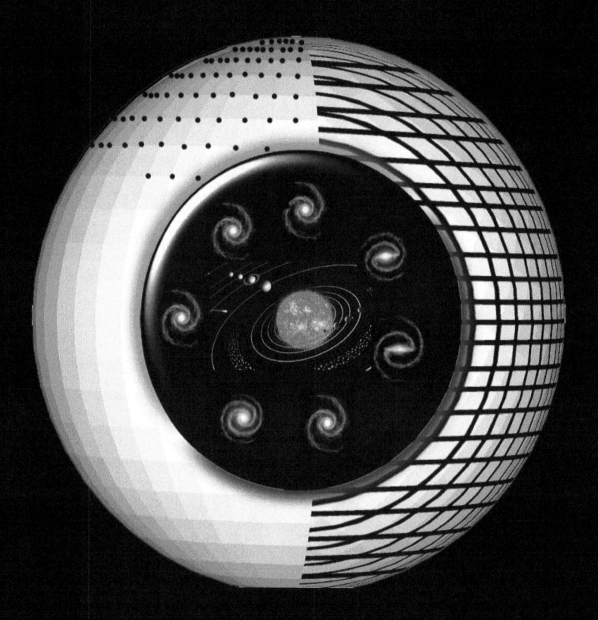

Plate 15: The Matrix of Creation

Plate 16: The enlightenment of Ani – from the Papyrus of Ani

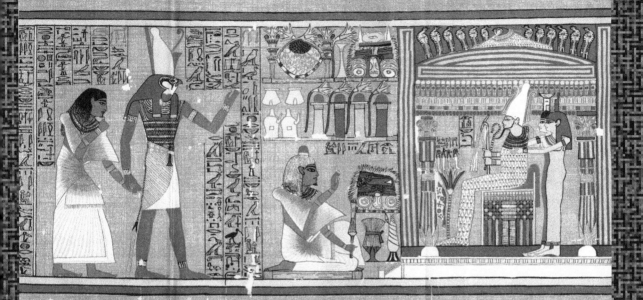

Plate 17: The Goddess in the Tree of Life

Plate 18: Three iconographical representations of the god Nefertem

Plate 19: The Dissemination and Lineage of Kemetic Spiritual Philosophy

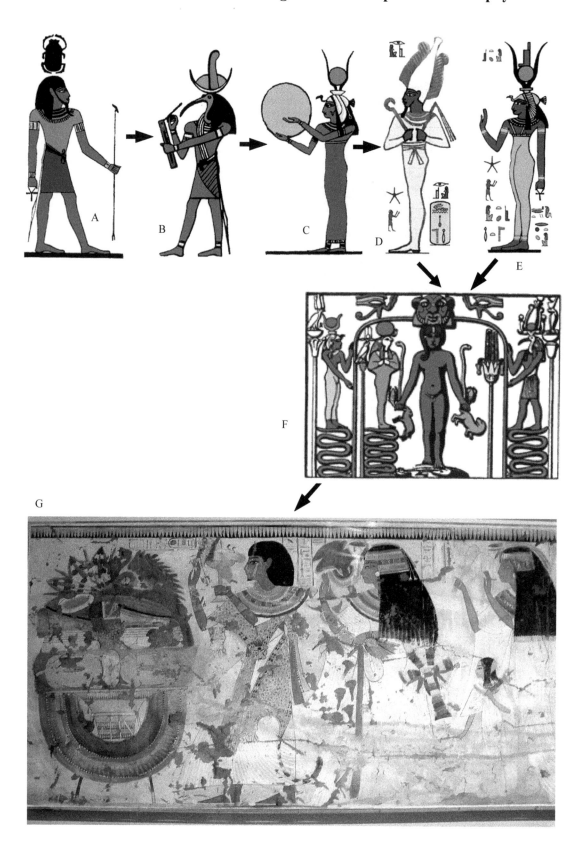

Plate 20: The Ancient Egyptian *Ben Ben* Stones (Pyramidion) (Capstone) in the Egyptian Museum, Cairo

Plate 21: *The Great sundisk (Ur-Uadjit) on the Ancient Egyptian Temple Entranceway*

Plate 22: The Great Sphinx of Ancient Egypt

The Great Sphinx, together with the Great Pyramid are marvels of engineering. In Anunian Theurgy they relate to the concept of a primeval hill and the union of Spirit and Matter where the harmony is discovered at the point where earth and heaven meet, the pinnacle of the pyramid, or at the confluence between the physical and the spiritual, the deeper meaning of the Sphinx.

Plate 23: Sebai MAA (Dr. Muata Ashby) teaching the philosophy of Shetaut Neter

The Anunian Theurgy Tree of Life picture should be treated as all other Kamitan iconographies in Temples (pictographs, reliefs, glyphs, and the images of divinities); it should be understood as a visual meditation. This is something that the Buddhists and the Hindus have been very big on but the Ancient Egyptians did it in grand and magnanimous style. The Hindus developed images called Yantras and the Buddhists developed images called Mandalas. You are supposed to sit in front of them, concentrate on them, and meditate on the deeper meaning. The Ancient Egyptian temples, icons and even the hieroglyphic texts themselves are meditative icons. The temples are giant visual aids to understanding, concentrating and meditating upon the teachings of Shetaut Neter.

An icon presented in a graphic form may be termed "iconograph." The Tree of Life form of spiritual iconography may be termed as "iconomythograph," since it conveys mythic information about a spiritual system, in this case, Anunian Theurgy in a graphic format. Our image specifically includes cosmological[20] information. So, a cosmiconomyth, in our context, is a visually schematized representation of the cosmos, characterized by a hierarchic and geometric configuration of divinities in different levels of existence. In Jungian psychology, such images might be thought of as symbols representing the effort to reunify the self. The Anunian Theurgy cosmiconomyth is in graphic form, so may more fully be described as, "cosmiconomythograph," as it includes macrocosmic information (about the outer Creation) and microcosmic information about the nature of inner human existence.

So, one of the purposes of this lecture series is so you may gain a deep insight into the meaning of this Tree of Life, which opens up other iconographies as well, of course, so that you can be able to delve into their

meanings deeply and make use of it on a personal level to promote your own mystic evolution. This image, of the Kemetic Tree of Life, is like a concentrated chemical formula. If you understand the meaning of its elements, then you can open up its mysticism, and thereby transcend in your meditation. This is the whole idea behind the yantra and mandala concepts in Hinduism and Buddhism respectively. If you go to a temple, it is one big mandala, one big architectural meditative image.

Let us proceed here with a brief general introduction to the Anunian Theurgy cosmiconomythograph, and then we will proceed into the specific aspects of the principles of the Tree of Life of Anunian Theurgy. We will go into the deeper aspect or personality of the tree, so that we may understand the deeper mysteries of it, because as you can see, the tree is actually a pathway, a vertical ladder from the earth to the heavens. If you were to understand the secrets of the tree, you would be able to elevate yourself through transcending the principles, the psycho-spiritual metaphysical aspects that are given in the tree. You would rise to the top of the tree, and of course the top of the tree is the source of creation.

---

[20] the branch of philosophy dealing with the origin and general structure of the universe, with its parts, elements, and laws, and esp. with such of its characteristics as space, time, causality, and freedom. *American Heritage Dictionary*

General Description of The Anunian Theurgy Cosmiconomythograph

The central image of the Tree of Life Cosmiconomythograph is of a *Technu*, an obelisk.[21] This is a reference to the Tantric philosophy contained in Anunian Theurgy, the sexual Life Force in a vertical movement, a movement of spiritual subtlety, of becoming subtle, of discovering the higher essence of oneself, moving from the gross to that which is more subtle and refined, as symbolized by the tapering format (larger at the bottom than at the top) of the obelisk. Therefore, The Tree of Life of Anunian Theurgy is a journey of self-discovery whereby an aspirant learns to discover and embody the principles represented by the divinities in the iconograph. It is a movement of increasing focus as one moves towards the top; the bottom being more spread out, more diffuse and the top being focused as it reaches a single point at the top of the obelisk. It is a philosophical, meditative discipline that is also to be applied in practice in the world of human activity. Let us proceed with the description of the images contained in the Anunian Theurgy Tree of Life Cosmiconomythograph.

The Anunian Theurgy Cosmiconomythograph top section

The top section has divisions of creation. The top is the subtlest, and the lower section is grossest. The top is the NuNu or the Primeval Waters, the Primeval Waters which contain within them, the essential innermost Divine Self, the consciousness that sustains Creation and the human personality as well. The Nun (NuNu) is like the body of the Divine Self.

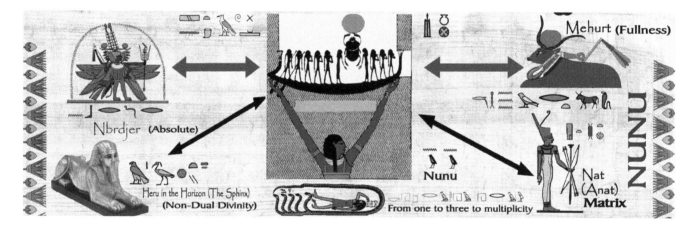

In the center of the picture you see the God himself, Nun, the personified Primeval Waters, pushing up the boat of Ra and Khepri is in the boat, and he is holding up the sundisk.

---

[21] *Technu*, an obelisk

The hieroglyphs to the left side of the Nun picture with the boat, which means Shetaut, and the ones on the right side means Anu, so Anunian Theurgy, or Mysteries of Anu. Now all of these other forms are either male or female aspects of the supreme Divinity that are integral to Anunian Theurgy.

To the left of Nun is the divinity *Neberdjer*. The literal translation of the name means "All-encompassing Divinity. *Neberdjer* is the aggregation of the attributes of all the gods and goddesses combined into one essence. More will be said on this in the final lesson.

Below, Neberdjer is depicted as the divinity Heruakhuti, also called Harakti, which means Heru in the form of the two horizons, meaning that Heru encompasses the opposites, encompasses both horizons, the dawn and the dusk, the beginning and the end. HERU is also the sun in the form of the great Sphinx. Thus, he is the two in the one, therefore a non-dual Divinity.

75

There is another divinity, Sekhmet- Bas- Ra, which is the same as Neberdjer and the Nun, but she is not present on this particular Anunian Theurgy cosmiconomythograph. However, she is presented here as an example of the dynamic capacity of Kemetic Spirituality to put forth an all-encompassing divinity concept with either a male or female tendency. Yet, both Neberdjer and *Sekhmet- Bas- Ra* may be thought of as representations of the idea of all-encompassing Divinity and both are to be considered as androgynous. She has all the attributes, all the scepters, all of the winds, and means all encompassing Divinity.

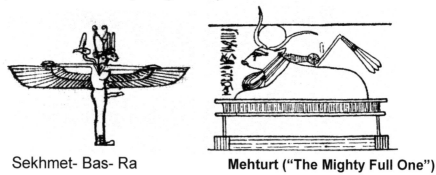

Sekhmet- Bas- Ra   **Mehturt ("The Mighty Full One")**

On the top right, we have Mehturt, the cow goddess aspect of Hetheru and Aset. The name is composed of the

word ⌒ Meht –fullness. In Ancient Egyptian the terms "Meh" means "full" and "urt" means "great," so we have "mighty fullness." And what this fullness relates to,and really, what the creation myth is

talking about, comes down to that which is the *Mehturt*. What I am trying to bring you to understand is that everything in creation is full of the Divine Self. There is no place, a rock, lizards, plants, the sun, even the very most inner part of yourself, that is not full of the Divine Self /Spirit. Even the space in between objects is also permeated by the Divine Self, and that is the Mehturt. You can't escape. God is everywhere and in all things. No matter how different or separate you think that you are, you can never run away…only by your own illusion, that is egoism. And the more deluded you are, the more prone you are to complexes, because you feel alone, abandoned, and separate. And you can delude yourself with all your religion, your complexes, your concepts, but all human beings are actually one in the Divine Self, regardless of whatever name they call It, and by ignorance only, can they feel separate from It. You are together here. You may think you are all different, white people and black people and Chinese people and Hindus and Muslims. It is all ridiculous in the ultimate realization of Mystical awareness.

Looking at the bottom right hand corner of the Nunu section of the Anunian Theurgy Cosmiconomythograph (top section) we have goddess Nat or Net. Net means loom, and she is a weaver. Net means matrix, referring to the matrix upon which all creation is created and sustained. She weaves the clothing "Garment of "Nun", in other words, the apparent creation (images of differentiation (objects separate from each other and appearing to be composed of different constituent forms of matter) which is the visible creation whose underlying essence is Nun or undifferentiated matter. She is also referred to as "Mesu Ra"…she gives birth to the sundisk, Ra…the energetic impetus that gives rise to this matrix (Creation).

Figure 11: Children-Scooter in a german amusement park near Schlangenbad in Taunus

When you go to a carnival and if you go on some of the safer rides like the bumper cars...you see the metallic mesh on the floor, and then there is a pole that sticks out of the car, and it touches a mesh up above on the ceiling. The mesh has the electricity running through it that allows the car to run. And anywhere on that mesh that the pole touches you can have an electrical connection. And that is like a matrix; there is a mesh with electricity running through it. Your consciousness operates through your body, your nervous system; your body is the bumper car, bumping against other people, and their other desires, feelings, etc.; it is enlivened by your soul and the life force energy permeating the universe. The reason that you can travel from here and go to, say, NY or Paris or Africa or even the moon or another planet and continue the existence of your life is because you are continually existing within the matrix of The Spirit. Your body is not alive because just because you eat food and that sustains it; the gross food sustains the gross physical body but what sustains the gross foods? Your body is alive because it exists within the matrix of Creation, sustained by the Life Force of the spirit that sustains every individual soul. If it were to leave the matrix your body could not remain alive because your soul, your spirit would not be there where the body was, sustaining it and being there to be conscious of whatever the body's senses were perceiving (which would be nothing-since it would be outside of Spirit and outside of Spirit there is nothing.). As a physical personality you are like that bumper car. And you are bumping yourself between other people and objects which all exist within the matrix, the fullness of Spirit. And so wherever you go, there you are; your soul is everywhere...not because you are carrying it around with you, mind you. Do you follow the difference? Do you understand the difference? You are not carrying your soul around with you in your body.

When you go to a carnival, if you go on the bumper cars...you see the metallic mesh on the floor, and then there is a pole that sticks out of the car, and it touches a mesh up above on the ceiling. The mesh up above has the electricity running through it that allows the car to run. And anywhere on that mesh that the pole touches, you can have an electrical connection. That is like a matrix. Your consciousness operates through your body, through your nervous system. In this example, your body is like the bumper car, bumping against other people, and their other desires, feelings, etc.; it is enlivened by your soul. The reason that you can travel from here and go to, say, to New York or Paris or Africa or even the moon or another planet and continue the existence of your life is because you are continually existing within the matrix of The Spirit. So your body is not alive because you eat food and that seemingly sustains it; it is alive because it exists within the matrix of Creation. If it were to leave the matrix, it could not remain alive, because your soul, your spirit, would not be there where the body was, sustaining it and being there to be conscious of whatever the body's senses were perceiving (which would be nothing-since it would be outside of Spirit and outside of Spirit there is nothing.). You are like that bumper car. And you are bumping yourself between other people and objects which all exist within the matrix, the fullness of Spirit. And so, wherever you go, there you are; your soul is everywhere...not because you are carrying it around with you, mind you. Do you follow the difference? Do you understand the difference? You are not carrying your soul around with you in your body. The Soul, the Spirit is everywhere, like the electricity in the mesh and the universe is the mesh, so wherever you go, wherever your body goes, that is, where there is Spirit (which is everywhere), you can perceive through the mind and senses of the body if you are dependent on the body to perceive with. If you go into outer space you are carrying your body with you not so you can exist out there, but so you can perceive with your body's senses. The existence of your body is predicated upon certain physical laws, the first one being that it must be sustained or enlivened by soul. And since Soul or Spirit is everywhere, you can go everywhere. But your body cannot go everywhere. Your body needs sunlight. Your body needs green foods to eat, but as long as you have those sustaining items for the physical body you can go anywhere and that is the matrix of Creation weaved by the divinities of Creation. However, what if you were to discover a higher body that does not need physical food to survive? What if you could stop living a pathetic and empty life like a hysterical child intent on crashing into others before they crash into you; having fun by knocking your car (your body) into others or being fearful they will crash into you? What if you could extricate yourself from the endless and mindless bumping of the world, banging your head against a brick wall, never being able to find or hold on to the objects you desire or be free from the dullness and nonsense of human culture, competing against others, fighting for resources, engaging in conflict and hurting others as well as yourself, through petty jealousies, greed, and the disappointments and frustrations of life? Actually you do have such a body, an astral body, and it can live on subtler forms of sustenance; and we will discuss more about such things in subsequent lessons.

At the center, the picture underneath the Nun is Khepri, in fact it is called ᙁ ᛁ ᛁ ᛁ ᛁ *Khepri Asha Hrau.* *Khepri* is lying on his back; he is actually lying on the Primeval Ocean. On his feet, lying there, are three symbols of body parts. So from the one he as become three, and those three touch the head of the cosmic serpent, the serpent that is in the Primeval Waters. The name of the serpent is ASHA HRAU, or "Many faced one". He (Asha Hrau) has 5 heads, but these heads represent *Asha* or manifold, in other words, multiplicity.

Next level down (see below), Anu, is the *Ben Ben* stone which is the top of the Techbu (Obelisk). The obelisk is an important Kemetic artifact that figures prominently in the Tree of Life iconography and spiritual mysteries. In Hinduism they call images such as these Yantras, these special geometric patterns that lead you to a deeper understanding of the mysteries of creation, and if you have studied the book *AFRICAN RELIGION VOL. 1- ANUNIAN THEOLOGY THE MYSTERIES OF RA,* by Muata Ashby, you would have seen a particular symbol of the god Ra, the circle with the dot in the center, ⊙. The dot at the center of the symbol of Ra is the same point at the top of the *Ben Ben* stone. From this ⌡ᴼ⌡ᴼ⌂ *Ben Ben* in the Kemetic philosophy, you can see the similarity to the concept that arose later in India called the "Bindu" in the Hindu myth and philosophy.[22] Actually, you can see the Ancient Egyptian Ben Ben point, the black dot, in the Hindu Yantra called *Sri Yantra.*[23]

---

[22] *THE AFRICAN ORIGINS OF CIVILIZATION, RELIGION AND YOGA SPIRITUALITY AND ETHICS PHILOSOPHY* by Dr. Muata Ashby
[23] ibid

Figure 12: *Ben Ben* **(capstone) of the Obelisk**

Anu means "the first place," "the original city," "the original spot," "the beginning place." And from this single point, all of creation comes forth, just like the big bang theory of the modern physicists…from one single point all matter comes, all the universe comes into being…it expands out of there. And the Kemetic tradition being the older brings forth the teaching for the first time in human history. From this *Ben Ben* point, (refer to top section of the obelisk), the golden point at the top of the Technu or obelisk symbol that is in the top-center of the Anunian Theurgy cosmiconomythograph, everything comes into being, into the physical plane mind you. Note that when we are speaking of the Benben we are referring to the pyramidion (small pyramid fitted at the top of obelisks and pyramids, but more specifically to the very top of the pyramidion, the uppermost point where the four corners of the pyramidion meet at one place, where the four corners, which represent the four cardinal directions and time and space reality come into existence when Ra made the first solid place out of the primeval ocean, but also where they dissolve at the end of the creation cycle. Therefore, the *benben* symbolizes transition point in a movement (downward) of creation and a movement (upward) of dissolution. If a human being were to discover the pathway of the dissolution that person would be able to dissolve the Creation and discover the transcendental nature of being. This is the objective of the Anunian Tree of Life mysteries and its mystical philosophical teaching. But this pathway is not just about philosophy. It is also about a meditative experience, an intuitional discovery of the Gods and Goddesses within oneself.

Diagram 4: Obelisk/Pyramid view from above showing four corners (A) meeting at one point (B)

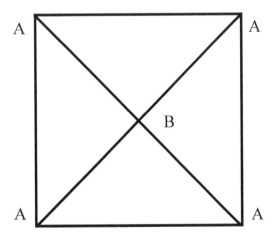

Figure 13: The Ancient Egyptian *Ben Ben* Stones (Pyramidion) (Capstone) in the Egyptian Museum, Cairo

In archaeological terminology, a pyramidion, (plural pyramidia), is a term used to refer to the uppermost piece of an Ancient Egyptian pyramid, also known as a capstone.[24] The pyramidions were called *benben* in Ancient Egyptian.[25] This placement of the pyramidion atop the pyramid served also to associate the pyramid in its entirety with the original sacred benben stone.[26] In the Old Kingdom period of Ancient Egypt, the pyramidions were usually made of granite, diorite, or fine limestone. Then the stone was covered in gold or electrum.[27] During the period of the Middle Kingdom era and down through to the rest of the Pyramid building period, the pyramidions were composed from granite.[28]

Not many pyramidions have survived to the present day. Most of the ones that have survived are composed of polished black granite. There are four pyramidia in the Egyptian Museum in Cairo's main hall. Among these four is the pyramidion that was placed on the so-called Black Pyramid which belonged to Amenemhet III at Dahshur.[29]

---

[24] Toby Wilkinson, The Thames and Hudson Dictionary of Ancient Egypt, Thames & Hudson, 2005. p.197
[25] Ermann, Grapow, *Wörterbuch der ägyptischen Sprache* 1, 459.13-14
[26] Wilkinson, op. cit., p.197
[27] an amber-colored alloy of gold and silver used in ancient times. *Based on the Random House Unabridged Dictionary,* © *Random House, Inc. 2006.*
[28] *Pyramidions* by Alan Winston
[29] editors Regine Schulz and Matthias Seidel (w/ 34 contributing Authors), *Egypt, The World of the Pharaohs,* Konemann, Germany: 1998. *Amenemhet III,* 1842-1797 BC, p.115

The top of the Tech004 of Anu, the obelisk of Anu, which is one of the only surviving objects from the ancient city where Anunian Theurgy was developed, is the *Ben Ben*. In earlier times, the temples of Anu themselves were actually different from the temples which were used in the later periods of Ancient Egyptian history. The remnants of the obelisks of the ancient Anunian temples have a huge fat base, and they were shorter, and the offerings were made to this Tech04 temple.

Picture 28: Basic Ancient Egyptian Obelisk Temple Complex of the Anunian Period

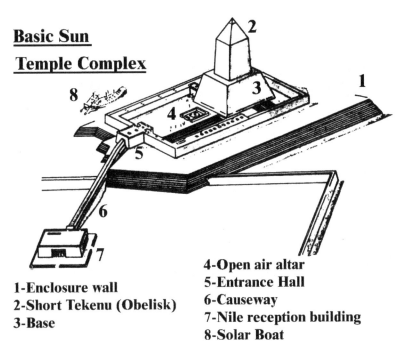

Basic Sun Temple Complex

1-Enclosure wall
2-Short Tekenu (Obelisk)
3-Base
4-Open air altar
5-Entrance Hall
6-Causeway
7-Nile reception building
8-Solar Boat

At the bottom of the Anunian Theurgy Tree of Life Cosmiconomythograph are two divinities we have not talked about but that are important to conclude this introductory level of study: Nbthotep and Iusaasety. These divinities represent other subtle emanations of Ra that he brings into existence. These three (Ra, Nbthotep and Iusaasety) form a subtle trinity composed of principles that are necessary for the Creation to exist. Nbthotep represents rest or sedentary nature and Iusaasety represents stimulation to motion, so we have stimulation and rest, the opposites of creation which constitute change in time and space and in fact are the cause for the existence of time and space. Imagine if things were motionless? How would there be any change, or any perception of change? Imagine if things were constantly in motion, how could things be stopped in order to study them? There would be no way, there must be both motion and rest in order to have proper perception which in turn allows proper cognition about the nature of reality and that we can call sanity. So they are the two important principles of Anunian Theurgy that are the crucial and essential ingredients that Ra brings to the Nun that allow it to be differentiated (clothing of Nun) into the forms we call Creation. In Anunian Theurgy and in this Anunian Cosmiconomythograph we are looking at one male divinity and two female divinities which compose an Anunian Creation Trinity. However, generally, in Kemetic metaphysics, the female divinities represent the movement, and the males represent sedentary-ness. This is why the god Geb, who represents the earth, is often depicted lying on his back and he is not moving around. Yet, his companion, Nut, is the sky which is always moving and changing. You will also see the divinity Asar often on his back as well. Actually, Khepri, as we saw earlier, is also on his back and doesn't do anything either. He is thinking all this "stuff" (Creation) and talking all this Nunu "stuff", undifferentiated matter into existence as the apparent objects of Creation, but the actual work of differentiating undifferentiated matter into the forms of creation is done by the sound vibration, charged with life force energy, directed by thought, which engenders the movement exciting the primeval matter and polarizing, coagulating it into the forms of Creation. In this image the voice of Khepri engenders part of his body to be moved by the primeval serpent. The serpent's vibration churns the ocean, making waves of varying shapes and sizes, where there was only a flat and calm ocean previously. The obelisk is Geb's penis, which is erect and copulating with the sky; this tantric symbolism signifies that so too a spiritual aspirant is to sublimate the sexual excitement for worldly sexual experiences into a sexual desire for reunion of the earthly nature with the innate divinity in the sky.[30] More will be given on the Tantric teachings of the TOL later. And this concludes this preliminary overview of Anunian Theurgy and its relation to the Anunian Cosmiconomythograph of The Tree of Life.

More Detailed Description of the Anunian Theurgy Tree of Life Cosmiconomythograph

Firstly, you should begin to notice that Kemetic Iconography is very balanced, very structured and very orderly in its depictions of males and females. The Anunian Cosmiconomythograph has a certain balance between the male divinities and female divinities which reflect and complement each other. This is due to the recognition that there must be a balance between the male and female elements in order to have a proper equilibrium and stability not only in the creation of the Universe but also in the promotion of beneficial culture and positive spiritual evolution. This balance was also reflected in the secular affairs of Ancient Egyptian life, in government, business, etc. wherein men and women were accorded equal legal rights.

The TREE OF LIFE teaching of Anunian Theurgy as depicted in the Anunian Tree of Life Cosmiconomythograph is based on the creation myth of Anu and the pyramid texts of Anunian Theurgy. Anunian Theurgy is one of the main theurgs of Kemetic religion, of Neterianism. Neterianism is the theurgy of Neter. All of the Kemetic divinities are called Neteru (plural). They are aspects of Divinity, of the one Divine Self: Neter (singular). The one Divine Self differentiates Itself out of the primeval, undifferentiated matter, the Nun. It creates aspects or forms of itself that carry out several different tasks or functions in order to sustain creation. These aspects manifest through cosmic natures and within realms or dimensions of existence. The cosmic natures are neteru and the realms are *Ta, Pet, Duat* and *Nun* (or *Nunu*). Here we will continue the discourse on the TOL with the Duat realm and move forward through the cosmiconomythograph of the Tree of Life.

Duat means "netherworld." Remember that all of the following divinities arise from the original, the non-dual Self that emerges from the homogenous, non-dual primeval ocean. The most important Duat divinities are the god Djehuti, and the goddesses Maat and Hetheru. Djehuti represents intellect; Maat represents order and balance, but in this context primarily order, specifically the ordering of the disordered (undifferentiated) primeval matter. Disorder is not necessarily a bad thing. It just means that it does not have a particular form. That is all it means. You should not give it a negative connotation when we are engaging in a philosophical study of this teaching, though from an egoistic perspective disorder or chaos can be troubling in some cases. So in our context it refers to unformed matter. Maat gives it form. Hetheru is the energy that sustains or that holds that form. Maat is the order itself. Now we will look at the *Pet* realm. The realms may be likened to the concept of causality.

---

[30] see the book *SACRED SEXUALITY: EGYPTIAN TANTRA YOGA: The Art of Sex* Sublimation and Universal Consciousness by Dr. Muata Ashby ISBN 1-884564-03-8

Planes of Existence from the Tree of Life	Metaphysical Causality Planes of Consciousness/existence
Nunu ⬇	**Absolute** ⬇
Duat	**Causal Plane** (Subtlest plane of Creation—center of consciousness and individuality.) ⬇
⬇ **Pet**	**Astral Plane** (Subtle plane of Creation where the mind operates with ideas, thoughts, imagination and dreams with the subtle senses.) ⬇
⬇ **Ta**	**Physical Plane** (Most dense plane of Creation where living beings experience physical existence with the physical senses.)

Pet means "heavenly". In the Pet realm we have: Space, Air, Ether which is Shu. We have Geb which is earth. We have Tefnut which is water. Nut is the heavens. Notice that we are moving gradually from the subtlest essence of the substratum, coming down to the more gross principles (elements) of the creation. This is what the sages have broken down creation into. This is what creation is made up of…these principles. Now we will look at the *Ta* realm.

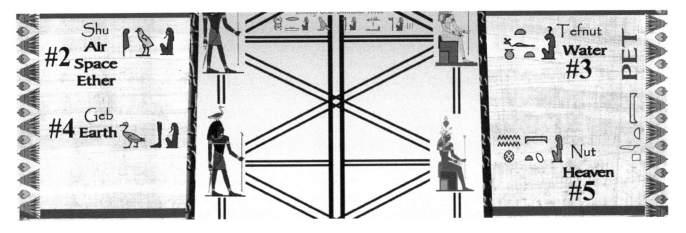

Ta means "earthly", worldly, in other words, physical. In the Ta realm, we have the divinities that go to compose the personalities of human beings and animals. Most importantly, *Asar* is the eternal soul. *Aset* is wisdom and intuition. *Set* is ego. *Nebthet* is mortality, and *Heru Ur* is king of the earth, master of the earth. And encompassing these male and female principles are *Nbthotep* and *Iusaasety* which are the most primeval opposites, if you will. They arise out of Ra directly also, and they are the principles of rest and movement, respectively. Nbthotep and Iusaasety may be thought of as foundational divinities that together with Ra orchestrate a triangle, a pyramid encompassing the matrix of Creation.

The Tree of Life of Anunian Theology (5,000 B.C.E.). From the book "Anunian Theology" by Muata Ashby ©2002 Sema Institue (305) 378-6253, www.Egyptianyoga.com

So they seem to appear at the bottom of the cosmiconomythograph instead of in the Dua realm along with Djehuti, Maat and Hetheru but in reality they are not at the bottom, they (including Ra) are surrounding the Creation as if the world is inside a sphere and in a sphere there is no top or bottom; they encompass Creation but we must also keep in mind that outside of this sphere of Creation (the universe) there is also spirit. Thus, spirit is within and without. However, in this three dimensional model, when lines are connected between them their trinity encompasses the obelisk and the creative principles contained in it; meaning that it governs them.

The goddesses Nebthotep and Iusaasety are important aspects of Anunian Theurgy and are closely associated with Ra. Together with Ra they form an important Trinity which circumscribes the nature of Creation. Creation is engendered by the primal force of Spirit, the divine fire of the Supreme Being, Ra through Hekau –Word-sound of Power. Time and space are actually relative aspects that come to exist through the motion of objects in space. Essentially, therefore, Creation consists of the ever-dynamic fire of the spirit which operates through energy, Sekhem, which sustains (Ankh (life)), the elements and the relative motion of objects within the matrix of Creation. However, the Spirit underlies all and therefore it can move nowhere since it is everywhere. Objects in Creation move in and through Spirit and are rooted (dependent) on Spirit for their existence. If objects were to be completely motionless in space there would be no existence. For example, all hearts would be still and no stars would burn, no heat would be produced and no life could exist because no metabolic functions could occur. If objects were to be in perpetual motion there would also be no creation because the motion itself would become a constant that would allow no awareness of existence and no replenishment, reorganization or recreation of elements, foodstuffs or fuels would be possible; all would be used up and all would cease. Awareness is a factor of relative motion. It is an action that the mind performs. If that action were to cease the world would also cease to exist from the perspective of that mind that has ceased to operate, to move.

Figure 14: The Trinity of Khepri (Ra), Nbthotep and Iusaasety

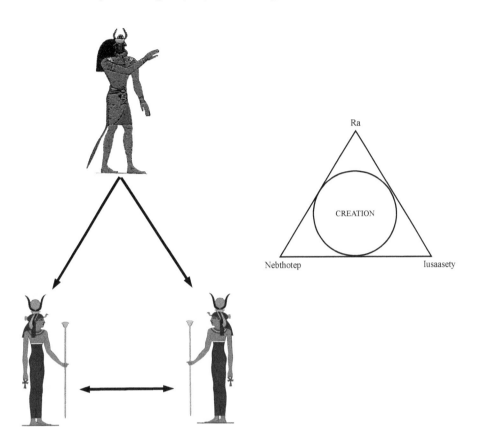

The task of the Creator is to balance the principles of **Nebthotep** and **Iusaasety** in order to bring about a universe in which consciousness can perceive it. Therefore, relatively speaking, there is motion and motionlessness. From an absolute perspective however, there is no motion since in reality no Creation has actually occurred. So if one were to discover existence beyond the apparent Creation, the motion of relative reality, one would discover the absolute and transcendental nature of existence. This idea will be expanded later. In ordinary human life there is more motion than motionlessness; from the time a person gets up in the morning until they go to bed they are for the most part, talking, thinking, desiring, yearning, imagining, remembering, hoping, etc. then at the time of sleep they dream which is another form of the same which occurred while in waking. For a short time the mind may experience dreamless sleep, a state which offers a respite from the constant movement of mind, but that is not enough to allow the mind to perceive higher consciousness (transcendental nature of existence), just enough to replenish the mind so as to allow the personality to continue to exist as an ignorant human being. The task of a follower of Neterian religion and practitioner of Neterian metaphysics is to find the place wherein there is motionlessness and then to discover that God is to be perceived and experienced there since God exists in the world of motion as well as out of it where there is no motion. If the human being were to discover that aspect of consciousness existing in motionlessness of mind they would also discover their own spirit essence outside of time and space, and thereby also their transcendental essential nature beyond the mortal and finite human personality (body, mind and senses). However, existing as an ego personality and perceiving with the mind and senses, which are in perpetual motion prevents a human being from perceiving the transcendental aspect of reality. So a discipline of ritual practice, purification, meditation and philosophical introspection is enjoined to enable the mind to slow and even temporarily stop, in order to discover the essential nature of the Self (Spirit).

These two places (physical realm, astral realm) are in the same space but in different dimensions. This program of discovery is accomplished through worship of the divinities,[31] learning about them,[32] meditating upon them with the ideal of identifying with them, embodying their characteristics and manifesting them, and finally mastering their principles and thereby rendering those principles effective. Beginning at the bottom, the personality discovers each principle on the Tree in a particular order and eventually the human personality, which was impelled by ignorance, becomes voided and the aspirant takes up her/his rightful place as one with the Neter, master of the gods and goddesses. Then in such an advanced aspirant the movements of the world as if cease and the rest of Spirit, which moves nowhere, becomes the ever-present reality.

Figure 15:: Khepri, Nbthotep and Iusaasety and the Anunian Theurgy Tree of Life Cosmiconomythograph

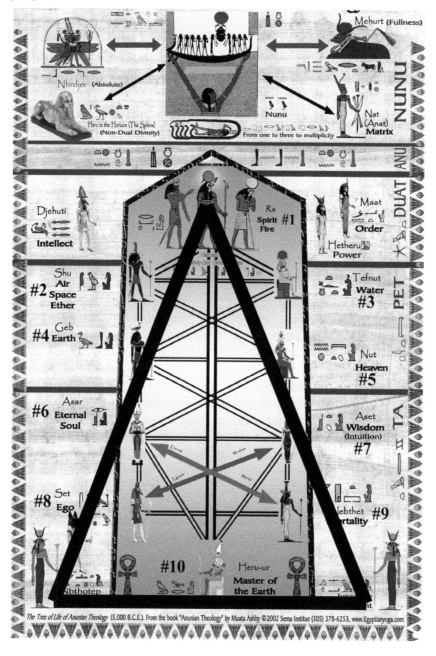

---

[31] See the book *GOD OF LOVE: THE PATH OF DIVINE LOVE The Process of Mystical Transformation and The Path of Divine Love* by Dr. Muata Ashby
[32] *EGYPTIAN MYSTERIES VOL 2:* Dictionary of Gods and Goddesses by Dr. Muata Ashby

86

In closing, you should be thinking of these icons, the gods and goddesses, as physical principles as well as concepts because they operate through physical creation, and everything has these aspects in some measure, if you delve deeply into all matter. Anunian Theurgy is important because it is the oldest Theurgy of Kemet, and it gives rise to all the other theurgies of Ancient Egypt. All the other theurgies have a basis in Anunian Theurgy. As you saw with the other iconomythograph, the one of the Gods and Goddesses and their relationships,(Plate 1) we demonstrated that all of the divinities of the varying Kemetic theurgys are related to each other. And you should understand the fundamental theory of Neterianism in this way. And that will actually simplify and clear up a lot of issues or confusions related to the so called polytheism of ancient Kemetic religion, and of African religion in general. This concludes Lesson 1.

Hetep -Peace

Questions and Answers

Questions:

Why is the *Ben Ben* placed at the top and why is the Anunian Theurgy Tree of Life cosmiconomythograph arranged in this way with divisions?

Answer:

The *Ben Ben* is the top of the Technu, the obelisk. The divisions as outlined in the Anunian Theurgy Tree of Life cosmiconomythograph are a 2D representation of a multidimensional creation Matrix (Nunu, Duat, Pet, Ra), so it is arranged for proper visual effect. The divisions represent demarcations between realms. Keep in mind that this is a 2-D icon that you are being given, that actually represents a 4-D concept, and actually also transcends 4-D as well. Really it represents the single point, if you can think of the smallest point that you can have at the top of the Technu. This is symbolized by a small pyramid at the top of the obelisk. If we were to represent Creation graphically we could metaphorically use the shape of a sphere containing the worlds and galaxies of Creation. We might see that the sphere has points everywhere that are connected to all the other points in a mesh, a matrix. Therefore, all points are connected and thus there is no particular center or we may say that all points are one with the center or we may say that all points are the center; in this way the Spirit is central to all, as it is the container and the connections between all and therefore it is the center of all and wherever it is there is the center and thus every thing and every human being in Creation is at the center of Creation.

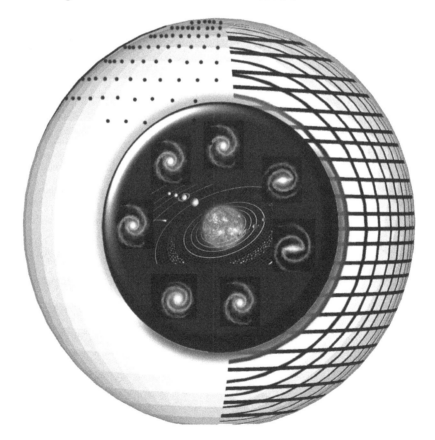

Question:

What is the symbolism of goddess Nat/Anat's weapons?

Answer:

For goddess Nat (Net or Anat), her main symbols are the papyrus scepter, which is in the center, and she has the bow and arrow. Also, she has the loom which she uses to weave. She, along with being the creator goddess…understand that all these are solar divinities...the Mehturt, the Nat, the Herukhuti, the Asha Hrau…they, and she specifically, represent the power of creation and destruction. In the Asarian resurrection myth, she has the power to destroy evil. And if you befriend her, if she becomes your mother, you have access to that power to destroy your enemies. But we weren't dealing with that aspect of her here. That is more of an aspect of how she manifests in the *Pet* realm. In the higher aspect she is the creator goddess. The loom is the most important symbol as it represents the instrument she uses to weave the matrix of Creation.[33] We will discuss about goddess Nat in the last lesson in more detail.

Reflection and Journal discipline:

1- **At the top of each page copy the following hieroglyphs to the best of your ability**

[***cht n ankh*** *" tree of life "*]

REFLECTIONS: What is this ancient teaching that has come to me through this book? How is it that my spiritual search has led me to this? Why should Creation be organized like a tree? Is it really possible for me to tread the path of the Tree?

After studying the Lesson proceed to answer the following question and write the answer in your journal.

What is the origin and purpose of the Kemetic Tree of Life?

What is(are) the main teaching(s) of this lesson and what do the principle(s) of the divinity(ies) discussed in this lesson mean in reference to my actions, feelings, thoughts and desires and understanding of the spiritual philosophy?

---

[33] see the book *EGYPTIAN MYSTERIES VOL 2: Dictionary of Gods and Goddesses* by Dr. Muata Ashby, **Chapter 5: Instruments of the Gods and Goddesses: Headdresses, Scepters and Weapons for Spiritual Enlightenment ; INTRODUCTION TO THE** NETERU OF THE GODDESS PATHS, The Goddess Tradition, Net (Anet)

Lesson 2:– Introduction To The Philosophy of Neteru and the TREE OF LIFE of Anunian Theurgy

In the last lesson we did an overview of a previous series[34] that we had done called *Introduction to Anunian Theurgy*. And in that class you learned about the oldest Theurgy in human history, the earliest known religion. This was not the earliest form of philosophy in ancient Kemet, but it was the earliest completely espoused and codified form of religious philosophy (Anunian Theurgy) and the god Ra is the central figure of that Theurgy…the High GOD or Supreme Being, the ultimate cause of everything that exists. And everything branches out from Ra as an upside down tree that has its roots (sundisk) in the sky and its branches (sunrays) reaching down to the earth, extending out, not just to the earth but throughout the physical realm. In fact the roots are in the transcendental worlds, in the Nun, and then come into the physical realm (Ta, Pet, Duat).

The realm of Nunu is the undifferentiated consciousness, that doesn't know anything, that doesn't do anything, is just sitting there. Its not in any kind of form, it doesn't care about holding any shape, its just there. And then some kind of impetus is applied to that substratum of existence, the undifferentiated matter. And then that matter, which was previously undifferentiated, begins to take varied shapes and forms and sizes and functions… and these impetuses that cause changes in the undifferentiated matter and cause it to become differentiated; we call them cosmic forces. The concept being related here is that of the extension of Neter through the neteru, the Neter (Supreme Being) branching out into the Creation by means of the cosmic forces (neteru). That is the basis of the Anunian Theurgy Creation myth and the foundation of the concept behind the TREE OF LIFE of Anunian Theurgy.

Now, these cosmic forces are governed by principles, and those principles are given names. Those principles denote the manner in which the energy of the cosmic force operates or manifests. You have already been given the name of these principles. In the Anunian Theurgy TREE OF LIFE, you know the main names already, Ra, Aset, Shu, Geb, Tefnut, Asar, Djehuti, Maat, Hetheru, etc.; these are all principles and cosmic forces as well as elements that have taken form out of the primeval matter. From an outer sense, an exoteric sense, people may look at this strictly as a religion and think of these as actual personalities, and in a sense they are, just like human beings have personalities but the Neteru are much more than that. Consider that people act in certain ways and society recognizes that and labels them in accordance with their way of action. For example, people on wall street… people who like to buy stocks and invest in a lot of things and spend a lot of money…they call them "bulls"… and if you believe think or act with that kind of energy your referred to, on wall street as being "bullish", and if you like to hang back and see what is going on before you invest and be cautious, they call you a "bear"…you're "bearish." Are you really a bear? No you are just acting like a bear, your force is bearish, the energy you are manifesting is bearish. The neteru are like that also; some carry with them certain energies. Ra is fire, Aset is wisdom, Shu is air and wind, etc. Those energies are to be understood and mastered by a spiritual aspirant and the aspirant should be able to manifest them at will.

When we talk about the principle of supreme wisdom, we are talking about goddess Aset, and she embodies the principle, feeling and actions of that. In a sense, yes…just like that Wall Street personality, he is a bull and at the same time he is John Doe….whatever his name is also. Essentially, especially in Maat philosophy, you are your actions, what you do. And as the saying goes, "morals are judged by deeds." Your internal morality is judged by the expression of that morality and that determines your fate for your future spiritual evolution.

The whole idea here is that if an aspirant was to learn the principles they would discover those principles within, truly, and not just intellectually; this is not just to know about them and to be able to recite the myths about them, or be able to discuss about them, their history, exploits, etc. and this kind of thing; this is not what we are talking about. To know something is to become one with it and to express it. That means that your thoughts become it, your words become it, and your physical actions become it… the three modes of expression. And if you were to learn and "know" that principle, you master it. You have heard master musicians talk about how they

---

[34] The Anunian Creation Myth: Series dates: 8/4/02 10015-10020, by Dr. Muata Ashby

do not think about music when they are playing it. They're doing it, they are it, and they become it. If someone was to ask you a question about the philosophy and you have to go look in your books or go back and ask questions about it, reflect upon it, seek council about it, you haven't become it. You are still in the effort stage, you are still striving. It's a spontaneous movement once you have attained it.

And once you have attained it, then you are ready to excel to other attainments, other masterships. And as you master, also you are able to harness. If you master the principle of Aset, then you can harness that principle, you can harness that cosmic energy, by the modes of action, but these are just supports for your will, and the Goddess Nat (Net, Anat), the progenitor of Aset, represents will, although right now we are referring to her transcendental aspect that we have talked about previously. On a physical level She also represents will and determination as well as clarity of purpose. This principle is related to the power that a person is able to harness once they have comfort in their knowledge, once they have security in their understanding; this concept is related to the term "Mn" or Mnnu" which means you are "firm" or the term "djed" which means that you are "established"... in your knowledge.

Religious practice has three steps, Myth, Ritual and Mysticism and it is to be made effective through three disciplines of *Shedy* (disciplines to penetrate the mysteries of *Shetaut Neter*); the disciplines are: Listening, Reflection and Meditation.[35] So in order to harness the power of a principle of the Neteru, you must know that principle, and to know that is to become it. In order to know it you must be able to philosophically deconstruct it and reconstruct it and also experience it as well as express it. You know it by studying the teaching related to it, by acting it, by thinking it, by speaking it. When your actions take on this quality of this discipline of the Tree of Life the actions now are the ritual actions in which you are taking the teaching, the philosophy, to the next level of religious practice. Your actions are also to become the day to day expressions of the teaching in your ordinary life situations.

The sacramental practice of propitiation and relation to a principle is that you should have a ritual related to the divinity, say goddess Aset for example. In the practice of the Anunian Theurgy Tree of Life spiritual program you offer libation, incense and light a candle and then utter Hekau (special Words of Power) to commemorate and invoke the energy (cosmic Force) of Aset and then you do readings (or listen to a live or recorded lecture), reflect on what you have read (or heard) and then meditate on what you have studied. But in your day to day life, you must also act like Aset. You must adopt the principles of her personality. Notice that you don't give up your personality to become her. You discover her essence within and your personality is transformed thereby. Remember that you already are an expression of the Divine...you're not becoming something else. When you begin to learn about the principles and you start to act and think in accordance with them you begin to "feel" them or rather, you begin to recognize them within yourself as your own deeper innate nature.

In this way you are becoming a master. Remember the saying, "Men and women are mortal gods and goddesses, and gods and goddesses are immortal men and women"...that is the Ancient Egyptian teaching...and a goal on the spiritual path. If you were to remove your ignorance and unrighteousness through the practice of Maat, the practice of Shedy, study of the teachings, and if you begin to practice as we are talking here today, knowing the divinities, acting like them, speaking their truths, thinking thoughts related to them, how they think, their rationale, learning to reason as they do, you eventually become like them...you become one with them.

There are cosmic forces in the universe that are positive and negative, but the negative cosmic forces are due to ignorance. Ignorance causes cosmic forces to be turned to that which is relatively negative. For instance, let's say you have a dam, and a town below. Let's say some evil person put a bomb on the dam. The power of the dam is there, and it's not doing anything bad. Actually it's serving a good, it's making electricity, it's holding up the waters, etc. And if somebody blows up the dam, then that same energy-force is used for something negative. What we are referring to here is that the cosmic forces, the neteru, are beyond good and evil, and they cannot be forced into negative actions. However their emanations can be turned by unscrupulous people, and some people

---

[35] *INITIATION INTO EGYPTIAN YOGA AND NETERIAN RELIGION* by Dr. Muata Ashby, MEDITATION THE ANCIENT EGYPTIAN PATH TO ENLIGHTENMENT by Dr. Muata Ashby

do it without knowing. There are people who harness vast forces, an example is Hitler. Actually, there is evidence that he tried to set himself up with astrology and he tried to learn eastern wisdom so he could harness those energies against his enemies and you see how he used the swastika, a Kemetic-Buddhist-Hindu symbol of cosmic forces which had nothing to do with racism, violence or hatred.

The people that were following him were ignorant, as there always are ignorant people in every generation, every society, they were like lost souls. They were people, not unlike many who are alive today, who had little knowledge of authentic religion and higher realms of being and therefore lived out of their fears which caused them to support demagogues and warmongers. When a generation of peoples develops in this way they then teach the same ignorance to the young ones, inculcating them with the same fear, hatred and egoistic ideals of racism, superiority and violence as a way of coping with the fears and ignorance, just like the racists in the United States… the KKKers, they inculcate their children with it, and then their children do not know anything else and they too become KKKers. Then they teach their own children, and so on and so forth. Getting a large group of people to think a certain way also draws the emanations of the cosmic forces in a big way and can affect an entire culture for positive or negative. So therefore, these forces can be harnessed for good or evil. So you can imagine therefore, that a person should not be taught this teaching unless they are pure of heart; that means they should be purified by practicing the disciplines of Maat, specifically observing the 42 Precepts of Maat and also Serving humanity (extending and sharing the three needs of human beings, as outlined in the *Pert m Hru* text, food shelter and opportunity).

There is an Ancient Egyptian parable that illustrates some important aspects of this teaching related to the cosmic forces and their control. This is a Kemetic story of the Old Kingdom period, the most ancient period of the dynastic era. There was once a story about a king who was bored. And he had a harem; and one of his ladies said "why don't you take a boat ride, and we'll play music for you as we sail down on the Nile, and we will have a great time." He said, "Excellent idea, lets go." So they went sailing down the Nile, and all the ladies were playing music, and they were relaxed and it was unbelievably calm. If you go to Egypt, you can just see it happening; you can sail just as they used to in ancient times. Now all of a sudden, one of the ladies stopped rowing, and then the rest of them stopped rowing, and the king asked "what is going on, why have we stopped?" And the lady said "I lost a great jewel that you had given me. It fell overboard. I don't see it. I don't know what happened to it." Then the king called one of his ministers, a priest, to see if he could do anything about this problem. He said to the minister, "one of my wives has lost a jewel that I gave her and she's very upset, and all the ladies are very upset and they have stopped rowing, and my whole wonderful day has turned into a nightmare, can you do anything?" So then the minister said, "I'll do the best that I can" Then he goes and looks overboard and then he utters some words of power, and all of a sudden, the Nile river stopped flowing and furthermore the waters started to part, from the middle, water from one side of the river rose up and went on top of the other side. There was a parting of the Nile. And so the priest got out and started walking on the bottom of the Nile, and he saw the jewel where it had fallen, and he went and picked it up and returned to the boat. The priest uttered some words and the waters came back into the Nile again and they started flowing down the river again, and the ladies started rowing and everything was fine from then on. And this story of course comes thousands of years before the parting of the seas in the Bible myth of the Exodus.

What I am getting at is that fantastic feats are possible if the cosmic forces can be controlled and harnessed; this includes feats such as flying through the air, making rain, causing earthquakes, storms, etc., the psychic powers and powers to control the forces of nature and such. Recall the movies of George Lucas, *Star Wars*, where he took up this theme of Life Force energy residing in the universe, that sustains all life, which the Ancient Egyptians called *Sekhem*, and called it "the force"…where special individuals can harness the forces of nature. This is where he gets it from…this is where the idea comes from and he admitted as much; it came from the ancient sages who discovered these forces and developed spiritual disciplines to discover and develop them. If you were able to know the principles and become one with them, propitiate them in a proper way, you could harness their power too; you could perform strange feats controlling the outer forces of nature or control and manipulate the inner forces, the subtle forces that are even more powerful and potentially more destructive to the human personality (egoism).

We should also not neglect that the subtle aspect of the myth is relating to the power of inner peace that leads to enlightenment. When the Pharaoh became bored it was his ego making his mind agitated. He had given away the jewel which represents the goal, the inner peace of self-knowledge. The ladies are the movement on the waters of life who bring solace, harmony, pleasure, desire but also progress on the waters. But that cannot work for long if the jewel is lost. To find that jewel it is necessary to stop the movement, the endless actions and futile pursuits of life, long enough to learn and utter the words that turn the mind towards the goal, the jewel, the Divine. Then the separation of the material and spiritual, the opacity of life, the waters, must be cleared away in order to see the way to the goal. Having attained the goal, the movement of life may continue with a higher perspective, a higher vision and a masterful dominion over life.

Now remember that history is cyclical...you know about the great year that I talked about previously[36]...the signs of the zodiac are an expression of the great year... it goes in a great year which lasts 26,000 years...each month in it is about 2500 years. We are supposed to be in the Age of Aquarius now. We just came out of the Age of Pisces, over the last couple hundred years, which is the age of the fish, which was supposed to be the age of Jesus ...which is the age of water.

Now, in certain periods of history, again, which is cyclical... in different periods of history (different great months), the cosmic forces are sometimes more and sometimes less accessible, easier or harder to harness, but they can be harnessed in any period. However, the harnessing of the cosmic forces for the purpose of performing psychic feats is neither necessary nor a prerequisite for attaining enlightenment, the highest goal of life. And just because you know about the cosmic force, that does not mean that you have full control of it. You can attain that control of it, but that has to be worked on. Yet, even if you can control it, even to a great extent, that does not mean that you have attained its wisdom. There are two important components needed to attain Spiritual enlightenment, the attainment of the wisdom of a principle and the mastery over its use. What I am getting at is that the knowledge of it, the wisdom of the cosmic forces, of the principles, that comes first, and then the mastery over it, the power, comes next...so the knowing of it is the first stage. This is important because the outcome could be destructive in the reverse. How would it be if people were put to drive cars before they were taught how to drive? Many people can produce music but without wisdom they produce music that is commercial and ego self-serving, to make themselves rich even if it's injurious to the listener. A wise person would produce music that is commercially viable and yet elevating. The wise person has mastered the wisdom and the usage of their gift, in this case over the force of music.

Of course from our perspective of the teachings, the mastery over the forces in order to use them properly in day-to-day living is important but the knowledge and wisdom of spiritual enlightenment, relating to the things that transcend the world of time and space, is most important. If you were to discover the knowledge of the principles of the Kemetic Tree of Life, they all lead you to understand the entire creation, the entire universe, and understanding the entire creation and universe, you understand also the ultimate, the cause, the ultimate source that we said before, is Ra, who emerges from the transcendent (Neberdjer, Mehturt, etc. On another level, knowing them means knowing yourself, because the essence of creation is you, or your higher self, your deeper self. Knowing a principle also allows you to have insight into the nature of the principle as it affects your life as well. Most people are unaware of how the cosmic forces are driving their lives and so they move on in life thinking of life as an uncontrolled and unfathomable river in which they become swept up with no control over their situations. This path is of mastery over the principles represented by each god or goddess and thereby becoming like them, or rather, discovering your divinity, them within yourself.

For example, if you want to know about Set, you get to know about your own egoistic nature...your desires and the futility as well as the illusory nature of egoism. Knowing about Nebethet allows you to know about death...about the transient nature of life. But all of these descriptions right now are really superficial. What needs to happen is that there needs to be a deep study of each principle, and after that study, comes reflection on that principle, and after reflection, comes meditation on that principle. Then, as your thoughts have been led

[36] See the Book African Religion VOL. 1- ANUNIAN THEOLOGY THE MYSTERIES OF RA, by Dr. Muata Ashby; and THE AFRICAN ORIGINS OF CIVILIZATION, RELIGION AND YOGA SPIRITUALITY AND ETHICS PHILOSOPHY by Dr. Muata Ashby

through this process, you manifest the principle through your physical organs of action (mind, body, speech). It means speaking in the way that the principle speaks. So, if you want to be like Aset, then you speak wisdom, you study wise teachings, you study wise thoughts, you speak them, then you act the way she acts, and you learn how she acts by studying her myths, and then you apply those ways in day-to-day life and eventually you discover her within yourself (whether or not you are a male or female aspirant).

Knowing the particular Neterian principle in its different forms is one of the first important steps in learning about a particular principle being spoken about. Again, you are to realize that knowing the neteru (gods and goddesses / cosmic forces) leads you to the Neter (Supreme Being / The Transcendent). As for the process enjoined in the Anunian Tree of Life, the pathway is simple but not necessarily easy, from the many (multiplicity and differentiation) at the bottom, to the One, the singularity at the top.

One thing you should realize, that we are emphasizing, is the importance of the rituals. The rituals reinforce the will, and the rituals also attract the cosmic forces through invocation. So if you are doing a program for the goddess, you do unveil images, readings, chants, songs, etc. related to the goddess, you talk about her myths, and you talk about her stories, and about her glories, sorrows as well as her triumphs and that attracts the energies that are related to the goddess.

Of course if you are fortunate (you have reached a certain level of mastery), it attracts the goddess herself too. And you harness those powers and then you can do goddess work, the kind of work that the goddess does. For example, if you want to destroy evil, then you propitiate the divinity that has the power to do that, the cosmic force that has the power to do that. And the cosmic force that has the power to do that with fire and physical fierce energies is the feline, the leonine energy. Of course that is goddess Sekhmet, an aspect of Hetheru, who is an aspect of Nat and Mehturt. If you want to use wisdom to overcome the adversity then that is the goddess Aset. Nevertheless, all are aspects of the ultimate goddess forms (Nat / Mehturt) and thus they lead an aspirant to the ultimate discovery as well as victory over the lower forces, the forces of egoism and degraded mind (anger, hatred, greed, jealousy, envy, etc.) which constantly thwart a souls attempts to attain spiritual enlightenment. Are you beginning to understand how this process works?

And once you have gathered those forces after your ritual, after your study, reflection, meditations, your uttering of the chants, etc., then you might unleash that power towards your objective. If you are an unscrupulous person, then you're going to unleash that power towards ends that feed your egoistic desires. And of course, when the Neter sees that, then that action is going to be turned on you and used to cause events that will go against your ultimate desires, even if you may seem to get what you want in the beginning and even for a time. If you use it for proper means, for proper goals, the cosmic forces are with you and the gods and goddesses approve and assist you to the extent that is possible based on your level of evolution and your spiritual needs, that may be in conflict with your apparently righteous desires. That's why it's better not to delve in these things unless you are secure in your knowledge, secure in your higher position, which means being secure in your virtue through purification by living and acting through Maat (order and truth). If you are an unrighteous person, a person who is not secure in virtue, there is a very good chance that you will use this force for a negative end, and that will lead you to a greater degradation later on. Even though in this present lifetime a negative act may seem that it's going to pay off and make dividends, and you might get a big house and get rich, eventually those gains turn into sorrows, worries, that prevent mental peace, which is the truly valuable attainment in life. And later, after suffering and not finding true peace in life, goddess Meskenet (an aspect of Maat controlling future birth) sends you back (reincarnation) and you may not like where you end up. She's directed by the gods and goddesses (Maat, Djehuti and others) to send you where you need to go to experience what they have decreed that you need to experience in order to grow as a spirit being. This can involve suffering after death and then reincarnation which may involve more suffering as well as opportunities for redemption (following Maat in a better way). So if you need to be humbled...watch out...because you are going to get experiences that are going to humble you, and you can trust that it will be a painful experience. That is the path of the ignorant, the arrogant, and the path of hard knocks.

So what I am getting at, is that all these studies that you have done and are doing, if you have not uttered the chant 10,000 times, the way it has been explained, 500,000 times, one million times...if you have not done the rituals lasting for days, the studies and meditations that go on for hours, for months, for years, you will not attain this kind of psychic power. It is hard for you to get it and it should be. But yet, you're doing a kind of ritual anyway, as an ordinary human being, that keeps you tied to and caught up in the worldly concerns; so you should do enough of the Shedy disciplines and Kemetic rituals to break the hold of the worldly rituals. The worldly rituals are the habits you indulge in that get you more deeply involved with the world and less with spiritual matters. When you watch television, you are filling yourself with ideas and energies and reinforcing these from day to day. If you are watching some x-rated movie, you are aligning yourself with lustful ideas and lustful energies/forces….those are being drawn to you and its going to exacerbate that aspect of the personality. Like attracts alike. So if you want to be wise, like Aset, you are to spend time with her, you attract her energies and they will guide you and impel you…they push you more. It works the other way also, for the negative energies as well as the positive energies. This is why the teaching of the temple of Aset (Isis) contains the following injunction: *"this knowledge the goddess invites us to seek after, as being near and dwelling continually with her."*[37]

And if you elevate yourself in virtue and through meditation, to the state above the waking state, you elevate yourself to the astral plane. There you are to remain awake and aware. It is important to remain aware all the time and not just to enter the astral plane and experiencing whatever happens because that would change the experience from a vision (opposite of a dream-where one remains aware it is a dream world and one does not get caught up in its happenings and actually one can control the dream world and shape it according to one s will in other words in one s mind one is the Creator, sustainer and destroyer, i.e. All-encompassing divinity [Neberdjer]- absolute master) to a dream (not aware of being in a dream world (astral plane). Through ignorance, and loss of higher awareness one falls from master to servant and from servant to slave to an illusion created by one s own ignorant fears, desires, weaknesses and delusions. This is not to be allowed   the discipline of the mysteries is designed to stop, reverse, and prevent this   the greatest prevention is enlightened consciousness   for when a dark room is lit with a light there is no place for the darkness (delusion) to remain. When the lights come on a little or illumine part of the room there always seems to be some other unknown lurking in the darkness but in that room {the mind} there is only what you have put there which turns out to be no-thing when you shine the light of wisdom and then spirit {AKH} on it. So if you remain awake, purified and fearless, you can have a direct contact with the presiding deities of the cosmic forces. You can converse with them.

If they feel you are worthy, they will give you some instruction directly. This was a popular practice by ordinary people in Ancient Egypt; there was even a practice of sleeping in temples so as to provoke a meeting with the divinity of that temple, in the astral (mental-dream world) plane. Of course it was then and is now ecognized that the Astral plane is the next plane of existence after the physical life in the physical plane. But you should not neglect the living sources of wisdom, the sages who can be conduits for neterian inspirations. And just like a jazz musician who can play jazz and without thinking about it improvise   and where does the music come from? Sages and saints can also be like that with the teaching, and as they speak, words are coming out that they did not plan to say. And where did those words come from? This is similar in a way but not the same as the concept behind channeling, in a sense, but from a higher perspective, the spiritually developing person is one who is connected to the higher principles, and becomes one with those. On an even higher level the sage is connected o the source, the transcendental origin of all things, beyond the *Ben Ben*, to the transcendent being. That is different than channeling. Channeling is like you are in individual, a medium. You are like a cellular phone repeater station. When you have a cellular phone, a cellular phone signal goes to one antenna, then that antenna boosts it and sends it to another antenna and another and another one until it gets to the person where the call is going to. A sage is not just a repeater but one with the source, so the words of such a one are to be treated like the source, as if the Divine itself was speaking directly.

When you develop fully, you're tapped in directly in other words. There are two ways to do it. Some psychics, they can be very sensitive to things, and they can be open to certain things, but you can tell that they are not wise people, they are not enlightened people. They are susceptible to human error and failings. They are being given the information, as it were, but since they have not had philosophical training and they have not developed that level of philosophic mind they are not living or expressing it. They are not being the source for it…finding the source for it within themselves, they are still operating out of ego instead of Higher Self. And so, this concept of

---

[37] disciplines of the initiates of the Temple of Aset – recorded by Plutarch, a student of the mysteries of Isis

the principles, the cosmic forces, the Neter and the Neteru…this is the presiding teaching. This is what all of the rituals are about. This is what all of the Kemetic Neterian writings are about.

"Gods are immortal men, and men are mortal Gods."

-Ancient Egyptian Proverb

This discipline of which we speak is embodied in a word that has been given to describe this Kemetic philosophy and practice of spiritual disciplines that lead to enlightenment and mastery is "Theurgy," or sacred Science, the art of learning and manipulating, controlling the Cosmic Forces. This is why human beings can be greater than the cosmic forces, because they can control the cosmic forces and exist on all planes of existence (symbolized by Heru at the bottom of the cosmiconomythograph to Ra at the top), as physical human beings and as divinities through development of the subtler aspects of their spiritual personalities. A human being who is a Sage or Saint is in a sense higher than gods and goddesses. The gods and goddesses rule in the Netherworld, and manage creation for the Supreme Being, and so they have their emanations that do their work, subtle energies that course through the universe. And these emanations can be manipulated and harnessed by mortal men and women to also do certain work, like creating positive vibrations to facilitate a program, influencing others, but also changing moods and engendering peaceful conditions but most importantly creating the energy or force of ⟨hieroglyph⟩ *Saa*. Saa means understanding. Having knowledge, information, does not mean having understanding. Understanding is important when studying the mystical philosophy and that is a certain form of energy or force that allows an aspirant to overcome obstacles on the path, like the lack of will to spend time reading or meditating or putting down the ego so that the intellect may have a chance to work out the mysteries of life. The application of the Tree of Life disciplines for spiritual evolution may be thought of as a scientific process

"Men and women are to become God-like through a life of virtue and the cultivation of the spirit through scientific knowledge, practice and bodily discipline."

"Knowledge is far different from sense. For sense is brought about by that which hath the mastery o'er us, while Knowledge is the end of science, and science is God's gift. All science is incorporeal, the instrument it uses being the Mind, just as the Mind employs the body."

-Ancient Egyptian Proverbs

If mortal men and women can discover their own divinity, this means that they rule on the lower planes, the planes of matter, physicality and mental instinct. In a sense that is what it means to become Heru Ur, "Heru the Great," and also this is what it means to be the Pharaoh, the king or queen, you preside over the world. In the meantime you are a prince or princess. You are aspiring to that position. If they discover the higher planes of existence they also rule on the higher planes as well, the planes of intellect and astral existence. In an upcoming class we will study more on Heru, who is king of the world, and how to become king or queen of the world. This concludes Lesson 2.

Om Hetep

Sebai Dr. Muata Ashby

Questions and Answers

Question: What is the tree of life in terms of a vehicle to achieve higher consciousness?

Answer:

The TREE OF LIFE is a ladder, if you will... it is a web of connections that connect the physical with the spiritual. A tree, in this sense, is like a ladder that makes a connection. Ordinarily you think of a tree that rises up from the ground and reaches up, it actually connects the earth to the sky. The tree comes up from the earth, from the seed. It raises up its trunk and then spreads out its branches. At the top of the tree you have the sky, at the bottom you have earth. And you can climb a tree and get to the top also. Likewise you can climb the tree of Anunian Theurgy. The Tree of Life of Anunian Theurgy is an arrangement of gods and goddesses, of Neteru, who are connected, and their connections, that which binds them, allows their principles to be understood in a wholistic manner by extending from one to the others in order to encompass them all from the heavens to the earth.

Figure 16: The Gods and Goddesses of the Tree of Life of Anunian Theurgy

Question: What is the purpose of the Neteru?

Answer:

The Neter or the single Supreme Being emanates cosmic forces, and those cosmic forces are called Neteru, or gods and goddesses. So from the Supreme Divinity come gods and goddesses, and those gods and goddesses are given a specific task. They are cosmic forces that have different vibrations, different manifestations in time and space. They also have particular colors and ways of feeling. For more insights into he Neteru see the following diagrams.

This picture displays the Pauti of Creation of Anunian Theurgy along with the underlying principles which sustain them. Pauti means "Company of gods and goddesses". As explained earlier, the Pauti refers to Creation itself. The deities of the Pauti are nine in number plus Ra the Creator, and include Shu, Tefnut, Geb, Nut, Asar, Aset, Set, Nebthet and Heru. Maati, Hetheru and Djehuti are not part of the Pauti itself. They are subtle principles which support its existence. Anpu (Anubis) is not a direct production of the Anunian Theurgy Creation myth Pauti (Company of Gods and Goddesses); however he is strongly related to the company as a product of the mating of two members of the company, Asar and Nebethet (Spirit and mortal life) and he represents instinct as well as purified mind. So he is a new principle emanating from Creation itself that represents the basic human mind at the level of instinctual behavior but not intellect or intuition. He expresses the canine cosmic force and represents instinct and sense awareness as well as correct discernment between right and wrong.[38] This right discernment is important as it is a necessary attainment for anyone who wants to enter into the obelisk and start the journey of the Tree of Life, the journey of self-knowledge and enlightenment. As the half brother of Heru, an aspect of him, Anpu (and his aspect Wepwat) is a preparatory step needed before engaging in the study of the first main principle of the Tree that allows vertical movement (Heru).

In order to successfully complete the journey everyone needs to evolve spiritually. So the characters of the myth of Creation and their various forms of interaction with each other are in reality an elaborate mystic code

---

[38] see the book *EGYPTIAN MYSTERIES VOL 2:* Dictionary of Gods and Goddesses by Dr. Muata Ashby

relating to the areas of human conscience which need to be developed in order to grow spiritually. The first thing that we notice when the divinities of the Ancient Egyptian Creation, based on the teachings of Anu, are placed in a hierarchical fashion based on their order of Creation by Ra and their mythic significance is that they are arranged in accordance with their level of cosmological density and psychic relevance. Density here refers to their order of their subtlety as the elements composing the Creation. Ra is the first principle which emerges out of the Primeval Waters. He is the subtlest, singular principle of Creation, the focus of oneness as individual Divine conscience in time and space. The ocean itself transcends time and space and is beyond existence and non-existence. Ra is the first principle to emerge out of the undifferentiated essence and his emergence signifies the beginning of existence.

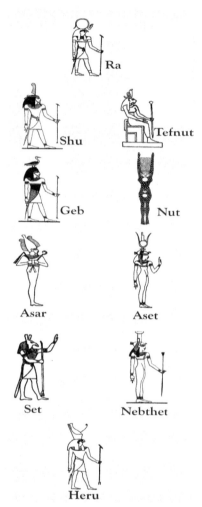

Figure 17: The Main Gods and Goddesses that make up the Anunian Tree of Life

The second important idea derived from the Pauti is that they represent a whole number, 10, and thus convey the idea of a special symmetry as well as the amount of numbers necessary to bring Creation into existence and also produce the seemingly endless multiplicity of forms in time and space (physical Creation). The highest level, Ra, is juxtaposed with the lower level of the Pauti with the image of Heru. So at one end we see the perfect singularity of the Supreme Self and at the other we see the perfect combination of Spirit and Matter in the form of Heru. So while the figure above may be understood as a reference to a "higher" and a "lower" idea, in reality the figure is not to be understood as a teaching of something that is above or better and something that is below or lesser. It is a teaching which expresses the essence of Creation, containing subtle as well as grosser objects which all emanate from the same source. The Ancient Egyptian teaching states that that which is above is the same as that which is below. If the Above and Below teaching is to be applied it should be understood as referring to the idea that everything in Creation is a reflection of the spiritual essence which transcends physicality. Therefore, that which produces "good and evil" in the terms that human beings conceptualize it is not God but the perception and actions of human beings. God does not have good or evil; human beings create that distinction through their actions, feelings and desires as well as their relative outcomes and their evaluations of them as these relate to the particular human being doing the evaluation. The physical universe is an emanation from the spiritual essence and as such is sustained by it. The very matter which constitutes Creation is in reality spirit in a condensed form just as when a person falls asleep their dream world is condensed out of their own consciousness, which is partially composed of subtle matter, individual identity and the person's desires. Nun is the underlying primordial consciousness of Creation. Ra may be seen as the Soul of Creation and Djehuti may be seen as the Cosmic Mind of Creation, Hetheru may be seen as the Vital Life Force of Creation and Maat may be seen as the underlying order of Creation. Djehuti, Hetheru and Maat, along with Nbthotep and Iusaasety are the underlying principles which sustain the Pauti, the forces that go to make up the forms of Creation.

Question: How are the gods and goddesses or cosmic force principles connected and accessed?

Answer:

Diagram 5: Pathways and Interconnections of the Tree of Life

On the Anunian Theology Tree of Life cosmiconomythograph you can see within the obelisk that there are 10 divinities (10 Neteru). The top five represent the subtler planes of existence and the elements of existence; the bottom five represent the human plane and the physical earth. Each divinity represents a sphere of cosmic force. They are interconnected in a particular way and that way is a path to their discovery by starting with one that can lead to the other and another and so on until all are known. We will study more about the pathways of the tree of life. You see all of these lines connecting the cosmic forces, the divinities. What do all of those mean? What are all of those interconnections? How does that give us insight into the interrelationships of the divinities? Because if we know those, and the myths give us those, then we have a roadmap as to how to lead ourselves from one to the other, and of course to the ultimate.

Question:

During the lecture you said that *"Ignorance causes cosmic forces to be turned to that which is relatively negative"*. What does "relatively" refer to?

Answer:

Consider that the blowing up of the dam, which we spoke about, is a bad thing if people live there and need it. If there are no people and nobody needs it and blowing it up does not affect anyone then the action has neither good nor bad implications does it? In the same way we should always try to remember that the teaching is relative; it has a relative meaning based on its perspective and it is not absolute; it relates to understanding the relative world of time and space which we have before us. But this world is not absolutely real is it? The absolute truth is neither good nor bad but transcendental; this does not mean we should promote bad things though, for obvious reasons. This is what it means to develop a philosophical mind. An aspirant must learn to think about things philosophically and that will allow her or him to make sense of the teaching and apply it properly in the world and then they will see fantastic results in their capacity to cope with and overcome the challenges of life and also they will gain the needed insight into the higher teachings of the mysteries.

Reflection and Journal discipline:

1- At the top of each page copy the following hieroglyphs to the best of your ability

[**cht n ankh** " tree of life"]

After studying the Lesson proceed to answer the following question(s) and write the answer in your journal. This exercise will require more than one reading and more than one journal entry, at least one page; write all you can find related to the subject of the question. Answer the question(s) first without referring to the text you just read. Then go back and see if you missed anything. This exercise is to be repeated until you become proficient with the principles of this sphere. The reflection exercise should be done after each reading or study session. Then you may practice meditation[39] on the wisdom you have learned. You may come back to add to your reflections even if you move on to other lessons.

REFLECTIONS: What is the nature of these neteru that fascinates me? This air that I breathe and earth that I walk on and sounds that I hear and smells that I smell and feelings and energies and all I know, is composed of these? Am I really one of them and them of me? I resolve to tread the path of the Tree to find my place among the Neters and all that I can be!

After studying the Lesson proceed to answer the following question and write the answer in your journal.

What kind of mastery is most important?

What is(are) the main teaching(s) of this lesson and what do the principle(s) of the divinity(ies) discussed in this lesson mean in reference to my actions, feelings, thoughts and desires and understanding of the spiritual philosophy?

---

[39] Explained in more detail in Lesson 15

Lesson 3: How to Understand the Cosmiconomythograph of the Tree of Life and the Philosophy of the Theurgy of the TREE OF LIFE

If we look beyond the outer manifestation of a myth and engage in serious in depth mythology, the study of myths, something most people are not usually willing to do, even though myth is the surface exoteric aspect of a religion, we discover a higher philosophical perspective and also a way to relate ourselves to the characters of the myth and thereby discover the same mysteries that the ancient practitioners discovered and find the same powers that they found. Many times when people look at Kemetic religion or African religion in general, or the Indian, etc., they see lots of gods and goddesses, and some people, as prideful Westerners, think they have "real" and advanced "religion" in the form of Judaism or Islam or Zoroastrianism or Christianity because it is supposedly monotheistic and it is supposedly based on a "real" god that supposedly existed and interacted with people at a specific point in history while the religions of others are, by comparison, only mere speculations, myths in the sense of fake or at least incorrect religious practices. This is, of course, a limited view but also an erroneous understanding based on the misinterpretation of their own religious concept. They don't realize that contained under the surface appearance of the many gods and goddesses there is a science, the sacred science, the Theurgy... "theo" meaning related to divinity, and "urgy" meaning science; the science of the gods and goddesses elevates our consciousness by showing us the intricate aspects of the neteru, the gods and goddesses, and what they represent, and if we begin to understand what they represent, then we'll be able to master those cosmic forces, in other words, understand Creation itself. In order to realize that there is a deeper aspect to religion we need to do what the ancient Egyptians called "Ab"[40], to purify ourselves first. Purification is through practice of Maat, righteous action, in the three aspects of action, your thoughts, your words, your deeds; then it is important to study religion beyond the limited stages of myth and ritual.

If you're practicing the theurgy (you act as a theurgist), you apply the characteristics of the neteru, the divinities, to those three aspects of your action...you start acting like them, you start talking like them, you start thinking like them, and then you start feeling like them, eventually you end up being like them. I have explained before that these are the aspects of being. Speaking in terms of worldly manifestation, what is being something? If a detective were to go into your house in an attempt to know about you they would say this is the kind of clothes this person wears, this is the language that this person speaks, and these are the kinds of things they think about, etc. They tell all that by looking at your surroundings...your clothing, by the music you listen to, the kind of people you hang out with, things you wrote or said that expressed your feelings; through all of these things the detectives can tell about you without you even being there and without them meeting you previously. Those are external things, reflections of your inner nature. But they are also disciplinary practices you can use to discover the inner reality; they allow a different form of energy, a different form of feeling to be discovered and experienced. For example, a person who grew up as a thug or thief looks, thinks, acts and feels a certain way but if they were to act in accordance with this teaching, to adopt the ethics, thoughts, looks, and feelings of the divinities those persons would change their external perspectives and they would eventually internally, psychologically and spiritually recognize that these other ways of being are more inline with their innate internal essential natures.

So you start acting like the divinities, thinking like them, speaking like them, speaking the truth that they speak...you gradually become them. Or, as explained before, you discover those qualities that are inherent in them, you find those within you, therefore you're finding the divinities in you. Having discovered them in you, you master that energy that they represent, that you are actually a manifestation of but which was dormant because you were lost in the ignorance and distractions of the world and your own egoistic notion. When you traverse the spheres of the Tree you are actually expanding your consciousness by discovering each divine

---

[40] means spiritual purification in Ancient Egyptian language and spiritual practice.

principle as you study, meditate upon and adopt the principles of each neteru. And since they are connected into other divinities, they give you entry into other levels and other aspects of Divine consciousness.

Of course, as you see the way that the tree as it is laid out, you naturally want to go in a vertical direction as much as possible, but really it is a process of mastering the horizontal levels, and then moving vertically to the next level above. The tree is laid out vertically, but it's on a two dimensional sheet, but you must really understand that it's vertical. If we were really to lay it out as it is, it should be like one of those children's books that pop up when you open it, the pictures pop out. It should be vertical, sticking up… perpendicular to the ground with some helical components.

On the highest level (this is also discussed in the Anunian Theurgy book as well–refer to it also), Ra is divinity number one, but recall that all of this that we are talking about, related to the tree, has to do with the realm of the Time and Space, the realm of generation. Beyond time and space is the Absolute. Beyond time and space there is no generation, meaning there is no generating of things, of forms, just the *Yanrutef* region.[41] "Yanrutef" means that place where nothing grows there, not even your thoughts…no words, no ideas, no concepts, there is nothing to differentiate matter and no differentiated matter [objects] there and since there is no duality, there is only oneness and that is the Absolute. That is where the Tree is taking us, out of the realm of generation and to the realm of the absolute. Now in the realm of generation, the area of the tree, the Absolute differentiates Himself/Herself into many aspects, many cosmic forces, many forms, many levels of existence of consciousness, and we are living here on the bottom most level, the *Ta*, the earth.

Now Ra at the top of Creation, is #1 and at the bottom of creation is Heru at number 10. As you can see, these two divinities are juxtaposed with each other. Now very briefly, the connections you see between these divinities, the horizontal connections first of all mean that the divinities are counterparts. They are either twins, or counterparts in sort of a mate or marital sense, however they are more of a counterpart in the manner of philosophical principles and energetic forms that they represent.

Vertical lines   = direct connection, gender compatibility
Horizontal lines= combination, mating
Diagonal lines   = product, offspring
Blue & Green arrows   = special philosophical principles of opposites

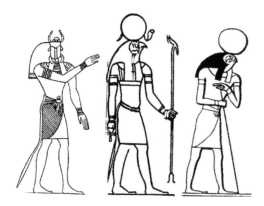

Figure 18: The Ra Trinity: (from left to right) Khepri, the Creator, Ra-Harakti, the sustainer and Tem the Concluder, one who ends, completes things

Ra is at the top of the *Techmu* {obelisk} in three forms. So first of all you see three divinities at the top of the obelisk. An Kemeti [Ancient Egyptian] obelisk is a tall quadrangular pillar which tapers towards the top. That is the central part of the graphic. There are two diagonal lines that are coming out of Ra. Ra has three aspects to his personality as you recall, *Kherpi, Ra* and *Tem*. He has three aspects, or three manifestations, but he is really one, and that is Ra. The vertical and diagonal lines can be movement of creation if we are moving from top to bottom, or movement of dissolution, if we are moving from bottom up. The vertical lines represent direct movement, direct connection and the diagonal lines indicate special interconnectedness and helical movement. Two diagonal lines come out of

[41] Ancient Egyptian - 'Growthless,' 'barren', 'Nrutef'.

that same Ra...these are the "generation" lines. If you recall the creation myth,[42] as the divinities were born, we were informed that Ra gave birth to Shu and Tefnut, and Shu and Tefnut came together and they gave birth to Geb and Nut. Ra gives birth to Shu and Tefnut, who are the #2 and #3 divinities. Here we have the first concrete trinity in Time and Space as we discussed in the Creation Myth.[43] The TREE OF LIFE philosophy is for the application of the teaching of the Anunian Theurgy Creation Myth, to make it effective and powerful as a living discipline for spiritual evolution.

So you see, we have two diagonal lines coming out of the Ra Trinity to Shu and Tefnut, and then we have a horizontal line connecting Shu and Tefnut. Two more diagonal lines come out of Shu and Tefnut, and they intersect and they meet, they mate, and they give birth to Geb and Nut. Two diagonal lines come out of Geb and Nut, and they intersect and they give rise to Asar and Aset. They also give rise to Set and Nebthet and *Heru Ur*. Actually the specific aspect of Heru is *Heru Khenti an Maa*, Heru the foremost not seer [more will be discussed about this form of Heru in a future lesson]. Two diagonal lines come out of Asar and Aset and they produce *Heru Pa khard* (Heru the Child); the lines meet at Heru Ur. Heru Ur is a higher aspect of Heru the child, who is the spiritual child, the aspirant who must grow and develop to do battle as *Heru Behudet* in order to attain higher consciousness. So, Anpu mind allows an aspirant to bring Asar (soul) and Aset (wisdom) together and that birth of aspi-rational (aspire to rationality (higher truth)) conscience in a spiritual aspirant eventually develops through the Tree until Heru reaches Ra and then returns to take his rightful place on earth as Heru Ur (Heru the Elder, the

Mature, the Great, Ruler of Earth, the Peraah (*Per-aah* – "Pharaoh"= "house" "great") King).

These are all connections that have been established by the myths of the gods and goddesses that were instituted by the Ancient Egyptian sages (Priests and priestesses) and handed down through history. It is their legacy and our inheritance as followers of this tradition.[44] There are vertical lines connecting all the male divinities. Notice also that there are vertical lines connecting all the female divinities. The male and female genders arise from the original transcendental divine act which produced opposites in an orderly balance. And all these divinities, relate to each other as a family, therefore they are all interconnected and ultimately, they all have the same source at the top who is Ra and the higher aspect of Ra is androgynous.

Now, Ra is in the realm of the *Duat*. In the *Pet* level of Creation we have the Cosmic Divinities that go to compose the main element of creation... Shu and Tefnut are the air and ether, and the cosmic energy that is termed as water, respectively. They also represent the elements of creation...from the standpoint of the physical universe, earth, water, air and Ra of course is fire.

The *Ta* section is most important for spiritual aspirants to concentrate on because you are beginning on the bottom of the tree....if you are not beginning on the bottom...if you are somewhere above, you don't need to be here. If you are at the top you are not an aspirant. You've already realized the higher truth. But if you are a neophyte, or an advancing aspirant, how do you get to the higher truth? You begin on the earth plane, where you are, and then you get to the Pet, the heavenly plane, and then if you are "able", meaning if you do your righteous spiritual work, the studies, disciplines, purifications, rituals, and meditations, you are able to enter into the Duat realm, there discovering singular divinity in Time and Space. Then transcending time and space you discover the all-encompassing divinity... the Mehturt, the Neberdjer, the Herukhuti, the Nat, or the Nun....all of these, they all mean the same thing...they are all related to the same thing...the transcendent.

As for the green and blue lines, the two lines that have arrows on both sides of them, connecting two divinities; these are critical for beginning the spiritual journey of the Tree and they will be explained in more

[42]The essentials have been presented earlier. For more details See the Book *African Religion VOL. 1- ANUNIAN THEOLOGY THE MYSTERIES OF RA,* by Dr. Muata Ashby, ISBN: 1-884564-38-0 and audio lecture series "Anunian Theology and the Anunian Creation Myth" by Dr. Muata Ashby
[43] ibid
[44] See the book *African Religion Vol. 4 Asarian Theology* by Dr. Muata Ashby

detail later since they relate to special relationships between those divinities that they point to. For now let us recall some of the fundamental aspects of the concept of the Tree. The Ta divinities come together to compose the human personality. The Pet personalities go to compose the physical creation, and the Duat divinities go to compose the subtle aspect of Creation that is behind the physical universe and the Nunu divinities compose the subtle principles…the substratum behind the subtle aspect of Creation.

Now, every human being has these Ta, Pet and Duat as well as the Nunu divinities within. If you did not have them you could not exist, very simply put. So the question is how to discover them? From this early position, the starting point, as Heru the child, we must understand what is above us, what is higher, what is to be striven for, what is to be achieved. First of all we must understand the Ta divinities and how they make up the main aspects of the earthly human personality. Let's look at Asar, his cosmic function is soul. Again, realize that we are talking about the Anunian Theurgy here; we are not talking about Asarian Theurgy. In Asarian Theurgy, Asar has an expanded role along with being soul. And in Asetian Theurgy, Aset has a different role along with being wisdom personified. Remember what we said in the first lecture on Anunian Theurgy,[45] that Anunian Theurgy is the seed for all the other theurgys…all the other theurgys take these Anunian divinities, aspects of the same Divine Supreme Being, and they develop whole theurgys around them… and that is how you should understand the interrelationships between the different theurgys of Ancient Egypt… In that way you will not confuse Anunian Theurgy with any of the other Neterian theurgys (theurgys of Ancient Egypt).

Furthermore, everybody has a soul, and that is Asar, even though they may not recognize it as such or call it by that name. Everybody has a Nebehet aspect, and that is your mortal existence. Everybody has the capacity to learn, to become wise, and that is Aset. And everybody has a Heru in them. If that aspiration (Heru) were to be perfected, you would become Heru Ur or Master of the earth. You would become the *Per Aah*,[46] the Pharaoh, the King.

And there is one more thing that you should know here, aspect #1 and aspect # 10 are genderless…they encompass male and female divinity. So Heru represents, in other words, kings and queens. Therefore a queen is also referred to as Heru. This is also why the kings and queens wore the *Nesubity*[47] symbols, also a word that means ruler of Upper and Lower Egypt, ruler over the duality.

If you are not a ruler, the king or queen, you are called *Hekat*. Heka is the word for the crook…not a robber, a crook is an instrument used by a shepherd for herding as in someone who shepherds sheep. And this is why the *Per Aahs*, the Pharaohs and the Queens, they hold the *Heka* and the *Nekaku*. Heka is the crook, and the Nekaku is the flail. Remember, the flail has three sections. The flail[48] is what you use to separate the chaff from the seed.[49] This means that the one striving for rulership needs to separate the truth from untruth of the three worlds, Ta, Pet and Duat. Then the mystical reality, the higher reality, the mysteries of life are discovered.

"Virtues fail that are frustrated by passion at every turn."

-Ancient Egyptian Proverb

---

[45] See the Book *African Religion VOL. 1- ANUNIAN THEOLOGY THE MYSTERIES OF RA,* by Dr. Muata Ashby

[46] *Per-aah* – "Pharaoh

[47] *"nesu bity"*- *"The King of Upper and Lower Egypt"*

[48] an instrument for threshing grain, consisting of a staff or handle to one end of which is attached three freely swinging sticks or bars. - flagellum "winnowing tool, flail," from L. flagellum "whip."

[49] grain husks separated from the seeds during threshing.

The action of the flail is self-discipline in the practice of the disciplines, of Shedy, in relation to the efforts in the application of the principles of each level of the Tree. And this action of the flail, diligence and discipline on the spiritual path, is what purifies you, separating you from the mixture that has developed, the mixture of your transcendental nature with the time and space objects, delusion of and mortal reality into an ever-changing, weak and ignorant personality {egoism}. Every human personality is a mixture of these qualities. Your soul is in there, your eternal aspect, your egoism is there, you have some intellect aspect, and you have some mortal aspect, and you have some bit of aspiration for something better. But always, with a person who is not pure, their aspiration is going to be eventually thwarted. If your aspiration is not pure, it is going to be thwarted. You are going to try to be a good person, you are going to try to do good things for other people, you are going to try to follow the path that has been laid out by the sages, you are going to try to stop eating meat…you are going to try to not do something that is going to cause you to end up in jail, you are going to try not to get into a fight, but your personality is defective and you will make mistakes. That is why there must be a process of *Ab*… Ab means purification. This is the first level of priestly service[50]; its objective is to render the personality morally pure.[51]

You must hit yourself with a flail, and the flail means self-discipline, following the teachings that have been laid out, listening, reflection and meditation and the rest of the disciplines of *Shedy*. *Sedjem*[52] means to listen and obey. This is what the sages have decreed. You must understand that you are not just a mindless human animal that has come into the realm of generation, the realms where things generate and multiply, the realm where you have sex and babies come out…where galaxies collide and they bring forth new worlds.

There is an aspect of you that doesn't generate, that does not bring forth any children…that has not been born…that doesn't do anything. Do you realize that if you come into existence, if you bring anything into existence, that thing has to eventually come out of existence, because it's not real, it doesn't exist in an abiding way, as an absolute reality. Only that which is absolute can exist forever and eternity, having no beginning and therefore also no end.

The flail discipline separates you from what is not real…from the aspects of your personality, the worldly from the spiritual. And what does it expect from you? Let's look at two specific divinities that relate to this point we are talking about right now. These divinities that are juxtaposed in the Ta realm, Set and Aset; there is an arrow pointing between them. These are the important connections that allow you to start your journey on the tree. Set and Aset are rivals or enemies, as it were, though the term enemy is not appropriate from a higher perspective, they are opposites. All human beings who have not discovered their higher nature live lives controlled by their egos to some degree; that is Set. So in order to counter egoism, which is were you are starting from, you need to apply wisdom.

What this means is that if you have more Set in your personality (egoism, emotionality, lust, desires, selfishness, etc.), you are going to have less Aset in your life and from a broad perspective Maat [order, righteousness, ethics] is included here since Maat is an aspect of Aset. So you also need to adopt ethical conscience and ethical behavior; this means following the precepts of Maat.[53] If you have more egoism, you are going to have less intellectual capacity to understand the teaching because egoism clouds the intellect, and without intellectual development there will be even less capacity for intuitional understanding about life. Wisdom occurs in the personality in direct relationship/proportion to the presence of egoism.

---

[50] *Uabut-* priestly service

[51] *uabti* - morally pure - noble

[52] *sedjm* {"heed} the teaching
[53] see the book *INTRODUCTION TO MAAT PHILOSOPHY: Spiritual Enlightenment Through the Path of Virtue* by Dr. Muata Ashby

And the same thing applies to Asar and Nebthet. The more consciousness of Nebthet (self-image as a mortal being) that you have in your personality the less Aset (wisdom) and the less soul awareness you have, that is, awareness as an immortal soul beyond the body. We will discuss these more in detail later but briefly Nebethet represents mortality, or your idea of yourself as a mortal finite being. The more of that that you have, the less of eternal soul awareness you have...the less Asar you have in your personality. When you attain wisdom you can overcome egoism and mortality and move from Aset to Asar. This concludes our lesson for now.

HTP

Sebai Dr. Muata Ashby

Reflection and Journal discipline:

1- **At the top of each page copy the following hieroglyphs to the best of your ability**

[**cht n ankh** " *tree of life* "]

   After studying the Lesson proceed to answer the following question(s) and write the answer in your journal. This exercise will require more than one reading and more than one journal entry, at least one page; write all you can find related to the subject of the question. Answer the question(s) first without referring to the text you just read. Then go back and see if you missed anything. This exercise is to be repeated until you become proficient with the principles of this sphere. The reflection exercise should be done after each reading or study session. Then you may practice meditation[54] on the wisdom you have learned. You may come back to add to your reflections even if you move on to other lessons.

REFLECTIONS: This theurgic philosophy is deep…it has a vast legacy which is being given to me. I resolve to become a philosopher of the Tree, like the Anunian Theurgists of ancient times. I will make it my own and climb the ladder of elements, the cosmic forces of Creation!

After studying the Lesson proceed to answer the following question and write the answer in your journal.

1-What is(are) the main teaching(s) of this lesson and what do the principle(s) of the divinity(ies) discussed in this lesson mean in reference to my actions, feelings, thoughts and desires and understanding of the spiritual philosophy?

2-What is the first level or principle that all human beings begin from on their journey of the TOL? How can an aspirant begin that movement and what is the objective of the movement?

3-" Every human personality is a mixture of these qualities."
What are these "qualities" and what do they mean to an aspirant on the spiritual path of the TOL?

---

[54] Explained in more detail in Lesson 15

Lesson 4: The Psycho-spiritual Journey Through The Principles of Creation.

The Tree of Life is a roadmap of a journey which explains how Creation came into being and how it will end. It also explains what Creation is composed of and also what human beings are and what they are composed of. It also explains the process of Creation, how Creation develops, as well as who created Creation and where that entity may be found. It also explains how a human being may discover that entity and in so doing also discover the secrets of Creation, the meaning of life and the means to break free from the pathetic condition of human limitation and mortality in order to discover the higher realms of being by discovering the principles, the levels of existence that are beyond the simple physical and material aspects of life.

Part 1: The Movement of Creation and the concept of Pauti

Every human being is on a psycho-spiritual journey. They are in various ways trying to discover happiness, peace and fulfillment. Most people search in the world for these coveted goals. However, invariably they can only find limited fulfillment at best and in the end all of a person's achievements, no matter how grand, are relinquished by them at the time of death. Mystical philosophy shows that people are really searching for a deeper happiness and that if they were to understand how to pursue it their worldly desires, actions and experiences would be directed towards an inner spiritual discovery. The fruit of this inner journey is the discovery that one has infinite peace and bliss deep within and the discovery of that is the true goal of life.

In order to successfully complete the journey everyone needs to evolve spiritually. So the characters of the myth of Creation and their various forms of interaction with each other are in reality an elaborate mystic code relating to the areas of human consciousness which need to be developed in order to grow spiritually. As explained earlier, the first thing that is noticed when the deities of the Ancient Egyptian Creation, based on the teachings of Anu, are placed in a hierarchical fashion based on their order of Creation by Ra is that they arise in accordance with their level of density. Density here refers to their order of subtlety of the elements in Creation which they represent. Ra is the first principle which emerges out of the Primeval Waters. He is the subtle, singular principle of Creation, the focus of oneness in time and space. The ocean itself transcends time and space and is beyond existence and non-existence. Ra is the first principle to emerge out of the Absolute and his emergence signifies the beginning of existence.

As explained earlier, the second important idea derived from the Pauti is that they represent a whole number, 10, and thus convey the idea of a special symmetry. The highest level, Ra, is juxtaposed with the lower level of the Pauti with the image of Heru. So at one end we see the perfect singularity of the Supreme Self and at the other we see the perfect combination of Spirit and Matter in the form of Heru. So while the Tree of Life cosmiconomythograph may be understood as a reference to a "higher" and a "lower" idea in reality the image is not to be understood as a teaching of something that is above or better and something that is below or lesser. Thou this does not mean that people who exist on the lower plane may not be degraded because they can be; however, Heru is on that plane too and he overcame his degradation. Therefore, degradation is not a rigid state; human beings can elevate themselves. It is a teaching which expresses the essence of Creation, containing subtle as well as grosser objects which all emanate from the same source. The Ancient Egyptian teaching states that that which is above is the same as that which is below. If the Above and Below teaching is to be applied it should be understood as referring to the idea that everything in Creation is a reflection of the spiritual essence which transcends physicality. The physical universe is an emanation from the spiritual essence and as such is sustained by it. The very matter which constitutes Creation is in reality spirit in a condensed form just as when a person falls asleep their dream world is condensed out of their own consciousness. Nun is the underlying primordial consciousness of Creation. Ra may be seen as the Soul of Creation and Djehuti may be seen as the Cosmic Mind of Creation, Hetheru (Hathor) may be seen as the Vital Life Force of Creation and Maat may be seen as the underlying order of Creation. Djehuti, Hetheru and Maat are the underlying principles which sustain the Pauti.

Figure 19: An image of the Company of Gods and Goddesses of Ra

The image above displays the *Pauti* of Creation along with the underlying principles which sustain them. As explained earlier, the Pauti refers to Creation itself. The deities of the Pauti are nine in number and include Shu, Tefnut, Geb, Nut, Asar, Aset, Set, Nebthet and Heru. Maati, Hetheru and Djehuti are not part of the Pauti itself. They are subtle principles which were created by Ra that support its existence. Anpu is a production of Spirit and mortal life. So he is a new principle emanating from Creation itself.

Pa → Pau → Paut → Pauti

The Ancient Egyptian words and symbols related to the Company of Gods and Goddesses (Pauti) indicate several important mystical teachings. The root of the Ancient Egyptian word Pauti is *pa*. Pa means "to exist." Thus, Creation is endowed with the quality of existence as opposed to non-existence. *Pau* is the next progression in the word. It means the *Primeval Divinity*, the source of Creation, the root of existence. *Paut*

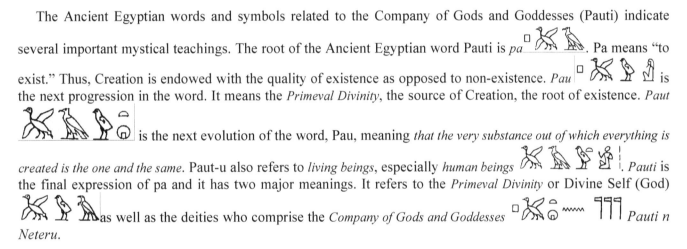

is the next evolution of the word, Pau, meaning *that the very substance out of which everything is created is the one and the same*. Paut-u also refers to *living beings*, especially *human beings*. *Pauti* is the final expression of pa and it has two major meanings. It refers to the *Primeval Divinity* or Divine Self (God) as well as the deities who comprise the *Company of Gods and Goddesses* *Pauti n Neteru*.

Therefore, the most important teaching relating to the nature of Creation is being given here. The gods and goddesses of the creation are not separate principles or entities. They are in reality one and the same as the Primeval Divinity. They are expressions of that Divine Self. However, they are not transformations of or evolutions from the Divine Self, but the very same Divine Self expressing as Creation {forms} through the acts *kpr* - creation, of the *Sheta Kheperu* – "hidden creator of forms." So even though God is referred to as a primordial deity who did something along time ago or set into motion various things, in reality God and Creation are one and the same. Ra is the God of primeval time as well as the gods and goddesses of Creation which sustain it all the time. With this understanding it is clear to see that God is not distant and aloof, observing Creation from afar, as is often conceived in orthodox religions such as the world religions of the Western countries. The Divine Self is the very basis of Creation and is in every part of it at all times. This is why the terms *Pa-Neter* and *Neteru* are also used to describe the Divine. Pa-Neter means "The Supreme Being" and neteru means "the gods and goddesses." Also, neteru refers to creation itself. So neter-u emanates from Neter. Note that the term Pa-Neter includes the designation "Pa" {what exists} and the term neteru does not. In this context it means that this is THE Divinity, the absolute. The others, the neteru, are not absolute, not abiding in and of themselves but rather in Pa Neter. Creation is nothing but God who has assumed various forms or neteru: trees, cake, bread, human beings, metal, air, fire, water, animals, planets, space, electricity, etc. the term "*pa*" {*the*[55]} as a grammatical term, in Ancient Egyptian, is used before singular or plural nouns[56] and noun phrases that denote particular, specified persons or things: *the baby; the dress, etc.* In the Kemetic language the noun refers to objects that exist as practical realities but when applied to the Supreme Being the grammatical particle "the" becomes part of the noun, thus signifying the exclusive designation of *Pa Neter* "THE DIVINE", i.e. "The Supreme Being". This is a profound teaching which should be reflected upon often so that the mind may become enlightened to its deeper meaning and thereby discover the Divinity in nature.

The Divine Self is not only in Creation but in the heart of every human being as well. Therefore, the very essence, the substratum of every human being is in reality God as well. The task of spiritual practice and Sema Tawi {Egyptian Yoga} is to discover this essential nature within your own heart. This can occur if one reflects upon this teaching and realizes its meaning by discovering its reality in the deepest recesses of one's own experience. When this occurs, the person who has attained this level of self-discovery is referred to as having become enlightened. They have discovered their true, divine nature. They have discovered their oneness with the Divine Self.

Ra, Asar and Heru and the Hawk Trinity

Ra represents the Divine Self, the source from which Creation arises. However, he is a High God who is the visible and dynamic expression of the formless and timeless Primeval Ocean, Nun. In any case he is still the singular essence of Creation. When he creates the other divinities it is only then that Creation comes into being.

Ra is also related to the nameless and formless concept of the Supreme Being which transcends time and space known as Heru. Heru (Divinity - The Sun Divinity). Heru means "The Supreme One who is above" or "That which is above." So Heru is the original pre-dynastic form of the Supreme Being associated with the transcendental Divinity. Heru (God) and Het-Heru (Hathor - the house of Heru) were among the first divinities to be worshipped generally throughout Ancient Egypt and as such, were the first theological expression of the duality of existence. The Supreme Being (Heru or Hor) lives within his own house (Het), the universe (goddess). Thus, God (spirit) and Goddess (creation) are in reality one and the same. In the pyramid texts, at the beginning of the Dynastic Period, the symbol of *Heru*, is used interchangeably with , *Pa Neter*.

The Divine Name, Heru, is related to the word for face, *Her* or *Hra*. The relation to face implies the idea that what is above (the sky, the heavens) is the mask of the Supreme Divinity. God cannot be seen but his/her mask, the physical universe, can be seen.

The god Heru (Horus) has several important aspects in Ancient Egyptian Mystical philosophy. In the Anunian Creation myth of the Pauti, Heru is incorporated as *Heru-ur* or "Horus the aged." In the Ausarian Resurrection myth the idea of Heru (Supreme One above) was incorporated into the myth as *Heru-sa-Ast-sa Asar* (Horus, the son of Isis and Osiris). In dynastic times Heru was associated with Horus as in the Osirian Mystery where he was represented in the form of *Heru-p-Khard* or "Horus the child," who later becomes Min, the *avenger of his father.*

The relationship between Ra, Asar and Heru is extremely important in the study of Anunian Mystical Philosophy and The Asarian Resurrection Myth. It is important to not only study the scriptures relating to the mysticism but the iconography needs careful study as well since the images sometimes convey teachings not contained in the texts and also messages that cannot be conveyed in text form, but which are complementary to the texts. One important symbolism (iconography) that provides insights into the nature and relationships of three

---

[55] the. (n.d.). *The American Heritage® Dictionary of the English Language, Fourth Edition.* Retrieved June 14, 2008, from Dictionary.com website: http://dictionary.reference.com/browse/the

[56] *noun* -any member of a class of words that are formally distinguished in many languages, as in English, typically by the plural and possessive endings and that can function as the main or only elements of subjects or objects, as *cat, belief, writing, Ohio, darkness.* Nouns are often thought of as referring to persons, places, things, states, or qualities. noun. (n.d.). *Dictionary.com Unabridged (v 1.1).* Retrieved June 14, 2008, from Dictionary.com website: http://dictionary.reference.com/browse/noun

special Neteru is the Hawk Trinity. Three male[57] divinities, Ra, Asar and Heru, display the hawk iconography, thereby, linking their essential natures within the context of the Tree of Life teaching.

 Glyph 1

The symbol of Heru (The One Above) is the hawk or falcon bird (Glyph 1). Hawks and falcons belong to the family of birds known as Falconiformes. Falconiformes are an order of predatory birds, comprised of vultures, kites, eagles, hawks, ospreys, and falcons.[1] Falcons possess special attributes. They have keen eyesight. They can fly at fast speeds. They have streamlined bodies, hooked bills for tearing meat and strong legs with hooked claws for killing and carrying their prey. A spiritual aspirant needs to develop determination, strength, physical health, and the ability to tear asunder the veil of ignorance and the negative aspects of the mind with the claws of wisdom, righteousness and goodwill. Glyphs 2, 3 and 4 (below) are some of the most ancient renditions of Heru. Glyph 5 is of *Ra-Harakty* or the combination of Heru and Ra, Heru with a sundisk.

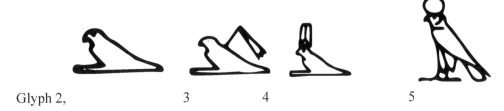

Glyph 2,   3   4   5

Figure 20: a picture of an Ancient Egyptian statue of Ra.

His distinguishing features are the head of a Hawk and the body of a man. His head is surmounted by a sundisk which is encircled by a serpent (*Uadjit*-Hetheru). He holds the *Uas* scepter (spiritual power) and also the Ankh (life). One more important feature is the bull's tail. The tail symbolizes that Ra is the "Bull of Creation." The Bull sires the Seven Cows of Creation and the Seven Cows are the goddesses which constitute the seven aspects of all existence, the manifested universe. Also, Asar is known as the Bull of Creation as well. Thus, Ra-Heru is the source and sustenance of Creation, it's Bull.

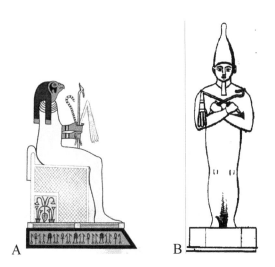

Figure 21: A -Left-a picture of Asar-Sokar (Osiris) in his aspect as the king of the realm of the dead (composite iconography). **B -Right-**Asar as resurrected King (anthropomorphic iconography).

---

[57] Aset also has an avian falconiform as a *kite.*

This form of Asar is known as *Sokar* or *Seker*. His main distinguishing features are the human body with mummy wrappings and the head of the falcon with the *deshret* or white crown of Upper Egypt (heart and origin of the country).

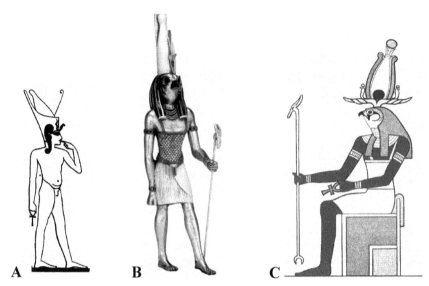

Figure 22: Above: forms of Heru, as a child(A), adult(B) and king (C).

Heru's distinguishing features are again the head of a falcon with the body of a man. He has the *wereret* crown symbolizing the union of upper and lower Egypt (Union of the higher and the lower self), the *Ankh, Uas* scepter and the bull tail.

So it is clear to see, based on the iconography, that the essence of Neberdjer, operating as Ra is reflected in Creation through the manifestations of Ra, Asar and Heru. The manifestation occurs in the form reflections of the Spirit into a Trinity distributed into the lower worlds of time and space in the following manner.

Neberdjer
(That which is imperceptible, formless, timeless and absolute, transcending all planes of consciousness while at the same time permeating them as the very essence or substratum which sustains them.)
↓
Ra
(The primordial singular essence, the soul of Creation, the first principle of manifestation by the Divine Self into the realm of time and space. In this aspect Ra symbolizes the Causal Plane of existence and consciousness.)
↓
Asar
(As the king of the realm of the dead Asar symbolizes the Astral Plane of existence and consciousness.)
↓
Heru-Ur
(The ultimate manifestation of the Divine within Creation. In this aspect Horus symbolizes the Physical Plane of existence and consciousness.)

Diagram 6: The order of evolution from Subtle to Gross and the Combinations that Bring Forth the Generated Divinities

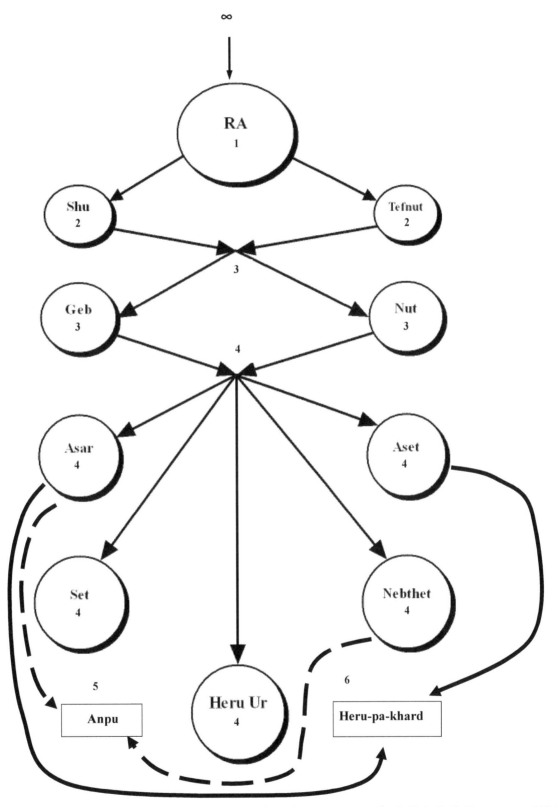

Six generations bring forth the main divinities of Anunian Theurgy. From the infinite[∞], Ra emerges[1]. He brings forth Shu and Tefnut[2]; They bring forth Geb and Nut[3]; they in turn give birth to Asar, Aset, Set and Nebethet and Heru Ur [4]. Asar and Nebthet give rise to Anpu [5]. Asar and Aset give rise to Heru-pa-khard [6].

Shu and Tefnut

Ra gives rise to Shu and Tefnut. Shu is the principle of air and space. Space is the first aspect/element of the Divine that is necessary in order for Creation to be possible. In Eastern mystical teachings this principle is referred to as Ether. The next principle of Creation is Tefnut. She symbolizes the subtle potential dynamic energy, the Life Force within all creation, *sekhem*. She is that which allows creation to have movement. She is represented as a lioness and she is related to the Ancient Egyptian goddess known as *Sekhmet*. Sekhmet is the goddess who presides over Sekhem or the Serpent Power Life Force of all things.

Geb and Nut

Next Shu and Tefnut give rise to Geb and Nut. Geb and Nut are the earth and the heavens respectively. So, from the subtlest essence of Creation (Ra) the subtle principles, space and life force energy, emerged. Now from space and life force energy even more dense principles arise and these constitute the physical world, stars, planets, outer space, etc.

Thus, from Ra the basic principles of Creation emanated and this sets the stage for the existence of human beings and the life forms of Creation. Notice that all of the principles (Shu and Tefnut and Geb and Nut) are pairs of opposites which have been given male and female iconographies. This points to the teaching that existence is a mingling of opposite principles which emanate from the single essence. However, in and of themselves they are not what constitute life from the human point of view because they do not contain the dynamic consciousness of the Self or Spirit (Ra) in the proper manner to allow reasoning, feeling, etc. to manifest. Reasoning, feeling, memory, action, love and other capacities are what constitute human existence. In order for these to manifest, the proper combination of matter and spirit must be present. The next five deities represent that melding of God and Creation which allows human life to exist and to be sustained.

Asar and Aset, and Set and Nebthet

From Geb and Nut arise Asar and Aset, Set and Nebthet. Asar and Aset represent the epitome of human existence. In the view of the myth Asar is seen as the soul of Creation, a reflection of the Divine consciousness (Ra). Aset represents intuitional knowledge, the wisdom which transcends time and space and is united with the soul.

Set and Nebthet represent the lower nature of every human being. Set is the egoistic will of a human being, that which is selfish, greedy, impulsive and full of desires for sensual pleasures. Therefore, Set is that aspect of a human being that is prone to becoming involved with and exacerbate the desires and egoistic tendencies of the mind. When this occurs a human being does not see things clearly and becomes enslaved, as it were, by his or her own desires, feelings/emotions and attachments for worldly objects and for worldly experiences. This is known as spiritual ignorance or bondage to the world of time and space. It is also the cause of reincarnation or the cycle of birth and death which every human being suffers until they attain spiritual enlightenment.

Nebthet represents mortality and all that is transient in human existence. She is physical nature itself which transforms itself constantly, bringing forth life only to see it die and be reborn again. Thus, she also presides over reincarnation but also she represents another important principle of human existence. Nebthet is the quality of Devotion in all life which is expressed in its highest degree through the emotion of love which manifests in every human being. Nebthet loves Asar, that is to say, she is devoted to him and wants to mate with him. In other words, mortality desires immortality, the freedom of the soul. When she mates with Asar they bring forth Anpu who represents right discernment. Therefore, upon discovering Anpu conscience no longer does a person desire worldly things for their own sake, no longer does a person care and think about the body, mortality and finite existence (principles of Nebthet) but they now turn towards what is true in life. Human love manifests in various degrees. Some people love themselves in a selfish way, caring for themselves alone. This condition is Set operating through them. Others love material objects and sense pleasures. This is also Setian although a more expanded manifestation of love. Others love family members and still others love their community. Love may expand to include one's country or even humanity. And the highest love in time and space is for God and transcending that is Neberdjer. As the feeling of love expands a person loves the earth and the heavens and then the subtle essence which enlivens Creation itself (God, and beyond that: Neberdjer). Thus, they grow in universal love and in so doing they are actually growing in cosmic consciousness because God is universal love itself, the cosmic expansion of love and devotion for all that exists.

Nebthet is the reflection of Aset. Her name means "Lady of the House." "House" here implies mortal or physical human existence which exists in Creation which is also time and space, whereas Aset represents the subtle spirit realm which transcends mortality. In any case they are one and the same goddess expressing in two forms, the subtle as well as the gross aspects of Creation in human consciousness. The fact that they are both consorts of Asar points to the fact that the Soul (Asar) is wedded to the subtle (Aset) as well as the gross essence (Nebthet) of Creation. It is notable that while Nebthet is supposed to be the consort of Set she is nevertheless drawn to Asar. Set produces no offspring with her. In the same way, a life of vice, egoism and selfishness (principles of Set) produces no offspring in the form of spiritual enlightenment, abiding joy, peace or happiness, but only illusory ego conscience, frustration, unrest and discontent.

Anpu (Anubis)

Anpu is the offspring of Spirit/soul (Asar) and pure physical/mortal nature (Nebthet). Anpu is often related to the dog or jackal deity. The jackal deity has two aspects, *Anpu* and *Apuat* (or *Wepwat/Wepwawet*). Anpu is the embalmer, the one who prepares the initiate, the *Shti* (one who is in his coffin-the body). As a neophyte, the initiate is considered to be dead (a mummy) since he/she does not have conscious realization of the transcendental reality beyond the ego-personality. He or she is an ordinary mortal human being in consciousness. At this stage the aspirant must be prepared through virtue and physical purification to receive the teachings, because without this preparation, the highest teachings would fall on deaf ears. In this context Anpu represents vigilance and the constant practice of discrimination and watchfulness (mindfulness) over the ego-self. Anpu represents the development of mental clarity {sanity} which unfolds within the human heart in degrees. Gradually, through the practices of discrimination and watchfulness, the ego-self becomes effaced and reveals the true self as one with Asar.

Anpu represents: "Control of the thoughts", "Control of one's actions", and "Devotion of purpose", "Learning how to distinguish between right and wrong," "Learning to distinguish the real from the unreal". Anpu is solely devoted to Asar, and as such, represents the process of concentration and oneness of vision which lead to Divine awareness (Asar).

Anpu also implies dispassion and detachment from worldly desires. This should not be misinterpreted as a pathetic development. Detachment from the world implies a keen understanding that the world and all objects in it cannot bring happiness to the soul, because they are transient and fleeting. Since the essence of all objects is the Higher Self, in detaching from objects you are merely detaching from the reflection of the Higher Self and attaching to the real Higher Self behind the objects. From the perspective of spirituality, the act of detaching from objects does not mean simply giving up objects. Rather, it means you now have a more profound way of seeing and understanding objects. You now have deeper insight into the true nature of the object; it is this understanding which allows you to detach from objects. You understand they are temporal creations from the source of all existence, your very own heart, as in a dream, and therefore are not abiding realities that can or should be possessed or owned.

Discernment, purity of mind, the ability to know right from wrong, truth from untruth, reality from unreality are the hallmarks of Anpu mind. These qualities are essential in the beginning of the spiritual journey as well as in the more advanced practice. In order to develop a mind that is capable of discovering the subtlety between the absolute reality of spirit and the subtlety of egoistic desires and the apparent reality of time and space, which are temporal and illusory, Anpu mind is required. Anpu as the preparer of the mind, the purifier of the mind, operates to allow proper discernment and right thinking about worldly situations and objects. As the warrior, Anpu mind, the capacity to confront wrong thinking, allows the aspirant to succeed against the incorrect ideas, thoughts and desires. Anpu as Wepwawet, opens the way and leads an aspirant to the land of spiritual enlightenment, the west, and Anpu of the West is the mind of the west, the place where life comes to a proper end in peace and spiritual enlightenment, perfection in understanding the nature of the transcendent. This capacity of mind to discern, operates in the intellectual processes of the mind as well and is a foundation for the capacity of mind to understand concepts as well as to separate understanding from egoism, the desires that skew the mind and cause it to make decisions that are partial to the desires and are not based solely on truth.

The qualities of Anpu assist in the spiritual movement since an intellectual grasp of mystical philosophy is necessary for progress on the spiritual path. However, intellectual sophistication, sharpness and subtlety are only a means and not an end in themselves. Spiritual evolution necessitates a transcendental movement beyond the level of the ordinary human intellect (the level of the mind and senses).

Now we return to the other aspect of Anpu, Anpu as the god of two faces, has a second aspect whose name is Wepwat (Apuat), which means "opener of the ways." Once the Anpu mind is engendered, the mind that knows truth from untruth, then the Wepwat aspect can lead the soul to the higher realms of existence, to the Netherworld. This is what Wepwat did for Asar after Asar was resurrected. In the same way Wepwat mind leads an aspirant on the right path for the spiritual journey. Then the movement of dissolution, the spiritual journey to enlightenment based on the pauti, can begin and have a positive outcome.

Heru and Hetheru (Horus and Hathor)

Heru is the epitome of all human qualities when they are sublimated, or harmonized. He is the offspring of the Spirit (Asar) and intuitional wisdom (Aset). When human beings evolves in consciousness to their full potential they become masters of their own conscience as well as of their own physical nature. They are the perfect blend of matter and spirit, desire, devotion, wisdom and power. They transcend time and space even as they continue to live in time and space. Such a life is glorious and it is the goal of all human beings.

The goddess Hetheru is the subtle essence of dynamic (focused) spiritual power in Creation, as symbolized in her form as the right eye of Ra {the sundisk}. The sundisk is the ultimate symbol of the dynamic power of the Divine Self which sustains all life. Her name indicates a close relationship with Heru. The name "Het-heru" means *House of Heru*. Heru is indeed the one who dwells in the *House of Hetheru,* in other words, Spirit {Heru} lives in creation {HetHeru} itself. Heru is none other than Ra in another form and Heru is also Djehuti. Heru is also Nefer-Tem. "Nefer-Tem" is the "beautiful completion", the Divine Self arising from the primeval waters, sitting on his lotus. Thus, every human being (Heru) is not separate from God but is essentially God, who arose from the primeval waters (Nefer-Tem) and is potentially able to realize their true nature. The Self manifests as the universe as well as the consciousness (Ra) and intelligence (Djehuti) which resides, lives and interacts within that creation.

Diagram 7: The Path for the Journey along the Realms of the Kemetic Tree of Life

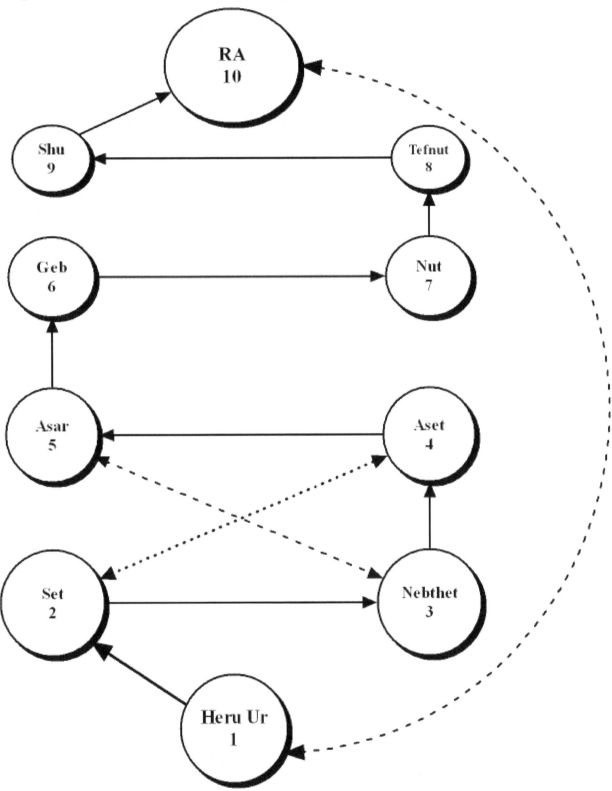

Part 2: The Movement of Dissolution, The Spiritual Journey To Enlightenment Based on the Pauti

The journey of spiritual enlightenment may be seen as a reverse of the creation process. In the creation everything emanates from the Nun or Primordial Ocean and expresses in the form of elements in succeeding levels of denseness. These elements also manifest in the form of opposites which appear to be exclusive and separate from each other, but which are in reality complements to each other. To counteract the movement towards ignorance and illusory divergence, the spiritual journey is based on first sublimating the ego and its desires, which cause a person to become entrenched, as it were, in the physical realm of existence and to be oblivious to the higher planes of existence. Spiritual practice consists in developing the intellectual capacity by understanding the illusoriness of the opposites of Creation. This leads a spiritual aspirant to develop mystic aspiration and the qualities to go beyond the appearances of nature and to discover the Absolute existence which is the real basis for all that exists.

Nun (10)
(Discovering the absolute and transcendental essence which is beyond even the singularity of consciousness (Ra)- beyond time and space and the opposites of creation (Shu-Tefnut-Geb-Nut) as well as the concepts of existence or non-existence.)

↑

Ra-Tem (9)
(Discovering the single essence which underlies the multiplicity of nature-Cosmic Consciousness.)

↑

Shu ⇔ Tefnut (8)
(Discovering the more subtle aspects of nature.)

↑

Geb⇔Nut (7)
(Discovering the gross aspects of nature.)

↑

Hetheru -Djehuti – Maat (6)
(Spiritual Strength - Right Reasoning - Righteous Action
These higher spiritual qualities allow a spiritual aspirant to discover the mysteries of nature— to pierce the veil of illusion which prevents the discovery of the underlying essence of nature (Creation)—God.)

↑

Heru (5)
(Advanced Spiritual Aspiration, having developed spiritual qualities such as purity, truthfulness, honesty, etc. to pursue a spiritual lifestyle which will lead to success in life as well as spiritual enlightenment—self-discovery.)

↑

Asar ⇔ Aset (4)
(Glimpses of the transcendental Divine Glory and initiation into the teachings of mystical wisdom.)

↑

Anpu (3)
(Intellect-understanding that the world is perishable and that there is something else which is abiding. Also, understanding the real meaning of life and the real goal of life—to attain enlightenment. Understanding what is real from what is unreal, truth from untruth.)

↑

Asar⇔Nebthet (2)
(Devotion to the Divine - Faith in the existence of the Divine Self and in the idea that Enlightenment is a real possibility.)

↑

Set (1)
(Sublimation of the ego and the lower self-control over the sex drive and the negative qualities such as anger, hatred, greed, covetousness, jealousy, etc.)

Diagram 8: the Realms of the Kemetic Tree of Life in Order of Increasing Subtlety

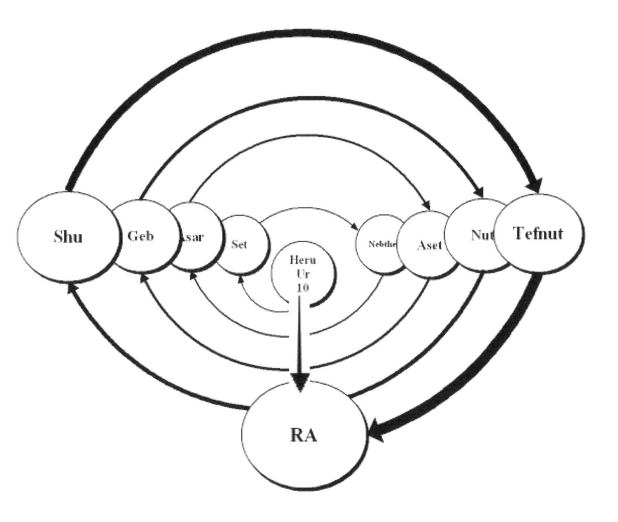

Reflection and Journal discipline:

1- At the top of each page copy the following hieroglyphs to the best of your ability

[**cht n ankh** " *tree of life*"]

    After studying the Lesson proceed to answer the following question and write the answer in your journal. This exercise will require more than one reading and more than one journal entry, at least one page; write all you can find related to the subject of the question. Answer the questions first without referring to the text you just read. Then go back and see if you missed anything. This exercise is to be repeated until you become proficient with the principles of this sphere. The reflection exercise should be done after each reading or study session. Then you may practice meditation[58] on the wisdom you have learned. You may come back to add to your reflections even if you move on to other lessons.

REFLECTIONS: The movement of creation is what I have known all my life. This teaching of the Tree brings me to know the movement of dissolution, the opposite of creation. With this teaching I will know how I have created things, situations, feelings and thoughts; I will now learn how to uncreate…to dissolve what has been formed, to see beyond the surface of things.

After studying the Lesson proceed to answer the following question and write the answer in your journal.

    What is an emanation from the spiritual essence and as such is sustained by it.

    What is(are) the main teaching(s) of this lesson and what do the principle(s) of the divinity(ies) discussed in this lesson mean in reference to my actions, feelings, thoughts and desires and understanding of the spiritual philosophy?

---

[58] Explained in more detail in Lesson 15

Lesson 5: The Number Order of the Divinities and the Mysteries of Number for Understanding the Levels of Creation and the Path for the Journey of the Tree of Life

The Principle of Creator and the Nine Divinities

Based on Anunian theology, as it is presented in the Theurgy of the Ancient Egyptian Pyramid Texts and other Kemetic scriptures, the order, nomenclature and attributes of the Ancient Egyptian divinities of the Creation may be viewed as follows. As with other African religions, Ancient Egyptian religion follows the format of recognizing a Supreme and transcendental divinity out of which "Lesser divinities" emanate or emerge. In the Anunian Theurgy Creation we are presented with divinities that compose the gross and subtle elements of Creation as well as the psychological principles that make up the psyche of a human being.

The Account of the Creation of the Gods and Goddesses of Creation According to The Creation Theurgy of Anu and the account of Plutarch

1. In the beginning, there was the primeval ocean, Nu, and from it arose Ra.
   1.1. Upon his emergence this magnificent God created all that came into being from his own self and he existed within his creation as one exists within one's own body.
   1.2. He sneezed Shu and spat Tefnut and they in turn gave rise to Nut and Geb.
   1.3. The goddess Nut and the god Geb were united in amorous embrace since they had loved each other so deeply from the beginning of time.
   1.4. Their embrace was so close that no other living being could exist in the world.

2. From their union Nut became pregnant, but Ra had decreed that they should be separated and that Nut could not give birth in any month of the year.
   2.1. At this time he also decided to retreat as an active participant in his creation and to abide in heaven wherein all who would seek him must go.
   2.2. From this position he supports creation as he traverses in the form of the sun making it possible for life to exist and flourish.
   2.3. In the morning he is known as Kheper, at noon he is known as Ra and at sunset he is known as Tem.

   2.4. Also from here he witnesses all of the activities and events of creation. In his absence he created Djehuti, his minister and messenger through whom he, Ra, would manage and sustain his creation.

3. Ra instituted himself as the sustainer of creation during the day and illumines creation as the sun, $\odot$, while setting Djehuti up in the form of the baboon to watch over creation at night as the moon, $\pmb{\mathbb{D}}$.

4. Having become pregnant as a result of her sexual union with Geb, Nut gave birth to Asar, Set, Aset, Nebthet and Heru Ur.

5. Djehuti, who being wise and caring for Nut, was able to win the seventieth part of each day of the year and to have these added up and added to the year.

5.1. These Epagomenal Days or "the five days over the year" he added to the three hundred and sixty days of which the year formerly consisted.

5.2. These five days are to this day called the "Epagomenae," that is, the "superadded", and they are observed as the birthdays of the gods.

5.3. On the first of these days, Asar was born, and as he came into the world a voice was heard saying, *"The Lord of All, Neberdjer, is born."*

6. Upon the second of these days was born Heru Ur (Heru the Elder).

6.1. Upon the Third day Set was born, who came into the world neither at the proper time nor by the right way, but he forced a passage through a wound which he made in his mother's side.

6.2. Upon the fourth day Aset was born in the marshes of Egypt, and upon the fifth day Nebthet was born.

6.3. As regards the fathers of these children, the first two are said to have been begotten by Ra, Isis by Djehuti, and Set and Nebthet by Geb.

6.4. Therefore, since the third of the superadded days was the birthday of Set, the kings considered it to be unlucky and in consequence, they neither transacted any business in it, nor even suffered themselves to take any refreshment until the evening.

7. They further add that Set married Nebthet and that Isis and Asar, having a mutual affection, enjoyed each other in their mother's womb even before they were born, and that from this union sprang Heru the Elder (whom the Greeks call Apollo).

7.1. Asar and Aset gave birth to Heru, and Asar and Nebthet gave birth to Anpu.

From the reading above we obtain the following schematic of the Cosmology of Shetaut Neter Theurgy

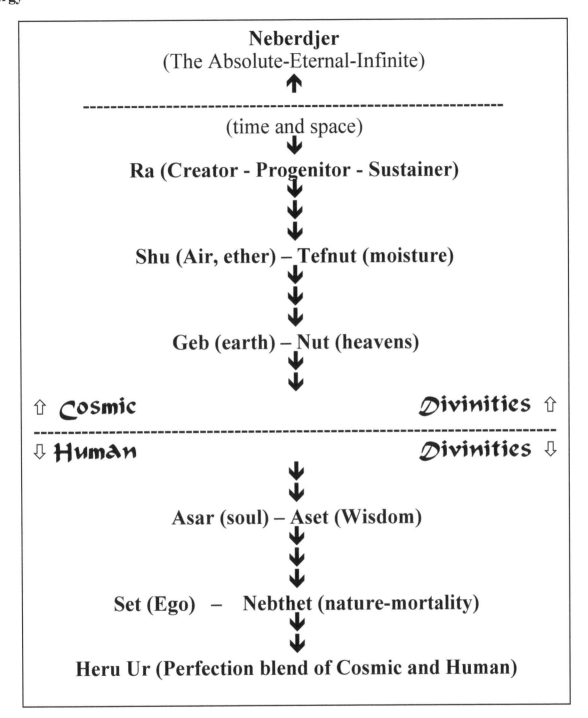

The Mystical Significance of Number In Creation

The Number 1 and The Number 9

There is important mystical significance related to the number nine (9) within Ancient Egyptian mystical philosophy. In the Company of gods and goddesses of Ra (Ra-Tem, Shu, Tefnut, Geb, Nut, Set, Asar (Osiris), Aset (Isis), Nebthet (Nephthys), and Heru-ur) there is a total of nine divinities and when we add the progenitor, Ra, who is the first and therefore is assigned the number one, we get a total of ten. The nine compose Creation itself and the first is the High God (or Goddess) of the system, who engenders and supports the existence of the nine. The number nine is to be found in the very heart of Ancient Egyptian Myth, the Cosmology and Cosmogony itself, because the number nine is the basis of creation. This is why the number nine recurs in nature, in chemical and physics experiments. Creation unfolds into nine relative aspects and they are all rooted in and sustained by the Supreme Being, the first principle. This idea is mythologically expressed as the emergence from the primeval ocean and the eventual submergence back into the ocean at the end of time, thus creating a cyclical movement of the spirit wherein Creation is continually emanated (created), dissolved and re-emanated again. If the gods and goddesses of the Pauti are assigned numbers their qualities explain the numerological aspects of Creation and these explain the cosmogony of Creation. The number of each divinity is assigned in accordance with their emergence pattern, mythic significance and psychic relevance, as stated in the Ancient Egyptian Creation myth and its traditional account.

```
                    Nun (∞)
                       ⇩
                  Ra-Tem  (1)
                       ⇩
        Shu (2)    ⇔ Tefnut (3)
                       ⇩
          Geb (4)  ⇔   Nut (5)
                       ⇩
        Asar (6)   ⇔  Aset (7)
                       ⇩
        Set (8)    ⇔ Nebthet  (9)
                       ⇩
                  Heru Ur (10)
```

In verses 5.3-6.2 of the Account of the Creation we learned the order of the emergence of the Earthly or Human Divinities; it was 1) Asar, 2) Heru Ur, 3) Set, 4) Aset and 5) Nebthet. But this is not the order format that is used for the Tree.

Examination of the Creation from the Original Papyrus Text written by the Anunian Priesthood

The foundation of the teaching of the Kemetic Tree of Life comes from the Anunian Creation myth. The name of the book is *The Book of knowing the forms of Ra.*

shat	*nty*	*rech*	*kheperu*		*nu*	*Ra*
Book	the	knowing	forms		of	Ra

The Book of knowing the creations of Ra is a cosmological mythic scripture. If it were to be compared to a biblical type scripture this would be the Genesis section. The portion below is part of the section that contains the segment that talks about the nature of Creation and the emergence of the gods and goddesses.

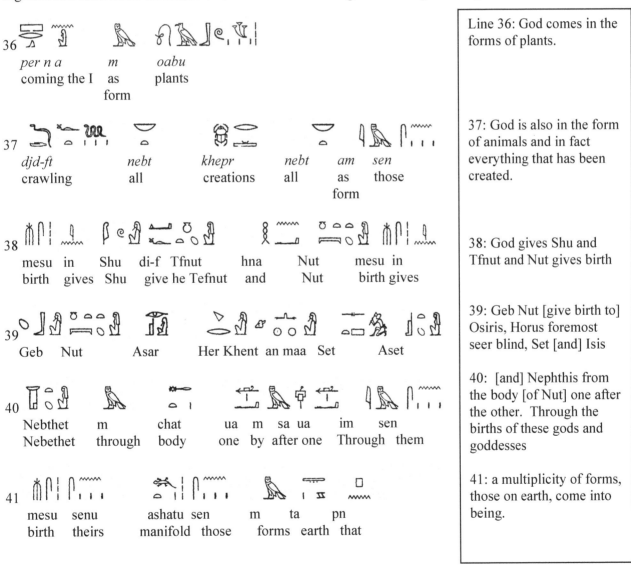

Line 36: God comes in the forms of plants.

37: God is also in the form of animals and in fact everything that has been created.

38: God gives Shu and Tfnut and Nut gives birth

39: Geb Nut [give birth to] Osiris, Horus foremost seer blind, Set [and] Isis

40: [and] Nephthis from the body [of Nut] one after the other. Through the births of these gods and goddesses

41: a multiplicity of forms, those on earth, come into being.

So, from this brief reading of the Creation Myth Scripture, we learn that God created the living beings on earth and that the varied life forms on earth originally proceed from the gods and goddesses that God created. This teaching explains an ancient Egyptian proverb that states: *men and women are mortal gods and goddesses and the gods and goddesses are immortal men and women.* This also explains how human beings are of divine origin but that implies also that men and women have a divine spark, a divine essence. It is that essence that the teaching is dedicated to rediscovering and the discovery which constitutes the attainment of the coveted goal of the mysteries, the mysticism.

In the Creation Myth Scripture line 39 the name of Set is given with a special determinative glyph. The determinative is the primary aspect of a word that assigns it's meaning. In this case the glyph of a man in the process of striking himself with an ax. is the determinative of death and also self-immolation, self-destruction. What is implied here is that the principle that Set represents the aspect of the personality that causes itself suffering; that is what the ego, based on ignorance of the knowledge of self and the desires of such an ego, leads to. In other words, the pain and sorrow that human beings experience is of their own doing if they live out of Set nature.

When we examine the text of the papyrus of the Creation we see a different form of Heru is given, *Heru Ur* [Horus the Aged(Elder), the King], in the section of the birth of the children of goddess Nut. How do we reconcile that with the account provided by Plutarch? The account given by Plutarch is based on popular legend or folklore and is valid. The account of the papyrus is theurgical and philosophical, so it is also valid. The form of Heru given in the papyrus is *Heru khenti an maa* or "Heru the foremost not seer", literally, means Heru the blind one. This form of Heru is of the full potential. The theological/philosophical/mystic interpretation of this form of Heru is an allusion to the time when the sun and moon set – meaning that when the eyes (sun and moon) are closed and looking internally, there are no objects since they need to be illuminated in order to be perceived, i.e. to exist as practical realities; this is the highest vision – i.e. the internal is foremost and not the external, so Heru in this form is "foremost seer." In worldly and ritual terms, the new moon period at night is a time when there is no illumination either from the moon or from the sun and this is known as the period of rebirth, i.e. the resurrection of the moon, the soul. The moon is a symbol of Asar, the dead and resurrected soul. When the two eyes close it is also a period of rebirth because the eyes are the sun and moon of the personality. *Heru khenti an maa* represents the potential of Heru to be born as *Heru Pa khard*, "Heru the child" [In Asarian Theurgy he is *Heru sa Asar sa Aset* (Heru the son of Asar son of Aset)] and then to grow up and become *Heru Ur*.

Having emerged alone, without a counterpart, and having the title of King, displaying falconiform iconography and being an earthly divinity and not one of the five cosmic divinities, *Heru Ur* belongs to the center and non-gender section [left or right sides] of the Tree cosmicinomythograph and thus he is placed at the opposite end of the numbering sequence from Ra.

If Set had not emerged at the proper time and right way and not in a wrong time and forced way (Verse 6.1) he would have been born in the fourth position instead of the third. The order of the Human Divinities in the Tree of Life is arranged differently from the actual order of emergence as recounted in the scripture in reference to the divinity Set because the same Account of the Creation informs us that Set emerged in an unorthodox manner which is shunned by the scripture and the practitioners of Neterian Religion (Verse 6.4). so the cosmicinimythograph depicts an idealized scheme and not a potential layout or literal arrangement but rather following the intent of the scripture based on the mythic narrative of Neterian (Ancient Egyptian) scripture and their own eschatology. According to the proper protocol for emergence, set should have been born after Aset (position number 4) but he jumped the order to position number three.

⇩
Asar (1)   ⇔   Aset (2)
⇩
Set (3)   ⇔ Nebthet (4)
⇩
Heru Ur (5)

Therefore, as a matter of mythic significance and psychic relevance Set is assigned the fourth position instead of the third and that resolves the mythic and psychic conundrum of the egoism and ignorance that was created by Set's wrong form of birth which mythically led to the falling out between him and Asar and concomitantly also the misunderstanding between the human soul consciousness and its ego conscience which has led to the miserable predicament of ignorance and suffering in ordinary human life. Thus, through the proper order of the Tree the mysteries of life may be resolved, which were created through the improper creation of them in the first place.

One's acts on earth are like a dream.
            'Welcome safe and sound!'
        to who ever arrives in the West.[59]

From "The Songs of the Harper" (Ancient Egypt)

The world is like a dream that arises during sleep. The dream may seem to be very real and abiding ("full") but when you wake up you discover that it is of lesser value than what you believed previously (hollow). The dream was an emanation from you and it has no reality unless you dream it, unless you support it and unless you believe in it. The dream is the realm of numbers and you are infinity. You are the "fullness" which gives rise to your dream. Following the metaphor, in the Creation myth, the Neter, Ra, is the dreamer, the "emanator" and the neteru, the gods and goddesses are the dream, the temporary Creation itself. So what is that Creation in terms of number? When the multiples of the number nine (number of the divinities that compose Creation) are added they all add up to 9. Also, every number that can add up to nine is divisible by 9. Thus, nine is the highest number.

The Creator, the Supreme Being is in reality not part of the Creation and in absolute terms is not counted as one of the Neteru. The Supreme Being is the transcendental principle engendering Creation. Nun is the infinite source material for Creation and Ra-Tem is the unitary and solitary individuating principle emerging from the Nun. Nun and Ra-Tem are essentially aspects of the same Supreme Being. Creation is given value due to the presence of the Self who is the Absolute Reality which sustains Creation. However, considering the High God, the Demiurge, who is the manifestation of the Supreme Being in time and space, as number one, the principle of fullness, Heru-ur then becomes number ten. This is why in Ancient Egyptian Mystical Philosophy the number ten is special to Heru. Thus, Heru signifies fullness and completion <u>in</u> time and space while Ra relates to fullness that transcends time and space. This is the original teaching whereby Buddhism and Hermetic philosophy (latest version of Kemetic (Ancient Egyptian) Mystical Philosophy), and the even later Christianity, derive the teaching

---

[59] M. Lichtheim, "The Songs of the Harper", *Journal of Near Eastern Studies* IV, 1945, p 178ff.

of "As Above, So Below" and "I am the Alpha and the Omega" respectively. Having discovered *Shetau Akhet*[60] and your Higher Self as being one and the same, you have discovered all that there is to be known, you have achieved the number nine.

The Sacred Numbers of Creation and their Important Subsets

Below Left: Number Correspondences in the Divinities of Anunian Theurgy
Below Right: Tree of Life of Anunian Theurgy

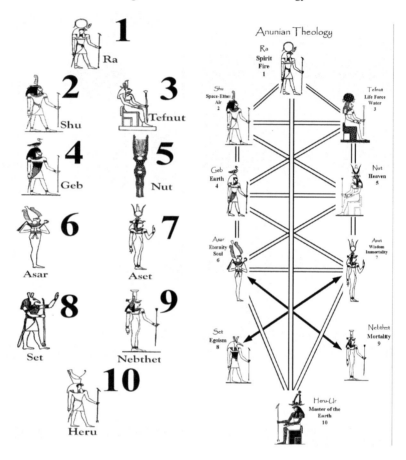

The Number 7

From the sacred numbers of the Pautti we are also given the number seven, the number of the goddess. The number seven relates to the seven aspects of Creation wherein human life has its manifestations. It is important to realize that Ra has seven *bau* or souls. The number seven is related to the seven psycho-spiritual energy centers which sustain human life, the seven realms of existence as symbolized by the seven Hetheru goddesses, the seven notes in music, the seven colors of the rainbow, etc. There are certainly more notes in music, energy centers and colors beyond the perceptible range but those are extrapolations of the same seven. However, the number seven denotes the perceptible range in which human existence has its mundane (typical of this world) manifestation and the other numbers are multiples or variations on the same seven. Seven times seven gives us 42, the number of ancient Egyptian Nomes or primordial settlements which gave rise to Ancient Egypt. Forty two is also related to the number of main precepts in Maat Philosophy. The number seven relates to the goddess of Wisdom, Aset in that with her basket, composed of a serpent that is coiled thee and one half times, relating to the spiral journey of the Serpent Power trough the psycho-spiritual energy centers as it enlightens human consciousness.[61]

---

[60] *Shetau Akhet* ⬚𓂝𓅓𓅪𓏤𓏭 ⬚𓏭 - hidden properties of matter (objects)
[61] see the book *The Serpent Power* by Dr. Muata Ashby

Figure 23: Basket of Aset

The Number 6

The number 6 was regarded by Pythagoras, an initiate of the Kemetic Mysteries, as the number of "full manifestation", the limit number. This idea is seen in music as the number six being the limiting factor of harmonies and there are only six harmonies in music. Thus, Asar, who symbolizes the soul, is fullness of manifestation of the spirit in time and space in the form of individual sparks of life that give rise to human beings. Put another way, each human being is like a wave in the ocean. The Supreme is the ocean and each soul is the limit of manifestation of that ocean as an individual.

The Number 5

In the metaphysics of the Anunian Theurgy Tree of Life the number five is significant because it incorporates or aggregates groups of Neteru into important dynamic fellowships. The grouping of subtle elements of Creation are five (Ra, Shu, Tefnut, Geb and Nut). The grouping of gross elements of Creation are five (Asar, Aset, Set, Nebthet and Heru Ur).

The Number 4

The number four is the number of Creation. Geb is the god of the Earth. Thus prayers are offered in a fourfold manner to the four cardinal points of the compass. This practice thereby fills Creation with the utterances and their vibrations. The number four is also significant in that it is represented in the four corners of the obelisk of Anunian Theurgy symbolizing the four cardinal points and thus also physicality.

The Number 3

The number three is the number of the Cosmic Trinity (Amun-Ra-Ptah) and of the Creation Trinity (Khepri-Ra-Tem). The Trinity relates to the modes of Consciousness (Seer-seen and sight or subject-object and interacting medium) and the modes of matter (Harmonious-Agitated-Sedentary). These principles govern the manifestations of consciousness as it differentiates into the various forms referred to as matter. Further, the number three relates to father, mother and child, {Asar-Aset-Heru} past present and future, and in space: length, height and width. Thus, in Kemetic religious practice, prayers are offered thrice daily (morning, midday and evening). In musical philosophy, the number three is the number of manifestation. No more than three notes can be combined to make consonances. This means that even though there may be a duality present (Self and Other), all you have is a unison of two which is essentially equal to the original One. There still cannot be manifestation unless a third principle is present, in other words the interacting medium, the capacity of awareness, to see separation between the two aspects of duality. In relation to the Tree of Life we have certain prominent Trinities incorporated into it; Khepri-Ra-Tem, Ra-Shu-Tefnut, Ra-Nebthotep-Iussasety, Asar-Aset-Nebthet.

The Number 2

From the number three we are further reduced to the number two, symbolizing duality. In Kemetic philosophy this number is referred to as the "two things that came into being in this land". The number one relates to non-duality. In Kemetic philosophy this number is related to the "first time" or beginning of Creation and referred to as the era "before two things had come into being in this land". Duality relates to the opposites of Creation (up-down, here-there, male-female, etc). Duality is the apparent existence of two or more items that can be perceived. So, a person who perceives their existence as an item, an object in Creation, among other objects (people, elements, trees, water, stars, etc.) said to be in a state of duality as opposed to non-duality, the perception of one essence manifesting through the apparent multiplicity of duality.

One and Ten

$$1 \Rightarrow \quad \text{Creation} \quad \Leftarrow 10$$

The number One is genderless and transcendental. In essence, all numbers are emanations from the number One. They are reflections of One in time and space, but the reflection is modified and conditioned, in other words, refracted or divided, fractionalized. The Divine Whole Numbers are the clearest reflection of the basic principles in creation. The numbers 100 and 1000 and 1000000 are related to the number 10 and 10 to 1. Therefore, all Creation and its infinite manifestations and vast quantities as well as its vast fractions can be studied through the numbers from One to Ten and ultimately reduced to the number one.

$$(\infty)$$
$$\Downarrow$$
$$(1)$$
$$\Downarrow$$
$$(2) \Leftrightarrow (3)$$
$$\Downarrow$$
$$(4) \Leftrightarrow (5)$$
$$\Downarrow$$
$$(6) \Leftrightarrow (7)$$
$$\Downarrow$$
$$(8) \Leftrightarrow (9)$$
$$\Downarrow$$
$$(10)$$

Figure 24: Heru Bhudet" (Heru the Warrior/conqueror)

The numbers One and Ten have a special relationship. Actually they are reflections of each other. Ten is the reflection of One. Heru symbolizes perfection in life which is reached by living a life of truth and righteousness, in other words upholding Maat. In the Temple of Heru in Egypt (city of Edfu), dedicated to Heru in the form of *Heru Behudet,* the Sanctuary (Holy of Holies) is encircled by a corridor and ten chapels. In the same temple of Heru there are reliefs in which Heru can be seen harpooning Set ten times. Set (8) is the principle of egoism and unrighteousness in the human personality which must be subdued and sublimated in order to attain higher consciousness, in other words to discover the mysteries of the other numbers and thereby attain spiritual enlightenment, discovering the Supreme Being as the support and essence of Creation. Ten is the number of completeness since we cannot count beyond it without combining other numbers and the other numbers are the same 1-9, not new numbers but the same ones as before – so nothing new happens after 10. Conversely, nothing happens before 1. 0 is "no thing"; 1 thru 9 are "some things". But in reality they are merely emanations from the original nothingness of undifferentiated potential. However, the number one is undivided and all-encompassing; it is all-encompassing and universal from a time and space perspective. 0 is undifferentiated and all-encompassing, as well as transcendental; it is all-encompassing and universal and from an un-circumscribed perspective it is transcendental and thus absolute and infinite. Therefore, Creation exists between One and Ten. As the characters of the Pautti are in reality aspects of human consciousness, the highest goal of all human beings is to attain the number Ten, in other words to become Heru or in other terms, to attain Heruhood and thereby reflect fully the glory of the Divine within themselves. Thus, the number one symbolizes the transcendent, in other words the absolute, and the number ten symbolizes perfection in the world of time and space. Thus, the task of every human being is to discover their absolute and transcendental nature, Ra-Neberdjer, and to become masters of their lives like Heru. In other words, the destiny of every human being is to discover their spirit nature and thus allow that nature to rule over the lower self, the ego, ignorance and vices.

Reflection and Journal discipline:

1- At the top of each page copy the following hieroglyphs to the best of your ability

[***cht n ankh*** *" tree of life"*]

After studying the Lesson proceed to answer the following question and write the answer in your journal. This exercise will require more than one reading and more than one journal entry, at least one page; write all you can find related to the subject of the question. Answer the questions first without referring to the text you just read. Then go back and see if you missed anything. This exercise is to be repeated until you become proficient with the principles of this sphere. The reflection exercise should be done after each reading or study session. Then you may practice meditation[62] on the wisdom you have learned. You may come back to add to your reflections even if you move on to other lessons.

REFLECTIONS: Like the song of the harper I will play the music of numbers; the numbers of the Tree which lead from the 10 to the 1 and beyond. The Creation is number and I am the sum of those…no longer to bounce between the numbers of Creating or playing at games of chance. This is a numbered map, figures of a formula, and I have the keys to understand them, and I shall know the numbers of Creation.

After studying the Lesson proceed to answer the following question and write the answer in your journal.

What is(are) the main teaching(s) of this lesson and what do the principle(s) of the divinity(ies) discussed in this lesson mean in reference to my actions, feelings, thoughts and desires and understanding of the spiritual philosophy?

Which divinity emerged in an unorthodox manner and how is that issue resolved in the Tree of Life?

---

[62] Explained in more detail in Lesson 15

Lesson 6: The Principle of Heru the Child and How to Start to Practice the Theurgy of the TREE OF LIFE as a Beginning Aspirant

The name of the god Heru is ⬡𓏤𓂀𓅭𓅆. It means that which is on high. Notice that the phonetic triliteral consonant 𓁷 *her* is part of his name. Her means person or personality or entity. All people are *her* or personalities. Heru is the highest personality, the personality of all personalities.

Figure 25: Heru-pa-khahard

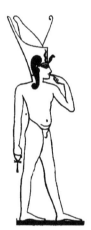

As an ordinary worldly human being your soul (Asar-eternity, immortality) has mated with Nebthet (worldly desires, mortality); in a sense you have taken on the role of Set, the divinity who represents egoism; you have developed throughout many life times in such a way that you have more awareness of yourself within the context of mortality and worldly desires and not so much as an immortal and infinite being. Now, the spiritual journey begins when, due to a certain attainment of virtue which you have attained, your personality becomes purified to a certain extent where you start to question the world and your self-concept with serious inquiries such as, who am I?, Why am I here? Why is there so much sorrow in the world? Why does the world seem so futile? What is life all about? What are these divinities?...I'm seriously interested in that...I want to know more about life, etc...and that's Heru being born and inquiring about the nature of life and aspiring to discover its secrets and master it's powers...when you start asking those questions but not just in a superficial way as most people do at some point in life, but in a serious way that you will do whatever is required to pursue the answers to the questions. Also, you are able to recognize people around you who are wise and who can lead you to others who are even more knowledgeable. So you are led eventually to Aset, the "Lady of Wisdom." And then Aset introduces you to her husband, her counterpart, who in this context really represents resurrected soul, the soul that has regained its immortal awareness. And then you begin to realize in small and not completely intelligible ways that...hey, there is some soul, there's some eternity here; there is something there beyond this death and mayhem and destruction and unhappiness that there is in this world. Aset also represents dispassion and detachment. And that is when Aset and Asr are able to come together, when the soul turns away from worldliness, Set and Nebthet, and turns to Aset. You see the diagonal lines that are emanating from them. They come together and they produce

Heru-pa-khard 𓅭𓏤𓏺𓂋𓐍𓂞 (Heru the Child), the prince, and Heru the Child is you, your newborn aspiration for self-discovery and self-mastery, and to become a true seeker of spiritual enlightenment. As Aset and Asar protected and guided him, you too are to be guided by them until you are ready to control the forces of nature (see

image below of Heru-pa- khard controlling animals (lower self)). Later, as the control of nature (animal desires and passions of the personality) and advancement in the philosophy of Aset are achieved Heru grows up (aspiration becomes mature) and an aspirant is ready to do battle with Set, in the form of Heru Behdet, to challenge for the throne of Kemet (to become ruler of the world (Lower forces) and become Heru Ur.

Figure 26: Heru-pa-khahard as controller of the forces of nature

Diagram 9: Origins of Heru and Anpu in the Tree of Life and the Pathway to Start the Journey of Spiritual Enlightenment

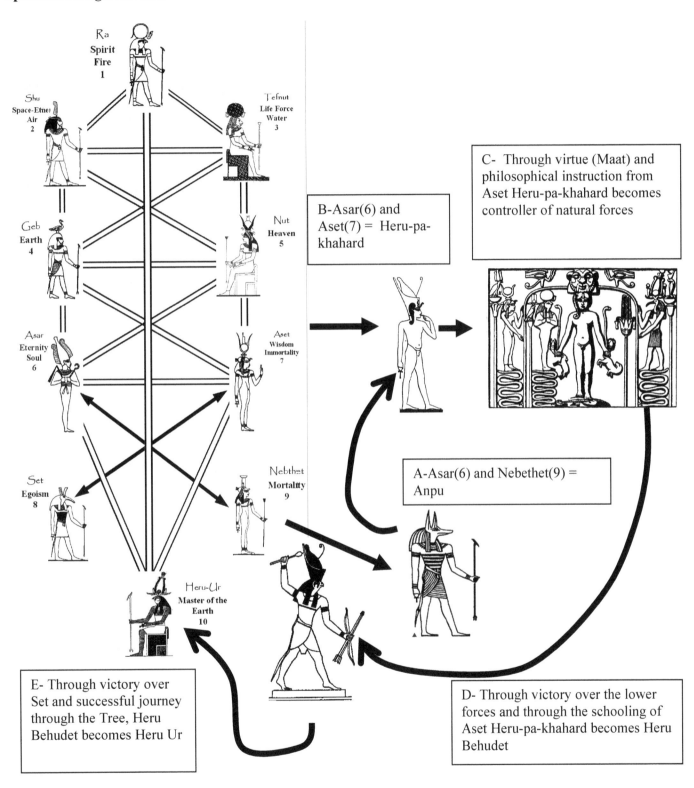

C- Through virtue (Maat) and philosophical instruction from Aset Heru-pa-khahard becomes controller of natural forces

B-Asar(6) and Aset(7) = Heru-pa-khahard

A-Asar(6) and Nebethet(9) = Anpu

E- Through victory over Set and successful journey through the Tree, Heru Behudet becomes Heru Ur

D- Through victory over the lower forces and through the schooling of Aset Heru-pa-khahard becomes Heru Behudet

Ra
Spirit
Fire
1

Shu
Space-Ether
Air
2

Tefnut
Life Force
Water
3

Geb
Earth
4

Nut
Heaven
5

Asar
Eternity
Soul
6

Aset
Wisdom
Inmortality
7

Set
Egoism
8

Nebthet
Mortality
9

Heru-Ur
Master of the
Earth
10

Heru pa khard – "Heru as the Divine solar child", has seven aspects which are a reflection of Ra's seven souls (*Sefech ba Ra*). Those seven souls are associated with the seven spheres of consciousness that are weighed in the judgment of Maat. The image of the Ancient Egyptian Papyrus Kenna (see below) illustrates the seven spheres as levels on the shaft of the balance scales of Maat. The Ammit monster demarcates between the spheres that represent the lower nature (3 lower spheres) and those that represent higher consciousness (4 upper). These spheres are related to the Ancient Egyptian concept of Arat Sekhem or Serpent Power.[63] When the spheres are superimposed on the nexus points of the Tree of Life their dynamic forces are graphically illustrated as references to energy forms (gods and goddesses) and elements that awaken the varied levels of higher consciousness. The image below depicts how the spheres or energy centers relate to nerve plexuses and glands of the human body, regulating the flow of Sekhem, Life Force energy that is needed for spiritual evolution. These centers must be opened and purified in order to allow the free flow of the Life Force power in order to be successful in the struggle to understand the philosophy of the path and have the stamina to endure the trials of the path, specifically, controlling the ego and the forces of nature.

Figure 27: The Life Force Energy Centers of the Serpent Power and the Human Body

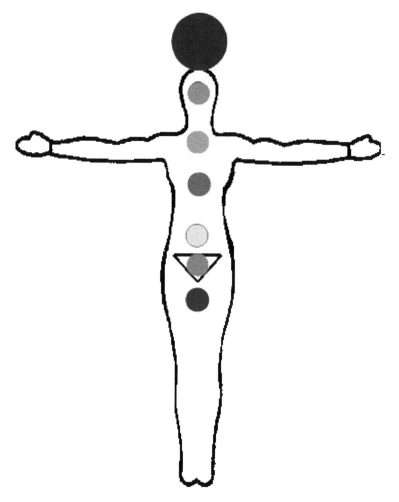

---

[63] see the book *The Serpent Power* by Dr. Muata Ashby

Diagram 10: Below-left-Central section of the Tree of Life Obelisk with the seven souls of Ra and the seven aspects of Heru the Divine Child.

Figure 28: Below right- Line art and Grayscale image of Kenna Papyrus

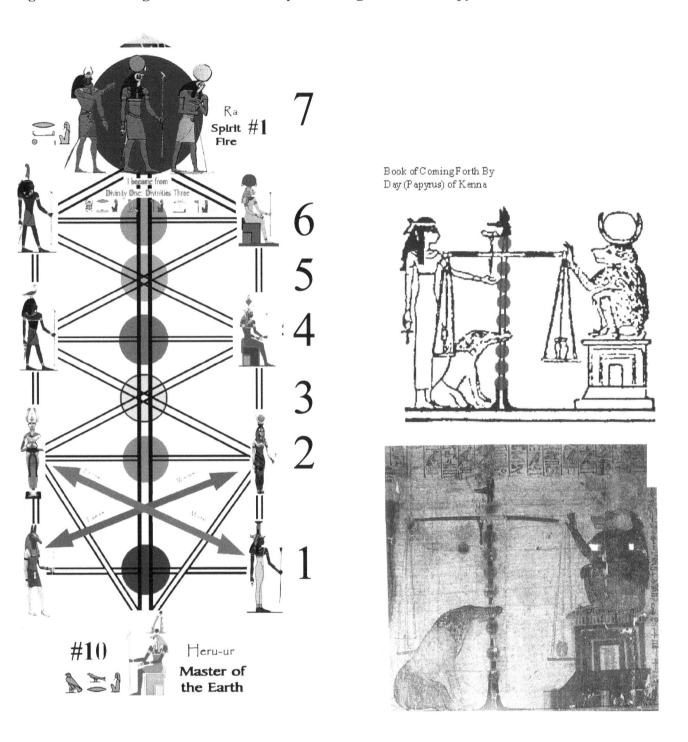

Sphere #1 (beginning from the bottom and moving upwards) includes the god(dess) Heru forms: Heru as a child, Heru Khuti and Heru Ur as well as Nebthet and Set. Sphere #2 includes Aset and Asar. Sphere #3 includes the nexus between Nut and Geb that brought Asar and Aset, Set, Nebthet and Heru Ur into being. Sphere #4 includes the principle of Geb and Nut [earth and heavens]. Sphere #5 includes the nexus between Shu and Tefnut that brought Geb and Nut into being. Sphere #6 includes the principle of Shu and Tefnut [air/ether and moisture/life force]. Sphere #7 includes the god(dess) Ra [here Ra is androgynous-containing male and female elements within himself until he engenders the first duality (Shu and Tefnut)].

In the *Pert M Heru* text of Ancient Egypt, *The Ancient Egyptian Book of Enlightenment,* the state of spiritual enlightenment is described in Chapters 83 where the initiate realizes that the seven *Uadjit* (Uraeus {serpents}) deities or bodies (immortal parts of the spirit) have been reconstituted (rediscovered):

"The seven Uraeuses are my body... my image is now eternal."

These   *Iarat sefecht* –seven serpent goddesses [seven Uraeuses, rearing cobras (rearing cobra is the primary symbol of the goddess in Ancient Egyptian iconography)] are described as the   *sefech Ba Ra* -*"seven souls of Ra"* and *"the seven arms of the balance* (of Maat).*"* These designations of course refer to the seven spheres of the balance scales of Maat which correspond to the seven Chakras of the Indian Kundalini system.

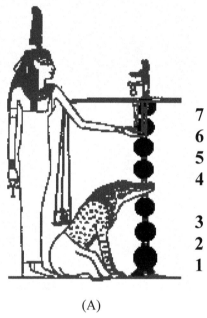

(A)

Figure 29: The figure (A) shows the scale of Maat displaying the seven spheres or energy centers called the *"seven souls of Ra"* and *"the seven arms of the balance (Maat)."* (Kenna Papyrus)

The process of the Journey of the   *cht n ankh* -*Tree of Life,* is in effect a method to make the seven souls of Ra part of one's body. Since an ignorant person, not having awakened the inner Life Force, is unaware of its existence it is as if dead to that person, not part of their life. Thus, the awakening of the seven energy centers through the disciplines of study, meditation on each principle, applying the maatian ethics and living in accordance with the wisdom of the *cht n ankh* will lead to the positive spiritual evolution of the soul and to its discovery of its cosmic true essential nature. Thus each level of evolution in the Tree is correlated to a level of evolution in the balance scale of Maat, which is composed of seven arms or spheres or levels of spiritual evolution.

You may have noticed that there are no diagonal lines between Nebthet and Set. That is because they do not produce anything. They cannot produce anything....anything real, that is. How can death and egoism produce anything real? Consider that...mortality is an illusion and egoism is also an illusion. Therefore, all they can create is illusions; but since illusions are not real, in effect nothing has been created! When a person gets upset over an object that was lost, that they desired, that is Set in them leading them to suffering –over something that is not real, since the object is an emanation of the Divine and does not have independent existence and since the only reason they desire it was because the mind is overpowered by setian ego conscience. Also, when a person grieves over one who has "died" they are acting in accordance with an illusory belief, because there is no such thing as death of the real essential nature of a human being. Only the generated part, the physical part can die and since that was never real even when it appeared in the world of time and space there is no such thing as death from an abiding point of view. Since the true essence of the soul of a human being is not generated, as an aggregate of elements, like a body, it is not mortal, it is part of the ocean of Spirit. A soul's concept of individuality is its only generated aspect, but the soul itself is not generated, it is only a confined portion of the Universal Soul (Ra). So when a human being discovers their transcendental nature their soul as if realizes their oneness with the vast Spirit, like a drop realizing it is part of a vast ocean. The misunderstanding of thinking it was alone was the illusion.

So when Asar comes together with Aset, they do generate something real, the aspiration for self awareness, the truth which *is* an abiding reality, so they lead us to Heru. The next thing you should know before we go any further is the arrangement of the divinities… this is crucial for your understanding of what I am about to say next related to the theurgy process…the science of the sacred worship. You need to understand that there are two main levels of the divinities. There is the Neter which is the transcendental, and then there is the Neteru which is the mundane, in Time and Space, the realm of generation. Note: even though from the perspective of the generated world we may consider the transcendent as a divinity, for the purpose of having a concrete vision and direction for the worship program, in the higher level of understanding that is not considered a divinity since it is transcendent of that concept. From an absolute perspective only the entities of time and space are considered as divinities but for the purpose of explaining the philosophy from the perspective of a person who is moving upwards on the Tree they may see everything above as a divinity until they are ready to understand the higher philosophical insight.

Therefore, since there are two kinds of divinities, the one that is the source and the ones that are generated by that source in a hierarchical format, there are two kinds of worship. The movement towards the Divine, on the spiritual path, necessitates the development of the feeling capacity and its emotion as well as the intellectual capacity and its understanding. An aspirant begins the worship aspect of the spiritual program by propitiating the divinities of time and space; this practice, when properly instructed and enjoined, leads to the level beyond time and space. The divinities of generation are to be worshipped with objects of the world of generation, objects from Time and Space. Since they are time and space divinities, they are to be worshipped in time and space, and with time and space objects.

So Shu is to be worshipped with beautiful fragrances, oils and incense. He is in the air. He is in the space. Geb is to be worshipped with things of the earth, and by cultivating the land, by planting beautiful plants and trees and taking care of them, watering them, etc. Nut is to be adored with paintings beautifying her body which is adorned with the stars, and there are many other aspects of her worship as well, like the incense, like the offerings such as the Hetep. This brings us to an important aspect of 𓏏𓅓𓍯𓀢 *Uash* – "praise worship, devotion", which is understanding about the Hetep offering. Hetep or hotep, also means contentment of the gods and goddesses through the appeasement offering you are giving.

You are giving these divinities their due, so that they will be contented…and they will not be obstructive in your pursuit of Higher Divinity. If you do not quell their desires, their energies in you…, in other words, if you have lots of egoism in you, that egoism is going to block you from discovering divinities that are higher than it…and virtually all the divinities are higher than Set…the egoism. Let us be clear here. The divinities are cosmic forces that course through the universe and within your personality. They are to be mastered by you and not the other way around. You are to become their controller, their master, and thereby you will rule and be free on the higher planes as opposed to being ruled and enslaved. It means bringing them together so that they merge and lose their gender, uniting in the oneness of Self and in so doing their energies within the propitiator coalesce as well.

"The wise ones serve the higher planes and rule the lower, in this way one operates the laws
instead of being a slave to them."

"Salvation is the freeing of the soul from its bodily fetters; becoming a God through knowledge and wisdom; controlling the forces of the cosmos instead of being a slave to them; subduing the lower nature and through awakening the higher self, ending the cycle of rebirth and dwelling with the Neters who direct and control the Great Plan."

"Mastery of self consists not in abnormal dreams, visions and fantastic imaginings or living, but in using the higher FORCES against the lower thus escaping the pains of the lower by vibrating on the higher."

-Ancient Egyptian Proverbs

So you must know how to control and to appease Set...the same with Nebthet and the other divinities. Now, the Divinity that transcends Time and Space is not to be worshipped with time and space objects. That is to say, you don't go burning incense to the Supreme Transcendental Timeless Formless Being. You are to worship that Divinity with things that are timeless, formless, undifferentiated, transcendental....and what are those things? One is Meditation. Not chanting...chanting is in time and space...it has vibration, it has sound, it has concepts, words...remember, for this level of worship we are going beyond the realm of generated things. But until you are ready for that level you must practice the rituals, and offerings of the lower and in due time they will lead you to the higher forms of worship, the transcendental forms.

Let me give you an example of what the higher practice requires. Meditation at the higher level, the transcendental worship level, implies leading yourself to a place that transcends consciousness of Time and Space...and meditation in that sense is the answer. The Kemetic sage AbAmon (also known as Iambliuchus) said that the Supreme Divinity is to be worshipped with silence, with nothingness...which is very hard to do...if you have not appeased the other divinities, the divinities of the realm of generation...that are coursing through your entire personality and mind as we speak; it will be hard to offer the higher practice...they must come to a peace...hetep. And they do that by your learning about them, mastering their principles, and thereby purifying them within yourself. This is purifying your lower nature.

Realize that if you master the divinities, you learn about them, you become wise about them, and automatically your lower consciousness about yourself is reduced. If you learn about Aset and Asar, those aspects of your consciousness, which are: intuitional wisdom (Aset), and soul eternity (Asar), are automatically enhanced and you are automatically discounting and minimizing egoism (Set) as well as worldly desires and (Nebthet) who represent ego consciousness and mortality. If you become wise, you realize that you should be caring not just for yourself. As you care for all people, you realize that you are the very essence of all people. This teaching of selfless service to humanity is a primary theme of Maat Philosophy.

Let's be clear on the definition of egoism from the perspective of this teaching. Egoism is the idea that you are an individual, and that as an individual you are not connected to others, to nature or to a higher Spirit. Egoism means seeing the world from the perspective of a finite and mortal individual. Your pleasure is first and of foremost importance and the welfare of others is secondary, so you need not care for them or about them. Or if you care about others it is because they mean something to you like the pleasure you get from their company or the idea that you are related to them through family ties, or something else YOU get from them, etc. So the study and understanding of these opposites of the Tree of Life also represent the antidote to the problem of human egoistic complexes, which came into being due to the separation of the principles and their misunderstanding by the mind. Human complexes are represented by the three lower divinities, and I include Heru, the child here, because before he is nurtured by Aset and Asar, Heru is in his state as an unenlightened human being; he is not Heru-Ur, the King; he is only a prince, an heir, but he must first prove himself before he can take the throne.[64] This is also a problem for you...he is you as you are if you are not an enlightened being. He is the totality of all the other divinities, but in an ignorant state that must be cultivated and trained to discover and realize the deeper aspects of life. Until that training occurs, Heru is vulnerable and so are you, to the shots by the ego, the

---

[64] See the book *African Religion Vol. 4 Asarian Theology* by Dr. Muata Ashby, See the book *The War of Heru and Set* by Dr. Muata Ashby

temptations, the fears, the lethargy, the procrastination, as well as the traditional fetters of the soul, lust, jealousy, envy, greed, hatred, etc. And really, Nebthet and Set, that is, the notion of mortality and ego-individuality, are the real problem, and if they are mastered and transcended, you are well on your way to discovering higher consciousness.

So for now we are leaving aside the transcendental realm and its worship because we will discuss it at the end…the special silence that encompasses all…for now we are talking about the worship of the divinities of Time and Space, which as we said, is the proper starting point. We propitiate them by using time and space objects such as food and drink, incense, etc. and when the energy of their name is used, as in chant, it invokes the physical presence of that cosmic force. One important item to keep in mind as you engage in this practice is if you are impure as you are engaging in that invocation, that energy is going to be tainted, and your use of that energy is going to be, therefore, also tainted. We already talked about the wisdom that the journey begins in earnest when you elevate yourself to Aset, and Aset introduces you to Asar. And then Set and Nebthet begin to get minimized. This level of spiritual practice is called striving, and this is what Heru represents in his not enlightened state, an aspirant. Effective aspiration leads to Divine Grace. Divine Grace is the minimization of the negative aspects and the elevation of the positive and the opening up of the mind to philosophical wisdom teachings that you were not able to understand before. Divine Grace is also increase in inner peace, reduction of entanglements and better physical, mental and emotional health.

Now we are going to discuss a feature of the Neteru that is implicit in the Anunian Theurgy Tree of Life Cosmiconomythograph. Think of it as an electrical transformer feature. When you are doing electrical work, the power companies have generators in their main building, and then they run that electricity through the wires, and then it goes through transformers. The transformers transform the voltage that comes from the power station into levels of electricity that you can use in your home. If it were transferred directly, everything would blow up in your house. If the Supreme Being which is at the top of the Tree were to appear here in full power it would destroy everything…blow everything up; it would also blow your mind. So therefore, It has created the Neteru who are like transformers of the energy. They control certain portions of the energy to carry out certain tasks…and those tasks are what uphold creation, that keep creation afloat if you will, that keep creation from falling apart. But it takes more energy to sustain the sun than it takes to make a blade of grass grow. If the energy of the sun were to arrive on earth without restraint all would burn up. The higher divinities have more power and are more subtle than the lower divinities. Ra passes on energy to the next lower divinities, Shu and Tefnut and Shu and Tefnut pass on lower energy than what they received from Ra to the next lower divinities, Geb and Nut and so on.

Now, beyond the highest main divinities, the are tiers of divinities, the Duat divinities, the Pet…and now we are coming down to the Ta divinities, and within the Ta realm, you have aspects of the divinities that are even more differentiated; this differentiation provides detailed insights into specific functions of specific cosmic forces. So you have many aspects of Heru.[65] And all these different aspects of Heru are like specific descriptions of a particular aspect of the Heru power. In this manner an increasingly refined knowledge of the powers can be attained by an aspirant. Since at this level of practice it is important for you to understand what being an aspirant is and what it requires it is appropriate to go more deeply into the nature of Heru which is your very own nature.

First of all we want to discuss what the name Heru itself means. There is a word in the Kemetic hieroglyphic texts, *her*, which is a person's face. It means person…it means personality. The name Heru is based on this root, *her* or *hra*. Also Heru means "face of God,"…this is another definition that is given in the text. Heru means that which is above…and all these terms give you an indication of the meaning of Heru. In a general sense it means the personality that exists and that is all of you who are listening to this or who will read this in the future. Also the scripture explains that one aspect of Heru, *Heru Pa Khard* (Heru the child) is the *Nefertem*. Pa Khard also means Ra when he is young, the solar child, so the descriptions of the names themselves are giving us insight into the connections of the Tree, because if Heru is allowed to grow up, who does he become?…Ra of

---

[65] For more details see the book *Egyptian Mysteries Vol. 2 Dictionary of Ancient Egyptian Gods and Goddesses* by Dr. Muata Ashby

course. In Anunian Theurgy Heru manifests as Heru; in Memphite Theurgy he manifests as Nefertem and in Theban Theurgy he manifests as *Khonsu*.[66]

Figure 30: Heru as Nefertem

Heru must grow up. In order for Heru to grow up, he must be nurtured and taught by his mother who is Aset. The first important aspect of Heru that we want to talk about is *Heru Kenti n Maa*. Heru the "foremost seer who is blind." And this is also explained as the new moon. Heru has two eyes. The right eye is the sun and the left eye is the moon. The right eye signifies fire and power of the life force that manifests through the sun. The left eye being the moon is associated with mind, with the god Djehuti as well as the god Asar. The moon also signifies coolness. When the moon shines full it signifies the fullness of the reflection of the sun but when it is waning or completely dark it signifies the loss of that reflection and hence represents growing ignorance and or weakness instead of enlightenment and power. In Memphite Theurgy, in the form of *Nefertem* {Nefertum} Heru is a solar child, the new born sun, which emerges on the horizon as if from out of the ocean. He points to his mouth, signifying his command over words of power to bring Creation into existence.

Figure 31: Eyes of Heru

 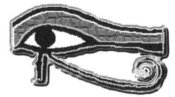

Figure 32: The God Djehuti

When Heru is blind, it means that he is in the new moon phase. The New Moon phase is a place of darkness and *there is no darkness like the darkness of ignorance* –Ancient Egyptian Proverb. But the New moon

phase is the prelude to the waxing period. The waxing period is where Djehuti comes in. Djehuti symbolizes intellect. The symbol of Djehuti is the crescent moon, so therefore Heru Khenti Maa is the new moon preparing to grow…the intellect increasing in knowledge of Self…increasing to fullness…to Full Moon period. One of the most important symbols of Heru and Lord Djehuti is

the crescent moon, ☽ , which Djehuti uses as his crown. Djehuti is the divinity that records teachings[67] and also espouses them in the form of a spiritual preceptor.[68] Djehuti represents intellectual development and that is promoted through writings and philosophical study but not just of the scriptures but also of the iconographies. Notice the following iconographies.

🌒🌒🌒🌒🌒🌒🌒🌒🌒🌒🌒🌒🌒   ○   🌘🌘🌘🌘🌘🌘🌘🌘🌘🌘🌘🌘🌘   ●

Waxing period   Full   Waning period   New

---

[66] these interconnections are dictated by scriptural teachings and are illustrated in the Kemetic Gods and Goddesses iconomythograph (Diagram 1) of this volume

[67] See the Book *African Religion VOL. 1- ANUNIAN THEOLOGY THE MYSTERIES OF RA*, by Dr. Muata Ashby

[68] see the book *TEMPLE RITUAL OF THE ANCIENT EGYPTIAN MYSTERIES--THEATER & DRAMA OF THE ANCIENT EGYPTIAN MYSTERIES* by Dr. Muata Ashby

Figure 33: The teaching of the Hauk iconography

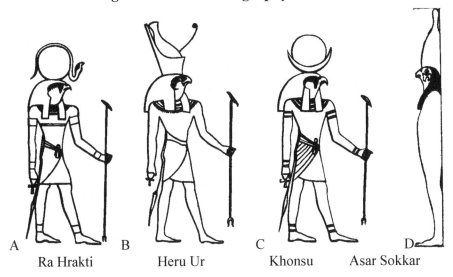

A   B   C   D

Ra Hrakti   Heru Ur   Khonsu   Asar Sokkar

From the icons above we can see one particular overriding feature that all the images have in common. They all display the Hawk iconography. This means that we have a direct line from Ra(A) to Heru(B) in Anunian Theurgy, Khonsu(C) in Theban Theurgy and to Asar(D) in Asarian Theurgy. We already saw how Heru is related to Nefertem of Memphite Theurgy. Therefore, the traditions are not as separate as they might appear to be to the untrained onlooker. More importantly, this feature running through all the icons means that each is a manifestation of the same solar principle, Ra(A). Therefore, Ra is the basis for all of them; Ra is the ultimate essence of all of them and as manifestations of Ra they are as Divine as Ra; so too every aspirant is also divine. In fact the manifestation is essentially, taking away the illusory misunderstandings, the same as the source. This wisdom, when fully understood and applied, should render the personality of an aspirant humbled and awed with the realization that while there is striving for attainment of realms of higher consciousness, the lower realms are also divine and worthy of the same respect; so even while striving to climb the Tree there should also be poise, balance and peace on the lower levels. There is no need to rush or be rash in the treatment of the teachings of the lower as these eventually lead to the higher, when there is patience, diligence and correct instruction.

Now, getting back to Heru Pa Khard, Heru the child; He is also known as the lord of animals. You recall the *Tjef Neteru* Postures Exercise program[69] of Egyptian Yoga, when we do the posture of the *Heru Pa Khard*

where he is standing on a crocodile and holds animals by their tails, that means he is a master of animals...meaning he is master of his lower animal tendencies, the animal, instinctual propensities. Heru Pa Khard also means the rising sun as we discussed, it means Nefertem, the child sitting on the lotus...the lotus of creation...his hand pointing towards his mouth, engendering the utterances that create the Creation.

Figure 34: Heru, as the Divine Solar Child, sitting on the Lotus of Creation that emerges from the Primeval Ocean

Heru Pa Khard is explained as having seven aspects, and those aspects of course are levels of growth from child to adulthood and they also represent the spheres...the Sefech Bas Ra, the seven spheres, the seven energy centers, the whirling vortices of consciousness as it evolves from childhood as a spiritual being to a spiritual adult. Heru has many other aspects besides those of

---

[69] See the book *EGYPTIAN YOGA The Postures of The Gods and Goddesses* by Muata Ashby

the childhood. If we think of the seven aspects as important phases in the development of the Heru principle we can realize the necessary aspects within ourselves that need to be developed in order to have a successful journey towards spiritual enlightenment. We have discussed several of the aspects that are important for spiritual evolution. One important aspect, is Heru Behudet.

Heru Behudet is the specific aspect of Heru that was worshipped in the city of Edfu. Edfu is where you have the main Temple of Heru. In that Temple, you can go to the interior side of one of the boundary walls, even today, and it gives you the story of the battle of Heru and Set. This brings up another important point about the Cosmiconomythograph, the assignment of numbers to the divinities. The numbers are assigned in accordance with the mythic scripture or temple inscription, which assigned them. The number of Heru is confirmed by the Temple of Heru. So, how do we know the number to assign to Heru is 10? On the wall of the temple, he is seen spearing Set ten times, who is in the form of a Hippopotamus, then he chains him, then he controls him. He does not kill him. Of course, adding to this, in the Asarian Resurrection myth and the account of the battle between Heru and Set, we were told that Heru took Set's virility...his testicles, and he has control over those, in other words he controls Set's power of generation, that is to say, Heru gained control over Set's power that Set had used to wreck havoc and promote egoism, murder, deceit and worldly illusions.

This battle between Heru and Set is said to have occurred over three days. Three days of course, as you recall in the Christian myth, is important...the time it took for Jesus to be resurrected. We know that Heru and Ancient Egyptian religion of Asar were prototypes for the Christian myth and religious practices. Heru's birth, persecution and subsequent redemption of his father is the same theme that was adopted by the Christians later in history. In mystical philosophy it means that you have had a battle in the three aspects of your personality...physical, astral, causal, in the three realms, Ta, Pet and Duat. It means a battle in all of these realms. And this *Heru Behudet* is called the great protector, because he vanquishes Set, and you cannot move forward on your spiritual journey until you vanquish Set.

There is the form of Heru called Heru Smai Tawi , Heru the uniter of the two lands. He is also known as Nefertem. He springs forth from the lotus each year bringing forth creation, and bringing forth enlightenment, unity of the Higher and lower Self, transcending duality. There is a form of Heru called "*Heru Nub*," the Heru of Gold. Nub means gold, as in Nubia, the land of Gold. Gold is the color of the sun. It is the color of perfection, the color of spiritual enlightenment. There is a form of Heru called "*Heru Mirti*," Heru of the Two Eyes...the two eyes being open, which is also an aspect of *Min*, or *Amsu-min*, and this ties Heru into Theban

Theurgy of Waset again.[70] Of course you know that Min represents the fullness of sexual power, male and female sexual power. So Heru has harnessed the power of sexual energy and employed it to the project of attaining self-mastery, the redemption of Asar within you.

Heru Sekhem is the Lord of the Uadjit, which means the Lord of the Two Eyes, the Power of the Two Eyes, the Power of the Two Serpents (Caduceus), who are also known as Aset and Nebthet...and furthermore are known as the two serpents that intertwine the central shaft, and connect the *Sefech Ba Ra*, the Serpent Power. These higher forms of Heru develop as an aspirant progresses on the path and with these developments an aspirant gradually wields more power over life and more understanding of the Higher Self within.

Figure 35: Images of the Caduceus (A) Contemporary, (B) The Caduceus and the Human Body, (C) The Ancient Caduceus of the Ancient Egyptian God Djehuti

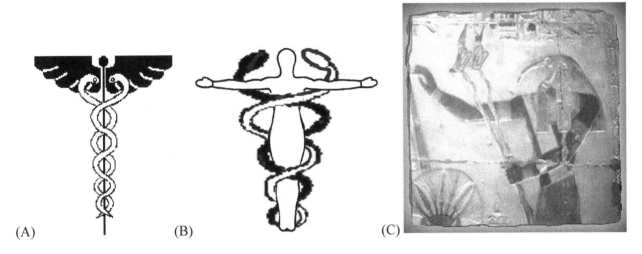

(A)   (B)   (C)

We have discussed *Heru Akhuti*, or *Herukuti*, as Heru of the two horizons. This is Heru uniting the forms of Ra, Khepri and Tem, the beginning and the end... the alpha and omega. This is the Heru that unites the duality and reconciles the opposites. Below: caduceus with single serpent wrapped around a stick, a piece of wood.

---

[70] *Amsu-min* is the son of the God Amun of Theban Theurgy

Figure 36: (on next page) The Great sundisk (Ur-Uadjit) on the Ancient Egyptian Temple ntranceway

Figure 37: Heru as the Ur-uadjit, is the Great sundisk

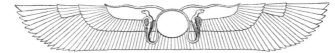

Heru as the Ur-uadjit, is the Great sundisk with the two serpents coming out of it…the form in which he defeated Set, in other words, the All-encompassing divinity. This aspect may be thought of also as a person whose mind has expanded such that it has moved beyond seeing him/her self as an individual being and now sees the world all together; the vision of separations, opposites, genders, etc., have subsided and have given way to the vision of oneself as embracing all that. In physical terms it may also be thought of as what happens when a supernova explosion occurs. When that happens a star expands to encompass all of the planets in a solar system, they, along with their differences in size, climate, colors, compositions, etc. are encompassed by the light but they are also burnt up (dissolve) into the essence of the singular luminary. And having discovered these aspects, Heru becomes the sitting king, and anyone who discovers there aspects and develops them within themselves become the sitting ruler, be they male or female.

The divinities are worshipped by studying their myth, these different aspects, understanding their power, applying their power in your life, speaking their power in your life, reflecting on their power, becoming that power. If you were to be able to do this…there is another central shaft in the middle of the obelisk that runs directly from Heru to Ra…there is a connection that opens up, and then it becomes, in the words of Djehuti, "as above, so below," that is, the one below becomes the reflection of the one above and vice versa. You have someone who is walking the earth, but yet their roots are in the sky. They are one with the Divinity of the Higher Nature. But all of the other divinities have to be learned and mastered, and then this channel opens to you, and you have a highway to heaven, if you will. This concludes our lesson for today.

Om Hetep!

Sebai Dr. Muata Ashby

Questions and Answers

Questions:

What is Ra in relation to the Anunian Theurgy…is he a supreme being or a God?

Answer:

Ra in time and space is the personality, *Bes,* the icon or image, that the Supreme Being (Neberdjer) has assumed/delegated to complete the work of creation of Time and Space. The specific Creator aspect is *Khepri,* the sustaining aspect is *Ra,* and the dissolving aspect is *Tem.* Those three are aspects of the one singular divinity when it manifests in time and space and this Trinity engenders and overseas creation through the other lower divinities. When the Supreme Divinity is not manifesting in time and space we call it Neberdjer, or Mehturt, or Net, etc. Ra is like a part of Neberdjer that has taken a form and become the delegated employee, shall we say, the minister of the Supreme and all-encompassing Being, of Neberdjer, and Neberdjer is the transcendental being, or Mehturt… or HeruKhuti. And Nun is another name which we may think of as even more transcendental in a sense, because Nun does not give you so much an idea of a personality, gender or form, even though there is a picture of Nun… really Nun is undifferentiated matter which has no form, it is abstract. The form is for the lesser advanced minds. But when you start thinking of Nun, with an advanced perspective, you start thinking of all expansive, transcendental, undifferentiated waters, formless waters…but within those formless waters there is a singular transcendental consciousness. When that consciousness takes on a personality, meaning that part of the undifferentiated matter takes a differentiated shape, (which human beings call "God") that is the beginning of time and space and form and of Ra. This teaching is supported by the Myth of Ra and Aset[71] where it is asserted that Ra is not the real name of the divinity underlying Ra. Ra is merely a front, if you will, a mask that appears in time and space but which is transcended when we move to the absolute, when we discover the true and unspoken name of Ra. More will be given on this when we discuss the principle of Ra in a future lesson.

Question:

Do all of these divinities have these different aspects?

Answer:

Yes, for the most part they all have different aspects or parts and some are more concrete while others are subtler. They also have some aspects that are more important than others, or rather we may say that some are more dynamic while others are more passive or more mundane aspects; and some are more important for aspirants at different levels when certain teachings are learned at different levels of spiritual evolution. And perhaps Heru has the most aspects or forms.

Question:

Does Heru principle have to be mastered before moving onto other divinities?

Answer:

Yes, because Heru is neophyte aspiration moving towards mature aspiration. If you don't have aspiration, how are you going to move onto discovering what the other divinities mean?

---

[71] see the book *THE MYSTERIES OF ISIS: **The Ancient Egyptian Philosophy of Self-Realization** by **Dr. Muata Ashby***

Goddess Nut is the one that brings you up to her...she raises up Asar...she does not raise up Set, and so one must be able to master how to be a righteous aspirant, how to practice the teaching, otherwise one's aspiration will be thwarted, and even one's very desire to study the teaching will be thwarted, because this is what Heru represents...one's very inkling to study the teaching. Also, if the desire for spiritual aspiration is tainted with Set, even if that person displays great devotion or they do good works, that will be contaminated with egoism so that spiritual practice of that person will be ultimately blocked because they will be prevented from moving higher. The desire for self mastery in a person, to become enlightened, is Heru conscience in that person. But if you pursue Heru in a wrong, ignorant fashion, you will be like those aspirants who come to the lecture, and start dictating to the teacher what the teaching is supposed to say and do. They will start talking instead of listening...because they have read some things and they think they know what the teaching is all about. They selectively follow the teachings they agree with or that go along with their egoistic desires or their intellectual convictions...and that pride, an aspect of egoism, will keep them from becoming humble enough to open up to real learning.

But also, aspirants are Heru in the lower aspect, however consider that people who have not been awakened spiritually, they are not even at the level of Heru. They are like blind people or animals walking the face of the earth, living their lives on the basis of instinct and ignorance that thwarts their intellectual capacities and ability to follow truth even when it stares them in the face. Here we will gain more insights into the number three. The three aspects of the Nekaku, the flail, are the areas to be controlled with the mastery, the physical, astral, and causal, your conscious, subconscious and unconscious aspects, corresponding to the *Ta, Pet* and *Duat* realms respectively. Another aspect that is represented here is that there are three basic modes of consciousness as it manifests in life on earth, one is the instinctive level, one is the intellectual level, and the third is the intuitional level. If you are operating at the instinctive level, you are no better than an animal, and people are called animals as we discussed previously. When you acted a certain way, they call you in accordance with the way you are acting. If you are a lustful man, they call you a wolf. If you are a heavy investor in Wall Street, they call you a bull.

And consider that your *Ka* , when you are caught up by the lower nature, the egoism of Set...when you are controlled by your animal nature, your *Ka*, astral/desire body (the word *Ka* is phonetically a pun on the Ancient Egyptian word for "bull") starts to take the shape of the animal that you are mentally embodying at that time, that you are emulating. This is why set has an animal head...he does not even have and anthropomorphic aspect, like Heru. That is why it is important for you to act like the higher divinities. If you are acting like a wolf, you're ka takes on the form of a wolf, and as you know, your Ka is that which gives rise to

your *Khat* or Physical body. If the Ka was powerful enough, it would transform the physical body into a wolf, in other words. And this should not be strange to you. Consider that ...there is a joke that people who have pets start to look like their pets. For example, if somebody has a bulldog...the owner will have a bulldog face. A person that has a poodle will have a poodleish kind of face....etc. And in the next lifetime, the people may become a bulldog or poodle. So watch out...think about what would you like to be? Would you like to be a poodle or Aset? Would you like to be walking on higher ground, or on the curb with somebody scooping up your droppings...as an animal...and that is if you are lucky, and you have somebody to take care of you properly and that's not the way that most animals are treated in the world, as possessions, slaves, sources of food, etc.

Figure 38: Heru-Set as two personalities in one. The Composite Divinity-Heru and Set in one personality.

As explained earlier, as an ordinary worldly human being your soul (eternity, immortality) has mated with Nebthet (worldly desires, mortality); in a sense you have taken on the role of Set, the divinity who represents egoism; so you have awareness of yourself within the context of mortality and worldly desires and not as an immortal and infinite being. The scripture also demonstrates that this combination of the Heru in you and the Set in you is a source of conflict that must be resolved. The composite image of Heru and Set is called *herfy* or "the two personalities". It illustrates, in an iconographic way, that Heru is afflicted with an alter-personality. He must do battle with that personality in order to separate himself from it, to throw off the unrighteousness of the personality, the egoism. He of course attains ultimate victory in the form of *Ur-Uadjit*, but the journey of self-discovery and the struggle for control of the personality is a lengthy and arduous one, requiring much patience, and repeated effort. Set is like an appendage, a popular term, "monkey on his back" would not be an inappropriate reference. Even though Set is an illusory divinity he has great power of generation, that is, the power to generate entanglements, desires, unrighteousness, etc. which lead a person to much expenditure of time pursuing futile opportunities for happiness and thereby eventually leading to frustration and sufferings. Set has that power because the deluded soul has given that power to him by believing in him, that is, believing in egoistic things and indulging and feeding the desires of the ego over a period of lifetimes. Set is to be overcome through

Maat, virtue, and through *Sbait* - spiritual philosophy instruction teaching education, the wisdom philosophy from Aset. As long as Set remains as an independent aspect of the personality outside of the control of the conscience of the personality, {Heru} of the aspirant, promoting desires based on ignorance of the Higher Self there will be conflict. Those desires thwart the spiritual progress, and there will be confusion and failure in the mind and consequently also in the spiritual practice. When Heru eventually is victorious over Set and gains control over him, Set's great power is harnessed and put to the task of the spiritual practice. This is strongly symbolized in two specific iconographies, the one of Set fighting against the serpent of Chaos on behalf of Ra and the one of the two divinities (Heru and Set) tying of the knot of unity of the higher and the lower self, the lotus and papyrus on the *Sma* symbol.[72] (See below) In that tying there is no longer disorder, but rather balance and unity and power. Here there is separation from Set and Nebthet and the capacity to move upwards and forwards, on the spiritual journey, towards Asar and Aset and beyond.

Figure 39: Above: Set protecting the boat of Ra from the forces of entropy (symbolized by the serpent Apep).

---

[72] *sma*(sema) or *smama*(semama)- union

Figure 40: Heru and Set tie the knot of the Higher and Lower Self

"Sema Heru-Set"

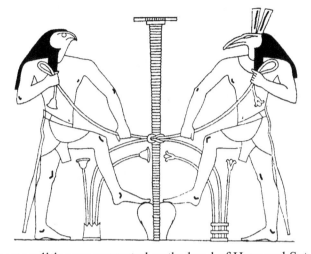

The image above is a rendition of the concept of reuniting of Heru and Set demonstrating peace between the two adversaries. The divinities representing Virtue (Heru) and Vice (Set) actually make peace and in so doing foment a "Sema" or union. They tie the lotus and papyrus plants (upper Egypt-Lower Egypt, Higher and Lower Self). In the same manner, the aspirant who wants to overcome the vices needs to engender a movement towards virtue. This allows the personality to be purified and the lower nature is subdued, and then the true essential being (Heru) emerges shining brightly to illuminate the individual and all who come into contact with him or her. This tying of the not is also a form of *hetep* {hotep}, the uniting of two opposite aspects into a unitary whole. In the special iconography of Heru-Set, presented earlier, the two personalities are presented as the head of Heru and Set in the body of Heru. This is to realize that Set is not an external entity but rather an outgrowth of our own personality and he is an appendage created by our own egoism that we must control and master.

Special Comment by Seba Dr. Dja Ashby based on Lesson 6

- <u>Sba Dja comments on how discipline and understanding are related and the importance of understanding in developing willpower and dispassion.</u>

One of the aspects discussed in the lecture was of the Nekakhu, the flail, and Sebai MAA (Dr. Muata Ashby) talked about the flail essentially separating the real you from the unreal you. And the flail symbolizes what? What did that flail mean to you as a child growing up when you saw it in your parent's hands? Discipline. And what was the aspect of discipline that it meant? Something painful…a painful blow that was going to come if you did something wrong. And you can see parents do that with their children. They can give them that look…that says…go ahead…continue…wait until we get home. Most of us know that "wait until we get home look"…as a child. So the aspect of discipline is part of spiritual growth, and it must be applied for you to be able to evolve properly. But you must understand that discipline is an initial stage in spiritual growth that you go through. As you grow, the other important word that was emphasized in the above lecture was your understanding, your capacity to understand. Your wisdom allows you to do that. As you grow in wisdom, as Aset opens the doors, and your understanding grows, the amount of tension you have to apply for the discipline aspect is going to proportionally be decreased. For example, suppose there is something that you really can't resist…in other words you are trying to do that raw diet, but there is still that chocolate bar every once in a while…or whatever it is…even a non-food item. It can be something in your life you are struggling with, that you want to get over, but every so often you feel yourself drawn to it, pulled to it, attracted to it. You go to a party, or you go visit family, and there it is staring you in the face, and yet you know you must be disciplined, you must resist it…but you struggle with the temptation.

Researchers did a study with little children where they put them in a room and they told them not to turn around, and they were being videotaped. And all the children turned around to see what was behind them. They could not resist the temptation not to do it.

So imagine you are in this room now, closed off, no body's watching you, no video camera…just you and this object with which you are having a difficult time resisting… and you can feel the tension there, you can feel the struggle. But now imagine…say this item is a food item…and you are in the same room with it… and someone tells you that this same food has poison in it. What happens to your struggle? What happens to your desire to go over and taste it? Your temptation, what happens to that? It's gone. Actually now you are repulsed by your object of desire. You don't want to be anywhere near it…you don't care about it. As a matter of fact, you would rather not be in the room with it. You can sit there all night and stare at it, and it can stare back at you, but you have no desire to go and take even one piece of it, because you know it will kill you.

So, the situation in both instances were the same, being locked in a room with an object of desire, but having the understanding that what you desire will be harmful for you takes away all the tension that would be there normally in the struggle if you were just trying to apply discipline and force to resist it. And this is what the teachings are about. This is what the teachings of dispassion are about. This is why when the sages talk, they talk horribly about the world of time and space, even though with the same breath they will tell you that the world of time and space is, after all, also the Self, the Spirit.

This is why in the story of Ra and Aset, Aset poisoned Ra, not the Transcendental Ra, but the world of Time and Space Ra. So you are doing the same if your understanding grows, if you poison the world essentially, through your understanding, through application of the principles, through understanding how the mind and senses get you all caught up in the unreality of the world. Sebai MAA talks about how, as Heru Ur, you sit on the throne of eternity, you are ever unaffected.

However, caught up in the world of Time and Space, caught up in all the mental projections of the mind, you are very affected by everything that goes on around you. You don't feel that you are just sitting watching the movie of your life unfold. Tragedy comes and you feel the pain. Happiness comes and you feel the joy and the laughter, as if you were in a dream almost. Or imagine you are in a theater watching a movie; you are sitting there watching the screen, and an event of tragedy unfolds. You become so caught up in the movie that the main character smiles when something good happens, and you find yourself smiling with that character, identifying with that character, you're relating to them because you have become so engrossed in the movie. And then something terrible happens to them, a tear jerking moment, and you start to cry also. Or in a horror movie, here comes Dracula...and he is about to bite the girl, and your mind starts to say no, no...everything in your body is caught up into that moment...yet there you are in the theater, and all you really are is a spectator...you are really just watching the show...seated...ever unaffected...but yet so involved in the projections on the screen that have no reality.

So you can imagine how complicated this is for most people why people have difficulty in being able to come to this level of spirituality ...because even in ordinary life...just watching a movie turns out to be like a rebirth, as if a reincarnation for them...they are caught up in another life, a whole other life, a whole other situation from the time they are caught up in the movie. And if you cannot extricate yourself from that, how are you going to extricate yourself from your own life, from your own projections that your mind is putting on you...your own drama that is unfolding in the world of Time and Space. How do you do it in the movie theater? There you are watching the show and you are all caught up into it. How do you extricate yourself from that, being caught up into it? What are some of the things you can do?

If for a moment you catch yourself, you can remind yourself, Oh, here I am. I am just seated here and it's just a movie. What else can you do? You can stop the projections by turning off the movie. What else? You can start poking holes in it. When you see the blood of Dracula, you can say, Oh...that's ketchup...that's really cheap make-up they have on, etc.

So you need to start poking fun at the world of time and space....start developing dispassion and taking account of all the things that people take for granted, all the things that are taken to be so normal, and see the illusoriness of them so that you may not find yourself getting caught up in the drama of the world of time and space. You need to start pulling it apart...and find a way to detach yourself...to bring yourself to that awareness. You can say things like, "hey, I am just seated here, and I am just the onlooker of this show that is going on. And the real me is seated and unaffected, and I am not caught up in these projections of the mind...these are just mental projections." You can get up and go turn it off, but you don't have to if you can get yourself to UNDERSTAND it.

You can continue to actually sit there, to watch the show unfold, and to not be caught up in it. Your mind has the capacity to do that. Likewise your mind has the same capacity to allow you to discover that aspect of your being that is unaffected, and even as the mental projections of the mind continue in the world of time and space, and the drama of your personality unfolds, you have that capacity to also be detached from it...to watch it as if you are watching a movie unfolding on the screen...to understand that is not the real you.

Also going back to the analogy of the dream character, while you are dreaming, you feel it's the real you, and if someone in that dream were to come and tell you it's just a dream, if you were really caught up in that character...you're still not going to believe them. So then, why is it when someone comes and tells you now that this is not the real you, why is it so hard to believe this...that the real you is sleeping on the bed of eternity or sitting on the chair of eternity...ever unaffected. What makes this believing so hard? Yet tonight, there you will go again and have a dream, and you are going to believe it while it is going on, that that is you, and whatever is happening there is really happening to you, and then you are going to wake up and say, Oh...it's not real.

So again there is a capacity of mind, you have that capacity of mind, through the process of understanding, to be able to bring the mind to an understanding that this is not real and that you are the one just witnessing all of this.

Hetep.

Sba Dja Ashby

Questions and Answers

Question:

About Heru, is he not seen as an avatar?

Answer by Sebai MAA (Dr. Muata Ashby):

Mythologically, Heru is seen as an avatar. In fact, all of the divinities are seen as manifestations or as emanations of the divine. However, Avatarism, in a specific context, means that the divinity comes down in human form, and this is why, especially the divinities of the Anunian tradition, are seen as avatars, because the scripture itself says that they came down in physical form, and that they manifested through physical human bodies.

I have spoken about this in the book on the Asarian Theurgy[73] as well as in the book on Anunian Theurgy.[74] In a future lesson we will talk about how Geb brought forth the Bennu bird, and the Bennu bird, the scripture says, is the living form of Asar. And Heru is also a form of Asar. Heru is the redemption, or the rebirth of Asar. So, you see, Ra is coming through and being born into time and space, into the physicality through Geb, and in a form of the Bennu, in the form of Asar, and the form of Heru. So, in fact, the ten male and female main divinities of Anunian Theurgy are all avatars in the true sense of the term itself. And that is what these divinities, these neteru, do in fact.

---

[73] See the book *African Religion Vol. 4 Asarian Theology* by Dr. Muata Ashby
[74] See the Book *African Religion VOL. 1- ANUNIAN THEOLOGY THE MYSTERIES OF RA,* by Dr. Muata Ashby, ISBN: 1-884564-38-0

Reflection and Journal discipline:

1- At the top of each page copy the following hieroglyphs to the best of your ability

[*cht n ankh* " *tree of life*"]

After studying the Lesson proceed to answer the following question and write the answer in your journal. This exercise will require more than one reading and more than one journal entry, at least one page; write all you can find related to the subject of the question. Answer the questions first without referring to the text you just read. Then go back and see if you missed anything. This exercise is to be repeated until you become proficient with the principles of this sphere. The reflection exercise should be done after each reading or study session. Then you may practice meditation[75] on the wisdom you have learned. You may come back to add to your reflections even if you move on to other lessons.

REFLECTIONS: I am this child, ready to grow and meet the challenges of life. I am the child of that lady with the answers to the mysteries and child of that lord of blackness and eternity. Let me be energetic like the child, innocent as the child pure as the child and shining free like the solar child. Let me see the light that is my solar self, and let me feel the wind beneath my wings as I fly up to the heavens and walk the earth as a spiritual warrior!

After studying the Lesson proceed to answer the following question and write the answer in your journal.

What is(are) the main teaching(s) of this lesson and what do the principle(s) of the divinity(ies) discussed in this lesson mean in reference to my actions, feelings, thoughts and desires and understanding of the spiritual philosophy?

What is an emanation from the spiritual essence and as such is sustained by it?

---

[75] Explained in more detail in Lesson 15

Lesson 7: The Principle of Set, and how to Overcome Egoism on the Journey of the Tree of Life

The first level that is above us, that is, human existence, is Set and Nebthet. Recall the picture of Heru-Set. We talked about Heru's aspects. Heru – Set is a combination of the two divinities. It is depicted as Heru with two heads. One head is the hawk head, and one head is a strange looking animal…his head looks a little like a camel, and like a dog as well as an aardvark. There is no record of any such animal existing in ancient Kemet, ancient Africa. It is a mythological creature that has no origin, no destination, and we will explain again why that is further on.

Figure 41: The Level of Set and Nebthet

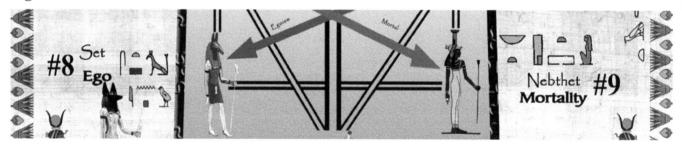

Figure 42: (below) The Composite Divinity-Heru and Set in one personality.

What does the struggle of life in terms of the successes and failures of maintaining virtue in life represent? What this means is that this wonderful spiritual aspiration that you have…you come here, you sit for the classes, you study the books, and you want to be an aspirant…all that kind of thing signifies that you mean well. But often, for most people, the next thing that happens is that you get caught up in the world…you get pregnant or you get somebody pregnant, you get drunk, or you eat too much or you smoke, or you got angry and you hit somebody…whatever it is…because along with that wonderful aspiration that is in you, there is something else…and that something else is called Set. So you have some positive aspects of your personality and that causes you to do good deeds and be altruistic. But there is another aspect that comes out once in a while (more often for lesser evolved people) that causes negative thoughts, feelings and actions. Notice that the image is of the body of Heru and that the head of Set is just an appendage. There is more Heru in Heru and only a head of Set coming out. But the head is all that is needed to send the personality for a loop. The presence of the head of Set means that the mind and the unrighteousness of Set can corrupt even the most perfect body.

There is an ancient Egyptian proverb that states "there are two roads of humankind. One is the path of righteousness, and the other is the path of unrighteousness." And this is your choice…your free will to take the path…but it's not as simple as your free choice, because you really don't have free choice. You think you have free choice, but you are kidding yourself…you are fooling yourself. Your choice is determined by the life you lead. A person's life is determined by their actions and actions are determined by thoughts and thoughts are determined by the philosophy a person lives by. Do you believe you are an individual personality in competitions with other individual personalities in the world or do you believe you are higher than that, belonging to something greater and more sublime than that? When a person performs an action, that action contributes to a building tendency to move in that direction if the action is repeated. If your life is virtuous, that set's up *Ariu*[76] of a virtuous tendency. If you do lots of good deeds, if you have lots of good thoughts, you have a tendency in that direction. If you are a negative person, you say hateful comments, you develop hate and tend to be a hateful person. If you are a lustful person, lusting after things, you develop more lust as your tendency. And that goes on even after death…that impels you in that direction.

Consider that you may think that you can make a conscious choice; how many times have you tried to stop smoking or stop eating meat and you can't do it? Somebody puts some meat in front of you, and you feel you've got to take it because you desire it, sometimes with rationalizing the action you know is wrong but which you can't stop yourself from doing….you have heard that kind of rationalizing speech… "just a little bite is ok, no big deal," or "just a little white lie," or "just a little bit of beer," or "just a little bit of that." Or sometimes you get sick and tired of hanging back and you plunge. You may say: "If I am going to commit this sin, let me just go headlong into it. If I am going to have a little affair, let me have an adulterous and fully lustful affair."

You give in, and this is where the Christian idea of the little devil sitting on one shoulder and the little angel sitting on the other shoulder comes from. But this teaching we have here is a much deeper conception because what we are talking about, is that when you have a thought, when you have an action, that action or thought sets up a residue in your unconscious mind. That unconscious impression that is left is attached to a cosmic force…a portion of an energy form. If you think lots of thoughts, you are accumulating more and more energy in that direction. It works for good or for evil, positive or negative. And this is the key to succeeding in transforming the *aric* (karmic) basis of your unconscious mind that impels you.

Virtuous people do not have to worry about being virtuous. They don't have to sit around and worry what would I do if this situation happens, what would I do if that situation happens…what am I going to say or do? They don't have to, because all that is going to come out is from the storehouse of what is there already, from the positive ariu that was created through positive thoughts and actions of the past. If you are the kind of person, who is getting into these things (the teachings), but you are coming from a place where you were cursing a lot…every other word is a curse word…you notice how sometimes you try to transform yourself, you try to become virtuous and righteous and all that kind of thing…and all of a sudden an insult or a curse word will come out…and you don't know where it came from, and you didn't mean it, and you tried to control it, but it comes out anyway.

And this is an effect of your unconscious mind that is tied to your mouth, your speech organ. You may try to control it, but you can't fully, because eventually your unconscious mind will compel you since the impressions are still there waiting to be expressed with the energy they have associated with them. This is why the unconscious mind must be cleansed. And what is the unconscious mind? The unconscious mind is the region of your existence where your unconscious impressions, your *ariu*, is stored. You have three main realms or planes in which you exist. One is the physical plane, and that is the plane that most people know about. There is an astral plane…that is the plane where your mind operates. When you have a thought, imagination, idea, or a dream you are operating in that plane. But where do those thoughts that come into your conscious awareness come from? They already existed as seeds in your deeper unconscious mind…a realm that you are not aware of. But every time you have a thought or you make an action, a residue or impression gets dropped into that unconscious area, and it sprouts forth when your current or future physical or mental energy or activity resonates with that *ari* (karmic) impression.

So, for example, if you like red sports cars you may be drawn to that. Suppose that when you were a child your big brother or big sister once owned and was infatuated with a red sports car. You heard that back then but now you may not be thinking about it, but you are walking down the street and a red sports car rides by, and you look at it and say, "Oh, I like that. All those cars I liked when I was young…" It starts to resonate and then you may feel like you would like to have it so you go pursuing actions to get it and that is what you get caught up in.

---

[76] *ariu-* {actions, deeds, [plural] and the unconscious mental impressions of the past that impel the desires of the mind} accumulated over previous years that impel and compel a person to future actions. This term is similar in most respects to the Indian concept of karma. See the book *Introduction to Maat Philosophy* by Dr. Muata Ashby

You may not be thinking of somebody who did some wrong to you a few years ago, but at the mention of their name or an associated memory related to them or if you meet a person who looks like them or acts like them the feelings come back and then the thoughts associated with the feelings come in and you may not know why you hate a person you never "met" before. Furthermore, the seeds of memories, the unconscious impressions, carry with them some portion of life force energy potential. At some point, if there is sufficient reinforcement of an idea, for example "I like red sports cars," "I like red sports cars," "I like red sports cars," "I like red sports cars," "I like red sports cars," etc., eventually the personality will be compelled to act on that idea even if the intellect says it's a bad idea. The force behind the idea can overpower the intellect and bolster feelings which express as uncontrolled emotional acts that can also be rationalized acts. You may feel compelled to go out and buy a red sports car even though you know you can't afford it and that your spouse will be upset when you bring it home.

Good actions and bad actions, your *ariu*…you can transform it by performing righteous actions today, suppressing the negative actions, and resolving those negative actions through understanding of their error. Egoistic actions are erroneous because they are based on unrighteousness, on error. If you hate somebody, understand that you are hating yourself. Your hatred is a factor of your own failure to seek truth to fulfill yourself in a righteous manner. Your failure to achieve happiness is the same thing.

You cannot achieve true happiness in the realm of generation as we discussed already. If you accumulate righteous thoughts, righteous feelings, righteous actions, good *ariu*, that begins to accumulate and it begins to outweigh the negative until the negative becomes diminished, weakened and dissipated. But it will not be completely diminished because there is so much of it. The only way to completely diminish it is to overpower it, to subdue it utterly. And the great weapons for the subjugation of negative *ariu* are the light rays of Ra, which are like arrows, this also recalls the arrows of goddess Net, the pinpoint strike of wisdom into the heart of ignorance.

Figure 43: The Ancient Egyptian God Set

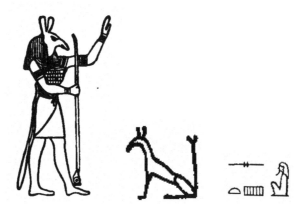

And that brings us to the Set character and what he represents. Notice that unlike Heru, who is related to an avian quality, Set is related to a four legged animal. So he is earthbound and thus related to the heavier elements like earth, metal, stone, etc., as opposed to Heru who can take flight and is thus capable of living on earth but also attaining communion with air and fire. So this means that Set represents what is gross while Heru has the capacity to operate in the gross as well as the subtle. Following this metaphor, the human body and its name are the grosser aspects of the personality while the ⟨glyph⟩ *Ba* (soul) and the ⟨glyph⟩ *akh,* (Spirit) are subtler aspects.[77] As we said earlier, Set is egoism…not ego per se, although he does have an aspect that is ego. Ego is the projection of your idea of self. What you know of yourself, as a limited being; that is your ego. That ego is the image of yourself in time and space and the ignorant as well as the wise have egos. The question is what is

---

[77]

egoism? When you live in a state of ignorance about your higher self you don't know of your other aspect, your transcendental aspect. Now, if you become egoistic, you start living as if this is the only reality, in a way such that you should seek pleasure just to satisfy your own personal desires, selfishness, nepotism, all of those kind of things…that is egoism and Set represents really both of those (ego and egoism).

The mother of Set was Nut. His father was Geb, and in the beginning he was a servant of Ra. His energy was in the service of the *Pauti*. He is known as the 𓂝𓂝 *"Pehti aah"*. *"Peh"* means strength and *"Pehti"* means "double strength." He is the "two-fold strength" one. "Aah" means "great." And he uses his strength to move the boat of Ra. The boat of Ra moves through the sky, as the sundisk and it shines and in doing so serves the needs of sustaining life on earth. He pushes the clouds out of the way, and the rain. So, set was a great and powerful force for good and for sustaining life. But something happened.

In the Asarian Resurrection myth we are told that he became jealous of Asar, and then he murdered Asar and wanted to take his place, to assume the throne of Kemet and become the king. And he no longer assisted the boat of Ra, he actually fought against it. He wanted to promote gloom and doom, and clouds and rain. This is what Set represents…coldness, opacity, ignorance, jealousy, envy, and not warmth.

And he did these things in his own form, as a composite zoo-anthropomorphic body of a man with head of an undetermined animal as well as in a form of a fiend or a demon called 𓃀𓄿𓃀𓄿𓃀 *"Baba,"* which is one of his main forms. Another form is ⊙⊙𓃀𓄿 *"Akh Akh"*. In this form he is a winged beast that harasses. This uncharacteristic and rare form, with wings, may be considered as an opposite and as a nemesis to Heru's earthly avian form only. In the *Akh Akh* Set has not lost his four legs nor has he made a full transformation to avian form; therefore we consider this form only as an earthbound mode of the setian character, like a bird that can fly in the atmosphere of the world but cannot leave the boundaries of the planet's environment, a form that is opposite to Heru's earthly form but not Heru's transcendental *Ur Uadjit* form. He is also a pig, 𓏤𓏤𓏤𓃀𓄿[78], associated with filth, and in this form, when he is in the battle with Heru, he threw excrement in Heru's eyes and messed up Heru's eyes. And so, from ancient times on, we don't eat pork for this reason. Of course there are physiological reasons, but this is the mythological reason. Furthermore, Set (ego) makes the eyes of the soul cloudy, opaque, and tainted; here we are referring to the capacity to see the truth and not just the physical capacity to see worldly objects.

Figure 44: Black pig of Set being shooed away from Asar by Djehuti who is in the form of a baboon

□ □ 𓆓 *Apep* is the great serpent that fights against and tries to stop and destroy the boat of Ra. Apep may also be considered as Set's lieutenant. Set has seventy-five other forms, because Ra has seventy-five forms. And so he has to have seventy-five names or forms to fight against Ra's seventy-five names. So the darkness fights against the light. And remember that Ra is a form of Heru. So the conflict is ultimately between Heru and Set. But it is also between the aspiration and the tendency towards darkness and ignorance within you as a spiritual aspirant.

---

[78] *Shai Kam* - black pig- Set - that was speared by Heru

Remember what the main weapons are: The Sun Rays, the light, the warmth and heat, the truth…and these are the weapons that Heru uses to harpoon Set. Also we are told that Set is the backbone of every human being. If your backbone is controlled by your ego, that means that your caduceus, your life force energy centers, your serpent power energy is going to be corrupted. Remember what we said previously, that "Heru as the Divine solar child", has seven aspects which are a reflection of Ra's seven souls (*Sefech ba Ra*). That energy, that backbone is to be harpooned, and is to be shackled and it is to be transformed by Heru. Remember that Heru harpoons Set who is in the form of a wild hippopotamus, which symbolizes uncontrolled lower self. It is interesting to note that the symbol for the word ⌐ 𝒵𝒶 "one" in Ancient Egyptian hieroglyphic is the "harpoon" ⤙, as in 𝒩𝑒𝓉𝑒𝓇 𝒵𝒶 𝓊𝒶 𝓊𝓇 𝓎𝒶𝓃 𝓊𝓇 𝓃𝓊 𝒻, *"God, the only one, the greatest one-nothing greater than he"* - in other words, God without a second. Thus, Heru spears Set with oneness, which neutralizes his multiplicity, his separateness, his opposite nature, which lead to separation, individuality and egoism.

There is a hippopotamus goddess, ⌂ 🐾 *"Reret."* Her main duty is to capture Set and to chain him and control him. This goddess form is an aspect of Aset. Notice that phonetically, the names of the two divinities are opposites, Set means to shoot out and Aset means "royal throne," "abode" and she is healer as well as "that which puts back together"; notice also that phonetically, Aset has the name of Set in her name. She stabilizes, controls Set and that is why Heru must study her principle in order to defeat Set. Set is also known as the ⊚ □ ∿ 𝄞 *"khepesh."*[79]

Figure 45: Hetep -offering table displaying the hieroglyphic symbol of the Khepesh

Hetep means peace brought about through union of the opposites; the opposites primarily are symbolized by the male and female gender. Khepesh is the thigh ∿ glyph that you see on a *Hetep* Slab. This means that he is the maleness. He is the force of the male gender… and we are talking about this in a sense like the eastern Yin and the Yang…Here he is the harshness, he is the coldness, the hardness. And he has different spellings to his names. In one of his names he is called *Setep* ⌐▭ 𝄞 , and there is a "p" in it which means a stone. So he belongs to the land of the stones and the harshness, and rockiness and dryness, while Heru belongs to the green areas, the fertile areas. Heru belongs to the greenery of the Nile valley.

---

[79] Khepesh - thigh region of northern sky - home of Set

Figure 46: Seven stars of the Great Bear constellation. Reret chains Set

Going back to the *khepesh*, the khepesh is also known as the constellation of the Great bear in the Northern sky. There are seven stars in that constellation. So he is a God of the north...the northern sky that is captured and held fast with the goddesses help and the spear of one pointed conscience. In this sense, when the moving, changeable and variable nature of Set, the wandering, agitated mind, the ego is captured, the mind can transform that into a more stable form of stellar conscience, as we will see next.

Figure 47: The Great Pyramid of Egypt with the Mystical Constellations (view from the South).

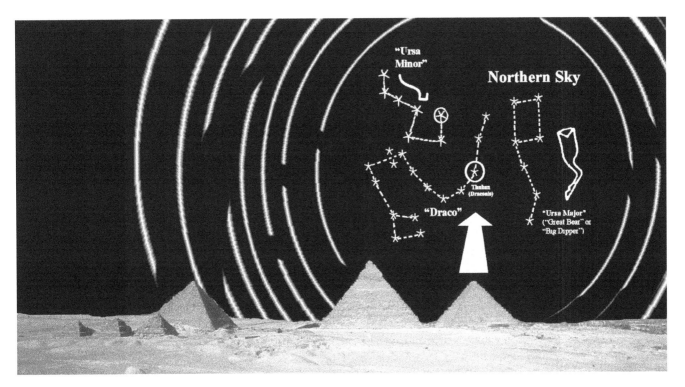

In the northern sky we have the North Pole. And there we can see different kinds of stars, the *Akhemu Seku* - never setting stars the imperishable ones, the stars that don't move (stars close to the center). These are also divinities that fight against Set. Then we also have the *Akhemu Urdu* stars, which means the never resting stars, the ones that set on the horizon, that go below the horizon and then come up again on the other side (stars further away from the center). If you look in the northern sky, and you look to the North Pole, you will see that...if you were to see a picture...(see above), If you were to use time lapsed photography of the entire sky, you would see that there are stars that appear to move in a circle around the world, rising in the eastern horizon (after the sun sets) and they go below the western horizon and they come up again. If you look in the dead center of that circle, you see there are stars that don't move. They stay in that circle...they don't go below the horizon and come up again. These are the

159

stars that are to be emulated, their steadfastness and abiding nature, as they do not die and come back to life again, as the other stars.

The khepesh is the power that must be discovered and mastered for succeeding on the spiritual path. An aspirant must learn to be diligent and unwavering in the practice of the teachings and the pursuit of truth. In this way such an aspirant will discover unchanging consciousness and not the type of conscience that most people have, that wavers with the times, sometimes being lucid and at others being clouded. Then the mind becomes awake to the teaching and not just intermittently or in a mediocre way, but in a mature and dynamic way that allows the teaching to become effective.

The Forces of Entropy

In Neterian religion, there is no concept of "evil" as is conceptualized in Western Culture. Rather, it is understood that the forces of entropy are constantly working in nature to bring that which has been constructed, that which has been made into a form, back to the original natural state (undifferentiated matter). The serpent Apep (Apophis), who daily tries to stop Ra's boat of creation, is the primary symbol of entropy. This concept of entropy has been referred to as "chaos" by Western Egyptologists, however, the term "entropy" is a more accurate reading of the teaching..

Apep

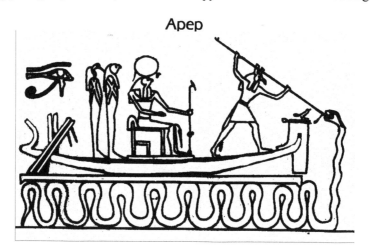

Figure 48: Above: Set protecting the boat of Ra from the forces of entropy (symbolized by the serpent Apep).

As expressed previously, in Neterian religion there is also no concept of a "devil" or "demon" as is conceived in the Judeo-Christian or Islamic traditions. Rather, it is understood that manifestations of detrimental situations and adversities arise as a result of unrighteous actions and their consequences. These unrighteous actions are due to the "Setian" qualities in a human being. Set is the divinity of egoism and the negative qualities which arise from egoism. Egoism may also be defined as the idea of individuality based on identification with the body and mind only as being who one is. One has no deeper awareness of their deeper spiritual essence, and thus no understanding of their connectedness to all other objects (includes persons) in creation and the Divine Self. When the ego is under the control of the higher nature, it fights the forces of entropy (as above). However, when beset with ignorance, it leads to the degraded states of human existence. The vices (egoism, selfishness, extraverted-ness, wonton sexuality (lust), jealousy, envy, greed, gluttony. Etc.) are a result. So, the principle of set is not inherently evil or bad but when ignorance takes over the personality and it forgets its true self, it can turn to egoism, selfishness and greed. Those are the causes of the bad things that people can do to each other, the world and to themselves. We are to turn that force of Set around and place it in the service of Ra, our Higher Self, by using it to fight off the egoism and the negative desires. In that way we will succeed on the path of the Tree of Life.

"Sety mer –n-Ptah"
"King Sety, beloved of Ptah"

Since Set {Sety} was originally a divinity of power that employed that power to assist the divine, who lost his way but was subdued, he is not seen as a divinity of evil like the devil in the western religions. Rather, he is a redeemed character; a personality that lost his way and was brought back to the path of truth. There is proof that Set's name was used by Ancient Egyptians, most prominently, the Pharaoh Sety Ua {Sety the first}[80] who had the name of Set incorporated into his own. This could not have occurred if Set was considered to be an inimical personality; he was and is a beneficial personality when properly mastered as outlined here. He therefore is a metaphor of all who have at some point lost their way or who have moved away from the divine who can regain their standing by allowing Heru in them to fight for order and truth. In so doing aspirants can redeem Asar within themselves and thus attain higher consciousness. As Set is an important divinity, we have discussed about him in previous lessons and we will discuss more about Set in future lessons but that is all for now. This concludes the lesson for today.

Om Hetep

Sebai MAA {Dr. Muata Ashby}

---

[80] Menmaatre **Seti I** (sometimes called **Sethi I**) was a Pharaoh of Ancient Egypt (Nineteenth dynasty of Egypt), the son of Ramesses I and Queen Sitre, and the father of Ramesses II. There was also a Sety **II**

Reflection and Journal discipline:

1- **At the top of each page copy the following hieroglyphs to the best of your ability**

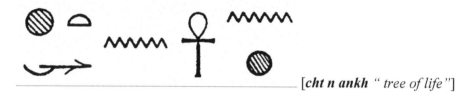

[*cht n ankh* " *tree of life*"]

After studying the Lesson proceed to answer the following question and write the answer in your journal. This exercise will require more than one reading and more than one journal entry, at least one page; write all you can find related to the subject of the question. Answer the questions first without referring to the text you just read. Then go back and see if you missed anything. This exercise is to be repeated until you become proficient with the principles of this sphere. The reflection exercise should be done after each reading or study session. Then you may practice meditation[81] on the wisdom you have learned. You may come back to add to your reflections even if you move on to other lessons.

REFLECTIONS: I have been Set…I have done Setian things in the past. Out of ignorance or greed or lust or whatever reason I lost the way and suffered my sufferings for it. Set within me will be controlled. He will be harnessed. He will be stopped by Heru and guided by Aset and his power shall be for the glory of my Higher Self and that is God. Let me purify Set and let his name be a source of power for the success in my spiritual journey!

After studying the Lesson proceed to answer the following question and write the answer in your journal.

What is(are) the main teaching(s) of this lesson and what do the principle(s) of the divinity(ies) discussed in this lesson mean in reference to my actions, feelings, thoughts and desires and understanding of the spiritual philosophy?

What force can overpower the intellect?

---

[81] Explained in more detail in Lesson 15

Lesson 8: The Principle of Nebthet, and how to Overcome the Seductiveness of Worldly Desires on the Journey of the Tree of Life

We continue today our studies of Anunian Theurgy Tree of Life Philosophy. Today we continue our exploration of the Principles of Creation. We have studied Anunian Theurgy in general and we have learnt about the origins of the neteru, the gods, and goddesses, who emerge as principles or else I would say the reverse, that the principles emerge and they are termed as gods and goddesses by the sages and this is done so that people can have an easier entry into the study of the principles, from a personal perspective that people can more easily relate to instead of an impersonal perspective that is distant. This is done because everybody has some understanding of personalities of people or aspects of the personality. Naming something is the first step in understanding it. This is a very great teaching, although it is misused or misunderstood by most people. They think that naming something gives them the knowledge of it and actually that is a superficial knowledge that you gain from naming anything. An object can be named but if its essential nature is unknown the name can become a label for the ignorance. A person can have a name and another person may trust them because they have a familiar name, but if the person does something bad like stealing then you hear "wow I never knew he had it in him; I guess I never really "knew" him like I thought I did." We can name the sun, but what do we really know about the sun, its origins, and it's internal operations? The concepts about the sun may be derived from scientific studies and extrapolations but they are all theoretical. Whatever the physicists can tell us about the sun is theoretical. To the ancients or in ancient times, for ordinary people these were great mysteries and the words used to name them were merely descriptions of their superficial appearance though for the sage, for the theurgical scientist (remember the term 'Theurgy' - the science of the worship of the gods and goddesses) this is a study of the internal properties of the principles, the inner-workings of the principles, and in order to have a full understanding of a principle, or in order to have full understanding of anything, you have to become one with that thing that you are trying to understand. Becoming one with something that you are trying to understand means, understanding its operations, its construction, its movements, its vibrations, it's way of being, existing, and, as you recall from previous lectures, that is done by, first of all, learning about or listening to the teaching about the object or the principle that you are trying to learn. Then you start purifying yourself through mind regulations and disciplines. Also, you start acting in accordance with the principle, you start thinking, or allowing your thought process to adapt to or to adopt the wisdom of that principle. You start feeling like that principle and you start being that principle. In meditation you also experience existence as that principle. If these principles were to be mastered, meaning that they are fully discovered by you internally, that means that you have attained the principle and transcended that principle; you are then moving further on the rungs of the tree or on the branches of the tree.

As such, we have studied the basic principles of the tree, which are ten in number and we began our study with a general look at the philosophy of the Tree and the neteru of the Tree. Lately we have concentrated on the lower principles of the tree, which are Set and Heru and we will come back to Heru. Last time we studied the Principle of Set and the Setian nature, the egoistic nature of life. Set is that principle which disintegrates, that principle which chops up the soul and, as you may recall, a lot of the insight that comes from the Tree of Life can be derived from the Asarian Resurrection myth. It is like a mythological explanation of the principles of the Tree.

Anunian Theurgy gives us the basis for understanding the elemental Creation neteru that compose Creation itself and the Asarian Resurrection gives us the mythological insight into the neteru that compose the human personality. Set, as you recall, in the Asarian Resurrection myth,[82] murders his brother Asar. He mutilated him; He chops him up into pieces. Recall that Asar is a reflection of Ra in the night and therefore he is the sun of the night and the Sun of the Night is the moon. The sun can never be chopped up, it shines always, but the moon can be chopped up, it has phases and so it can be chopped up into fourteen pieces and Set is the agent of that chopping up process and conversely Heru - this is all explained in the mythic scriptures- then Heru is the one who is the redeemer. He and Aset and Nebthet and Anpu, put the pieces back together and primarily Aset through

---

[82] See the book *African Religion Vol. 4: Asarian Theology* by Dr. Muata Ashby

Heru, these principles (meaning aspiration joined with wisdom) put together the pieces of the soul (Asar), which had been torn into pieces, back together again (Asar-Sokkar). When you are torn into pieces, it means that you are disintegrated, your consciousness, your ego, which is your concept of self, is disintegrated and you are susceptible to the realm of generation. You are not one in the universal sense, you do not know yourself as one with all; you think of yourself as separate and as an individual among individuals; that is what the ignorant ego does to the soul, which is, in reality, one with the transcendental Spirit. That means you are susceptible to the world of time and space and to desire. Time-space is the realm of generation, where things generate from each other. If you were to experience yourself as a whole principle, the reason why you transcend that principle is because you have discovered the fullness of that principle. If you are lacking in some aspect of the principle, that is going to mean that you are going to desire to be whole and you will search, firstly therefore, in the realm of time and space for wholeness. If you experienced yourself as, for instance, pure soul, you are not going to need to add anything to yourself, you are not going to need to desire anything of soul nature. However if your soul has the experience of itself as pieces, as non-whole, as something that is missing, that is when Set has come into your life and when you act egoistically, when you have egoistic desires, and when you move through life in a way that is disjointed, that is un-holistic, that is when your conscience, guided by egoistic thoughts and desires for wholeness, leads you to search hither and thither in the world of time and place for fulfillment. The way to overcome this problem is to transform the desire for wholeness from that which is illusory and cannot provide wholeness (Nebthet), worldly objects and people to the desire for truth and wisdom; that is Aset.

Consider the following; in the beginning you are going to have some special dish of food that is going to make you happy. So one day you go out for Chinese food. If that was going to make you happy and whole then you should eat Chinese food forever, every day for every meal. But you know that if you are tired of that then you go to Burger King or then you go to an Indian restaurant, etc. Hopefully one day you would go to a health food store where you could find true wholeness and nutrition in the food that will give you a feeling of true fullness. Then you don't have to go wandering around in the world. There are jokes about that, people who have money, they are in New York in the morning, and then they go for lunch in Paris, and then they go to dinner in Rome so they can experience all the "different" dishes and actually what they are experiencing is all the same molecules and atoms because all that food is composed of only a different arrangement of spices and organic material. But all of it is composed of spices and organic material which is all constituted by the same atoms and molecules that compose every other food on earth. That wandering behind the different arrangement of things, to try to satisfy your desires, your ego concepts, is a feature of the disintegrated soul which gives rise to a disintegrated mind and mental disintegration gives rise to delusion because the disintegration creates illusions of thoughts in different parts of the mind, like a house of mirrors at a carnival; one image reflects on another and the happiness seems possible if the mind were only able to grasp the fleeting reflected image in the mind, the idea of what would bring happiness. But only the reflection is grasped and that is never satisfying, so the mind sets off again looking for another delusion to run after. This is caused by a feeling of being un-whole, of not being whole due to spiritual ignorance, and as long as that continues, the consciousness is disintegrated, the mind is distracted and you are not able to seek or to discern truth in a fully effective manner, and this is what Set does to the soul.

A certain level of maturity is required on the spiritual path. It allows the personality to be sensitive to the words of wisdom and when there is enough maturity, certain higher wisdom comes to be desired by the personality and that is the Aset principle and then that Aset principle begins to elevate the consciousness, but we are not going to get into the Aset principle today. That is for a future lecture. Today, we are going to discuss the Principle of Nebthet.

Nebthet is, as we recall, one of the five divinities that go to compose the human personality. Now, there are ten divinities. There are five above and five below; five cosmic and five worldly/human, if you will, personalities. Recall that Geb and Nut gave birth to five divinities – Asar, Aset, Set, Nebthet and Heru. Set and Nebthet represent the first tier or level or we may also call it the first rung on the ladder of the Kemetic Tree of Life of Anunian Theurgy and every rung has two connections in the ladder, to a male and a female principle. We discussed Set previously and now we are discussing Nebthet and this completes the first level of the Tree so that the climbing process may take place.

Nebthet is explained to be the counterpart of Set, although when considering these principles, you should not understand them as being opposites in the sense of equal and opposite, though they may be so in that sense, that is, suppose for instance, when if I ask the opposite of good you might say bad, or the opposite of up and then the answer would be down. These are, if you will, complimentary opposites in a sense. They are equal but opposed and complementary.

Heru and Set are complimentary opposites and Set and Nebthet are mated principals, if you will. They are counterparts. Set and Nebthet are said to be husband and wife, and yet they have no children as it has been explained to you before. Their union bears no fruit in the form of other divinities, as per the Anunian Theurgy. However, as we introduced earlier, Nebthet and another divinity do bear offspring.

First of all, in relation to the principle of [hieroglyphs], or [hieroglyphs] Nebthet there are two basic issues that need to be discussed about her and one is her name itself which is composed of two parts, [hieroglyph] "Nebt" and [hieroglyph] "Het." "Nebt" means mistress or Lordess (as in Lord) and "Het" means house. To that effect she is the Lady, the mistress of the house. And what house are we talking about?

Before getting to that, let us briefly discuss the aspect of her twin sister Aset so that we may gain a deeper insight into the nature of Nebthet via comparison. Aset is the twin sister of Nebthet and they are said to be physically identical twins. The only difference that is possible to use in order to tell them apart is their headdress.

Nebthet has a symbol of the Nebt and the symbol of the Het [image] and Aset, her twin sister, has a symbol of the throne chair [image], which means "abode" so we can consider that Nebthet represents the totality of the house, which is a metaphor of the physical realm and Aset represents the supreme abode of wisdom of the physical Creation which is in the one place that rules the physical Creation, the throne. So in essence, Nebthet represents duality and Aset represents non-duality. Aset is the Goddess of the single point and Nebthet is the goddess of the multiple points in space; Nebthet is the goddess of the ever moving stars and Aset is the goddess of the non-moving stars.

One of the hieroglyphic terms of the goddess Nebthet is the symbol of the serpent or the cobra which is the symbol of all. What I am getting at here is the understanding of the complimentary nature of Aset and Nebthet. This is going to play into the discussions related to Aset and Asar. Nebthet is therefore the mistress, the ruler of the world and we are thinking of her here as the grossest aspect of the world because, recall that we have Geb and Nut and they are solar principles of physical Creation. Nebthet really represents the grossest principle of time and space because she includes not just the gross elements but also the gross mental thoughts and worldly impressions of the mind; and from a human perspective, the grossest principles of time and space are the body conscience (idea of self as the physical body) and the principle of mortality (concept that I am alive now, I was not alive before and one day I will die). In fact one of the definitions of her name is end of things. The meaning is something like that of the god *Tem*, in a sense, that really means she is like a physical death, the culmination of physical life. Tem means the end of creation as a whole, the end of the whole day, the end of a creation cycle and so on and so forth. Nebthet therefore, also represents the end of physical life.

The end of physical life is a strange passage-way of the soul when it goes on its journey into the astral plane and on to experiences in the astral worlds in the nether world as explained in the story of Sa-Asar which we went through, I believe, a year and a half ago.

Nebthet opens the door, as it were, to death and there is also a mystical relationship of Nebthet with sexuality but a lot of people who study ancient Egyptian Mythology don't realize it. In the Asarian Resurrection Myth, for those of you who recall the lecture series or have read the book, you know that, one day, Asar was sort of intoxicated because he liked to have parties and he was a very jovial personality, very happy go lucky and he went to bed and then Nebthet (remember that Aset and Nebthet are twins) came into his room and he thought that she was Aset and he made love with her, with Nebthet, and they had a child called Anpu. Now recall that we said previously that Set and Nebthet had no children. However Asar and Nebthet did produce a child, Anpu.

Anpu is known as a God of two faces. He represents the principle of mental opposites, also the principle of righteousness, knowing right from a wrong at the most basic level, the level of basic instinct, as the instinct of a dog. This is a capacity of righteous discrimination, between truth and untruth. Also he serves as the divinity of embalming the dead body and leading the soul to higher rungs of consciousness. So, through Nebthet, the soul

gives rise to higher capacity through death, because, what we are getting to here is that, when you are studying Nebthet, it really means that you are studying death and that really signifies the death of worldliness, death of the search in the world for happiness and fulfillment based on egoistic desires. Moving beyond physical death occurs when your sexual energy is cultivated and channelized into the death experience, which occurs in meditation; meditation is actually a death experience. This change represents an inverting of the movement of creation to a movement of dissolution. In the discipline of the Serpent Power, there are two serpentine forms of movement, downwards and upwards. Aset and Nebthet are the goddesses of the serpent power.[83]

Figure 49: (above) Caduceus with two serpent goddesses, displaying upwards and downwards movement

Figure 50: (below) Goddesses Aset and Nebthet as Serpent Goddesses

Below- A-The goddesses Aset (Isis) and goddess Nebethet (Nephthys) depicted as the dual serpent goddesses which are B- in reality manifestations of the one singular essence.

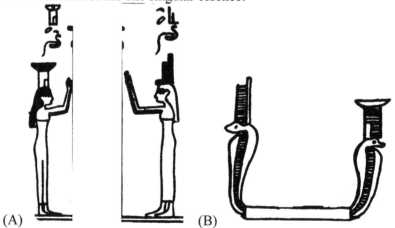

(A)   (B)

Nebthet and Aset are the goddesses of a serpent power. In this form they are known as *Nebty nebty* ('Two Ladies')- and the two serpents 𓏤𓎼𓃒𓃒. The two serpent goddesses are one and the same but operating

---

[83] see the book Serpent Power by Muata Ashby

oppositely. One serpent represents downward movement (Nebthet), the movement of Creation and the other represents upward movement (Aset), the movement of dissolution. If you are able to elevate your consciousness to the level of transcending your lower energy centers (energy spheres of the souls of Ra (*Sefech ba Ra*), called *Chakras* in Indian Yoga), you begin to die to the world of time and space, the Nebthet aspect, which includes the physical body, the physical nature and mortality, finiteness, the fleetingness of the world. This allows you to begin to die to the world to give birth to that Anpu right thinking consciousness within you, that righteous mind, the discerning mind as opposed to the mindless mind, that acts on impulse based on egoistic notions and desires; Anpu is an instinct of ethics as opposed to an instinct of ego {Set} based on ignorance that may be defined here as "Absence of the knowledge of the Higher Self." The discerning mind is just like a dog, a canine being, which Anpu is. It cuts off that which is untrue and it has clarified that which is true and follows that. That kind of mind leads you to higher consciousness {Heru}. And so through Nebthet all that is possible. Actually Nebthet is an extremely important and necessary principle, because if you do not have that kind of death you will be running around horizontally, if not downwardly in the world of time and space indefinitely and never have any abiding vertical movement, and that sexual energy, that we discussed, will be expended in the world of time and space and it will be impelling the personality ever forward into all kinds of adventures, dramas and all kinds of time consuming and wasteful searches for fulfillment in the world of time and space, but not upwards and in a meaningful or fulfilling way.

Now, another important nomenclature or terminology that is given related to Nebthet is *Neb Khat* which means lady or lord-ess or mistress of bodies and where this epithet comes from is that she is given the title of Fashioner of the bodies of the gods and goddesses and by implication she fashions all bodies. And we realize that this teaching is similar to another Theurgy (for those of you who attended previous studies), where we did the studies of the god Khnum and Khnum is the potter who fashions human bodies (not souls) out of clay, in other words earth. That is in a related mythic system of Neterianism (Shetaut Neter, Ancient Egyptian Religion). So don't confuse the two).

So, Nebthet is known as the creator of bodies; she creates the bodies of the gods and goddesses, and realize that the images (iconographies) of the gods and goddesses represent principles, and they need to have forms that they can embody so that the human mind can understand them because otherwise if it is too abstract it is too difficult for the untrained mind to understand. So therefore, that principle that Nebthet represents as creator of bodies is extremely important, otherwise it would be beyond human ability to understand those beings, and those principles (the neteru) and from a practical perspective, without Nebthet human bodies could not take shape in the world of time and space. However, as the Lady of the House and as goddess of earth, the temporal and fleeting, so too her creations, including her bodies are temporal and fleeting; thus, the bodies she creates are not immortal but mortal and finite. So therefore, as Neb Khat, lady of the bodies, she has an extremely important role in the Kemetic Religion.

Another important aspect as we have discussed above was the aspect which cannot be understated, that the goddess in conjunction with goddess Aset are also Serpent Power goddesses. Serpent Power is the form of Life Force that is used by the Creator to create Creation. It is also the same energy that sustains human life and which a human being uses to create. That creation can take the form of offspring or can also be ideas, works in time and space or spiritual enlightenment. The creations in lower time and space, the physical world (the Ta realm), occur when the Serpent Power is allowed to flow downwards, the Nebthet direction; creations in upper time and space, (the Pet and Duat realms) occur when the Serpent Power is allowed to flow upwards, in the Aset direction. The Nebethet movement represents physicality and ego production; the Aset movement represents dissolution towards that which is spiritual and ultimately enlightening. So, these two goddesses are the embodiment of the serpent power energy that has been divided into two aspects. One is a downward moving aspect and the other one is an upward moving aspect. These are complementary opposites also, one is a cooling aspect (Nebthet) and one is a fiery aspect (Aset). One is a coagulating aspect (Nebthet) and one is a disintegrating aspect (Aset). If these two principles are mastered and balanced, then that allows the personality to, as if, congeal the two energies and this is the principle of the Maatian form of the two goddesses. The two serpents collapse into one force and that is the one serpent that moves up the balance scale of Maat, in other words the spine. The balance scale of Maat is actually the central shaft of the human spine. The two goddesses preside over that creative or dissolving movement depending on a person's level of spiritual maturity which is dependent on their level of self-knowledge, which in turn affects their behavior, how much they adhere to or stray away from a path of order and truth (Maat).

So therefore what this means, in a practical sense, is that working with the lower serpent allows one to develop and do works in the realm of time and space. Doing those works in a manner based on truth allows one to have entry into the subtle form of the second life force energy which is represented by Aset and therefore, this is why Aset would be the next principle in the path of the Tree of Life system.

Now, Nebthet, therefore, represents the mysteries of another aspect she has which is symbolized in her relationship with Asar. This is the aspect or feature of the voluptuous nature of the world, the seductive nature of the world and without you're actually knowing it, you have fallen prey to it when you succumb to the desires for the world and its objects and/or belief systems (relative realities). You are actually dying and when you have sexual experiences and actually, all experiences are really aspects of sexual experiences because they relate to acquiring something to make yourself whole and the life force of Nebthet sustains that process. For example, when you eat something, when you hug someone, or when you go out and feel the warmth of the sun or think about a garden and smell the roses. If you like the change of the seasons or if you like being by the beach, all these things are seductive and all these things that are wonderful and beautiful about the world, the stars and the wondrous universe, etc., all that beckons you come outside of yourself and that is a death to the inner higher self. What we are talking about here is that, if you were to discover the wholeness that you are, you do not need to be looking into anything in the world and you will not care about anything in the world. You would be indifferent to it all; if it is there it is fine, if it is not there it is also fine. You are not desiring to go to Hawaii or to Bahamas to experience the so called wonderful beaches and the sunshine and the atmosphere and the food and all the people you can meet and make friends and those kind of things so you can "enjoy" life and have "a good time" etc. But if there is that call to go out and have experiences and enjoyments, that call is beckoning to you to the death of your soul, of your higher personality because it causes you to degrade yourself and be dependent upon limited and finite experiences for your enjoyment, for your sense of worth and dependence upon the delusion that life is meaningful and worthwhile if you can only "enjoy" it in accordance with the desires of the ego self within you. But those limited and finite experiences can never lead to fulfillment so the soul remains disintegrated with Spirit. Integration is life and disintegration is death because it leads to the notion of mortality {Nebthet}; integration leads to the understanding {Aset} of immortality and transcending death.

Those who are seduced by Nebthet like Asar, are led to death. Recall the Asarian Resurrection myth; Set was a jealous person and he envied Asar. Set wanted to be king. So he was jealous and he was leading himself to a road of negative thinking to begin with and when the *setian* principle, which is the ego, is lead through unrighteousness through *an-maat* (unrighteousness-the opposite of *Maat*) to entertain thoughts of self-importance, jealousy, envy, these lead to anger, hatred, violence, and so on, to disaster. These thoughts will eventually compel the personality to take actions that are unrighteous, due to passions based on delusion supported by ignorance and vices. This lead to Asar's death and this beckoning of the world of time and space leads to the death of human being and not just a single death but they reincarnate [*uhm ankh*] and have more death experiences and it is like a constant killing process that you are doing to yourself; constant suicide. That is what happens to an ignorant soul. When you are indulging in the world of time and space, out of ignorance, it leads to suffering and death, but that is not necessarily a bad thing if it leads to a process of increasing wisdom. However, it can be a process of interminable suffering if the wisdom never dawns. So, Nebthet's principle of death is supposed to be a good thing. This should not be thought of as a bad thing. Through death, but a real death to worldly desires and egoistic ignorance, the soul can be led to a spiritual awakening through Aset. That is what happened to Asar, as we learn from the Asarian Resurrection myth.

For ordinary people, who are caught up in the world, the prospect of saying goodbye to worldliness, worldly pleasures and the pursuit of egoistic desires is inconceivable. For sages and saints, people who are enlightened, the conception of death to the world of time and space is wonderful and something they look forward to, something to run to and to promote. For those aspirants who are increasing in understanding, they look to the sages to teach them more of this philosophy so they may learn to avoid the folly of most human beings. The ordinary (spiritually ignorant) people, egoistically and ignorantly, think that they are going to find some peace and calm and quiet in the world, some fulfillment. There are many people, for example, who take a vacation, say to the Bahamas, and they may have a good time, being away temporarily from their job, family worries and personal anxieties, so they see how "wonderful" things seems to be there so they try to move there and after going through all the trouble of moving they discover they have the same problems plus possibly some new ones they discovered once they began to live there, all the things that you didn't realize; the same family issues, work related issues are there and new troubles may arise, like you may have too many mosquitoes, or a war may break out or something else may happen that is unforeseen. The idea is that, like the ancient Egyptian proverb states, *"Searching for one's self in the world is the pursuit of an illusion."*

So, the real death that Nebthet should be leading to is a death of the illusoriness of the world that leads to discernment, and that death of discernment means learning truth from untruth which is going to lead you to not pursue the superficial pleasures of the world of time and space. That is the kind of death that is to be sought through a righteous cultivation of your personality and through the disciplines of Kemetic spiritual aspiration which is Heru and when that happens, that discerning insight of Anpu develops. That ability to know right from wrong and then to follow the path of righteousness develops. This is what Anpu represents. Although he is not a direct divinity, per se, of the Tree, he is an ancillary divinity, if you will, of the Asarian Resurrection Myth and the Tree. So he is an important principle in our studies.

So this death that Nebthet is beckoning us towards is actually a wonderful mystery and this is one of the reasons why sexuality is given as one of the symbols of Nebthet. Sexuality between her and Asar is paramount in the understanding of the fact that the sexuality in the world of time and space is that the Principle of Generation in the realm of time and space and it operates in many human pursuits but most grossly in the physical sexual act of intercourse between two physical bodies (animals, humans, insects, etc.) and leads to the generation of offsprings. All generated things, including offsprings, are "things" that come "out" of other "things." Only things that are whole do not come out of other things and do not give themselves to things that come out of other things. So what I am getting at here is rather like a riddle but if you are whole you are not going to indulge in things that are un-whole. But somebody comes to you and asks you to go out partying with him and to go and have a "good time" and you say "well I am already having a good time here. I don't need to be going out with you." That person is going to be going out to the bar today and then tomorrow they are going to go across town to another night club then they are going to go flying to New York or some other city in search of more enjoyment, more entertainments and in reality more distractions away from what is real and true. Consider that if you have a mature attitude about life and insight into the teaching you gain pleasure and peace from meditative practice, study of the philosophical teachings and you get enjoyment from looking at the iconographies of the neteru and listening to or reading about the myths about the neteru and their teachings. That person is in the pursuit of generation, the fragmented reality of life, and you are in the realm of seeking the whole based on the higher truth of the underlying Spirit in which all things are connected. That pursuit of wholeness gives you peace of mind as supposed to that person's distracted and undiscerning mind. That person has a clouded intellect and a wrestles heart. You have a clear intellect, and therefore, you have death to the things that that person is into. However, that person is giving himself to death but really unable to fully fulfill the promise of that death, so he must continue pursuing enjoyment after enjoyment and then at the end of life also come back to do it again, to be reincarnated again. So in life there will be no abiding peace for that person and in death there will be no peace either, only more coming to the world again to run like a hamster on a wheel, doing a lot of activity, running fast but getting nowhere! Now that is a pathetic situation and most people in the world are in it; that's how they live and that is why the world is in the condition it is in; it is filled with people pursuing egoistic desires and not listening to the voices of reason, wisdom and enlightenment.

In other words, the Anpu principle or quality has not been born in them yet, and therefore, their death is a form of suffering but the death of the authentic spiritual aspirant is a boon. It is a pleasurable experience; they don't have any feeling of missing anything in the world or a feeling of desiring anything in the world. To them all the money that worldly people can have cannot compare to that peace.

Set and Nebthet are the divinities of time and space of the gross ego consciousness. Asar and Aset are divinities of the higher aspects of the ego consciousness. They are higher aspects of the personality. As we said before, when Set and Nebthet are mastered and when Asar and Aset are discovered then the higher aspect of Heru is born and one eventually becomes the master of one's personality and the lower realm of time and space of the gross physical world.

I want to give you here a preview of an extraordinary aspect of the teaching related to the goddesses. I will mention a special secret of the goddess Aset. You must realize that the special secret that I am about to reveal to you and which I will elaborate on next time is predicated upon the idea that you as an aspirant have mastered the teachings so far, that you have purified yourself to a certain degree, that you have sought to act in accordance with the ways of the teaching; that you have sought to purify your body, your mind, and your actions in accordance with the teachings through study of the philosophy; and that you have sought to promote the righteous worship of the divinities of the divine within your self and so on and so forth. Otherwise you will not realize its full meaning yet; the secret will have no use for you, even now as I tell it to you, you will not be able to have sensitivity to realize the worldly death and the importance of what has been said. This has been said already and yet I am putting it in such a way and I have made you wait a whole week to hear about it, but you are not going to hear about it fully today because the teaching should be given in order so that you can build gradually on a teaching and lead yourself to fully be able to appreciate it. If the teaching is given to you too soon you will not fully appreciate it. You will not be able to. You won't even know if you should or not.

We talked previously about the secret of Aset that allows the personality to have respite, a break from the realm of time and space and there are two specific occasions in which Aset performs the special *act* and this is related to the aspect or the epithet of Nebthet referred to as Urt Hekau. Aset is also known as Urt Hekau and she is the most popular divinity known as Urt Hekau. Urt Hekau means great goddess of verse or great of chant/words of power. On two specific occasions which I will tell you about next time in detail, Aset used her words of power in order to stop the realm of time and space, the realm of generation. With her words of power, she was able to stop the mental distraction to stop temporarily the realm of generation in order to give the soul a rest so that it could penetrate into higher realms of consciousness. It is as the ancient Egyptian proverb states: *"Virtues fail that are frustrated by passion at every turn."* You should realize that if you are constantly, and we emphasize the word "constantly" here, distracted by the realm of time and space, it will thwart the positive spiritual movement. That would be like being in the back of a pickup truck without having a chance to get seated properly. Someone makes you jump in and right away they step on the gas and they tell you to hang on somehow, and you are trying to find a way but you don't have a seat belt on, you don't have any kind of a protection and they go over a bump, so you go flying. Now on the other hand, suppose you had been able to take a seat, secure yourself and then go. This metaphorically speaking would be like calming the waters as it were, of the mind, in order to have peaceful time where you are not overburdened by the realm of time and space so you could gather yourself and reflect on the deeper realities of life and the secret of causing that to happen is uttering the chant. If you were to practice those as they have an outlined eventually what will happen is that your mental operations will cease and you will have an entry into the nether worlds, into the higher consciousness leading you to a brief communion with your Higher Self, with Asar and the Yanrutef and this is the great secret of Aset and the aspect of Urt-hekau but we are going to discuss those in particular next time.

As the teaching goes, as the scriptures say many times, -for those who have ears let them hear – if you realize the importance of what has been said you should be looking at all the books I have written and look into all the things I have said about hekau and especially in the initiation book and realize that it has to be practiced in a way by mature and purified individuals, otherwise it can have deleterious effects. So therefore, this is why you are told to practice the chants as enjoined and that way they will have a full and total effect on the mind and we will discuss this in detail next time.

And that, for now, is the aspect of Nebthet in the Anunian Theurgy Tree of Life and the mysteries of life and death.

HTP
Sebai Dr. Muata Ashby

Special Comment by Seba Dr. Dja Ashby based on Lesson 8

I just wanted to read a proverb from the Egyptian Proverb book, from the new version, on page 86 in the section on controlling the emotion senses that relates to everything that has been said in this lesson.

It says, *"When ye have served your time, and have put off the world's restraint, and freed yourselves from deathly bonds, pray that GOD may restore you pure and holy to the nature of your higher self, that is of the Divine! Those who have lived in other fashion - impiously - both is return to Heaven denied, and there's appointed them migration into other bodies unworthy of a holy soul and base...souls in their life on earth run risk of losing hope of future immortality."*

So Sebai MAA (Dr. Muata Ashby) talked about the process of *uhm ankh* incarnation when you allow yourself to become seduced by Nebthet, seduced by the world. Sometimes it does not seem so bad, because you may say "Oh I will come back, Oh I will just try it again. I will just get a new body and go on, but you must always remember that to have any human birth is a very special experience and occasion and it is not a guarantee that in one's next lifetime one will be born into a human body. You don't know what the *ariu* is and still has a and what will come out and what you would be reincarnated as in the realm of time and space. And as the proverb says – you run the risk of coming back in to other bodies that are not worthy, they are not worthy of a holy soul and base. You may come back as a rat, as a cockroach, and also you must remembered that when we talk about leaving the realm of time and space or getting away from worldly pleasures, not allowing yourself to become seduced by them that there are two aspects to that. One is the physical aspect of moving away from that which you are easily seduced by if you cannot control yourself mentally. One can move away by putting a limit on it; physically you actually take yourself away from the scene before the crime occurs, so to speak, before you indulge in whatever passion it is, that you may befall. So, this is where good association comes in. Good association[84] is keeping yourself in contact with associations that are positive, that promote the higher aspects of your being. So good association in itself means gathering to hear the teachings, in *Shedy* meetings, that have been espoused. You are actually practicing moving away from the physical world, the seduction of the physical world, in a positive way. Some people will do it, instead of going to the *shedy* meetings, going to good association, where they can actually be learning how to develop from the physical to the mental control, some people actually move across state or move out of the country to try to escape from whatever it is that they are trying to run from or divorce this person to get away from this person and think this person is a bad person and go marry someone else. They may kill their spouses thinking that the spouses are the source of burden in their life. All sorts of unrighteousness can occur. Really, physically he can never run away from it. Don't try to run away from what bothers you or what is bugging you. This is like running away from your shadow; because really, the source of the bother, the source of the seductiveness, the source of the succumbing to the passions, is in your mind. The *ari,* the residues[85] that we talked about in previous lectures, the mental impressions from performing actions and allowing yourself in the performance of the action to say "I am really enjoying this" and "this is really good" to feed into the ego personality and that builds the delusion into the personality, and the delusion becomes so thick, like fog, that you cannot see through it clearly; just think of Asar when he was intoxicated.[86] How he allowed himself to be seduced by Nebthet. So when the mind becomes deluded, intoxicated, the normal reasoning capacity becomes obscured. And you may think this is why people fall pray to the world all the time. Right, I guess in AA[87] there are some people who are "on the wagon" and "off the wagon." I met people who said "O I stopped smoking for four years and then one night I went to some party and somebody gave me a cigarette, and I have not been able to stop since then". Probably in that same party, they got a little drunk, they got a little intoxicated. Everybody around them was smoking and carrying on and there was somebody who lit up a cigarette and then they said "oh I

---

[84] 𓏲𓈖𓅓𓏏 *knumt-nefer* –"good association, divine association, joining others, together."

[85] *ariu* –psychic impressions left in the unconscious mind by previous actions, thoughts and desires – may be thought of as a residue that remains.

[86] In the Asarian Resurrection myth the god Asar became intoxicated with enjoyments and he was seduced by the goddess Nebthet.

[87] Alcoholics anonymous

will just have one." And here they are now, four years later, still having that "one." So one has to be very careful with allowing oneself to fall in with the negative associations, to make that association even for a moment. One should never test oneself and say "well I've been good for so long" I have not done this bad thing. Let me go and put myself in that situation and let me see if I can control it, or overcome it or if I can stay away from it, if I can restrain myself. One should never do that. At some time the divine will appropriately test you in a natural way. And you will have your chance and if you allow it to occur in that way you will be more than likely to be ready to have a capacity to overcome it. So, physical withdrawal is one aspect, but the higher aspect is actually developing mental detachment, mental withdrawal and thereby not being susceptible to the influence of the tempting objects of the world, the objects of desire of the personality. This occurs in different levels and it occurs in degrees. The highest occurs when one understands one's highest nature because, as Sebai MAA (Dr. Muata Ashby) said, when you understand your true essence you become one whole. There is no more desire. There is nothing that you want; there is nothing you need to complete yourself. So there is nowhere to go and there is no where to not go. There is nowhere to be and there is nowhere to not be. There is not one place to be versus another; like being in the ocean. Which part of the ocean is better than the other? It is all the same water. So one must strive, really, if one wants to over come this seductiveness this attachment of the ego personality, to the body consciousness, not to kill one's body, which is not going to work; (You are just going to get reincarnated and as I said, you might be into something worse than a human body, than even a lowly human body.) but rather, one must strive to eradicate the subtle unconscious impressions of the pleasures of the senses. So in essence, as one must continue one's practice of *shedy* until the *Nehast* is attained and the movement should not stop until that point.

Reflection and Journal discipline:

1- At the top of each page copy the following hieroglyphs to the best of your ability

 [***cht n ankh*** *" tree of life"*]

After studying the Lesson proceed to answer the following question and write the answer in your journal. This exercise will require more than one reading and more than one journal entry, at least one page; write all you can find related to the subject of the question. Answer the questions first without referring to the text you just read. Then go back and see if you missed anything. This exercise is to be repeated until you become proficient with the principles of this sphere. The reflection exercise should be done after each reading or study session. Then you may practice meditation[88] on the wisdom you have learned. You may come back to add to your reflections even if you move on to other lessons.

REFLECTIONS: Let me know the Lady of the House…let me see the truth of her charms and the glory of her body even if it will die one day as I will die one day through her auspices. But let her lead me to her child of righteous mind and to her sister of wise truths and let my death be a death onto the life beyond and not to the ignorance below!

After studying the Lesson proceed to answer the following question and write the answer in your journal.

What is(are) the main teaching(s) of this lesson and what do the principle(s) of the divinity(ies) discussed in this lesson mean in reference to my actions, feelings, thoughts and desires and understanding of the spiritual philosophy?

What is the problem with wandering behind the different arrangement of things?

---

[88] Explained in more detail in Lesson 15

Lesson 8: The Principle of Aset, and how to Discover and Adopt the Cosmic Wisdom That Leads to Enlightenment on the Journey of the Tree of Life

We continue now, our studies of the Anunian Theurgy, Tree of Life spiritual evolution system. Before we lead into today's topic I would like to reiterate a couple of points from last time. These are a couple of key points about the principles of Aset and Nebthet. One aspect of Aset that I don't believe we touched on, well we touched on in previous lectures in a different series, is the principle of the fetters of Set, the *Saiu Set*. Saiu Set means "the bandage that goes over the mouth; you can see that in the system of gods and goddesses [Plate 1]. The Gods and Goddesses iconomythograph relates all of the main divinities of Neterianism and it shows their interconnections. On the bottom of that diagram, you will see all the main forms of Heru in the three major theurgys. The Anunian Theurgy, Memphite Theurgy and Wasetian Theurgy. The child aspect of Heru, who is the divine solar child of the Anunian Theurgy, who we discussed in the Anunian Theology lectures series is that aspect of in Memphite Theurgy called Nefertem and in Theban Theurgy the same Heru is called Khonsu. In Asarian Theurgy he is Heru sa Asar sa Aset (Heru the son of Asar son of Aset), and Heru Ur, among others.

Figure 51: Heru as Nefertem, sitting on the Lotus (the Creation) that arises out of the Primeval Ocean

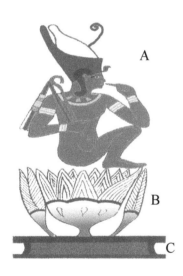

In this iconography, the Divine Child(A) is the master of Creation, the Lotus(B) is Creation itself and the Primeval Ocean (pool symbol (C)) is the substratum from which the Creation arises. As the Nefertem aspect, he points to his mouth. He utters Heka (words of power) and the world comes into being and Set is the opposite to that. Remember that we talked about the opposites of Creation in the form of the divinities as well as complementary opposites or direct opposites. In this particular point we are discussing, Set and Heru are direct opposites. Heru is the one who speaks and whose words bring forth creation into being and Set is the divinity that stops the speech and we know this because it is specified in the myth of the Asarian Resurrection. Now in this series, the pointing to the mouth conception or teaching, relates to *ra* – ra is the mouth or *ro* – in modern Coptic language. When the divinities speak their words can affect Creation because they have power. Ordinary human beings also have power in speech but not so much to bring physical items into existence, but they can bring ideas and feelings into existence and those can have great consequences in the physical realm. The reason why the mouth brings forth powerful words, the words that bring creations into being, is because it is tied directly to the unconscious mind. The unconscious level of mind is the subtlest and therefore the most powerfully vibrating energies are there. But if the unconscious mind is clouded, and is beset with egoism, with anger, hatred, greed, lust, envy, jealousy, etc. then those creations, are going to be curtailed, limited and tainted. Yes, you will create all kinds of unrighteousness. But unrighteousness, since it is not ultimately real, cannot be said to be a creation, speaking from a philosophical perspective. So, that is Saiu Set. On the other hand, spiritual aspiration, what Heru represents, is antithetical to the Saiu Set and antithetical to the fetters and each fetter has a corresponding virtue. So the way to confront the fetters is with the practice of their corresponding virtue. Therefore, if you hate somebody you should practice love, if you are a violent person, you should practice non-violence. If you do the opposite, you will neutralize the fetters and if you continue on this process, going beyond just the neutralization effect, which means, not just being a good person, a compassionate, loyal, ethical, etc. person it will bring positive situations in life. That is a good thing but that is not going to liberate you from ignorance that causes sorrow in life and the cycle of birth and death; it only brings you peaceful conditions and prosperity more than sorrow and pain. It is not going to lead you to enlightenment and immortality in other words. You must go beyond just being a good person and that happens when you grow in wisdom, the studies of the mysteries of the mystical philosophy such as the teaching of the Tree of Life. We saw how Nebthet facilitates that passage. She is the doorway. You know how some people are, they want to go to heaven, but they don't want to die and you have to go through Nebthet because she is death in order to experience the bliss of the transcendent. She is therefore a beneficent being, meaning, she does away with your physical body so you can experience the higher forms of consciousness; but if you go on holding onto your egoism that curtails your spiritual evolution.

So, we talked about the mysteries of death and how when the soul, in the form of Asar is intoxicated with the world, how it becomes seduced by the worldliness and since Asar's heart was pure, that led him to the resurrection. However, for most people, it leads them to reincarnation. And again this process was discussed in the story of *SaAsar*. This teaching talks about the levels of consciousness that the soul experiences after death and the passage way into another world.

But here, as far as the Anunian Tree of Life is concerned, with the divinities, the emphasis is on understanding that this level is the first level [Set and Nebthet] that we are trying to climb over or to raise ourselves through on the path to reaching the highest, which is Ra. This is the level of worldliness and egoism, the vices, the worldly desires and so on and so forth and by becoming virtuous, we over come those.

It is important here to understand the principle of virtue as the goddess of Virtue, Maat {Ma'at}, is an aspect of the goddess of wisdom, Aset. Virtue, Ma'at, meaning truth, order, justice purifies the soul so that it can contemplate through mental clarity, the higher perspectives of life. In other words, it develops spiritual sensitivity. Otherwise, if the personality is controlled by Set and Nebthet, the mind remains nebulous and the conception of soul and wisdom escapes you. Asar and Aset escape you, they are beyond your capacity for understanding. They are like some kind of the theoretical conception that is not really clear to you. How is this problem to be overcome?

In order to be able to achieve the proper understanding of the Neterian philosophy it is necessary to cleanse the personality. The personality is cleansed through the "liquor of Ma'at," as the Ma'at teaching says, which is given to you in the writing of the Maat Papyrus.[89] Maat is a goddess, a cosmic force operating in the universe, a spiritual principle of ari {karma} and reincarnation as well as a philosophy of order, balance, truth and reciprocity operating through virtue and wisdom or disorder, imbalance and misfortune operating through vice. The "liquor of Ma'at" is a kind of aura that envelopes a person with positive feelings and virtuous energies and thoughts that counteract and wash away iniquitous feelings and thoughts due to unrighteous actions of the past and unrighteous, selfish thoughts and forms of understanding that cloud the intellect. The "liquor of Ma'at" is acquired through ritual and action as well as study of maatian teachings based on maatian principles. The Maat papyrus says, "Maat neb bu ten" {Ma'at is everywhere}. "Cha hena Maat" {rise in the morning with Maat}. *"Ankh hena Maat"* {live with Ma'at} and then "Ha sema Maat" {means your body becomes one with Ma'at, your very actions, your very thoughts and your deeds, and your speech become "Ma'atian" in nature}. Part of the maat teaching refers to the lower practice. These relate to the previous levels of the teaching, when you are rising with Ma'at, when you were living with Ma'at, when you were practicing truth from the 42 principles of Maat and then the teaching of righteousness and so on and so forth. They relate to the level when an aspirant is learning that "Maat Ankhu Maat," realizing Ma'at is the source of life. All these are lower aspects, lower rungs on the practice of Ma'at' philosophy. This is when you have been following Ma'at and being a good person and you should be doing that and so on and so forth, but up to this level you don't really have an advance idea yet, any conception of the higher perspective of life or mystical awareness of transcendental being. When you start having "Ha sema Maat," that is when the mysticism starts kicking in, when you start becoming one with Ma'at; knowing by

---

[89] See the book *introduction to Maat Philosophy* by Dr. Muata Ashby

becoming one with divinity you start perceiving Ma'at within yourself, as yourself and as your actions. Your personality becomes purified as it becomes blended with Ma'at. A cosmic communion or union occurs between you and Ma'at. Since Ma'at is one with the universe, one with all, and since she is an aspect of God, then of course you become one with God as well.

Figure 52: Goddess Maat, a form of Goddess Aset

Now, acting with truth and order and righteousness is one of the first steps that lead you to understand the philosophy of Ma'at. Ma'at, of course, is an aspect of Aset, this is told to us in the scriptures. Ma'at is a manifestation of Aset, a form of Aset. As discussed previously. There are two Maat Goddesses, referred to as "Maati" and you may surmise that the two Maat goddesses are indeed also Aset and Nebthet but we are mainly here talking about the Aset form. Having mastered the principle of Set and Nebthet, or having overcome the egoism and vices through the aspiration of Heru, and having accepted, at least philosophically, if not yet intuitionally, the wisdom of the illusoriness of the world and having developed an aspiration to transcend the world of time and space and everything that it represents (pain and sorrow of the world and ultimate physical death) an aspirant can have entry into the wisdom of Aset. Now, I told you about Nebthet which is the principle of worldliness and death as well as destruction, pain and sorrow of the world. Having decided that you want to die to the world you are preferring to give the soul life instead of allowing your soul, your immortality, to die because that is what you are doing when you indulge in worldliness in an ignorant way. When you promote ignorance you are allowing your immortality to die in you or it is dead to you. Of course when we use the term "die" it is metaphorical because the soul remains after the passing of the physical body since it is immutable, and transcendental but, to you, as a personality, your soul and it's peace, immortality and transcendental awareness are as if dead to you, unreachable for you. So your worldliness through Nebthet is killing your body and your egoism through Set is killing your ability to perceive eternity. That is the worldly perspective of life, the predicament of worldly people, how life is when you are a worldly conscious person, aware only of time and space and individuality, even as the body deteriorates with old age. This is a cause of the deterioration of the mind in older people. For those who are advancing spiritually, their minds become stronger as the body grows older.

For true aspirants, the passage from life to death through Nebthet, as we discussed last time, through turning the worldly desiring mind into a Divine Self desiring mind. Meditation on the divine and higher principles of life, allows you to awaken to your higher nature and this is what happened to Asar. When his physical body died or was killed by Set it actually led to his resurrection in a higher and more powerful form. How did this come about? Did it happen on its own? Nebthet was the agent of the death and Aset was the agent of the resurrection. The resurrection is promoted through the wisdom and energy transformation of the personality that occurs through the mechanism of the Tree of Life system of spiritual evolution, meaning the whole cycle, the spiritual mechanism that we have been discussing; including all these principles that are psycho-spiritual metaphysical and mystic principles and how they interact and transform the personality from lower being to higher being. If you known the secrets of how they interact you also known the secrets of how to understand their inner workings within you, your own mind and you also discover their transcendental aspect within yourself.

When Asar and Nebthet came together, they created Anpu as we discussed last time. As introduced earlier, discernment, purity of mind, the ability to know right from wrong, truth from untruth, reality from unreality are the hallmarks of Anpu mind. These qualities are essential in the beginning of the spiritual journey as well as in the more advanced practice. If you have developed this capacity then you are well along the way to opening the doors to Aset. If you have not developed Anpu mind you are incapable of discerning truth from untruth you are gullible, you believe anything your friends say, politicians say or religious leaders say, you believe everything they say on television, the advertisements, you go and buy whatever they tell you. Externally you believe anything that is put before you. Internally you believe the voice of the ego because the ego tells you I desire this or that and whatever I desire I should have because I want it and it is ok to want whatever I want. This delusion is reinforced by the idea of death, that you should enjoy life and not waste the opportunity to experience pleasure, as if you cannot experience pleasure any other way than through the body and at the time of death all opportunities for pleasure and happiness end. Of course this is proof that, even though people may say they have faith in God, they may say they have faith in an afterlife, etc. in reality their hearts are filled with doubt, fear, ignorance and loathing about the prospect of death so they want to take advantage of doing whatever they can while alive. If you want to have a sports car, you say "I have to have it, I want it and I would enjoy that." Or if your ego tells you or it agrees with others that have told you that you are a terrible person, will you believe that too? If you become depressed or suicidal, because you are denigrated or attacked or because you feel like a failure because you have not acquired the things you desire, will you cut yourself with a razor blade, will you take pills and drugs to relieve yourself and so on and so forth? Of course, given the nature of the world as we have explained it here, to be running after it for pleasure and happiness is a ridiculous ideal. This understanding needs to be firmly grasped by the mind of a spiritual aspirant. Otherwise there will be no progress on the spiritual path beyond a certain point.

This entire world which is created by the supreme divinity is a manifestation, as we discussed, of all these principles which are vibrating, like waves in an ocean, and Nebthet had given them these vibration bodies that we can see. The counterpart to this conception in the Memphite Theurgy is where the god Ptah utters the names of the divinities and as the sound vibrations pass through his teeth out into the environment – they take on clothing and the clothing is every thing that you see. Everything physical, that you can perceive, and the non-physical that you cannot, for that matter, are the bodies of the subtle principles that are behind them. The physical world in other words, are the elements vibrating at different rates, which is why they appear to be different from each other and the elements are the gods and goddesses, the neteru and the neteru are manifestations, projections of the Transcendental Divinity. This is consciousness vibrating at different rates and we call them neteru and when the sustaining consciousness that is behind these principles, the neteru, withdraws them the entire so called hard cold realities, the solid, concrete, distinct objects that you perceive dissolves. That same consciousness that is behind the entire universe is the same consciousness that is the inner deepest reality within you. Therefore, if you were to realize the higher essence within yourself, you would be able to also withdraw your consciousness from this reality and make it disappear. If you were to succeed in the practice of meditation, this is exactly what happens. This is what was meant when we said that meditation is a pathway to death, an entry into Nebthet and through to Aset also.

Nebthet represents death to the lower aspect, to the physical world and Aset represents a kind of resurrection into the subtle aspect, the netherworld, to the higher consciousness. This is the high teaching, the great philosophy behind the secret that we talked about at the end of the last lecture. If you were to understand the wisdom of mind, if you were to be able to control, to cleanse the personality (the personality is like a pane of glass and you have different layers) you would have clarity, realizing that the opaqueness of that glass is merely an illusion created by your own dirt, the impurities of the personality are the dirt.

Before going into the principle of Aset, let us discuss the concept of mind to know where Aset fits in. In Neterian conception, the philosophical mystical conception, there is the basic level of mind and that is Anpu and different levels that animals have also, instinct. You do need to know distinct reality and to have a demarcation between yourself and the objects of the world as well as your desires and feelings about the world. You also need to be able to discern what is a need versus a desire. You need to see clearly what is right from wrong, I am hungry or not hungry, this is a friend or this is an enemy, I should bark or I should not bark – the basic level of mind – I am in pain, I am not in pain, etc. Human beings have another capacity which is the intellect. Animals do not have intellect. Intellect is presided over by the divinity Djehuti. Intellect, in our context, is defined as the ability to put meaning to your thoughts or to your perceptions about the world, to evaluate them in reference to your ego personality and the world as well as to the past, present or future and also in relation to desires, values and or aspirations and imaginations; of course we are putting these things in cut and dried ways but most people, and of course, this includes yourselves, have mixed mental capacity. Some things are very clear and some things are clouded. Some things people have power over, to control – they can control not smoking, but at other times they can't control sex. Some persons if they can control sex they can't control smoking. Some can control anger at another person but cannot control deceptiveness, deviousness. Some can be compassionate to others but not to themselves. This complexity of the human personality occurs because the *ariu* have been layered at different levels in the unconscious mind, the *ab*, which is the container of the impressions of thoughts, desires and intellectual concepts the personality has believed in throughout many lives and these are lodged in the mind.

Beyond intellect, we have Aset. Aset means wisdom. It means knowledge. But this is a special form of wisdom, the kind that is known and not just by experiencing it but being it –this is called intuition and it transcends the thinking process – thoughts are not part of the intuitional realization. An ancillary aspect to Aset is ▱▱⊠ *saa-*{understanding}. ▱▱⊠ 𓅮 *Saa-ndjs* means "to not know, not understand, ignorance, smallness-pettiness in knowledge, weakness and evil." **Saa** is the "aha!" moment that you have when you realize the truth of something, what it is, how it works, etc. Aset is the knowing that occurs upon becoming one with what is known. This is called "*gnosis*" by the followers of Gnosticism. Gnosis is the basis of Gnostic spiritual traditions (Gnosticism) which are based on knowing the divine by being one with it. The opposite of Gnosticism is agnosticism. An agnostic is not necessarily a person who does not believe in God or a divinity, but a person who does not believe that God can be known or the ultimate reality can be known. Gnosticism is the practice of leading the mind to know. As you can see, Neterianism is an Ancient Egyptian Gnostic tradition which was practiced thousands of years before the later Egyptian and Greek Gnostics of the pre Christian era developed as a distinct group. Gnostic Christianity was one of the sects of Gnosticism that developed in the late period of Ancient Egyptian history related to the concept of Jesus.[90] Specifically, it was strong in the Ancient Egyptian city of Alexandria.[91]

So, from Anpu, we go to Djehuti, and from Djehuti we go to Saa, from Saa we go to Aset, and then from Aset we go to what we termed as *un ren Ra* or the transcendent name of the God Ra, the Creator and High God of Gods. This is the ultimate reality of the name of Ra. If we were to raise ourselves up to a level of Aset which is like a jumping off point into the transcendent, then we would be able to stop time to make the creation disappear to discover what lies beyond time & with it, space. Space has no meaning without time; without the passage of time things do not change and their meaning comes in only with the movements and changes and without time there can be no movements or changes so without time the objects of space revert to undifferentiated matter, the primeval Ocean, the Nun. Now we are going to see how that happens.

First of all we will introduce the glyphs of goddess 𓊨𓏤𓆓 *Aset* {the goddess}. The Goddess Aset has three main hieroglyphs related to her; one is the throne chair 𓊨 (which also means abode, dwelling place) and that is actually what is called in Ancient Egyptian grammar, a triliteral or triphonic[92] sound sign because it has the sound of three consonants. It is a group of three consonants in one symbol "Ast". The vowels may or may not be written along with the consonants. This entire word can be spelled out or can be contained in that one symbol. When spelled out it has the ⊂ symbol the symbol for the letter **"t",** and an ○ egg and symbol for a woman, 𓁐, any female. Notice that if we look at the symbols of the headdresses of the goddesses Aset and Nebthet we obtain the same throne symbol in both. The headdress of Nebthet contains 𓉗 *het,* which means house. If we clear off the top and left lines of the house of Nebthet we obtain 𓊨, which is the hieroglyphic symbol of Aset 𓊨 *ast,* meaning throne. So Nebthet means house as in a building that contains an abode. That abode is the throne, Aset. Aset means point or focus of rulership, the throne seat upon which the soul, Asar, resides; it is its abode. In this sense Aset is not bound by the enclosure; her dominion is unencumbered, she is the queen of all through her wisdom while Nebthet is Lady of the House. The house here is a metaphor of Creation itself, but Aset's wisdom transcends the dominion of Time and Space.

The symbol of the throne is important here. As discussed last time, Nebthet is the lady of the house, lady of the physical world, the physical realm. Aset is not that, she is lady of the point, the spot, shall we say, and that is the chair which symbolizes the throne from which the ruler rules over all, the seat of power from which all the activities of the dominion are directed.

---

[90] see the book *Mystical Journey from Jesus to Christ* by Dr. Muata Ashby
[91] ibid
[92] see the book *Ancient Egyptian Hieroglyphs for Beginners* by Dr. Muata Ashby

Now if you want to attain  *rechtu,* which means "wisdom," you must follow the teaching of Aset. Rech is associated with the term *rechat,* which means "wisdom personified, Aset, Lady of Wisdom" and this is one of the titles of Aset. The understanding of what Aset represents gives an indication of the path to wisdom. You cannot be all over the place in the world, you cannot be worldly, indulging in the seductions of Nebthet and also at the same time pursue wisdom. There are two ways that this can be handled, either you, in a disciplinary way, curtail your worldly activities or you psychologically cut them off. You can cut them off physically and you can cut them psychologically. But if you do that physically, by avoiding the worldly situations that might force you to confront the worldly people, objects and situations that could get you caught up in dramas or distract your attention and may possibly allow you to indulge in desires for the objects of the world, there is a problem because you cut off interacting with the world. If you don't go to work you can't make money, you can't pay your rent, and they come and kick you out, you would be on the streets. When winter time comes you will be sleeping on a park bench and when winter comes you will be shivering and you won't be able to think about any higher philosophy at that point. If you say you can go to a shelter and then they will give you some soup and a bed what about the down side? You don't have a private place of your own, you don't have clothes, you smell, you have lice, you could have people pick-pocketing you or beating you up, or worse. What we are getting at is that even as the teaching is studied and the philosophy applied in life a practical way of engaging the world is necessary; a certain level of interaction with the world to sustain yourself is required and also beneficial. In any case, most people are unable to work on their fetters without interacting with the world, so the world has its purpose in the divine plan for the spiritual evolution of a human being. However, some physical distance needs to be maintained in order to have separation from the world so as to be able to work on the fetters of the soul; otherwise there would be confusion in the mind as to where the personality ends and where the world begins and that will thwart the spiritual movement. The teaching says that you should "live by love and necessity." You don't live to become rich, you live by working to take care of your necessities; to that extent you involve yourself with other people, your family members and the practical realities of life, like having a job. So you try to minimize those so they don't take your attention away from the important things of life. If you are able to accomplish that, that will lead you to clarity. The other way is, you can go through philosophical insight, realizing your way beyond the reality of the world and you are able to shut it off that way too but that is not so easy.

Through the wisdom of Aset, things will happen in the world, objects cross your path, thoughts and feelings come and go and philosophically you can get to understand them to be illusory in a way so you don't let yourself be bothered by them. This is an art, the way of handling the mind, it is a practice that you get better at over time and the discipline you follow for your spiritual development has to be a blend of those two, the practical and philosophical/psychological. Eventually, the psychological becomes more powerful and then whether your physical aspect is involved in the world or not you will be able to maintain yourself above it; then you are able to disengage and be free of it. In order for that to happen you must understand the philosophy of Aset, which relates to the philosophy of the wisdom about the nature of Creation and the nature of who you are essentially, which is not your ego conscience or your individuality, your body, your name, your relationships, accomplishments or anything about your personal history; all that is "what" you are but we want to know "who" you are? Before going into that, we will discuss the iconography of Goddess Aset.

Figure 53: Headdress of Goddess Aset

First of all, Aset is most often represented as a woman, as a physical and anthropomorphic personality. There are three different from of iconography in Ancient Egyptian imagery, anthropomorphic, zoomorphic and composite (combination). The Zoomorphic is like a "zoo," it has to do with animals. The term anthropomorphic has to do with human beings and therefore, the human form. Many times you will see combinations (composite forms) in Neterian religious art and hieroglyphic texts and you also find that in the iconography of Aset. The

vulture headdress ![vulture headdress image] is another important image of Aset. The vulture is a pun of the word *mut* [moot]. Mut means mother. The vulture is the one who eats carrion and turns that back into something alive. That is a process of renewal of life, the resurrection of life. In the Asarian Resurrection myth she resurrects Asar.

Figure 54: Aset as the Cow headed Goddess

Sometimes the crowns may be combined, displaying her multidimensional aspects and how they are dynamically present at the same time. She is at times represented as a lady with the head of a cow or a lady with a woman's head and a headdress of horns and sundisk in the middle. This headdress gives us an understanding that she is the lady of the Trinity – the trinity is contained in the two horns representing past & future and sundisk representing the eternal present. Sometimes she has two plumes, which is the mastery over duality. Sometimes she has the double crown of upper and lower Egypt as the ruler of the "Two Lands". The term "Two Lands" refers to, in a practical (mundane, exoteric) sense, Upper and Lower Egypt but mythically it also represents the physical world and the spiritual world. So she is a lady of non-duality. The two crowns of Upper and Lower Egypt represent duality. When they are worn by the same personality it means that that personality has united those two principles. They become one in that personality and that is what the king and queen, the ⬚ *Peraah* (Pharaoh)[93] does as well, what Heru Ur, the prototype for all Pharaohs, does also, by wearing the double crown of Upper and Lower Egypt.

She is the paramount representation of the principal of motherhood, faith, and devotion which is amply displayed by her actions in the Asarian Resurrection myth as you should recall what happened when Asar was murdered and his body was severed into pieces, what Set, the ego does to the soul. In this aspect she is the diametric opposition and opposite of Set. So, as we explained earlier, Aset is opposition to Set, the one who breaks things into pieces, as he chopped the body of Asar into 14 pieces. She is "one who puts pieces together." She assembles things, like broken pieces of a body but also broken knowledge and that includes the highest knowledge, the knowledge of the whole soul, which has lost its identity having been fragmented into believing it is a finite limited being and yet desiring something more abiding, more transcendental to hold onto; which is why most people search after answers in religion or some other spiritual pursuit. They somehow think they are more than just physical beings even if they do not have a real idea about what that means because their religion cannot help them since it does not have true and powerful mysticism that can enlighten them.

Set chopped up the body of Asar into pieces and strewed them all over the world and then Aset went all over the world looking for them. Set means shooting out, scattering, and so on; Aset means gathering, reconstitution and the like. If you are the person who practices the wisdom teaching, you are a spiritual seeker, you go all over the world putting the pieces together; you may go to universities, visit museums, monuments and special archeological sites, seek out wise people, read many books in many libraries, acquire even more books from bookstores, etc.; all that is really you attempting to put the pieces together of yourself, your soul; and that is Aset energy within you, working in you to put together your conscience of your true Higher Self. When you try to learn anything in the world, you are trying to put back together all the pieces of Asar. If you are an engineer, or you are a veterinarian, or you are a lawyer, a doctor, or even a clerk, a factory worker or an kindergarten school teacher, etc. you have pieces of knowledge of the world. What ever you may be you have a little bit of knowledge but nobody has enough space in their mind to figure it all out especially since they are accumulating relative knowledge from the world of time and space, which is a relative reality to begin with. This is like the parable of

---

[93] The title of "Pharaoh" actually comes to us from the Greek language and its use in the Old Testament. It originates in the Egyptian Per-aa, meaning "Great House" The Kings (Pharaohs) of Ancient Egypt by Jimmy Dunn

the five blind men. There were five blind men who were taken to an elephant so that they could feel it up, so they could discover what it was. One touched the legs and said it was a pillar; the other one touched the tail and thought that was a broom. Another one touched the side of the elephant and thought that was a wall. One touched the ear and thought that was a fan. One touched the trunk and said that was a snake. They were asked what is this? They said a wall with a pillar, fan, broom, and snake attached. Then somebody who was not blind was brought in. The person with the sight said this is an elephant. Intuition is that capacity which allows the human mind to transcend the ordinary intellectual capacity that perceives elements and relative concepts, to see beyond the illusory surface of the relative reality and perceive a whole. However, most people are like the blind men or like a person with a mental impediment called simultanagnosia.[94] In reality, most people suffer from spiritual simultanagnosia in their inability to see how the apparently varied objects of the world are really made up of the same substratum, the same stuff, atoms electrons and neutrons that are in reality all made up of energy and that is sustained by consciousness. In reality the mind is not equipped to simultaneously look at the world and perceive its unitary whole nature; that capacity exists in the intuitional aspect of the personality, that is Aset.

Many people think that they can intellectually discover the secrets of the world and of their selves through disciplines like the sciences. Intellectuals have brought forth many reflections about the world and scientists have discovered many things about the world. However, the power of intellectualism has not led them to mystical insights about Creation or ways to bring harmony and peace to the world or the knowledge of the secret to creating life. Some of the most powerful intellects in the world have caused much destruction of the world, much violence in the world. If this is what can be accomplished with brightness of intellect and self-important ego (superiority complex), imagine what could occur with strong intellect combined with the depths of dullness of ego (disposed to depression, sociopath, sadism, greed, irrational hatred)? Intellectualism is not necessarily good nor will it automatically lead to spiritual enlightenment or positive evolution; it can in fact lead to devolution and intensification of the ego. Look at the state of the world today, at the brink of global environmental disaster, economic collapse, health crisis and religious crisis, all led by people with advanced intellectual capacity!

So you must understand that mystical wisdom is supernatural wisdom. It's not what you see in the world of time and space or in the ivory towers of learned scholars. There are people who think they are wise, who know lots of things about the world. That's one thing. Mysticism puts together all those things and wraps them up into one neat little package. All that is to be known is known by that person who has achieved *rech* and the understanding of this teaching is given to us by the Goddess in her own myth. The myth of Ra and Aset is where she pursues the transcendental knowledge of creation and in brief, the story is told of how Goddess Aset was brought forth in physical form; this is why Set was able to kill Asar. They had physical bodies as physical beings, with flesh & blood like us. In fact they had been divine beings before coming down to the world. As per the myth, Aset and Asar were installed and enthroned in Egypt to rule. They did so wonderfully for a long time. Aset was reduced in consciousness in order to be brought into physical form but she had aspiration to the knowledge of higher nature. So she craved for that knowledge of when she was not in physical form, so she learned all she could. She learnt all the knowledge of human beings, engineering, medical science, law, etc. and she became bored with it, she became disappointed with the world because that worldly knowledge did not lead her to the beatific state which brings supreme contentment and peace. She became dispassionate about it. She thought, "If this is what the world is all about, then there should be something more than this. I want more, I want to know the ultimate truth, to become not just master of worldly knowledge but also master of transcendental wisdom." So, she developed dispassion, detachment, and these are some of the first qualities to be developed on the path of Aset.

This process of developing dispassion and detachment and increasing focus of mind leads a person to one pointed movement of the thought process instead of a scattered mental thought process (due to running after worldly desires, worries and anxieties) and that leads one to be able to pursue the ultimate reality and this is what she did. She pursued her great great grandfather, Ra. Aset sought him out so that he might tell her the ultimate

---

[94] Difficulty seeing how the parts fit into a whole. Inability to recognize multiple elements in a simultaneously displayed visual presentation; the ability to appreciate elements of a scene but not the display as a whole. **Form agnosia**: Patients perceive only parts of details, not the whole object.

truth. Knowing a name is like knowing the named object's essential nature and understanding its reality and this kind of understanding bestows the ultimate understanding of life and the nature of the universe and with that, contentment and peace. The ultimate truth is the transcendental name of the Divine, the name which opens the understanding of what the Divine and in fact what everything is as well as the meaning of life and the ultimate fulfillment of life. So Ra is not the transcendental name of the Divine. This is what the myth clearly tells us. This concept is called ⌇⌇ *bes* or *bas*. "Bas" means an image an outer representation of the inner reality [⌇⌇ *bes neter* –visible image of god]. The same concept is present in the term *tut* ⌇⌇ (form-image), as in *Tut-ankh-Amun,* "The Living Image of Amun". Ra refused to tell her the name. He said "O you are a little girl. You see yourself as dispassionate and you think that you are ready for high knowledge". So he put her off. Then she developed a plan. She watched him and studied how he goes through his particular path every day; he followed the same course through the sky in the form of the sundisk. This study and effort of the goddess metaphorically relates also to astronomy and the study of the movement of the heavenly bodies and the wisdom that bestows but also how that study can unlock the knowledge of those heavenly bodies. However, any scientific study be it astronomy (hard science) or philosophical study (soft science) of the world leads to the unlocking of the secrets of the objects being studied. So he was walking down on the path, through the sky, shining on the world, and he was getting a little older and tired in the afternoon and became an old man with spittle coming out of his mouth. Remember the three aspects of Ra at the top of the obelisk? The first form is the dawn, the creation of the day, the second form is the noon sun, the sustenance of the day and the third form is the setting sun, the dissolution of the day. In the morning Ra is a baby he is a child, the solar child (Nefertem) and he is also the Creator (Khepri). He is a grown up man at midday and in the evening he is an old man with a walking stick. So he was drooling. Without his knowing it, she caught some of his spittle, mixed it with a little bit of clay, which is earth element and she formed it into a serpent and that next day she left it on his path and when he walked on his path across the sky it bit him and poisoned him mortally. When that happened he could barely continue, he was so sick that he was on his death bed. The poison was going to the depth of his bones and he was in pain and all the Gods & Goddesses came to help him but they could not do anything. He had been poisoned with the duality of the world. His spittle represents the spirit; the earth, the clay represents the physical body and the two blended together in an androgynous unitary[95] mix poisons the polarized objects in Creation. So, Ra as a polarized object, a manifestation in time and space as a personality, was poisoned, that is, his image in time and space was poisoned and increasingly unable to sustain the relative reality, the illusory state of manifestation; but that would be bad for the world because it would leave it without a sun, without illumination and without the capacity to function since awareness of time and space can only occur in the realm of illusion, the realm of duality. So she went to him. He finally called her and said "can you help me, I am dying and I am in pain" and then she said "tell me your real name and then I will take this pain away from you and take this poison out." Then he finally agrees. He has no other choice. So he says, "ok, but the name cannot be spoken so may my true name be passed on to Aset within me, within herself." They joined, Aset went into Ra's heart, they became one briefly and had a communion and she learned the true name by experiencing oneness with it, leaving her personality and blending with the transcendental nature of Ra (which is the same transcendental nature of all in Creation.).

This mythic teaching is extremely important in order to understand the principle of Aset and the path of mystical wisdom. The dispassion, and detachment first of all, and next the tenacity to go after and to destroy the outer image of this Divine in creation leads to the revelation of the underlying truth or reality behind Creation. What she did was poisoning the world; she was destroying the illusoriness of the world so as to become dis-illusioned about the world and not just disappointed as most people are, who are frustrated but still keep on searching for fulfillment through worldly objects and worldly relative realities. So through her dispassion, detachment, her tenacity, her desire, and her aspiration to know the truth and finally discovering that truth, the wisdom of mysticism, she became enlightened, a goddess one again. By developing the necessary mental skills and performing the correct ritual of creating a blending between the two worlds (discovering spirit and integrating that with matter, as opposed to living in the material world and thinking that that is all there is or that spirit is something separate from nature that can be known when nature is forsaken) in order to dissolve the opposites and entering into a meditative mystical experience with Ra she attains that knowledge which cannot be spoken. She had to experience it by becoming one with the Divine, by transcending time and space, and that bestowed the

---

[95] Having the nature of a unit; whole; as opposed to opposites

knowledge, the Gnosis, the *Nehast* ⟨hieroglyphs⟩ (spiritual awakening, enlightenment). It is important to understand that the discipline of wisdom, the study of the philosophy and the living out of that philosophy works to render the personality detached and dispassionate and this is a prerequisite for coming into the higher knowledge of self which allows a person to become fully disillusioned and free from the spiritual ignorance. After she had this communion, she uttered special words of power, Hekau, to heal Ra:

Hekau For Aset Meditation from *matnu n Ra n Aset* [Myth/Story/Legend of Ra and Aset][96]	
Hieroglyphic text Transliteration Literal Translation Contextual Translation	⟨hieroglyphs⟩ *Ra {n} ankh metut myt* Ra {to} live poison death {to it} [may Ra live and may the poison die]

This specific formula is given to us in two major myths, the story of Ra and Aset and the story of the Asarian Resurrection. These are the special secret words of power that are to be uttered. They allow what the goddess did, the resurrection, to occur, but the words of power must be backed up with the accumulated energy of repeated effort in the studies and disciplines that cleanse and infuse the mind with positive *ariu*.

We did not speak about Aset's special power to stop the world. The question is, what kind of dispassion and detachment do you really have about the world? If you are partly caught up in worldly desires, worldly ignorance, your words of power are not going to have the full power. What is your level of tenacity? What is your level of determination? What is your capacity of one-pointedness of mind to concentrate on the goal of destroying the illusion of the world of time and space? Is the world bothering you? Are you bothered by people on your job, the injustices of the world, your health? Are you a doctor or a lawyer and do you have those kinds of worries? What are you going to do with your employees and your job and your this and your that? No matter how bad the world might be, if you apply this teaching properly, with sufficient power, sufficient determination, sufficient feeling, then you can stop the world cold and this is actually what Goddess Aset did when her son died; when that happened she could not help him. She had to stop the world, stop time and space in fact, and this is a great teaching. Stopping the world occurs when the mind transcends the senses and time and space. Having achieved this feat the personality can discover a heretofore unknown region of its existence beyond the world and henceforth remain separate from the world, regardless of its condition. Of course, the body, family and other circumstances of a person are part of the world of time and space. So through this discipline a person discovers their nature beyond the waking personality alone, which is the only idea of self that ordinary people have. This is why when ordinary people die they feel they are losing all of their existence since they have no knowledge of their existence beyond the physical components (*ren*-name, *khat*-body, *ka*-mind[97]).

The capacity of Aset to control and heal Ra underscores her nature as a healing agency. Aset is one of the primary divinities presiding over health and healing. In an Ancient Egyptian text we read: ***Oh, Aset, Great of Heka! Heal me, Release me from all things bad and evil!*** [Pap. Ebers, 18th Dyn.]

Aset's wisdom itself is a healing power which can heal the ultimate malady, human spiritual ignorance. That is what the healing of Heru and Ra by Aset represents.. Aset stopped time and space, that is the power of her voice. In the time just after Heru died and after trying in vane to revive him Aset cared for nothing of the world and her attention was directed exclusively to the boat of Ra. She withdrew all awareness of the world and its drama and she became fixed on the boat and on Ra. When that happened, the boat, whose sailing causes waves on the Primeval Ocean, causing it to maintain the shapes of Creation and the movement of time and objects changing

---

[96] Translation ©2007 Sema Institute (Dr. Muata Ashby)
[97] see the book *African Religion Vol 2/Egyptian Yoga Vol 2 Theban Theology* Elements of the Personality, parts of spirit

in space could not continue. Anyone who has the capacity to emote in this way can stop time and space, the waking conscience, and enter into the astral plane. From there they can commune with gods and goddesses and other spirits as well as the impressions of the subconscious mind. From here one can travel to great distances and discover expansiveness. From here also they can traverse to the realm beyond, to the transcendental, dissolving into the Primeval Ocean, like Ra at the end of Creation. Thus an adept aspirant can cause the Creation to come to an end and in so doing stop the worldly process that has killed Heru, and discover the goodness, peace, humility, joy, and universal love of the soul that resurrects and nurtures the soul, that comes from deepest Spirit. Having achieved this experience the aspirant can eventually (when fully established in this experience-the meditative experience needs to be repeated over a period of time) come back to the world of time and space with renewed and reconstituted soul, with invigorated fortitude and indomitable will.

HTP

Sebai MAA (Dr. Muata Ashby)

Questions and Answers

I want to expand on a particular question that was asked last time. It was a question about the seductiveness, the sexuality of the world embodied by the principles of Nebthet which manifest as all the things in the world that entice you and that sexually interest you, be it a wonderful sports car which has all the nice curves in it or nice clothing or a person. How to deal with that? How to overcome that? As we discussed, there are two levels of handling the world. One is in a disciplinary way by abstaining. But this is not going to work forever if you do not have higher mystical insight. It is not going to work very long, it will eventually fail. You can abstain but deep down you are going to continue desiring because the fundamental cause of the desire has not been resolved. Your desire is going to build up and will explode. There has to be regulation. For example, if you are a person who is constantly having sex on a daily basis bring it down to every other day then break down to one time a week, etc. If you do it regulate yourself. If it's four to five times a month, do it two to three, that kind of thing; this is control. Controlling whatever the vice is allows the personality to gain space, a separation between the senses and the objects that agitates the mind and resonates with the unconscious impressions that impel the personality to continue pursuing it's illusory fulfillment for pleasures and or happiness; this is the disciplinary aspect that needs to be practiced first. If you begin to understand the illusoriness of what you are pursuing, the illusoriness of your desires, whatever they may be, you can begin to understand how much time you are wasting on them. If you are pursuing the world you are pursuing something that cannot fulfill you. The people who pursue illusions are the people who are in the dark, people who are caught in a delusion. Delusion may be defined as the inability to perceive and act based on truth. Realizing you are following an illusion helps you to reduce the intensity of the psychological aspect of desires and that affects your physiology, your physical cravings and dependence on the pursuit of fulfillment of desires as a means for satisfaction.

If someone asks you to put out a fire would you want to throw gasoline on it? A person who doesn't know what Gasoline and Fire will do together would go and do it because they are ignorant. They don't know any better. And you will also do it if you have forgotten, if you don't remember, because you have put it out of your mind for a long time. Also, you would do it even if you know what will happen if you can't control yourself, because the pressure of psychological and physical craving can become irresistibly strong since it was allowed to build up over a long period of time. This is what most people do with the world. They are like dogs; they eat something that makes them sick and then go back and eat it again after they vomited it. With human beings in the world the problem is compounded because sometimes people do things they know are wrong but do them because their desires overwhelm their capacity to exert will-power over their own personalities and act in accordance with their intellect's dictates.

There is another aspect that needs to develop. This may sound strange to you but it is actually spoken of in the scriptures, it is disgust. You must learn how to be disgusted with time and space, disgusted with your own fallibilities, your own foibles, your own ignorance. In the Pert M Heru text, the Book of the Dead, this is referred to as "excrement". Then learn how to practice pursuing the truth tenaciously like Aset. Then eventually you will find that you have something else to hold on to that is more satisfying in other ways, more attractive in other ways. Those who have developed their higher capacity, they have discovered something that is even more enchanting than the worldly physical pleasures that never lead to abiding happiness. This actually can be another problem because there are mental pleasures, higher mental seductiveness aspects of time and space that are actually a bigger problem than the physical ones, believe it or not. But the Lady Aset transcended all of that. Aset, before she regained her full Goddess stature, put all of that aside. She was a revered healer, master sailor, scientist, and she had many other achievements. She was looked up to, revered in the world and she gave all that up. She could have anything that she wanted to have but she gave it all up to have *rech*. So, what will you give up in order to transcend? Would you sit around saying "the world is so strong and I cannot overcome that, I have to give in to desire, all the men and women are throwing themselves at me and I can't do anything at all." What does that say about you who cannot resist? What are you training your mind to? You have the capacity, you have the choice of what you will turn your mind to, your *ari.* What will that be? How would you act? Who will you pursue? Remember the Wisdom Texts, the instructions of *Meri-Ka-Ra* tell us that the *ariu* stays with us even after death if it has not been resolved. The *ariu* that you perform stays with you as a residue in your unconscious mind.

When it comes time for your judgment the *ariu* steps forward and bears witness to what you have done in life. Goddess *Meskhenet,* an associate of *Maat*, directs you where you need to go, to be reborn, based on that *ariu.* So, you have the capacity to control your direction, your personality based on the *ariu* that you engender based on the deeds that you perform from day to day. The *ariu* that becomes part of the content of your unconscious mind can be changed by your present actions, feelings, desires and understanding and that is the way to control your own destiny and change your fate, because when you change your unconscious mind you change the desires and your outlook as well as understanding of the world and consequently how you will approach the world. This concludes our lesson for today.

Reflection and Journal discipline:

1- At the top of each page copy the following hieroglyphs to the best of your ability

[***cht n ankh*** *" tree of life"*]

After studying the Lesson proceed to answer the following question and write the answer in your journal. This exercise will require more than one reading and more than one journal entry. This exercise is to be repeated until the principles of the sphere are mastered. This reflection exercise does not need to be done every meditation period. You may feel free to skip this section and go directly to the meditation practice. The reflection exercise should be done after each reading or study session.

REFLECTIONS: Oh Lady of Wisdom, first among knowers, glorify your child with a word and then with the silence of knowing without words. Let me attain your position on the gloried Tree by becoming like you, being near to you and to your infinite mind. Lady of Truth and balance and order and light, enlighten me for knowing the road ahead, enlighten me for knowing Self! I am your child and humble servant!

After studying the Lesson proceed to answer the following question and write the answer in your journal.

Why does the complexity of the human personality occur?

What is(are) the main teaching(s) of this lesson and what do the principle(s) of the divinity(ies) discussed in this lesson mean in reference to my actions, feelings, thoughts and desires and understanding of the spiritual philosophy?

Lesson 10: The Principle of Asar, The Secret Wisdom of the Soul and the Key to transitioning from the Ta Region to the Pet Region on the Journey of the Tree of Life

We are now continuing our study of Anunian Theurgy - Tree of Life Mysteries of the Neteru. Today is a new lecture and continuation of the series called Anunian Theology - Tree of Life, the lecture related to the Principle of Asar.

First we will have a brief review of where we have been so far. The creation and all the forces that sustain and maintain it are related to us in the most ancient spiritual tradition in our current human history, Anunian Theurgy. These forces are called neteru, and for the English language these neteru can be, in a mythical sense, loosely translated as "gods and goddesses" and in a metaphysical sense, "cosmic forces." But, also, they have a deeper and more mysterious function, a deeply philosophical, deeply mystical, and wholly mythological essence for different people at different levels of spiritual evolution. Different people at different levels of spiritual evolution need to adhere to different levels of the teaching because they are at different levels of spiritual evolution and those levels of evolution determine what they can understand and assimilate. This means, for example, many people will read this book all the way through, thinking that if they get to the more advanced lessons they can get the knowledge and elevate themselves, this without studying closely the beginning lessons and heeding their words, applying its philosophy. This is a typical mistake in modern culture, which is usually based on instant gratification. Well, authentic spiritual evolution in mysticism does not work that way. It requires time and dedication and purity on the part of the aspirant and it also requires an authentic teacher who can explain the teaching. Not all can be gained from a book unless one is already highly evolved, which only applies to perhaps one out of a million people. So you are advised to follow the instructions and concentrate on each lesson and not progress until you have thoroughly studied its wisdom and have confronted and become competent in recognizing and managing if not controlling each principle discussed in it. What does this mean in a practical sense? You can know when you are ready to move forward by receiving council from a more advanced practitioner of this teaching, a priest or priestess who is versed in this path and can answer questions so you may gauge when you are gaining understanding. You can know when you are gaining understanding if you know an answer or partial answer to a question before it is asked and before you receive an answer that confirms what you already figured out on your own. As you advance your internal answers become more complete and the completeness brings more closure to the mental unrest from quandaries, worries, anxieties of ordinary life and also about the spiritual journey. Eventually, you get to a point where you only need your internal answers to be confirmed and when, after a time, you do not have new questions but only a few of a more advanced, subtler nature that need to be confirmed. When this occurs you are ready for the next level of the teaching. Now, when does a person reach a level to be on their own if necessary? When an initiate reaches a certain point where they can consistently intuit the answers directly without the need for a spiritual master, a guide, and when the egoistic tendencies of the mind no longer control the personality and the moods of the mind does not cause the personality to lose sight of the logic and philosophy of the teaching and cannot break the connection to an internal peace and devotion to God {Goddess} even if the personality is under stress, sick or otherwise indisposed in suffering or exposed to pleasurable conditions, then this person is going to attain enlightenment and there will be no turning back and he/she is ready to be on his/her own if necessary.

We discussed in previous lectures how, if these principles are mastered, one can conceivably master the entire Creation. That is why, the Neterian tradition, rituals and propitiations of the divine are performed so as to attain physical, psychological, and finally spiritual mastery over these cosmic principles; but one of those propitiations is the practice of *shedy,* the practice of disciplines that allow one to penetrate the mysteries of life. A person who masters the cosmic forces becomes more powerful than those forces. So therefore, human beings can actually become more powerful than the gods and goddesses. Why? Because they innately embody all of the principles already but have not discovered them due to ignorance, manifesting through egoism, loss of memory and clouded intellects which have been atrophied because of harboring undue desires in the mind. So instead of being a master to the forces the forces control the personality; while the mind of such a person operates in the state of ignorance, those principles, governed by ignorance, hold sway over the human psyche. If that human psyche were to be purified and were to be rendered subtle and lucid, then the knowledge of the self, the empowerment of the self would be attained by that person.

As you know, we have been moving up the *tech016* or the obelisk and following the schematic of the neteru, which represent a visual and metaphysical/informational diagram of Creation that has been placed for you in the Tree of Life cosmiconomythograph, which we likened to a *mandala*. It is at once a philosophical, mystical and meditational iconomythograph to be contemplated just like any section of an Ancient Egyptian Temple wall. For our study of the philosophy, we have traversed through the principle of Heru as the child, Nebthet, Set and Aset, and now we have reached Asar. With Asar, we conclude our study of the human principles. We recall that there are 10 principles in all: the lower five are human principles and the upper five are cosmic principles. However, as we said before, the human personality contains all of the principles, all ten. But the lower five relate more closely to the elements that go to compose the human psyche.

We discussed the pathways in which they need to be discovered and mastered. By developing a certain sensitivity, we have become Heru. We have asked our mother Aset to lead us to mastery over the Principle of death, Nebthet, and the sensuality of the world as well as the egoism of Set and the selfishness, the greed of Set. As we saw in the Principle of Aset, the attainment of knowledge occurs through the experience of Heru, the Battle of Heru, and that leads us to attain the experience of Asar, which we have been discussing for the last two lectures.

We have also discussed the peculiarities of each principle, the teaching that each principle represents. And to some degree, but not completely, we discussed some of the objects that the principles represent. We talked about the concept of worshiping the principles, the Neteru; the higher and lower worship; the concept of the realm of generation and the realm of absolute consciousness and how each one is to be approached, each with its kind. The neteru of the physical realm are to be approached with physical objects and the Neter of the transcendental realm is to be approached with no-things. Now, let us look into the mysteries of Asar by beginning to look at his hieroglyphs and most important iconographies.

Figure 55: Asar holding the Heka and Nekaku

Asar is usually presented as a man wrapped in mummy swathings. His skin color is either green or black depending on the iconographical teaching being expressed. He often wears the crown of Lower Egypt and he holds the crook and flail. Asar has two principal objects: the *heka* and the *nekaku*. Heka is the crook which is used to herd animals, so, he is known as the 𓏏𓆓𓈖𓏏𓀭, 𓇋 𓈖 "Asar the good, the beautiful," 𓇳 — 𓅆 𓅓 𓅆 𓀭 𓈎 𓏏 *Asar Saa*, "Asar the Shepherd." This is where the concept was adopted for use in Christianity - the Good Shepherd, the one who leads his flock. It also means royalty; meaning, he is able to lead others. He is the wise ruler. He is the heir, the rightful heir of the throne, as you are. You are the rightful heirs of the throne of Spiritual Enlightenment. This is why initiates into this tradition are also referred to as Asar.

in threshing, from worlds, the philosophy and thereby

The other object that he has is the *nekaku* or flail. Again, the flail is an object that is used separating the chaff from the seed, which means separating truth from untruth, reality illusion. The object itself has three sections. The three sections symbolize the three *Ta*, the *Pet*, and the *Duat*. Becoming a Pharaoh means mastery over these. So with this of the three worlds, you are able to master duality, which manifests as the three worlds discover non-duality, absolute truth and Spiritual Enlightenment.

The truth and the untruth in the mind of an ordinary human being are blended. Any person on the street, or family members, a friend, etc. has some good qualities and some bad qualities. Most of the time you lean on the good ones and you try to overlook the other ones. Sometimes people may do some bad things to you, they may insult you or they do something you do not like, something that hurts you. And also some of the times they do what you consider to be nice things to or for you; they may buy you a gift and they are good to you and nice to you.

Then you yourself, you have some good points about yourself and bad points that you do not like. Even further, consider your mind; sometimes you are angry, you wake up in the morning and you are angry, then something happens and then you forget about it and then you feel relaxed and jovial, then angry again. These are mixed energies coursing through the personality and the mind; this is because you have positive and negative *ariu* in your unconscious mind. It is layered on because you have laid it on in your own mind in a layered way, over many life times. Sometimes you do good actions that give you pleasure, and then you feel good and you allow that feeling and memory to be lodged in your mind. You put a good layer into your consciousness, into your conscious mind; it then moves to the subconscious level and from there as a seed or residue it embeds in your unconscious level of mind and in so doing it conditions it, changing it from unconditioned consciousness to consciousness affected by shapes and forms dictated by desires, memories, feelings and delusions. Then the next hour, you may be doing something negative, like maybe arguing with somebody and you are annoyed, and then that goes on there as well, you allow that feeling and memory to be lodged in your mind. These experiences are based on and as a result of the mental food (worldly interactions) you allow your mind to consume but your moods can also be affected by the physical foods you consume (which is also controlled by your past *ari*). So your entire consciousness is mixed and has been so for many lifetimes. This state of affairs may lead to erratic behavior and cause psychoses. This predicament causes turbulence in the mind along with fluctuating emotions, indecision, lack of will-power and mental agitation, intellectual bankruptcy and other foibles of the personality including moodiness.

You may even realize that the roller coaster of highs and lows experienced by the mind, the up-and-down experiences are ridiculous; but who knows what the problem is? Most people say "Oh that's just life, take the bitter with the sweet." But, there are people, in the general society, who live in a more balanced way, what does that mean? It means that there is another way, human beings DO <u>NOT</u> HAVE TO live on a roller coaster of emotions, mental instability, weakness and ignorance. So, when you really begin to "know" that you are seriously able to start pursuing a way out of the dilemma of seemingly endless human suffering and ultimate death you can consciously move in a better direction in life. If you do not pursue this course of dissolution that the TREE presents, then you just keep on going like the masses, wandering in ignorance and calling that wisdom and never discovering true peace, prosperity or happiness; Your language is a language of "if only": if only I could find some money or if only I could create a favorable situation or if only I could get a good relationship or if only I could find a good job –then I could be happy and secure- if only I could do all of these; if only things would be okay, things would be good; if only I could get a better wardrobe, I would feel good about myself and I would be a better person; if only I can have a child, that would make me a better person, or things would be good and I would have someone to love me. If only I can become born again –then all my troubles would go away and Jesus would come and take me and I would go to heaven.

The wise forget about these "if only" words. The wise reflect as follows: "If I can understand all the things that happen in the world - the good and bad things, the stupid things and the smart things, the happy things, sad things and the insane things, the peace and the fighting –abiding happiness has never been found by any human being in worldly objects; if I discover the real reason for human suffering and the true essence of the universe and the inner spirit within me I would realize that the worldly pursuits, philosophies, pleasure seeking, prejudices, desires, hatreds, and sufferings are all ridiculous. Why run after those things that do not bring abiding peace and happiness and cannot be held onto anyway? Everything is connected so why see separations and segregations? It is all the same since everything comes from the Nun and is composed of atoms, electrons, neutrons and protons and all that is really the Divine Self. Why hoard things that other people need and why not help everyone to have a good life and discover peace and fulfillment? So living like the masses, with the "if only" mentality is all nonsense because in the end it does not mean anything real or true."

Now, how do you go through all of that? How do you achieve that level of awareness, confidence and peace? Well, you have to begin by practicing regularly at the teaching, do the disciplines, the meditation, reflections and the studies, such as reading this book. This process leads to *Saa* –understanding, and *Saa* leads to *Nehast,* enlightenment.

Sometimes you may have layered it on so thick that it may take you years to overcome, years to cleanse your mind. It may take you generations. It may take you lifetimes to study and to purify yourself. You must develop patience because even while you are doing something that is pure, like studying the teachings, you may be even still layering on some impurity and ridiculous nonsense, ignorance because your understanding is not pure. The best you can hope for is to do better and better and better, bringing yourself closer and closer to the truth, diligently as Aset did, tenaciously seeking out the truth and not allowing yourself to be sold a bill of goods, that are in reality lies and deceptions of the world that you have fallen into because of the desires that have clouded your mind and atrophied your intellect. Aset did not put up with that. In the same way you too should not put up with that.

When Heru was in the midst of the battle with Set, he sought Aset's counsel. She told him about the mysteries of life and combat, where he needed to attack, how to attack, when to attack, etc. That is the voice of wisdom, coming from intuition. Remember that wisdom is a child of training as well as the implementation of the training and the experience of the results of the actions. Without attempting to implement the teaching and experiencing the results your knowledge will not be true wisdom. Remember that wisdom is the result of knowledge plus action, it is experience and understanding the higher meaning of it. Recall the story of Aset and Ra. Aset did not become enlightened just by magic, just overnight, just by desiring it. She had to do many things. She followed a path of life founded in pursuing wisdom tenaciously and performing the actions that poisoned the illusoriness of the world of time and space, and so must you.

So this path, in our discussion today, leads us to the Principle of Asar. Today we are going to deal with some defining issues, issues that are of paramount importance in understanding the journey of the TREE like, the color of Asar as well as the principle of sexuality in relation to the teaching of Asar and Aset, and some other important points. Mind you, the information related to Asar's myth, contained here, is merely an overview, to the extent that it relates to the TOL, since the Asarian Resurrection book *Asarian Theology* has much more detail going into the myth.[98] We are discussing the aspects that are pertinent to the Tree of Life mysteries. However, our lecture series contains some teachings and facts that were not in that book also. So they may be treated as complementary texts

Next, the colors of Asar are *wadj* 𓇅 "green" and *kami* (kam) 𓊹𓄿𓅓𓏏 "be black –blackness." Asar's picture is usually either green or black. Let us begin with the color green. In the resurrection reliefs of the death and resurrection of Asar, and you can see one reproduced in the *Kemetic Diet* book, you can see a particular picture of Asar's dead body, which is buried in the earth and wheat is growing out of it. We are told that Asar is the essence of the greenery of the world. Spirit/soul itself is the essence of the green. Have you ever thought about what makes a seed turn into a plant? You might say, "Oh, it is water, or, it is earth, or, it is sunlight or maybe all the three." You have water you have earth and sunlight around everywhere. How come you do not have plants growing everywhere, greenery growing everywhere, coming out of everything? You have to have spirit and a particular arrangement of physical elements in order for conscience to manifest as a life. It's the same with a human being. You can go to any funeral home and/or morgue or hospital and look at some dead bodies. The ears are there, the nose is there, the heart and lungs are there, the two legs, brain, eyes etc. are there. Why is it that the eyes cannot see, the ears cannot hear, the lungs do not breathe? They have the same things that you have but they are not functioning but you are. What is the difference? *Wadj* is that difference.

The greenery that gives you *ankh, udja* and *seneb*; *ankh* is life, udja is vitality, seneb -- or *senab,* is health. That is what Asar is. Asar is the source of all of that. That is what your soul is. Your soul sustains your entire

[98] See the book *African Religion Vol. 4 Asarian Theology* by Dr. Muata Ashby, See the book *The War of Heru and Set* by Dr. Muata Ashby

191

personality. Without your soul, your mind, your heart, your physical body, your personality cannot function; it cannot exist. Your soul goes away, your body is like a rag doll and it will collapse. It will go limp. Your awareness of the world ceases.

As far as blackness is concerned, as we talked about it a little bit in a previous lecture, Aset refers to blackness, "nothingness." Nothingness here is referring to no things, no concepts, no objects, an absence of conditioning, forms. And that is also what the soul's innermost reality is. If you knock into a door by accident, the door hurts your body and it actually changes it. It actually conditions it; It causes it to have a different form, you get a welt. It may get black and blue and might get a big blister; your face might get puffy eyes. The soul inside you does not change though, but your personality, your body, changes. Something happens in the world and your mind gets all ruffled up and upset; it changes its form, like a calm ocean agitated by a storm. But deep down your soul does not change. It is witnessing all of this. From that blackness, from that no-thingness, things can come but those things are temporary. The source from whence they came is abiding. How do we know that this teaching is true? We can know because those who learned the philosophy and who practiced the disciplines of ethics, detachment, dispassion and meditation discovered the inner reality beyond their mental fluctuations. They discovered that they were not the same as the contents of their minds, that they are something else, something higher, something more abiding. When that realization dawns in a personality that person can take a step back and contemplate the mind and not act on every impulse. They have created a distance, a demarcation line, a border between the temporal and the abiding. That awareness grows until such a person is completely free from the illusoriness of the world and the delusions caused by egoistic desires that overwhelm the ordinary person's mind.

All things are created from that realm of full but unconditioned consciousness. If you were to discover that full unconditioned consciousness, you are discovering the primordial self that you are, and that is your deepest innermost reality. That is Asar within you; that is the blackness within you. If you were to realize, if you were to be able to stop the illumination of the thoughts in your mind, what would be illumined in your mind? There is energy that goes to shine on your thoughts so you can see them when you close your eyes; if those thoughts were to cease to be illumined, what would happen? You get to the place that is called -- or you would experience a state that is called in the scriptures, 𓇳𓆑𓏏𓀀 *urdu-hat*. *Urdu* means "stillness". The *ab* symbol means heart. 𓄣 *Hatti* means your heart and your lungs; this is one of the main titles of Asar, *the one who is still of heart*.

So that is blackness, the blackness that you are trying to get to when you practice meditation; to get to a place where your thoughts cease to burden you and you realize that you are innately undifferentiated, free of forms. Therefore, your name is not Joe or Cathy, Jane, etc. These are conditionings. The truth is the Asar in you. That is accessed through stillness of heart, which occurs when there is death but also when there is practice of a philosophy that renders the mind pure, then the desires, thoughts and other conditionings cease. Also this happens when the special breathing exercises are practiced that slow the breath and heartbeats to a level wherein a meditative state is induced and the world of time and space falls away from the mind.

The next point to discuss related to Asar, about the blackness and the greenness, is what these two colors signify as different functions at different times. Sometimes, you may be green; sometimes, you may be black. Green should be your worldly activities and black should be your inner mystical practice. Black is *Kem*; Kem as in Kemet (Egypt), the Black land. So when you are eating you should eat greens and not meat. Greens are the things of physical life and blacks are the things that sustain and nurture spiritual life. So for the spiritual life one should consume blackness in the form of peacefulness, ethics, stillness of heart, introversion and withdrawal of the senses from the physical body. This is a very great teaching that should be reflected upon keenly before reading on.

Now, related to the principle of sex, there are three forms of birth that are recognized in the scriptures. There is a cosmic kind of sexuality, a birth that is expressed in all traditions but most so in the Asarian, which relate to Asar and Aset, and in the Wasetian[99] teachings, which relate to Amun and Mut. In fact, in the form of Min (a form associated with Heru), Amun brings the world into creation through an ejaculation, an orgasmic act. He ejaculates into his very own hand, which is his wife. And this is why they call the goddess (Mut) or the high priestess that takes care of his icon and temple, they called her the "hand of the god." This kind of creation occurs daily. Every morning the temple is opened and the Shrine of the Divine Being is opened and the dust is dusted off and the clothes are changed and cleaned and offerings are made, divine food and water and so on and so forth. This is done so that the creation process may be orgasmically engendered once more. The cosmic creation is the high, and then the lower kind of creation is the human kind of creation, the creation performed by two human beings that get together and they have sexual intercourse and they produce physical children.

Then there is another form of creation; this is the one that we are particularly dealing with right now, which is the creation of what happens when there is intercourse between soul and intuition, between Asar and Aset. We discussed that in this process there is an intercourse between mortality and the soul and that brings you to the physical creation as symbolized by Anpu. In reference to Aset and Asar coming together, even with all her wisdom, Aset cannot bring forth Heru without Asar. In other words, Asar is the spark that gives life to her wisdom and together they produce Heru. Without the soul there is no life. Also, without the soul, wisdom, like everything else, is meaningless and therefore useless.

Speaking from a transcendental standpoint, there is no life in wisdom, anyway. Wisdom is a construct and constant (since it is based on truth) that applies to time and space as long as time and space exists. So is ignorance; ignorance is a construct of time and space but since it is illusory it has no constant of truth, but, like wisdom, has no meaning unless you have time and space and also a soul to give it meaning, albeit due to ignorance and delusion. But the soul exists whether or not there is time and space. This does not mean that we do not want wisdom or that wisdom is useless; you should be thankful and grateful that there is something called wisdom, illusory as it may be, as long as you exist in this "insane" world of time and space because, otherwise, you are doomed, without a way to understand it and become free from it. Otherwise you are doomed to experience all the pain and sorrow from time immemorial till time inconceivable.

Figure 56: Below, Goddess Aset Hovers over Asar

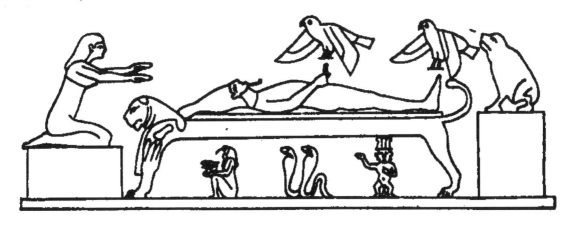

Hetheru kneels before Asar, who is conceiving Heru with Aset, who is hovering over him in the form of a kite(falconiform bird-like Heru, Ra Harakti and Asar Sokar) *as the frog God at the foot of the bed looks on. Below the bed* –from left to right- *the god Djehuti holds an Udjat (Eye of Heru) along with the double serpent goddesses and the god Bes.* [relief from the Temple of Hetheru {Hathor} at Denderah.

Moving on, if you look at the *African Religion Vol. 4 Asarian Theology* book and in the *Egyptian Book of the Dead* the *Pert em Heru* text,[100] you will see images of Asar who is lying on his back and with an erect

---

[99] theurgy of the Ancient Egyptian city Waset (called Thebes by the ancient Greeks)
[100] Egyptian Book of The Dead by Dr. Muata Ashby

penis.[101] Note that Asar is on a leoning bed; this means that there is Sekhem or Life Force power behind him, a force he rests on and which he channels through his body which he uses to make food in the form of wheat or ejaculate {life creating substance} to impregnate Aset and bring forth Heru. Aset may be seen in a posture sitting on or hovering over him in the form of a woman or in the form of a kite, an avian image, which is a form of hawk. So with this avian quality, that seed is taken and it flies. It is given the capacity to take flight. The symbols (iconography) of the soul are important for our understanding of its nature and relationship to the personality. Here we will focus on the avian principle.

Figure 57: Ancient Egyptian depictions of the soul

(A)   (B)   (B-1)

In Neterian Theurgy we are given the understanding that there is a (A) *Ba Neter* or "Soul of the Divine, in other words, ther is God, a "Universal Soul" and there are various *Bau* (B, B-1) souls of individuals, which emanate from the Universal Ba. In the *Pert m Hru* or *The Egyptian Book Of Coming Forth By Day* (also known as Egyptian book of the Dead) and in other hieroglyphic texts, the individual Soul is often depicted as a human headed hawk (Heru) with the head of a man. In this manner, we are led to understand that the individual soul is in reality a manifestation of the universal soul, the High God, Ra, who is the soul of everything and is symbolized as a hawk-headed man or as a hawk. In its highest aspect, the individual soul cleanses itself from its association with the mortal body-consciousness and achieves identification with the Universal Ba, the universal soul of Ra [who is the highest expression of Heru].

Figure 58: The initiate addresses the gods and goddesses and the souls of Ra and Asar (far- right) meet in Djedu of the Netherworld. (from the *Pert m Hru*)

If you look in the *Pert em Heru*, you can find a picture of Asar in the form of a soul, which is a hawk - a hawk body and a man's head, wearing the headdress of the king. That soul meets Ra (hawk with sundisk headdress). So Asar also has wings. But, as I said before, Asar does not do anything. He does not move. So what kind of form is this that Asar has? This is the soul form, not the body, human/king form; this represents the individual soul, the soul of every human being. That form has wings. It can fly from one place to another, from one realm to another. The soul can fly from one body to be associated with another when a person dies. It is often depicted as being present at the witnessing of the judgment of the heart, the *ab*. The iconography of Aset hovering over Asar is a great mystery teaching, and is related to the sexual mysteries -- of course there is more to it than this that is available in some other lectures as well as in the book *Sacred Sexuality*.[102] Here I will just give you an overview of the great mysteries of sex.

Figure 59: Asar Ani enters the Inner Shrine and Becomes Anointed

[101] see the book *SACRED SEXUALITY: EGYPTIAN TANTRA YOGA: The Art of Sex* Sublimation and Universal Consciousness by Dr. Muata Ashby ISBN 1-884564-03-8
[102] book by Dr. Muata Ashby

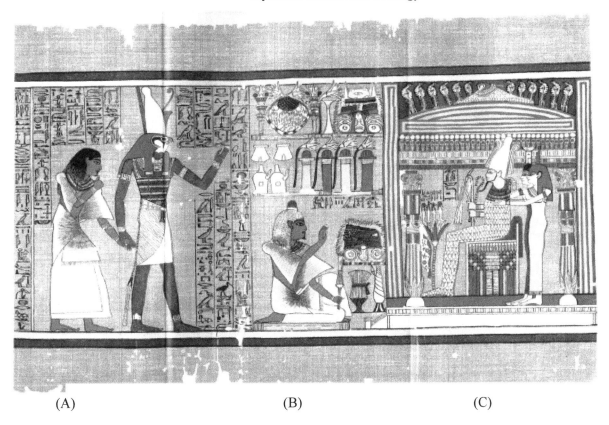

(A)   (B)   (C)

When this great wisdom, of the unity between Asar and Aset, is promoted to its highest it brings forth a spiritual orgasm, the blossoming of wisdom into intuitional realization of self, as opposed to ignorance and the egoistic search for pleasure in the world of time and space, which culminates in an ejaculation into a world of time and space. When wisdom brings forth an orgasm, there is an anointing that occurs and an intellectual glow that illumines and brings contentment the mind. Look at the *Pert em Heru* again and you will see where *Asar Ani,* the person for whom this particular text was written, before entering the inner shrine (A) displays black hair and upon coming into the presence of Asar (B), who is seated in the Inner Shrine, becomes anointed. His anointment is depicted as hair that turns all shiny and white due to the dripping down of an unguent cone that has been inverted and placed on his head, symbolizing the divine anointing, a dripping down of nectarine subtle life force energy that occurs when the individual soul has communed with the Universal Soul. [(C) Asar in his shrine, with the goddesses Aset and Nebethet]

These were the same mysteries that were performed or were adopted by the Greek mysteries of Dionysus and also in some mysteries that were performed later by non-Christian Gnostic and Gnostic Christian practitioners. However, many of them have become degenerated and people use those sexual mysteries, calling them Tantrism, as an excuse to engage in sexual intercourse or to engage in orgiastic kinds of rituals, or for enhancing sexual pleasures and that is a different kind of pursuit.

I will explain further so that you will not have any misconceptions about it. When this kind of anointing occurs, there is a special secretion that happens in the astral plane, from the subtle spine, the Djed pillar of Asar. This kind of ejaculation is the same as what we were talking about, how when the seventh psycho-spiritual consciousness energy centers and the serpent power is pierced, allowing a showering of a divine life force to take place. And, of course, it is beyond comparison to a worldly physical sexual orgasm. That would be like comparing the explosion of a dynamite bomb to the explosion of a nuclear bomb. As spirit is limitless the orgasm of the soul and spirit can be limitless and as spirit has no regulation it can be more powerful than the body could ever endure. So this occurs in the plane of the soul and not the physical plane of existence.

Moving on, the objective in the principle of Asar is to discover yourself as a soul. That means discovering motionlessness, that you have a consciousness beyond the movements of the physical body and

195

beyond the movements of the mind, the thoughts and desires of the mind. That means the mummy posture, one of the main postures of the god Asar, and the practice of a meditative discipline wherein you stop all movements. The motionlessness of the mummy means to be swathed, to be wrapped by mummy swathings. Swathings, in this context represent that which binds you, specifically the *saiu Set*[103] binding, which is the binding that goes over your mouth. This is why Asar, in the form of a mummy, is motionless; this means that as far as physical life goes, he is immobilized. He cannot move or speak but he can think, that is, until the *saiu Set* is removed, and then he can speak again; and in this context speaking is expanding in consciousness, essentially a resurrection in consciousness. When the *saiu Set* is in control the deeper essence of the personality, the soul, cannot express itself because the ego is in control. As physical beings we are limited and ego bound, like Set. How is his mouth, the mouth of Asar and all who are like him, all of us, unfettered? This is done by study of the philosophy of Maat, cleansing the mind and body, living less egoistically and more ethically, by necessity instead of by feelings and emotions and desires. Next, from a ritual point of view, offering libations, incense and chanting the divine name as well as practicing the mummy posture to attaining the state of *urduhat*. Remember that Asar is also *urdu-hat* {"still of heart"}. The practice involves removing the swathings and being free, removing the egoistic restrictions, and also becoming purposely still to the point that the movements of the heart slow down and the physiology of the body slows and the heart beat and the processes of the body become imperceptible and inconsequential. In this manner the attention is turned away from the lower aspects of personality and the higher, internal are perceived, discovered and explored. I am not going into details into this practice, of the meditation in the mummy posture, because this is advanced practice, reserved for higher initiation. Those who read the books on meditation and the Serpent Power may figure it out for themselves. Otherwise they can attend classes and be initiated into this meditation teaching.

Suffice it to say that certain disciplines, after purification through the diet, through your practice of Maat (ethics, righteousness), involve learning how to control your mind, relaxing your personality, serious determination to attain the higher essence of the teaching, act to bring your physical body to a balanced and lower state of operation. Through this practice, in meditation your heart beating becomes shallower, your breathing shallow, and everything comes closest to an actual death state. As we have discussed in previous lecture series, your personal diet and fasting and other practices are part of this discipline and they all lead you to loosen the bonds between your personality, your psyche, and your soul. Your soul is able to free itself from the earthbound, the worldly, and take flight.

Moving on, Asar is also known as *Sah* or *Sahu*. Sahu is Orion, three stars ★ ★ ★ in what is called Orion's Belt. Orion's belt has the three famous stars, correlated to the great pyramids in the Giza plateau in Kemet. From these three stars, if you look to the South-east, point to another star which is *Sopdu* or Sirius and that is a reference to goddess Aset. Its symbols are related to Aset and are sometimes used in her name, *Sopdu* or Sirius has actually two stars and the other one is called Heru. So three stars point to one star which is in reality two stars ★ ⋆, a brighter one and one that is related and much denser. These associations, of the teaching with the stars, point to certain conjunctions that lead us to astronomically understand the Path of Enlightenment, to become an *akh*, to become a "shining spirit" like Asar, a star in the sky. That is what meditation on the *urdu hat* and *Sahu* leads to, and this is what the chambers in the Great Pyramid, which is actually a temple, and not a tomb, is designed to facilitate.

---

[103] Fetters of Set, bandages placed over the mouth of the deceased

Figure 60: The Djed Pillar of Asar

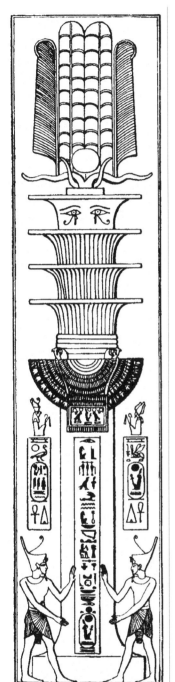

Asar is also the *Djed* Pillar. The Djed Pillar, as you know, has four tiers. It is a pillar which is also known as the backbone of Asar. It is also a city. The city is called *Djedu*, the city of the Djedu is one of the original places of worship of Asar. I will discuss with you how this djed is the actual central shaft of your back and goddess Aset and Nebthet are the two serpents that, together with the pillar, to form a caduceus in your body. Remember that these are the different ways to discover and attain the Principle of Asar. They lead to the opening of the Tree path, into and through the Principle of Asar. The four upper Psycho-Spiritual Consciousness Centers are highlighted in the Djed of Asar. Those who exist in and through these principles are elevated beings. They are called ⸢𓀃𓅓𓏲𓊃⸣ *djaasu* –sages, wise ones.

Asar, first of all, has more names than Ra. Ra has 75 names; Asar has more than 75 names. Asar is the soul of all of Ra's creations. Actually, he has a shrine in every city and goes even beyond after that. In the title, Asar ⸢𓊨𓂋𓈗𓇾𓈉⸣ *Asar m taiu nebu – Asar in places within all the lands* we find a pantheistic international, universal conception; *taiu* means lands, and *nebu* means all the various places, so we have Asar, in all the lands and places. It means that Asar exists everywhere. There is also ⸢𓁹𓂋𓅜𓅬𓅬𓀾𓄿𓊨⸣ *Asar Zaa* - Asar the shepherd; ⸢𓊨𓃀𓂋𓂧𓂋𓊨⸣ *Asar Neberdjer* "Asar All-encompassing Divinity" (in other words Supreme Being in the name Asar), ⸢𓊨𓂋𓋹𓉗𓂓𓊪𓏏𓎛𓊨⸣ *Asar m Ankh m Het Ka Ptah* "Asar the life in the house of the Ka of Ptah" in other words the God Ptah, ⸢𓊨𓂋𓉻𓊨⸣ *Asar m Anu* "Asar the one who is in Anu" in other words the god *Ra*, and ⸢𓊨𓂋𓇼𓊨⸣ *Asar m yanrutf*, "Asar in the place where nothing grows." Thus, Asar is where Ra, and Ptah are and the place beyond places. There are many other insightful epithets of Asar which enlighten us as to Asar's true identity and meaning. From the ones given above we can see that Asar is all encompassing, existing in and as Ra, as well as the land and in the transcendental places of existence.

So, Asar in one way is the physical being that came to earth and became the first king of Egypt. However, when he died his body became motionless and inert. Yet, through Aset, he came back to life; not the physical life but the after-physical life, in the netherworld {*Duat*}. There he is the soul of all, there he is in the land and in the heavens, in the souls of people and in the souls of the gods and goddesses and in Ra and all that emanates from Ra. So Asar is the key to breaking through from the *Ta* region of the physical world and the realm of human beings to the *Pet* region, the realm of the subtle elements and the lower Astral worlds. Therefore, we must grow to discover Asar and when we do we see the rest of the road ahead, from what we are, the soul to Ra, the Spirit, that which manifests in and through our "soulness." Then, as we continue on the journey of the Tree of Life, we will know the inner most reality of our selves and the extent to which we are in all things of Creation as well; and knowing this we will know all there is to be known. With this we conclude our lesson for now.

Questions and Answers

Question:

My question has to do with the Asarian Resurrection and the principles of the personality, Asar, Aset, and Nebethet. In the union of Asar and Aset vs. the union of Asar and Nebethet is one union seen as a righteous and as a correct union, and the other one is perhaps not supposed to be?

Answer by Sebai MAA (Dr. Muata Ashby):

Mythologically speaking, in a mythic sense, the unions have a philosophical meaning, a mystical meaning, an esoteric meaning behind them. And if you try to apply the ordinary, limited human social morality based on a particular culture, then you're going to come up with different answers and lose the mystic teaching. For example, the people who follow Islam are going to look at that and say, "Oh, wow, this is some wild orgiastic demoniac religion" or whatever. When I was in Egypt I heard that kind of statement from people there who are Muslims. And the Christians may think so as well. The Hindus may not because they have similar traditions. Metaphorically, a myth has a teaching that is behind the events, plots, themes and relations contained in it. And I explained this a little bit earlier in this series, and I explained it also in prior classes, that when you are, it's called reading a myth, you're trying to read and understand what the sage has brought forth metaphorically and metaphysically, as well as philosophically. If you try to – as I say, apply the social morality based on some conception of time and space [phenomenological] interpretation, then you're going to come up with something mundane, and something that is going to appear primitive, as well as gross, and perhaps even vulgar. And this is how many in western culture have tended to look at these things and in general anything that is not originated in western culture. Those of us who have been reared in western culture, in whole or in part, must take care not to apply that standard but to see with the Ancient Egyptian proverb says, "Strive to see with the inner eye, the heart. It sees the reality not subject to emotional or personal error; it sees the essence." Intuition then is the most important quality to develop.

So when we're looking at the union of Asar and Aset, we're looking at the creation of Heru. Asar, the soul comes together with intuition, with wisdom. It brings forth aspiration and the desire for enlightenment. When the soul comes together with death {Asar and Nebethet}, it opens up the door to discernment, because the soul realizes that it is not the body, it's not eternal in the body, so it starts to ask the questions that lead to knowledge of right and wrong, and truth and untruth and wisdom and ignorance, which eventually lead to spiritual enlightenment. So, from this higher perspective you can go back and look at where I talked about the principle of Asar and the principle of Nebethet as the principle of death and mortality and the means for Asar to reincarnate. One can see this death as a detrimental aspect but actually the principle of Nebethet potentially opens the door for the soul, to redemption, to eternity. And otherwise, if there was no Nebethet, the soul would be caught in physicality forever, and would not be able to escape the pains and sorrows of life as well as the delusions of human existence. Therefore, it is not a question of if one relationship is good and another bad but the reality is that both are necessary and therefore what is going to be the quality of the relationships? Will it be based on ignorance as most people do, so that they do not develop dispassion or wisdom and keep on suffering and reincarnating or will it be more elevated as we are discussing here?

Reflection and Journal discipline:

<u>**1-**</u> **At the top of each page copy the following hieroglyphs to the best of your ability**

[***cht n ankh*** *" tree of life"*]

After studying the Lesson proceed to answer the following question and write the answer in your journal. This exercise will require more than one reading and more than one journal entry, at least one page; write all you can find related to the subject of the question. Answer the questions first without referring to the text you just read. Then go back and see if you missed anything. This exercise is to be repeated until you become proficient with the principles of this sphere. The reflection exercise should be done after each reading or study session. Then you may practice meditation[104] on the wisdom you have learned. You may come back to add to your reflections even if you move on to other lessons.

<u>REFLECTIONS:</u> Lord of the Black, the nothingness of deep being, I come to you for knowing I am more than the death of bodies. Lord of the Netherworld, lord of the land of no thought open my eyes to the worlds beyond and to the glories of immortality! As you were once dead but now live let me live! Let me be green as you are green; let me be black as you are black…and let me see the way to be ever free, the gateway to the darkness and the light!

After studying the Lesson proceed to answer the following question and write the answer in your journal.

What is urduhat and why is it important?

What is(are) the main teaching(s) of this lesson and what do the principle(s) of the divinity(ies) discussed in this lesson mean in reference to my actions, feelings, thoughts and desires and understanding of the spiritual philosophy?

---

[104] Explained in more detail in Lesson 15

Lesson 11: The Principle of Geb, and Freedom from the Earth Realm

We continue today picking up where we left off in the Tree of Life series of Anunian theology, Ancient Egyptian studies that have taken us to the very beginning of Neterian culture and philosophy, specifically focusing on the *Tree of Life of Anunian Theurgy*, the religious science of the priests and priestesses of the city of Anu in Ancient Egypt. Let us begin with a brief review of some major teachings we have discussed in previous lessons. This lecture series is based on the *African Religion Volume 1: Anunian Theology* book, and the conception of the Tree of Life within the teaching of Anunian Theurgy. Anunian theology, is the study of Anunian Theurgy (Anunian religious science and philosophy of Ancient Egypt) and Anunian philosophy is the earliest advanced and recorded religious teaching known in human history. It's called Anunian because it began, or it was created, in the city of Anu in ancient Africa by the Ancient Egyptians. Anu is a city in the northeastern corner of the continent of Africa, the land which was later known to the world as Egypt, the land of Kemet. Anunian Theurgy states that in the beginning, there was a watery mass, and then from that watery mass emerged the Supreme Being, and that watery mass was its body. And by its desire, by its action, it turned that watery mass into the forms of creation. And how did it do so? By creating nine principles, along with itself, making ten. These nine principles represent the elements of creation.

Now, most of you have heard that there are four elements: earth, water, air, fire and maybe a fifth one, if you add ether. And is this only half of the teaching. From the Tree of Life series, we have learned that there are actually ten elements that go to compose our reality, because if you have ether, air, water, fire, earth, what does it mean? What can you do with that? These five are just the basis of creation, the building blocks of physical objects. In order for a human being to have an experience of creation, to perceive and relate in time and space reality, they need to have five more elements, and those elements we have introduced already in this series. There must be the element of Asar, the principle of Asar, which is soul. If you don't have soul, you can forget having experience as a human being. You can forget your senses. They won't help you. They won't do you any good. You'll be just like a corpse. A corpse has nose to smell with, fingers to touch with, skin to feel with, eyes to see with, ears to hear with, and so on and so forth, but those senses do that body no good. They do that personality no good because there's no soul. And beyond that what sustains the soul? The higher principles and most of all Ra, sustain the soul and its existence.

Now, what if you have a soul, and you have the elements, but you don't have wisdom? You'd be running around like an animal, living off of instinct. And what conscience does an animal have of the world? This is what makes human beings different from animals. You have intellect; you can cognize; you can reflect. But what good will the capacity to reflect be if you don't have Nebethet? If you don't have death? It will not be useful because all your reflections are going to be about life, and not about the opposite. They're going to be one dimensional.

"Evil as well as good, both operate to advance the Great Plan."
-Ancient Egyptian Proverb

And what will you do without Set, without opposition? Without that which is negative? If there is no trouble in life you'll never come to the temple of Aset and listen to the teaching, because everything's going soooo good for you; because there's no trouble, and Set means trouble. And Nebethet means death. Nebethet is like the failsafe. If Set doesn't teach you your lesson in one lifetime, Nebethet has to come along and kill you so that you will come back so that you will die, and come back another day, and have the struggle again.

Also, death is there so that we can give other souls a chance to incarnate, and put their two cents in about how they think that the world should be, imagine if the same people were alive all the time, and no one was to ever die. It would be a pathetic situation. Without death you would never grow, never change, because death is a passageway into a dynamic kind of transformation, and at least a possibility for that ultimate transformation but in any case a forced transition from one personality to a different one, so either a vertical movement or at least a horizontal movement through reincarnation. There are certain transformations that people cannot do while they're alive. They're locked in. They're locked in by their mental complexes, by their parentage, by their family, by their traditions, by their cultures. So together with goddess Nebethet and goddess Ma'at, goddess Meskhent pushes you on, so that you can be born into a different family, born into a different situation, born as a different character, but still possessing the same soul, albeit ignorant of it's true nature beyond the personalities it operates through. In one likely you'll be a mother, one likely you'll be a father, and in another lifetime you'll be a sister, in the next a brother, in the next a government worker, in the next a farmer, in the next an enemy, in the next a friend, in the next healthy, in the next sick, etc. So, through this process, you can get all the realms of experience so you won't be one-sided in your experience. And the broader your experience becomes, the more expanded your consciousness. But what good is all this possibility, to gain all these experiences, if you don't have any spiritual aspiration, if you don't have the desire to achieve the ultimate freedom, and that is Heru Ur? What would be the purpose of life if you are born just to face the insecurities and anxieties of growing up, go through the toil of raising children, suffer the ravages of old age and disease, love some people, hate others, desire objects of the world and be forced to run around competing with other people just to get pleasures and accumulate objects only to give them up at the time of death?

The answer is that there would be no real purpose to that kind of life. The wisdom that comes from the study of the gods and goddesses gives life meaning but even more than that, it provides insight into a means to experience the meaning; so this is not just an intellectual exercise that leads nowhere or a psychological delusion such as is experienced in faith-based religions. In the center of the Anunian Cosmiconomythograph, it has a great obelisk and the ten neteru or gods and goddesses of Anunian theurgy. And they're called a paut, or pauti. Pauti means company of gods and goddesses. And, of course, as you know, that is from a religious perspective, we call them gods and goddesses. From a metaphysical perspective, mystical perspective, we call them principles, cosmic forces. And as you enter into these studies, we get into the esoteric aspect of Anunian theurgy, and Neterianism in general. Neterianism is the religion of ancient Africa, ancient Egypt.

We talked, in earlier classes, about how to worship the divinities, how to master these principles, emulating them, purifying yourself through Ma'at, allowing yourself to embody these principles, acting with these principles in your day-to-day life. We also talked about the conception that there are two forms of worship. *Ushet* or *Uashu* is the term for worship. You worship the divinities with the elements that are related to the divinities, and these elements are related to us in the scriptures as well as the myth and stories of the divinities, the iconographies, the hieroglyphic texts related to them; The symbolism of their very appearance, their interrelationships, mythically, give us insight. Those divinities that are of a lower nature, provide insights into the nature of the lower and they are worshipped with lower forms of artifacts. And the term "lower" here does not mean, necessarily, low as in base or degraded. What it means is that it is in a position lower to other positions in a relative hierarchy of Creation. The grosser aspect of creation is a lower form, and the subtler aspect is the higher form. It's a matter of relativity.

And you see the Tree of Life. The five lower divinities are divinities of the grosser realms, they are divinities of the earth realm. The higher divinities are more subtle conceptions, and they are divinities of the heavenly realm and the transcendental netherworld. The five lower divinities are actually lower forms of divinity, divinities of the material world, and are to be worshiped in a lower way, with lower articles of the material world, with incense, with burning fires, with uttering chants, audibly, and so on and so forth. From a relative perspective, the lower the form the more material worship is enjoined and the higher the lesser. From a mystical absolute perspective all ten belong to the realm of time and space and so are to be worshipped with time and space objects and in time and space ways. But some of them are subtler than the others, so the means and objects of their relative worship is adjusted accordingly.

Now, if we worship the divinities that transcend time and space, then we must use means that transcend time and space also. We cannot even use mind to worship those divinities. The highest form of worship is the worship when you embody the divinity, when you become one, when there's no more you. And the highest divinity transcends all thoughts and conceptions of embodiment or non-embodiment and so on and so forth. It's abstract.

And that is what the symbol of the scroll ⌐ means in Neterian Theurgy. The scroll means abstract. And the scroll is also a symbol of wisdom. There's an aspect of wisdom that is concrete and time and space related, and also there's an aspect that is transcendental and abstract. The abstract, the transcendental, cannot be related directly in words. But it can be talked about; it can be explained indirectly in parables, in riddles, paradoxes. It can be pointed to. But it cannot be named. And, in the same way, the transcendental divinities have an earthly time and space name, but they also have an unnamable name. However, as the transcendental aspect of the cosmic forces, is rooted in the same source they all unite in the transcendental oneness that is the Neberdjer.

All this and more we have discussed in our journey through the Tree. But today we have a special treat for you. If you have not gained an insight already into the masterful synchronicity of Neterianism you will be rewarded today. Neterianism is the spiritual system related to the gods and goddesses of Ancient Egypt, who are referred to as neteru. Neterianism is Shetaut Neter, the hidden divinity, the formal name of the religion. And as we continue today, you're going to see more of this synchronicity, how the interrelationships work, and how the study of the divinities leads us to know ourselves, and to attain spiritual enlightenment.

So, today, we are going to study the divinity Geb. Recapping again, we discussed how Ra came from the primeval ocean and his body itself was a primeval ocean. He turned part of his body into the divinities, the elements and cosmic forces. First, he engendered Shu and Tefnut, which we're going to be discussing in future lectures. Then, Shu and Tefnut came together and they gave birth to Geb and Nut. Geb and Nut gave birth to Asar and Aset, Set and Nebethet and Heru-Ur. And we have been going from the bottom up. We have been discussing the Tree of Life, the journey of the Tree of Life, from the bottom up. From top down, the journey is of creation. From down up, the journey is one of dissolution, of dismantling creation so as to discover its constituent parts and by deconstructing it, to learn of its secrets, in order to not be deluded by it, in other words, to know the higher truth beyond it.

As you study and learn about the divinities, about the concepts and the principles – actually, what is happening is that they are being deconstructed in your mind. If you listen to the teaching well, we are deconstructing these conceptions, these principles, and at the same time Creation itself is being dismantled in your mind, that is, the illusory understanding about Creation that you have developed is being torn down. We are dissolving them in your mind, and as that happens, you, as a personality, also dissolve, and what is left at the end of that dissolution? What is left is supreme and transcendental being which is the reality behind all of the principles. That's how it's supposed to work.

So now, with the last lecture, we concluded the lower divinities, the divinities that come to make up the human personality. You have all the elements within you, but the lower five mostly represent the prominent aspects of your personality as discussed – soul, which is Asar, wisdom which is Aset, egoism, which is Set, mortality, which is Nebethet, aspiration and redemption which is Heru-Ur. As we break through the level of Asar and Aset, now we move into the realm of heaven, the heavenly worlds, the cosmic divinities, the principles that transcend this little world, the physical world that you're on, your little ego, and your little soul, and your little wisdom about life, and your life and death, and your aspirations, which, in the end of it, is all one little insignificant grain of sand in the midst of the world, and the world is an insignificant little grain of sand in the midst of even our own galaxy. Our own galaxy is an insignificant grain of sand in the midst of the whole universe and the universe is a thought in the mind of the Supreme Being. This brief set of reflections is to give you an idea to show you how little you are as a personality, and how significant you are as a Cosmic Being because the Cosmic Being that permeates and sustains the Creation is the innermost identity of the soul of everyone. In other words, as you expand to encompass the entire creation, then it's a different story.

So, now we move into the cosmic principles. We begin with Geb. Geb is the earth, element. And his wisdom is related to us in the Pyramid Texts. In the Pyramid Text of *Unas,* which is the earliest extensive spiritual text and earliest comprehensive Neterian writing in history, he is related as the king of the gods and goddesses. Why, you may ask, is that so? Was it not established that Ra was the king of the gods and goddesses? We are going to discuss that later.

Figure 61: Forms of The Ancient Egyptian God Geb

The main symbolism that they use for the headdress of Geb is a goose and/or the crown of lower Egypt, the area with the delta in the north, the crown, the red crown of the papyrus swamps. As we said before, his element is earth, that's what he represents, that's his principle, his cosmic force. And earth element is everything physical, everything that comes out of the earth, that's in the earth, metals, minerals, vitamins, plants, everything that lives off of those is presided over by Geb. The earth itself is called *het-geb,* or the house of Geb. There are no special temples of Geb, like, for example, Asar, who has a special temple, Aset who has a special temple, and so on. Geb is one of the universally worshipped divinities. He also presides over the *neter-khert.* The term Neter-khert is composed of neter, which means "divinity," and khert means "under." The symbol for that is like a kilt, a skirt, what is under your skirt. As opposed to over, on top. So it means "the divine realm that is below," that is the graveyard, the tomb. So Geb presides over the earth and what is below the surface, the grave.

And another term that is given for Geb is *smam-ur.* This comes from *"smam"* or unite, make union. Smam-ur means the powerful holder(uniter) and in the *Pert M Hru*[105] text, the initiate says, "I have asked Geb to open my jaws. I have asked Geb to open my eyes. I have asked Geb to loosen up the bandages that are wrapping my body as a mummy." And the reason why the initiate does this in the *Pert M Hru* text is because Geb is the Smam-ur, he's the great holder. He holds the key to the bolt that either opens or closes the earth realm into the netherworld.

So Geb "holds" the unworthy soul on earth just as the earth "holds" down objects that are not attached to it, from flying off into outer space. The god Geb has to aspects; one aspect is the physical objects and the earth itself. The other aspect is the magnetism of the physical objects. That magnetism works on objects and the grosser the object the more it can affected by the power of the magnetic force. Since mind is composed of subtle matter but matter nevertheless, it can be affected by "physical" magnetic forces. Magnetism is one of the most pervasive forces in the universe and the magnetism of one object can affect another across great expanses of space. For example, galaxies billions of miles away actually have a subtle effect on our galaxy and on us as well. It is important to understand that everything composed of physical elements is an object; therefore, even the human body and the mind, are objects. So if one is attracted to a person or another physical object the principle is the same. Again, the mind, being composed of physical elements can be affected by a magnetic force. But the subtlety or grossness of a person's mind is determined by the understanding of life and the kind of desires and objects that the mind holds dear or to be repudiated.

To the extent that the mind holds grosser mental elements (thoughts and feelings based on ignorance [desires, passions, longings, jealousy, envy, lust, etc.]) the mind is more susceptible to the worldly magnetic forces as opposed to a mind that has achieved clarity and has let go of illusory desires and egoistic sentiments. Magnetism operates in two modes, attraction and repulsion, which constitute a duality of perception. But just as the movement of attraction and repulsion both cause planets to remain apart (not physically touching each other) but still together (in locked orbits around each other), so too this duality complex (attraction and repulsion) operates

---

[105] See the book The Egyptian Book of The Dead Mysticism of the Pert Em Heru " by Dr. Muata Ashby, ISBN# 1-884564-28-3, CHAPTER 13 {Generally referred to as Chapter 26.} Words for giving a heart to Asar in the Neterkhert.

to keep the souls in a state of apparent individuality (distinct) separate from other souls and worldly objects but at the same time attached, dependent and entangled with them.

So attraction and repulsion are actually aspects of the same movement, away from transcendence and freedom because they both represent mental vibrations, mental accumulations of matter that cloud the higher vision of Self beyond time and space and cause the personality to perceive objects as being distinct from itself and itself also as a distinct entity among a myriad of other distinct personalities and this state of belief causes it to move towards or away from objects in an attempt to achieve its personal goal, in relation to those objects, which is impossible to achieve since the object of attraction or repulsion is illusory. The thought/feelings of attraction and repulsion, related to worldly objects and situations, that operate in the conscience of a human being are factors (due to ignorance (absence of the knowledge of the Higher Self)) based on the human being's level of spiritual evolution [or lack thereof] towards self-mastery and self-mastery here means self-sufficiency due to self-discovery through the inner fulfillment that comes from the revelation of the Higher Self. That inner fulfillment allows the mind to relinquish the illusory thoughts and feelings in order to discover the higher realms of being. Most people experience egoistic attraction and repulsion when they encounter worldly objects and situations and this produces more worldly entanglements because running towards an object or running away from it are both affirmations of its reality which is actually illusory and this is therefore, a fundamental cognitive error that leads to spiritual stagnation and worldly entanglement.

To be free from this cycle of ignorance the illusory reality itself needs to be rejected. This principle of attraction and repulsion can be applied to promote spiritual enlightenment rather than worldly entanglement. Though attraction and repulsion are both factors of illusory mental operation, yet, the attraction of the personality to the world which is also the cause of repulsion of other objects of the world must be confronted with repulsion directed towards the fundamental error, based on wisdom and not egoism. If the personality were turned from attraction and repulsion related to worldly objects and situations to attraction for the transcendent and repulsion for worldly ignorance and egoism, which lead to suffering, frustrations and disappointments, then the personality would be able to develop indifference and freedom from either worldly attraction or repulsion and those factors of mental operation [attraction and repulsion – based on egoistic illusory understanding of the world] will then no longer promote ignorance and lower consciousness in the form of gross content of mind that would be attracted or repulsed by worldly objects and be susceptible to the magnetism of worldly objects; the mind would instead be sensitive to and influenced by the magnetism of spirit which is subtler but more powerful than the ephemeral and enticing worldly objects and situations.

Table 1: How Attraction and Repulsion Operates in the Mind

Attraction	Repulsion
Unrighteousness	Righteousness
Desire	Indifference
Ignorance	Wisdom
Delusion	Understanding
Attachment	detachment

Geb holds the key, and he is the one who opens the door so that the light of Ra can come through every morning, and shine on the earth. He is also the one who holds the key to allow righteous souls to leave the earth realm when their time is up on earth, or he holds them if they are unrighteous souls. He holds them fast, he binds {smam} them to the earth. They have to "hang around" on earth, that is to say, in the lower netherworld, so they can suffer their fate or work through certain issues so they can then move forwards. They have to live another day, so therefore the initiate in the *Pert M Hru* says, "I am the heir of Geb." And you know who the heir of Geb is. The son of Geb is Asar, and Asar is the resurrected soul.

Now, how does this resurrection occur? In the *Pert M Hru* it says, one "Must live on the bread of Geb." The bread of Geb is purified divine food. This is the food that has been created with righteousness. Geb as *Per-*

204

aah, king of ancient Kemet presides also over righteousness – he is known as the King of Righteousness. Now, how did he become king? Before we continue, let's get on to that. In the writings of Manetho and in the Pyramid Texts, it also tells us that Ra came into being in the form of Khepri –Ra-Tem, he was the king of the gods and goddesses that he created, that he brought into being. And this is the earliest period. This is about 36,000 B.C., or prior. Then, there's the next period that comes through, when the gods and goddesses ruled the earth, and this mythic history is related to us also in the history of Manetho[106] and story of the divine cow, known as the story of Hetheru and Djehuti.[107] Then, at some point, also, Shu, his son became king. When Shu had his offsprings, Geb and Nut, Geb became the king. Geb and Nut have their children, and so Asar became king and of course Aset was queen. Asar and Aset had their baby, and that was Heru so Heru was next in line to be King.

When Ra was king, it talks about how he's king for thousands of years, and people had long lives, and then they started to ridicule him because they became arrogant, thinking they were as good as him. So one of the reasons why people are not allowed to live as long as they used to, they used to live hundreds of years in the past, is that you can live a thousand years, and if you're not a righteous person, if you're not on the path of spiritual enlightenment, you'll be just as ignorant and unrighteous on the last day of your life as you were on the first. You can live for ten thousand years and still remain ignorant and egoistic, and this is why death is there to force a person to think about living for something other than the little ego and its illusory desires.

Without death there would be constant misery because life is mostly misery punctuated by death. So death is actually a blessing. Not that you should run out and commit suicide, or go and slit your throat, or take a bunch of sleeping pills or anything like that. Suicide cannot help you from a philosophical perspective. The reason why it's not good is because you have to live out your life and you have to learn certain things. Otherwise, killing yourself and having your death is not going to help you, because Geb is going to close the bolt on the door and you're going to slam into it and you're going to be repelled back into the earth realm because you are not worthy to go to the next level, the higher realm of being, the netherworld.

So, then, after the time of the gods and goddesses, then we have the time of the *shemsu Heru.* This means "followers of Heru." We discussed this in a lecture series on how to be a Shems, how to be a follower of the teaching.[108] The whole philosophy of being a spiritual aspirant has been discussed. The *Shemsu Heru* were sages who lived in ancient times and they continued the divine tradition through a lineage. Then came the realm of the time of mortal kings and queens.

Now, there is a legend or story about Geb and Nut. This is a very subtle story, and I'm not going to go into the details of it here because some of you are at different levels. Some of you who are at a certain level will get what is being said. Some of you, it'll pass right over, and then you'll have to read to this lecture and the whole Tree of Life series again and again, and read some of the books over, and study and listen to lectures for a couple of years before you can get it.

The story is about how Geb and Nut came together and they laid an egg. This is aside from the other children that they had, Asar, Aset, Set, Nebethet and Heru. They laid an egg, and this egg turned out to be the egg that gave birth to the Bennu bird. The Bennu bird is what the Greeks called the Phoenix. The Bennu is similar, in some ways, to the sunbird of the Native Americans. The Bennu is a bird that resurrects every day with the newborn sun. It is in fact the newborn sun. Suffice it to say, for now, that he laid an egg. This is why they call him the Great Cackler. This is why his symbolism is related to the goose. He engendered an egg. He and Nut laid an egg. And this same Bennu bird, who is the fiery sun god, is also Ra. So you see, there's a little paradox

[106] see the book *THE AFRICAN ORIGINS OF CIVILIZATION, RELIGION AND YOGA SPIRITUALITY AND ETHICS PHILOSOPHY* by Dr. Muata Ashby
[107] see the book *TEMPLE RITUAL OF THE ANCIENT EGYPTIAN MYSTERIES--THEATER & DRAMA OF THE ANCIENT EGYPTIAN MYSTERIES* by Dr. Muata Ashby.
[108]**Ausarian Resurrection Shemsu Series—How to be a Shemsu of the Divine** (Available from the Sema Institute) **www.Egyptianyoga.com** Audio lecture series
330 A & B How to be a Shemsu (Devotee) of the Divine Part 1
331 How to be a Shemsu Part 2: Being Free of Desires
332 A & B Being a Shemsu Part 3

here. How can Geb give birth to his own father? It also relates to how can you discover your own power to create yourself?

Figure 62: The God Bennu

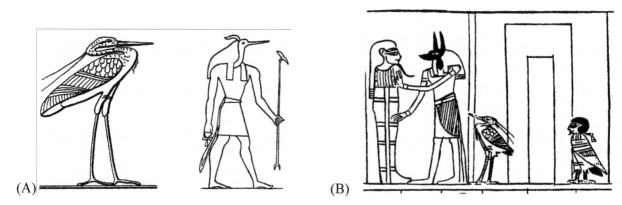

Figure 63: Above –left: the Bennu as (A)bird and as (B)bird headed god.

Figure 64: Above –right: Anpu places the mummy in the tomb while the Bennu and the Ba {soul} look on.

Figure 65: Bennu from Pert m heru Chapter 4

Moving on; we therefore call Geb the *Gen Gen Ur*. *Gen Gen Ur* means Great cackler, as in quack, quack, the sound that the goose makes. He's the great one, because he laid the big egg. Another important symbolism of Geb is the Technu ᵐᵐᵐ ℮ ⌐. Technu is the obelisk. Technu, also, if you recall, in the Kybalion metaphysical series lectures,[109] relates to the term *techn*, which means to vibrate, and Geb vibrates the earth realm,

the earth element. The term *techn* is related phonetically to the term ◎ ⌐🗕 *dchn*, which means to vibrate as in playing a musical instrument. When you utter words of power, Geb is the power that you are using in those words that shakes your earth element. This is what is being done with the sistrum, shaking the sistrum; you are shaking your upper psycho-spiritual consciousness centers to move that earth {physicality} of our body, and it's like an earthquake, and the same idea is related to the planet. It is said that when Geb moves, we have an earthquake, and when there is thunder, and the whole earth realm shakes and shudders it is Geb we are feeling.

[109] Teaching of the Kybalion – Ancient Hermetic (Djehuti) Text:
Series dates: 3/24/02 to 4/14/02 Available through Sema Books www.Egyptianyoga.com

And when you see him in the creation papyri, and this is in your Anunian Theology books, and also in the *Pert m Hru* text, the picture where Geb, Nut, and Shu are shown, you are essentially looking at the creation of air/space, earth and the heavens.

Figure 66: Shu separates Nut (the sky) from Earth

Before Geb was created, it is related in the myth of the creation how Geb and Nut were locked up in a sexual embrace. Geb's Technu was stretching forth out of himself into the sky, so Geb's Technu is also known as his penis, sticking out into the sky, and the sky is Nut.[110] Ra sent forth Shu to come between them, to separate them, and when Geb came out of Nut, the five children of the human personality, Asar, Aset, Set, Nebethet and Heru Ur came out. This is what the Pyramid Texts tell us.

Now, this is all related to tantrism, but we are not going to get into that aspect of the Theurgy right now because in this particular lecture series we're learning about the principles, and how to practice their wisdom which leads to mastering them. And to the extent of what you already know related to the tantric aspect, it will suffice for now.[111]

Up to this point, Geb was recumbent. He was calm and unmoving, but at this time when Shu comes along, and makes the movement, he pushes them apart, then Geb starts to move, and the heavens start to shake also, the sky and the earth. In relation to the Tjef Neteru Postures of the gods and goddesses, Geb has some important postures that are important to our study, and when you practice the Geb postures, when you're doing the Geb spinal twists, when you're doing the Geb plow posture, you are creating a movement in your body that is in opposition to being a couch potato. When you're a couch potato, you know what happens, you get lazy. Your belly grows big, you become like Sage Amenemope says, "a mass of food." You get caught up in the fatness of the world, the seemingly pleasurable but intrinsically illusory fancies of the world. If you do the movement of Geb, you're shaking off sedentariness. And if your movement is righteous, if your food of the earth is righteous, then you have good health.

---

[110] see the book *SACRED SEXUALITY: EGYPTIAN TANTRA YOGA: The Art of Sex* Sublimation and Universal Consciousness by Dr. Muata Ashby ISBN 1-884564-03-8

[111] see the book *SACRED SEXUALITY: EGYPTIAN TANTRA YOGA: The Art of Sex* Sublimation and Universal Consciousness by Dr. Muata Ashby ISBN 1-884564-03-8

So Geb is also related to Aset in the teachings of health and of course Aset is one of the primary divinities presiding over health and healing. Recalling the myth of Asar, Aset, and Heru, it relates that when Aset was fleeing away from Set, he wanted to kill her and the baby Heru. She came along and one of Set's evil scorpions had stung a baby, a child. And it was said that Geb gave her the words of power to heal the child, because, again, he presides over the herbs and minerals as well as poisons. There is another myth, remember how in the myth of Ra and Aset, when Ra takes his daily walk, he goes on his journey through the sky, he was actually taking a walk through the sky on his prescribed path. Before he would come out, over the horizon, he would ask, "Geb, where are all your serpents? Where are all your snakes? I don't want to be bitten today." And Geb would go and look for them. Well, of course, on this particular day, Aset created a special serpent and put it on his path that he could not see, and it poisoned him. But that's, again, another myth, a spiritual teaching contained in a legendary story of the gods and goddesses of Ancient Egypt.

This brief rendition was just to show you how it all meshes together. It's called synchronicity. Going back to the Bennu, it is Ra, the newborn Ra as the fiery sunbird, the phoenix. The text also tells us that this same Phoenix – follow this, now, the same Phoenix, the same Bennu is the soul of Ra. And, the same soul of Ra is the living Asar; what we have here is the divine spirit coming forth, being born into the realm of time and space through Geb, the Bennu and then Asar; and of course there is Heru, who comes from Asar and the Kings and Queens of Egypt are incarnations of Heru. Ra, Geb, Asar, Heru, they're one and the same. And the followers of Heru are one and the same. And *Peraah* (Pharaohs) are one and the same. And those who follow the path, as it is taught in the Asarian myth, the myth of Asar who is the Shepherd who holds the flail, which means self-discipline, and the crook which means princeliness (princessness), (in other words, discovering one's royal nature as heir to the throne of Asar, in other words discovering one is Heru), they are a heirs to the throne, that is to say, the wisdom of Aset. You follow the discipline, the *shems* [devotee, follower] path, and you become a prince or a princess, which means that you are next in line for the throne; and this is why the initiate says "I am the heir of Geb".

So the movements of Geb relate to the movements of the solid aspect of creation. So, to recap, we have Ra, Shu, Geb, and the Bennu coming forth, and the soul, through time and space, then being born as Asar in the living form, dying and being resurrected, redeemed as Heru and then maintaining as the Peraah, the Pharaoh.

Figure 67: The God Geb in the Spinal Twist Posture

The movements of Geb, finally, relate to three important aspects. It comes down to what it means to master the element of the earth. The first movement is the creation movement. When you do the first posture of Geb, the first of the two main postures of Geb, you're entering into a creation movement, a creative space. If you move into that creation realm you can also uncreate. You're creating a dissolution movement. The next thing you want to do is to have a movement of unbolting, or taking the lock off the door between the earth realm and the heavenly realm. This is accomplished by promoting flexibility in the physical body, especially the spine; it also means purity of the body through fresh herbs, greens and fruits that Geb produces. You want to open the door so the light of Ra can shine on you, and also, you want to be able to finally escape the earth realm.

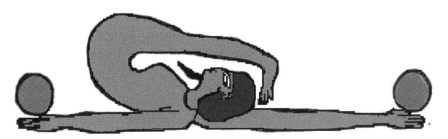

Figure 68: The God Geb in the Plough Posture

When they shoot a rocket out into space, it has to achieve escape velocity. Otherwise, it'll be like when you throw a rock up into the sky, it falls right back. That happens because it does not have enough escape velocity. If the rock had escape velocity, it would go straight through into outer space. It would escape the gravity of the earth. And if you have not become subtle as a human being, if you have not practiced righteousness and truth and fasting from the activities of the earth in your life, your conscience, your body, your mind becomes very sedentary, very heavy; your body becomes physically fat and your mind and soul become weighed down with complexes and sorrows and desires, regrets and ignorance. Spiritual development is a movement of increasing subtlety. And if you become subtle enough, you're going to achieve escape velocity. This means not holding on to earthly things, gross things, by means of your desires born of ignorance and delusions. It means realizing that earthly things belong to the earth and heavenly things belong to heave and making the decision that you want to belong to heaven {higher realms of consciousness including becoming one with the Divine} instead of belonging to the earth.

Ba ar pet shat ar ta
Soul to heaven, Body to earth

Now, keep in mind that we are giving a metaphor here; your physical body does not escape, though some of the subtle parts of the personality do escape. Remember the ancient Egyptian saying, "Body belongs to the earth, the soul belongs to heaven." But on the other hand know that as long as you are caught up in unrighteousness and are ignorantly holding on to earthly objects and worldly concepts, the Smam-Ur is going to come and grab you and hold you, and those mummy swathings will never be taken off. You will not be like the resurrected Asar but rather a reincarnated soul; that is called *Uhem ankh* –"To Live again – Reincarnation."

Mastery of the earth element means also mastering your cravings for food and earthly desires. Mainly the issues of the three lower psycho-spiritual consciousness energy centers [*sefech Ba Ra - "seven souls of Ra"*] must be mastered. The first issue is food. The first psycho-spiritual consciousness center relates to food. Overeating is a problem in which the food has mastered you. The food has control over you and in a negative way. Fasting is a method of controlling the earth element. Exercise in moderation is another. Eating pure and unprocessed foods is another. Along with these the philosophy of the teaching that promotes dispassion and detachment also must be practiced in order to render the objects of the world powerless to arouse unwanted and uncontrolled interest in you. The nourishment of the spiritual teaching is a food of mind.[112] And, of course, Geb presides over uranium and other naturally occurring elements that are toxic to the human body. He also presides over the elements that were unrighteously combined by chemical manufacturers and corporations that put out toxic waste and chemicals that are also harmful. You can take note that Geb puts the chemicals in their place in the earth. He doesn't put them in your environment, he doesn't put them in your body, to begin with. People recombine things and ingest the toxic chemicals, due to ignorance, delusion and greed. With Geb

---

[112] see the book *The Kemetic Diet* by Dr. Muata Ashby and see the book *The Serpent Power* by Dr. Muata Ashby

the earth is ordered. The earth realm is righteous. Putting pesticides and preservatives in your food, cooking it beyond the capacity to retain its life force, all this is unrighteousness of food. You're poisoning yourself. People can also poison themselves with unrighteous thoughts and unrighteous speech, as well; this is the subtle food but we are concentrating on right now physical food. All these things are ways to weigh the soul down on earth.

Controlling earthly pleasure and the desire for sexuality is related to the second energy center. [113] here also are those who desire to live in comfortable conditions, who feel that everything should be posh and comfortable. These are counterproductive things for you as an aspirant. You don't want to be living in terrible conditions, in a war zone, things like that, but you don't want to actually also be having people wait on you and do everything for you and all that kind of thing either. If you do you become soft, conceited and delusional about the reality of the world which is in reality not wholly pleasurable for anyone from an egoistic perspective. If you did that you would be sheltered from the reality of the world and the spiritual challenge cannot be made effectively under those circumstances. Under those conditions Heru within you cannot have a challenge to come forth and redeem you as Asar. Heru had to suffer defeat and failure in order to discern the correct path to success. [114] Mastering the earth element, the principle of Geb, allows you to achieve that success also.

And, in closing, in the teaching in the *Pert M Heru* it states, "I go into the *het* (house) of Geb, the earth, which is the *Neter Khert*, (which is the grave) the tomb." It says, "I go in as a hawk, and I come out as a Bennu" meaning, I go in as a challenger, as a redeemer, and I come out resurrected, enlightened, and transcendental." Therefore, by practicing the wisdom of Geb, purifying yourself in accordance with his tradition, in body and mind, and growing in detachment of worldly things, practicing his postures and propitiating his forms, realizing yourself in them ultimately as Ra, leads you to escape the earth realm, you move beyond the grave and the surface worldly existence and enter into the arms of mother Nut, the sky, who takes you up to the heavens and to your rightful place among the stars.

This concludes our lesson for today.

[113] see the book *SACRED SEXUALITY: EGYPTIAN TANTRA YOGA: The Art of Sex* Sublimation and Universal Consciousness by Dr. Muata Ashby ISBN 1-884564-03-8 and see the book *The Serpent Power* by Dr. Muata Ashby
[114] See the book *African Religion Vol. 4 Asarian Theology* by Dr. Muata Ashby, See the book *The War of Heru and Set* by Dr. Muata Ashby

Special Comment by Seba Dr. Dja Ashby based on lesson 11

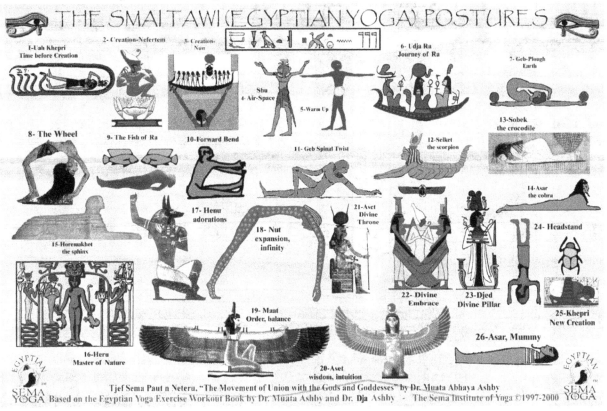

Figure 69: Tjef Neteru system of Ancient Egyptian gods and goddesses postures

Sebai MAA (Dr. Muata Ashby) spoke about and related the aspect of Geb, the principle of Geb, to some of the postures in the Tjef Neteru system, specifically the posture of the spinal twist, and also the posture of the plow relating to the earth, because what do you do with a plow? You dig into the earth with the plow, so likewise, you're digging into your unconscious mind, the depths of your being, when you practice this posture as well. The other thing about the earth element and the earth itself is that, as you know, one of the things that us humans do is that we take our garbage and we throw it in the earth. And the earth has a great capacity to take all the different objects and forms and names that we throw at it and it breaks them down into the very basic bare constituent elements, and then, from that, it has the capacity now to use these elements and actually produce and support new forms of objects that actually become nourishment to sustain our human lives. They produce trees, plants, plants that serve us food for humanity, for animals, trees that help to produce oxygen to nourish, again, human beings, and as you know, even the act of composting is possible.

You take your food, the parts of the food you don't want, you put it in a pile, and then it breaks down and that food actually becomes nourishment to the earth, and through that more food comes forth that actually will give you nourishment and be able to sustain you, and that is one of the principles that also you can derive from Geb, because, in your own life, in daily life, as you are in the world, how many times do you feel fed up. "I'm tired of taking everybody's garbage. I'm tired of taking everybody's crap. I'm tired of taking it – everybody dumps on me." Think of what we do to the earth, how we dump on the earth, as I said, how we give it our crap, we give it our garbage, and what does it do?

So, a lesson also of the principle of Geb is the capacity to transform all the negativity that you feel is coming at you. Actually allow it to come into you, but then, through your consciousness, through your vibration, your mental vibration, to allow it to be actually broken down. And what you give in return, when somebody's giving you impatience? What can you give to that person? You can give to that person patience. You can break it down, transform it, and naturally, just as earth gives beautiful fruit and oxygen and food, you can actually give them things that will actually nourish their soul as well. They're giving you anger and frustration. You can give them silence. You can allow them to get it off their chest without taking it personally. You can give them compassion. You give them understanding.

And then also relating to the aspect of Nut as the heavens, as the sky; there's also another great lesson in there, a lesson also on effectiveness. Because think of the sky; The sky is there. The heavens are there. When you look up, every day it's not necessarily clear. Some days there are really dark clouds and all sorts of clouds can be there. They may be obstructing your vision of the sky. And what do people say? "Oh, the sky looks terrible today. Oh, the sky looks horrible today", but in reality, the clouds are different from the sky. The clouds are beneath the sky, and Nut, the sky, she's ever unaffected by these clouds.

But think about a human life – in your own life, how human beings react when there are dark clouds in their life, dark clouds of trouble. Dark clouds of problems, or what they consider to be problems in their lives, situations in their lives that are troubling them. How does that person feel? Who is affected by it? Are the clouds separate from the personality? Or do people take it personally and egoistically, concentrating on the "I", saying: "I" have these problems, "I" have these worries. "I'm" so troubled by it. "I'm" so burdened by it. "I'm" so affected by it. Oh, everything in "my" life is terrible.

So Nut also relates to an aspect of separation, of being unaffected, being detached from your situations in life, the clouds that come to you. Sometimes, it's good situations. Sometimes it's a really little light cloud, or a fluffy wonderful cute little cloud; they may be all the different wonderful shapes that you like. Sometimes it's a dark and troublesome cloud that comes to you, but whatever the cloud is that comes to you, you must know that you are the Self, the immortal soul. You are the unaffected self, unaffected by all the different clouds in life. The real you is unaffected by the good and the bad, actually. You're separate from your situations. You're the unaffected self.

Questions and Answers

Question:

In reference to the principle of Geb, as some of the disciplines needed to master Geb are of the lower principles, seeing that Geb is of the heavenly realm, I was figuring his principles might have been mostly a mental or astral nature, bearing in mind it will also take that concerted effort of will power to master the forces of Geb.

Answer by Sebai MAA (Dr. Muata Ashby):

That's a point well taken. We shall consider something that I was alluding to in the lecture, that with Geb, even though you have the earth element, which relates to everything that is physical, that is grossly physical; recall that I also talked about the grossness as well as the subtlety of the neteru, the principles of Creation. The grossness of your body, the bones, the skin, muscles, and your flesh relates to the physical aspect of you, but also there is a subtle principle behind your physicality from which physicality emanates. Even your conception of physicality is included, your idea of physicality itself. This is where we get into more of the astral or metaphysical conception behind Geb.

Mastering Geb means mastering the gross physicality, which means that even the physical food that you eat, as well as the mental food, as well as the spiritual food that you consume are all included. So the principle of Geb implies all of that, and mastering the earth principle in its higher sense really means mastering the conception of physicality, the idea that you are an earthly being in and of itself, which is actually the bolt of Geb that holds you on earth itself. That is an aspect of you – it's your very conception, your very ideal of yourself, your very erroneous concept that you are the body. And recall that we talked about the teaching of the body; the body belongs to the earth, and the soul belongs to heaven. And Geb is like the gatekeeper between the earth realm and that heavenly realm. Therefore, mastering Geb means mastering the capacity to escape the earth, to escape the physicality of the earth.

In mastering Geb there's a two-fold process, and that is mastering the physicality, the gross physicality as well as the subtle physicality, and that's what I was implying during the lecture where I talk about the grossness as well as the subtlety. And when we are moving towards the higher divinity, the cosmic divinities, we may see their principles reflected in the lower, because all those are being projected downwards onto earth. But what we're seeing in the higher divinities is the subtle power of that principle that is manifesting in a gross way in the lower ones. As we get more and more subtle, we get to the Supreme Being, and another thing that you should be keeping in mind is that as we move also higher on the Tree of Life, the force or power of the cosmic principle becomes more intense also, so the power of physicality is more powerful in the subtle regions than it is in the gross regions. And the reason that is, is because the power of mind, the astral plane is stronger, it is greater than the power of the physical coagulated world. In fact, the gross physical realm is the least powerful; the more powerful, the more subtle and the higher your vibrational rate that you're tapping into.

Question:

Since this wisdom you are teaching of the Anunian Theurgy comes from the ancient texts, which are written in the Ancient Egyptian hieroglyphic language, would it not be better to learn the language itself? If we learn Medtu Neteru, the Ancient Egyptian Hieroglyphic language, can we automatically get the wisdom of the Ancients?

Answer be Sebai MAA (Dr. Muata Ashby):

You could also consider that the same language as the Greeks (which we are using-the western tongue), when used righteously can convey true wisdom. All the ancient Egyptian books that we have produced are not 100% in medtu neter, even though we use English mostly, for 95% of it, it is used in a righteous manner, following the teaching and not western culture or western values or philosophical principles. So what I'm getting at is that we should not just immediately think that just because we may learn medtu neter that we are going to automatically attain enlightenment or automatically attain higher consciousness. One still has to work to attain understanding of the concepts; one still has to strive and practice the disciplines as a spiritual aspirant. It helps to use the medtu neter because it is a more conducive language but in and of itself it is not enough, it is also important how it is used and understood and understanding requires additionally a living teacher who can explain the teaching. For this purpose, conveying the teaching, language is a tool and there are better tools than others to do particular jobs. The purpose of a language is to promote understanding through communication. It means to bring thoughts into speech. Some languages may be better than others because they may be more in tune with reality and with truth, and medtu neter is one of those, as opposed to languages that have many concepts and words related to illusory aspects of the world such as romance and the legitimacy of the pursuit of worldly desires.[115] But all languages can reflect truth. Some people think that you can only gain the essence of a teaching with the language that the teaching comes from; Islam is such an example wherein people believe one must learn the Koran in the original Arabic, otherwise, you can't truly understand Islam. Some practitioners of Hinduism present the same argument. They say the Gita must be in Sanskrit. All of this is ridiculous nonsense for the most part. But there are certainly some aspects of a teaching that the native language can convey; for example, the speech pattern of medtu neter is different from the western pattern and that affects the manner in which thoughts are cognized and reflected upon. Also, the feeling and point of view that the culture provides can be conveyed through he native language. So language can convey the feeling of its culture and feeling is an important component of a religion but less important in a philosophy. What it will do is it'll give you more feel for the culture and that facilitates your understanding, and that is what we're after also. However, if the teacher is well versed in the culture of the teaching and in the culture that the teaching is being translated into the teacher can skillfully relate the teaching in a format that is true to the teaching and its culture for the people of the "alien" culture who are receiving the teachings a correct understanding can be engendered. In such a case this can be accomplished using key scriptures, utterances and phrases of the native language that will provide foundation and structure for the teaching which will be constructed with the foreign language. Of course, we may expect that the more the original language is integrated into the teaching given through the foreign language the higher the quality of the teaching will be.

---

[115] see the book *Comparative Mythology*

Reflection and Journal discipline:

1- At the top of each page copy the following hieroglyphs to the best of your ability

[***cht n ankh*** *" tree of life"*]

After studying the Lesson proceed to answer the following question and write the answer in your journal. This exercise will require more than one reading and more than one journal entry, at least one page; write all you can find related to the subject of the question. Answer the questions first without referring to the text you just read. Then go back and see if you missed anything. This exercise is to be repeated until you become proficient with the principles of this sphere. The reflection exercise should be done after each reading or study session. Then you may practice meditation[116] on the wisdom you have learned. You may come back to add to your reflections even if you move on to other lessons.

REFLECTIONS: Oh Lord of earths and king of Neteru and holder of souls! I am your devout child and heir who comes to you cleansed and wise and dead but yet alive. Release me to the worlds beyond. To my mother above to walk on starts straight on. Judge of souls and material of every place of standing, release your child to be free! Let my meditations here on earth be released from the gravity of worldly thinking and feeling…let my meditations soar to touch the sky and let my mind experience that which is more than my physical self.

After studying the Lesson proceed to answer the following question and write the answer in your journal.

What cannot be related directly in words?

What is(are) the main teaching(s) of this lesson and what do the principle(s) of the divinity(ies) discussed in this lesson mean in reference to my actions, feelings, thoughts and desires and understanding of the spiritual philosophy?

---

[116] Explained in more detail in Lesson 15

Lesson 12: Goddess Nut and the Mysteries of Expansion

We continue today our studies in Anunian Theology on Anunian Theurgy and The Kemetic Tree of Life. Today our studies will continue by penetrating the principle of Nut {pronounced with the "u" sounding like the "oo" in "m<u>oo</u>t"}. The phonetic aspect of the name of goddess Nut is contained in the ancient Egyptian hieroglyph of a vase ⎕ (phonetic *nu*)- a vase that contains fluid - water, the sustaining fluid of life and the vast energies of the sky, the heavens. Another main symbol of Nut is a plank ⎓ *Pet*, that has two ends that extend downwards, and this means 'sky region' or 'sky city'. It is the region between the East and the West - the eastern mountain, which is called *Bakhau* and the western mountain, which is called *Manu*. If you were to draw a line into the sky beginning from east to west, that would be the center of Nut - the center of the body of Nut - going from east to west, like a meridian.

Figure 70: Goddess Nut (sky/heavens) stretches over the God Geb (earth) [Temple of Aset (Isis)]

Figure 71: Metaphorical depiction of Goddess Nut stretching across the world (Geb) Goddess Nut stretching accross the sky from one horizon to the other

Nut and the God Geb came from the separation of an androgynous divinity (Nut-Geb) as we learned in the previous class. Shu and Tefnut came together, and they produced a kind of mass – like a plasma, if you will – solid parts and some not so solid parts. Then Ra, in order to create the two separate divinities, ordered Shu to get in between Geb and Nut to separate them. That separation constitutes the first act of physical creation in which we now have – Geb and Nut who represent the physical

216

universe, but as you know, they also have a cosmic aspect. So at once they are the physical, tangible aspect of the universe; but, as you know, also if you were to study, as modern physics has shown, the physical universe, you quickly realize that this physical universe is not physical at all. It is composed of particles of energy, and those particles are composed of even smaller particles the essence of which is energy, and the essence of that energy is consciousness. The consciousness sustaining both of those, Geb and Nut is Shu and Tefnut. And the energy sustaining – or the essence sustaining - both of those is Ra.

Figure 72: Geb and Nut just after their separation, depicting the penis (Tech024) of Geb

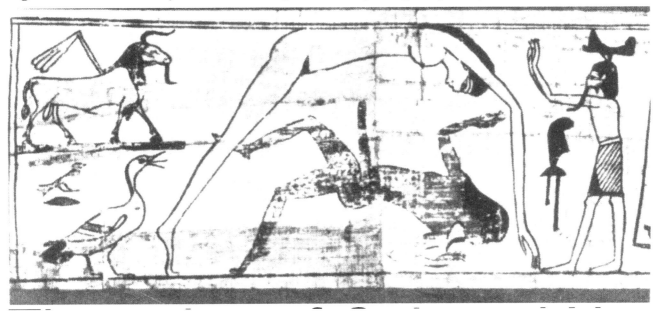

There are two Ancient Egyptian myths that talk about the nature of Nut. It is a creation myth that says that Geb and Nut were together, locked in a sexual embrace,[117] and that Ra decreed that they should be separated. He told Shu, {air, space} to get in between them and from that separation came forth the Heaven and the Earth. He also decreed that since they were locked in a sexual union Geb had made Nut pregnant and that the children that were to come out of Nut should not be born on any day of the year. The Kemetic year, was based on twelve months with 360 days. That's where the twelve months idea comes from for western culture. And so Djehuti had to, through his magic, create something like one seventy second part of a day, and he created five extra days for the year. And through those five extra days the other five divinities, the worldly/human personality divinities, came into being – Asar, Aset, Set, Nebethet and Heru Ur.

Now, having created those days, the 365 total now – having created Heaven and Earth, having created the five worldly divinities – the Ta divinities – so now human beings can exist on earth, Nut takes on a complementary role to the god Geb, which we learned about last time. Geb is the lord of the earth. Based on your life of righteousness or unrighteousness, he holds you fast in the ground, or he allows you to be free. He opens the bolt of the door to freedom from the earth realm.

[117] see the book *SACRED SEXUALITY: EGYPTIAN TANTRA YOGA: The Art of Sex* Sublimation and Universal Consciousness by Dr. Muata Ashby ISBN 1-884564-03-8

The scripture of the Pyramid Text says that the door itself is Nut. The door itself is the sky. The sky is a pathway to the Netherworld, and for this reason, in the pictures of Nut's body – she is depicted as studded with stars. Those stars are also souls {of her children} who have died and been elevated from the earth to the heavens. For this reason the image of the goddess was painted in ancient times on the inner lid of the coffin wherein the body of the deceased would be placed so that it would be able to receive its son or daughter just as she received Asar.

Figure 73: Goddess Nut in the Tomb of Seti I

Nut has a crown that has a sun disk and horns, like the goddess Hetheru. She may also wear a crown consisting of a vulture – like the goddess Mut or the goddess Aset. She also may appear as a cow with four legs, - outstretched from Bakhu to Manu – from the eastern horizon to the western horizon.　　　But the center of her worship is Anu, henceforth, she is a goddess of Anunian Theurgy.

Another primary symbol of the goddess Nut is the sycamore tree. And this tree is also known as the Tree of Life *cht n ankh - tree of life*. The goddess herself is a tree, and if you go to that tree she gives you two kinds of food – special kinds of food – that will sustain you up in the sky on your journey to the Netherworld - primarily air and water. So Nut is the goddess of the sycamore tree, the tree of life, from which she provides food and drink to righteous aspirants.

Figure 74: Goddess Nut as the Life Giving Tree {From the Pert M Heru text}

Nut is thus the protector of the dead. She protects aspirants from their enemies and provides the subtle food for existence in the *Pet* (heavenly) realm. She also allows souls to have movement in the *Pet* plane of existence. She was often depicted as the coffin lid with open arms (see below) ready to embrace the aspirant's body and receive the aspirant's soul to lift it up to heaven so that it might become one of the Akhu, luminous beings –enlightened souls who live in the sky as the stars. See the illustration of the interior of a typical ancient Egyptian coffins showing spiritual texts of the Pert M Heru (Coffin Texts) and the female figure inside, as if receiving and embracing the body of the aspirant. This is goddess Nut. Thus, Nut is the Coffin itself.

In the Pyramid texts it is stated that Nut lifts up righteous aspirants who have been allowed to transcend the earth realm by Geb. She is the pathway that is opened to aspirants so that they may depart from the earth plane. That is the same door that is closed when the bolt of Geb obstructs the movement of an unrighteous aspirant. Nut is the blackness of night and thus her children are also dark in complexion. Asar is referred to as "The Lord of the Perfect Black" and it is said that when Aset was born Nut exclaimed "look at this black child of love."

Nut is the same Divinity manifesting in all of the major forms of the Goddess including: Aset, Nebthet, Taurt, Hetheru and Mut. Nut most importantly represents the subtle principles of physical expansiveness. These are the principles to be mastered by a spiritual aspirant. Nut is the power behind the effectiveness of Hekau (words of power) of the Pert m Heru wherein the aspirant states the desire to live in the Duat. This occurs under the dispensation of Goddess Nut for she provides the sustenance for those who live there. This brings up another issue. A departed personality may reside in any venue of the Creation if they so desire or if their *ariu* will allow it or dictate it. However, any realm of the Time and Space (Ta-Pet-Duat} is considered ephemeral even if it lasts for billions of years. So one can direct oneself to living in heaven or to join with Asar or otherwise join with Ra by mounting his boat and that is an abiding outcome, as they term it in religious studies, this is one of the possible eschatologys of Shetaut Neter (Neterian Religion of Ancient Egypt).

Figure 75: center and far right- images of the Goddess Nut painted on the Inside of a Coffin (at left-line art image of the same)

Specifically, in reference to this question of what is the Neterian eschatology, the Ancient Egyptian myth of *Sa-Asar*[118] informs us directly and specifically about the possible fates of the personality after death. A human

---

[18] See the book *THE AFRICAN ORIGINS OF CIVILIZATION, RELIGION AND YOGA SPIRITUALITY AND ETHICS PHILOSOPHY* by Dr. Muata Ashby

being can control their destiny but once their life is over they experience the consequences of their actions (the actions while alive or in previous lives, guided by wisdom or ignorance constitute their working out or creating their destiny) and the destiny leads to the outcome which is the fate. There are three fates possible; for those who are unrighteous the fate is to suffer hellish conditions, being tortured by the gods and goddesses for negative deeds; for the moderately righteous they can live in the heavenly plane and worship and serve Asar or Ra until they are purified enough and then experience higher consciousness. For those who are purified {lucid, virtuous, wise, etc.} the fate is to go directly to sit in the throne of Asar or mount the boat of Ra, which is the same as saying to become one with them.

The gods and goddesses consume foods, as we've learned from Chapter 175 from the Pert m Heru. I think we have a different Chapter number for it in our book. In the Chapter the initiate goes and asks the God Atum, "Atum, what is the nature of this life? What is this world that I'm coming to?" Because the person, after they leave their earthly body, they go to the netherworld and appear before the god Atum. Atum is the third aspect of the Ra Trinity, the primordial self and an aspect of the Creator, who handles the dissolution of things, the completion of things. Atum tells them, "Well, you don't have physicality here, so therefore, you don't need physical food, you don't need physical air, physical vegetables or physical water. You don't have any need for having sex in this realm – you don't…" – so on and so forth. So Atum is indicating that there is a special kind of food that the personality lives on in the higher realm. The same thing when you go to sleep – consider that when you go to sleep at night, having a dream and if you think that you're eating, you're having a nice meal – a nice vegetarian meal – you're eating your lettuce, you're eating your carrots, drinking a glass of water, etc. – what is the substance of those items in the astral plane where you are in your dream? You're not drinking physical water. You're not eating a physical carrot. Actually, we may say that the physical carrot and water are reflections of the astral carrot and water. And the essence of that astral carrot and water is found in the higher and causal plane. The substratum of that is found in the higher transcendental realm beyond.

Nut provides that astral sustenance – the sustenance that occurs by mere thought. And the more powerful your thought, the more substantive the food. That's why stories are told of sages who can subsist on air alone, on water. We talked about this in the Kemetic Diet also, being sustained with the subtle aspect. Your physical body needs to be sustained by the physical aspect. If the thought were strong enough it could summon energies and cause them to coagulate, to coalesce into the form of physical food. Another way is if you were to make your physical body subtle enough, if you were to be able to find a pure enough environment in the physical world, you could live more on the subtle and less on the gross physical; also if you were even subtler, you could actually transform yourself from place to place physically. You could transport yourself and make yourself rematerialize elsewhere and so on and so forth. It's a psychic power.

The goddess Nut is the principle that allows that to happen, that allows you to raise yourself up. Once Geb opens the door for you, once you have the right to attain escape velocity from the earth, the goddess Nut stretches out her arms, and she reaches into the grave and she pulls you up. Now, don't go believing she is going to pick up your embalmed mummy or your rotting corpse! She comes for your soul, the subtler essence of who you are essentially. This is why, if you go to a major city with an Egyptian museum – go and look at the coffins. You'll see that many of them have - as well as sarcophagi - many of them have depictions of the goddess Nut outstretched the same way as the mummy that is placed in there. And her arms are open – she's embracing and receiving that mummy, that personality. She is receiving and taking her child – Asar. And Asar becomes *Sahu* at that point and becomes a star, a shining divinity, and *Akhu* in his spiritual body. Sahu is also the name of the three stars commonly referred to as "Orion's Belt." So you see, metaphorically, Asar was lifted up and took his place among the immortal stars, he attained immortality and transcended the earth realm.

As the goddess Nut, in her form as a cow, with her four legs or in her form as a woman with her two arms and her two legs in the bent over posture, form the four pillars that sustain the sky. And these pillars are reinforced by the four suns of Heru. They as if stand holding each pillar. These mark the cardinal points of the compass. And when this happens, the sundisk of Ra is able to sail through the heavens and bring warmth to creation. When Nut and Geb are together, the sailing process of the boat of Ra is not possible because they are too close. When they are separated, then Ra can sail forth through the sky or in-between the sky and the earth.

There are two myths about the posture, the position of goddess Nut in the sky. One tells of how Ra, in his boat, sails from east to west over the body of goddess Nut. Another one tells of how the boat of Ra sails through the body of Nut. Nut eats Ra in the sky and gives birth to him. One myth tells about goddess Nut's head as being in the east and one tells about goddess Nut's head as being in the west. So why do these descriptions appear to be contradictions and why is this important? Because if her head is in the west, it means that when Ra is done sailing and comes to the land of Manu, the west, and he goes over the horizon he is consumed by her, she eats him. He then sails through her body and then she gives birth to him as the morning sun in the east. He comes out of her vagina in the eastern horizon.

But isn't this confusing, didn't we say that her head was in the east also? If her head is in the east, how is she going to consume him in the west and then give birth to him in the east? Is she going to regurgitate him? You see, it appears backwards. And the fact of the matter is that if you look at it correctly there are two symbols for the goddess Nut, there are two symbols for the sky. One is called the 'day sky' and one is called the 'night sky'. And so therefore, goddess Nut has two aspects and they mirror each other. They face each other. When the boat of Ra, the sun disk, comes through the land of Manu, the west, and goes into the night sky, and is consumed and then he journeys through it, this is the same Netherworld, the Duat, that he goes shining forth through, the same land of those who live in the astral plane, the dead, he shines on them also. So right now, because it is nighttime where we are on earth, he's shining on them. Those who are not dull, as you recall from your Pert m Heru text, they're able to hold onto the tow rope, and they're pulled up onto the boat, the boat of millions of years, and they sail on until the end of time and beyond. As he finishes his nighttime journey, she gives birth to him in the east, and he sails up along her back.

In iconographies you will often see it depicted as one body, but actually in a few (see below), Nut is depicted as having two; it's two if you understand the mysticism correctly. Ra sails on her back, but her body is full of stars. This means that she is the sky and there is a mirror image. And as we know, the physical reality is a reflection of the astral reality. If you understand the physical reality, you can understand the astral reality. The astral reality, as we said, is more subtle, but yet more powerful and therefore more real than the physical reality.

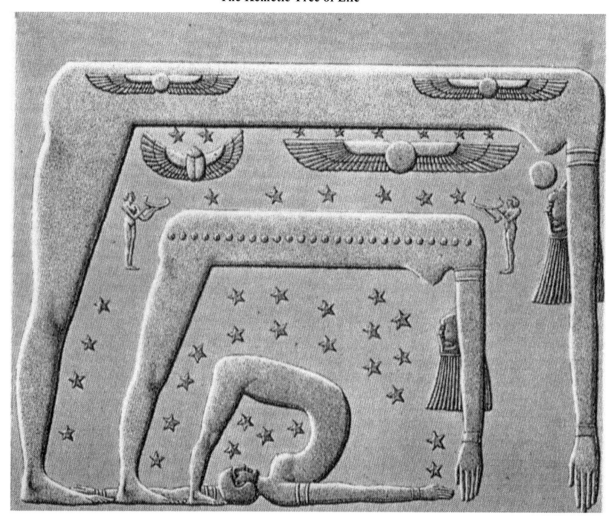

Figure 76: The Double Nature of Nut

So, the conception of Goddess Nut is that she has two aspects, the day sky and the night sky. If her image is as sky goddess is reversed and juxtaposed against that given in the scripture we see two Nuts facing each other over two sides of the earth, the day side and the night side, each lasting roughly 12 hours, hence the Kemetic creation of the 24 hours of the day. In this way of looking at Nut when she gives birth to Ra he sails over her body. When she eats him he traverses through her body and that is the night Nut.

Day Nut

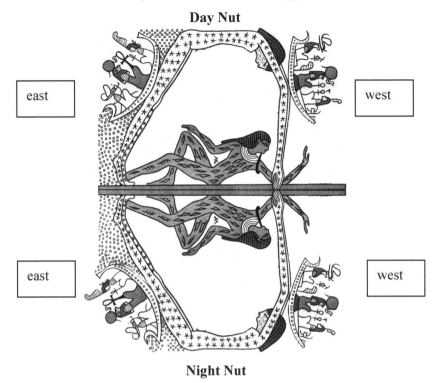

Night Nut

The image above can be viewed diagrammatically and when the movements of the boat of Ra, the position of the goddess and the realms or planes of existence are mapped, out the teaching related to Nut and the other divinities becomes clearer.

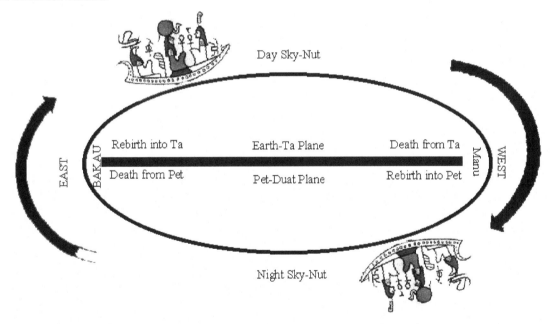

The birth of the morning is actually a death to the night just as a person's dream personality dissolves in order to give way to the daytime personality. Likewise the daytime personality gives way at night. When a human being dies it is merely an expression of being born into another plane, for sleep is a form of death that human beings experience every day. The death at the end of physical life is simply the same process but without coming back the next morning to the same body as before. Instead, at the death of the physical body {*Khat*} they remain in the *Ka* body and from there they may move on in one of the different bodies, *Ba* {soul}, *akh* {spirit}, *sahu* {glorious body}, in accordance with the ariu and level of spiritual evolution or, of course, they may dissolve into the Divine Self in the *yanrutf* realm.

So, therefore, as aspirants and initiates progress through life, they practice the rituals of Nut, emulating her principle: expansiveness. These arms of Nut are outstretched to them, the arms of outstretched expansion, to pick them up from the world of time and space. And the door is opened, and they are lifted. They are born just as Ra is born, with the stars. The daytime is like your life, your physical life. The nighttime is like your astral life, your sleep time, and your next life - how the stars are born. And you become like an *Akh* (shining spirit).

So Nut is propitiated in all her different forms. She is the mother goddess. She is also known, as I said, the mother of Aset. One story that's told of Nut relates to how the gods and goddesses of the earth, Asar, Aset, Set and Nebethet and Heru were born on different days. On one of the days, Nut was traveling through Egypt, and she came to the city of Denderah, the city of Hetheru. And she went to Hetheru's temple, the same one we visited on our trip to Egypt, and she had a baby there. And the scripture says that when the baby came out she exclaimed, "*As*...behold!...this beautiful blackness!" And the child was Aset. Aset is a beautiful blackness to behold. It is a derivative of the term *As!* And we know that Asar is the lord of the perfect black. So Nut is black, like outer space, and gives birth to these black children, to these children of the black, the blackness of undifferentiated consciousness, of transcendental consciousness.

And so the Pyramid Text say that the initiate should propitiate Nut, saying, "I am the child of Nut. I am Asar. Lift me up as you did Asar to be one of those stars in the sky. Protect me from the evil doers. Protect me like you did Asar. Provide for me that subtle food that you provided for Asar at that sycamore tree." The sycamore tree was sacred in ancient times, and it was a place to seek shelter. Just like the animals seek shelter in the hot summer, they go under the tree and they rest. And in this aspect of the Theurgy the final rest occurs in the trunk of the tree in the form of a coffin in which she embraces the deceased but the soul is resurrected and liberated (by Geb). So, for the living as well, the goddess Nut stretches forth her arms, her branches, and she provides shade, coolness and comfort as well as sustenance. And she allows you to have movement in the Duat, movement in the astral plane. If you do not have that kind of comfort, eventually the enemies, the thirst, the hunger, the unrighteousness, will eventually subdue you.

At that point, how will you survive? How will you make it through? You will be at the mercy of the inimical forces. In order to have a viable spiritual practice there must be rest; there must be a refuge. You can go to the Tree of Life for refuge, and sustenance, both physical and astral, to rest, meditate, receive teachings, and be elevated. There must be a place where you can go relax and reflect. Otherwise, it will do you in. And this brings us to a discussion of the matter of how to master the principle of Nut. Nut represents expansiveness, stretching herself forth from end to end, from beginning to end, what the Greeks called Alpha and Omega. As her arms end where her legs begin she forms a circuit wherein her expansion leads to infinity and eternity of Ra. And at the end of infinity, you come to the beginning of infinity, just as a straight line meets its own beginning in infinity.

How can you attain this? What I am going to say now applies in principle to how all of the neteru, the principles of the Kemetic Tree of Life, are to be approached and mastered. How can you master this principle? Firstly, you must worship, propitiate Nut as we've discussed. You must act as Nut, which means that you too must stretch forth, both physically and psychically. One of the exercises, the physical exercises, the posture of Nut that's practiced in the Tjef Neteru system, is part of this practice, placing your physical body in the same posture, in the same movement as the goddess Nut,[119] visualizing yourself as extending from one end of the world to the other and realizing now, taking the next step further, that one end or the other touches the other end back to the beginning. So, it's actually a circle. It's actually leading to infinity. There's no end to the circle, so she is also, in the deeper analysis, an expression of eternity if her expansiveness is realized to it's fullest extent.

If you are to master these principles, what Nut represents, then the scripture says that you have the power to make your *hekau* affective. Remember the *hekau* with in the Pert m Heru. "Get back you crocodile of the north! I don't belong to you. You can't consume me. I am one of those righteous spirits who comes forth from the land of the dead; reborn to eternity. Take me up goddess Nut, as you did for your son, Asar." All these words

---

[119] See the book *EGYPTIAN YOGA The Postures of The Gods and Goddesses* by Muata Ashby ISBN 1-884564-10-0

will be ineffectual if you do not understand or master the principles of Nut, this means listening, reflecting and meditating upon the nature of Nut and practicing the principles of Nut in your day-to-day reality.

How many times in a day in your life do you feel belittled, do you feel curtailed? You've got a mortgage to pay. Someone is obstructing you, you're in a car driving and the people get in front of you, it's a mess, it's a big traffic jam. And everyone has gotten there, in front of there, just to block you, just as a nuisance to you personally. How many days did it happen to you that you have a feeling, "Oh, I'd like to do that, but I can't do that. I can't make it through that course. It's too much for me. I can't do that job. That's beyond my capacity, my capabilities. I can't get in there because those people are waiting for me to slip up and then I'm going to fail. I won't make it." You are limiting yourself. How many times have you said to yourself "I am this individual. My name is such-and-such. I came from this place, and these are my people. They live in this town. I'm going to die one day. I didn't exist before, and I'm going to die one day and that's going to be the end of it."

Where is your eternal thought? Where is your beginning-to-end thought on that? Beginning-to-end, beginning-to-end and so on to infinity. Where is that? Where is your conception of your own immortality, your own divinity? Every time that you belittle yourself, every time you limit yourself, you are reducing the power of Nut within you. You're curtailing, and you're digging the hole in the ground, in Geb, deeper. And you're piling it on. You're causing Geb to say that this person is not ready to escape. They need to be held fast. And, actually, it is the principle of Geb within you that is doing that, the earthliness within you, the ignorance within you, and the misconception within you.

Mastering the principle of Nut is mastering the concept of expansiveness and living on the subtle sustenance of Nut as opposed to the gross sustenance of the world, meat, cooked foods etc., but also fat things of the mind, the vanities and egoistic ways of thinking such as that you are better than others, or thinking that you are lower than others, thinking that the teaching is too hard for you, or that you deserve to experience the pleasures that wealth can bring or that you are a bad person and deserve the worst. These are all fat ideas that bloat your personality, swell the head and inflate the ego. These things are in contradiction with the principle of Nut. Goddess Nut represents physicality, but a diffused physicality, the physicality of the vast outer space, which is not void but subtle matter. Just as you eat physical food, you must learn how to eat subtle food and derive sustenance off of that. The air and water of the world are themselves gross matter; the subtle air and water that goddess Nut presents to you is actually, even still, a gross aspect of an even subtler sustenance that's provided for you by Shu and Tefnut, that we're going to discuss next time.

You must learn how to oppose ignorance. You must learn how to oppose limitation, the thoughts of limitation, the negative chant of limitation. When you say "I can't" do this or "I can't do that," etc., etc. that is a negative chant, a chant that produces negative energies and counter-evolutionary spiritual movement. The positive movement happens when you strive for wisdom and when you practice righteousness, when you practice order and peace, study the wisdom teachings, chanting the philosophy, etc. Then gradually you have an expanded capacity to understand. You start to feel yourself as not being just a physical personality. But there is more that extends beyond. That extension is the arms of Nut.

If you were to obtain this even before the time of your death, then death has no affect on you. If you lived in a closed house with no windows and someone came to your house with a bulldozer and crashed your house, that would be pretty frightening, pretty gruesome and shocking. But if you have a house with windows and once in a while you look out, you may not go out, but every once in a while you look out, you may open the door and see that you can go out any time you want. If somebody comes with a bulldozer, you can go out the back door. Or your house blows up or burns down, you say, "O.K. well I guess I needed a new house anyway. I'll just have the insurance come and they can pay me some money and I'll build a new house." But what if you don't have any insurance? If you could not afford it you must philosophically accept the loss and be pleased you survived with strength to rebuild because you had the windows. The windows are your capacities to see beyond the confines, to see a grander reality and also you have the capacity to see what is coming and thereby get yourself ready for it. What is coming is death and the windows are your freedom, the insight into the spiritual teaching and the inner experience of Nut in your deeper self as well as the unburdened feeling from being released by Geb.

You must try not to let one moment go by in your life where you are minimized. You must learn how to feel *ur,* magnanimous. *Ur,* from the term "Heru Ur", this is the theme that needs to be followed, greatness, not littleness, not pettiness. Even as you may have to deal with petty things, with little things, you should feel extraordinary, even though you may have to cut the grass, even though you may have to do dishes. These things are worldly things, and they have nothing to do with you except to the extent of sustenance needs, the practicalities of your physical existence, the physical aspect of your personality in accordance with the precepts of Maat. That's it! Another example of this way of thinking could be for example, who knows about a little girl who saw an ant for the first time in her life in the year 1550? What does it matter in the grand scheme of things, this is a little speck of dust in the vastness of time? In the end it has no bearing on anything, anything substantial. Who cares about lawsuits that occurred back in the 1800's? Who cares about anything back in the 1400's except those people who live in the past, those people who are holding on to their worldly existence? From a cultural perspective, there may be some validity to that because some things that happened then have bearing on what is happening now but many other things have no meaning now for individuals especially of other cultures. For example, what does a person in china care about who was the King of the Zulu nation in the year 1300? Another example, there was a person who lived in 1840 who went to the yard and carved his name into a tree. The tree was cut down 50 years later and made into wood for a house roof, the house burnt down 20 years later, the ashes decomposed and became part of the earth. What does the carving matter? Think about the fact that all the events in your life are going to seem insignificant to someone living 2,000 years from now; think about it! From a mystical perspective, there is no validity to any of that history, neither the relevant parts nor the irrelevant parts. If you live in that kind of reality, believing that worldly events are real, abiding and meaningful eternally then you are not fit to practice the teaching. Because you are not going to allow yourself to lift off, to be released from the bondage to the earth. When goddess Nut comes to pull you up, the god Geb's hands are going to be holding your legs down on the earth. You are not going to be able to take off, to take flight. The wisdom reflection would be to visualize yourself now as if you are looking at yourself from 20 years in the future in the same manner as you would remember yourself of 20 years ago. Think about all the things that were meaningful to you 20 years ago and how those things have passed on or have been forgotten and think of the things of today as being just as fleeting and thus illusory. Feel yourself of today, now, as you will feel about you of today 20 years in the future, feeling that the things you are involved with today, right now, are illusory. And of course, 40 years in the future even the 20 years in the future you will be illusory also, but we will wait for that in 20 years, you see where this is going right? This exercise will allow you to let go of the worldly interests from an egoistic perspective and look at them from a more objective and expansive perspective.

You should practice breathing exercises. These exercises allow one to discover the subtlety of breath and that leads to the subtlety of higher energies and planes of existence. Watch your breath, allowing it to go on with its normal rhythm. See if you can discern the subtle aspect of breath in the air that you breathe. The scripture says that Nut allows you to sniff the air of the astral plane, the air of the sky, that she herself lives on. And of course, Nut is beyond the realm of Shu so what air is she sniffing? It must be mighty thin air since we are talking about the expansiveness of outer space. In outer space there is little air but within the vacuum of space there is something, there is *sekhem* {energy} and *Nunu* {consciousness}.

Make yourself quiet in your coffin, that is your meditation place. Stretch out your body and allow yourself to be motionless for several minutes. And then place your attention on your breath. Allow yourself to perceive the subtle aspect of breath, not the air, but the sustaining power that is within breath, *Sekhem.*

If your body is allowed to remain in this posture long enough, like a half hour to an hour, your body will fall asleep, but your mind remains awake. What is the subtlety, what is the air that you can perceive at that point? You can enter into the astral plane and experience the air and water of the astral plane.

The water that she gives is the sustaining force behind your blood, behind the fluids in your body. That is the same life force that sustains the universe. What is that sustaining you when you are not aware of your body, a state of consciousness that is experienced when, through meditation, a person loses body consciousness? That is what you must learn how to find out. What you find out at that point also is that your serious as well as your petty troubles of the world, such as, there is somebody suing you, you are suing somebody, your car breaks down, your house has termites, your neighbors are noisy, the world is going to war, crime is rampant, whatever it is – in that state all of these worldly situations, they become nil, moot. Not the goddess *Mut*. It becomes unnecessary to speak of it and inconsequential and therefore irrelevant.

The practice, therefore, of attaining that level of consciousness that allows you to experience expansiveness should be the focus of your life. That is the practice of the principle of Nut. If you have convinced yourself, if you have experienced and you retain a perennial awareness of your own expansiveness, then you have mastered the principle of Nut. And she will pull you up, as she did for her son, Asar. And you will live on as a shining star in the heavens, as all Asar personalities have done throughout history.

Hotep - This concludes the lesson for today.

Questions and Answers

There are a couple more things I'll add based on what we spoke about last time. In reference to the egg - Goddess Nut gives birth to the egg – and from that egg comes the Bennu, and that Bennu is the newborn son, the morning sun. The egg that is engendered by the goose, that is Geb. Now, there are two main symbols that are used and would it not be expected that the symbols used would be of an anthropomorphic (mammalian) birth as opposed to the egg? You can watch anthropomorphic births on the TV shows every day. You can turn on the medical channel and see it or you can go online, on the internet. It shows you how the child is born and there's no egg involved, there is no egg like a chicken hatching or a turtle hatching, etc. A human being does not grow in the mother like an egg, like a chicken or a crocodile or a being like that.

So why did the ancients choose the symbol of the egg and the symbol of the cocoon, which is used by the scarab? It's like an egg also in a sense. The reason is because there is an incubation period that you must have, and that aspect of human spiritual evolution is metaphorically similar to the egg concept or the cocoon concept. In the egg, there is an enclosed environment wherein you have a chance to examine the teachings in peace and quiet. Everything is given to you there to transform yourself in quiet, in darkness, at rest and with the sustenance for the time required. Now, you may say that you are quiet in your mother's womb and you are at rest; well not so, not in the same sense. When you were in your mother's womb, your mother was running around, she's walking, doing things, talking to people, watching TV, etc. and you received sum subtle influences from that. Also, you experience some of her feelings, good or bad, and you also experience the food that she ate. When you are in an egg, you are self-contained, in silence and you are by yourself. The animal may sit on top of you, to keep you warm, but that's about it. You are there by yourself.

This points to the concept of the meditative practice, allowing yourself to consume the elements that have been placed around you. Meditation allows you to consume subtle energies in your mind; it allows you to consume, to eat up the fatness of your mind, negative impressions and gross desires and illusions. And when you've eaten up all your thoughts, when you have eaten up all the gods and goddesses and you have assimilated their wisdom and their power, what have you then? What more have you to do? You are ready to be born. You are ready to break out of the shell.

These transcendental thoughts that I have given you lead you closer to infinity, eternity and magnanimity, etc. These thoughts cancel out the negative thoughts like: "I am an individual." "I am alone in the universe." "I am little." "I am weak and limited." "I can't do this." "I can't do that" etc. When there is nothing left, you are able to have the higher experience, and that breaking of the egg is the beginning of the birth of higher aspiration. That is the metaphysical practice that leads to enlightenment. You come shining forth as the *Akh*. And this is the practice that must be enjoined.

Question:

Can it be said that mastery of Nut then is that principle that allows one to transcend the causal plane?

Answer:

Using the parameters and nomenclature of the Anunian conception of the Tree of Life, there is a physical plane (Ta), Astral plane (Pet) and the Causal plane (Duat). And strictly speaking, the answer is 'No' to that question. Mastering the principle of Nut allows you to transcend the physical plane of the human personality divinities. Look at the cosmiconomythograph and see how the principle of Geb and Nut really allow you to transcend the physical plane. In order to transcend the Duat, Shu, Tefnut and Ra must be mastered. And then you are able to transcend the causal plane. Mastery of expansiveness leads one to discover infinity. When you master the principle of Ra, then you transcend the principle of the causal plane into the transcendental reality, the absolute, the named nameless, and formed formless realm, the Nun. Mastering Heru, Asar and Aset, Set, Nebethet, and Heru Ur enables you to grow beyond the human and physical plane. You cannot transcend the physical plane until you are lifted up. And you cannot be lifted up until you are purified through Maat and wise through Aset.

You should think of it also as follows, strictly speaking, there are three main plains: the physical, astral and causal, but then there is the transcendental, which may be considered as a fourth from the perspective of the time and space reality, but which is strictly speaking, not a plane. It transcends a conception of even a plane of existence. Strictly speaking, all planes are causal of the subsequent plane. The substratum of all planes is the transcendental. The next lower plane for that is the causal. The causal is named so because it causes the astral. But the astral is also causal to the physical.

Earlier, in this process we were discussing the concept of dissolution. In reverse manner, the lower planes are causal to the higher planes. Your entry into a higher plane is caused by your dissolution work, your spiritual enlightening movement, at the lower plane. You may understand this from a creation perspective that is the downward movement. From an enlightenment perspective, the creation of expansion, dismantling the illusory construct of the physical, astral and causal relative realities, this may be seen as upward movement.

Hotep- Peace

Reflection and Journal discipline:

1- **At the top of each page copy the following hieroglyphs to the best of your ability**

_____ [*cht n ankh* "*tree of life*"]

After studying the Lesson proceed to answer the following question and write the answer in your journal. This exercise will require more than one reading and more than one journal entry, at least one page; write all you can find related to the subject of the question. Answer the questions first without referring to the text you just read. Then go back and see if you missed anything. This exercise is to be repeated until you become proficient with the principles of this sphere. The reflection exercise should be done after each reading or study session. Then you may practice meditation[120] on the wisdom you have learned. You may come back to add to your reflections even if you move on to other lessons.

REFLECTIONS: Oh Lady of the sky, mistress of heaven, goddess of blacknes and stary night, stretch out your arms, extend your beautiful hands to reach down to earth. Grab hold of your child, I am your child, who was born on the day of separation. Lift me up to your realm so that I may be among the stars…not like those stars that go up and down, back an forth, being born and ever dying again and again…let me be like those special ones those that are always awake, always aware, always knowing and always here! Let my meditations lift me up and let me abide there in the stars, knowing myself and being myself always!

After studying the Lesson proceed to answer the following question and write the answer in your journal.

How should one propitiate Nut?

What is(are) the main teaching(s) of this lesson and what do the principle(s) of the divinity(ies) discussed in this lesson mean in reference to my actions, feelings, thoughts and desires and understanding of the spiritual philosophy?

---

[120] Explained in more detail in Lesson 15

Lesson 13 Part 1: Shu, Tefnut and Ra and the Mystic Wisdom and Meditation Teaching for Transcending the Tree of Life

We continue now with the next lesson in our studies of the Anunian Theurgy Tree of Life philosophy. This has been a journey that has taken us through the oldest religious system in this particular human history, a journey of discovery of the principles of creation, the very fabric that composes this universe and, indeed, ourselves – what we are composed of, what we are made of. We have seen how the Supreme Being emerged from the primeval ocean, from the primordial stuff of which all is made, from the Nun. From that ocean of consciousness, the Supreme Being emerged in the form of Ra, a focus of conscious intelligence. And then that creative principle gave rise to nine other principles, and those are the principles that we have been studying in the last several weeks. Together they form ten principles, ten elements of creation, ten aspects that go to make up existence.

As you may recall, there are two movements in Anunian Theurgy. One is the creative movement. The other is the dissolution movement. The path of studying Anunian Theurgy involves both understanding how things came into being and understanding how they go out of being; "Being," being a relative term. What I mean by this is that the term "Being" relates to the living as the Neterian philosophy states, that is, those who are in the realm of manifestation, generation. That which is in the transcendental realm are neither being nor not being.

In the *Pert m Heru* text, the Ancient Egyptian Book of the Dead, the realm of the Ta, the world where human beings interact and live, that is called the land of the living. But does that mean that if you are dead or, that is, not living on the earth plane, does that mean that you do not exist? Obviously it does not mean that because there are higher planes of existence. In the Ta realm, that is where you have human life, human existence. In the Pet realm you have astral existence. In the Duat realm there is an even subtler form of existence and in the Nun realm you have an even higher form of existence, a more subtle form of existence.

As we have been studying the principles, beginning from the lowest, which is Heru and coming up to the highest, which is Ra, that is, the highest within time and space, we have discovered an increasing level of subtlety, an increasing level also of power, and an increasing level of expansion and self-knowledge, which encompasses the levels that came before.

The downward movement, the creation movement, is a coagulating movement. It is a contracting movement from the very subtle Nun, which may be likened to what some physicists may call dark matter and dark energy. Really, consciousness is even subtler than these, coming all the way down to the very physical and most gross elements and compounds such as lead, metals, steel, granite, rocks, diamonds, and other dense, compacted items. And that compacting can be very dense, in other words, gross. For instance, there are some stars that are so compact in their elements that one cubic inch of that star material can be heavier than this entire world. Can you imagine that? And yet, the subtlety of consciousness passes through even the densest solid matter. And that is what we are heading to find in our journey of discovery. What is that subtle principle that pervades all? Because that which is subtler can pervade that which is gross. For example, gamma rays coming from the sun are subtler than granite so when the sunrays come to the earth they keep on passing through the granite as they hit the earth. Another example that is well known in modern culture is lead. Lead is denser than x-rays so the x-rays cannot pass through. However other radiations are subtler than x-rays so they can pass through the lead. In the same way, the consciousness of the Supreme Being is subtler than all the rest of the gross objects of the world so that consciousness pervades all and even sustains it, by virtue of it's presence. In a higher sense, the coagulation of subtle matter into solid matter is not an abiding reality since as soon as it occurs it starts to break down into its constituent parts. It may take millions or billions of years but the breakdown occurs. So it is as if for God, who has created the universe, this universe is like a mere dream or a thought and for us it lasts billions of years but for God, who is eternal, it lasts merely an instant. That instant is what beings in the realm of time and space call "time and space." Within that instant all the histories, events and dramas of the world occur and when the instant occurs it is like a dream with all of its seemingly real objects, events and situations that never really happened after a person wakes up. So, if that is the case, why should a person live life as if it is abiding and everything is do or die or as if everything that happens is the be all and end all. The answer is that they should not live that way. But after many lifetimes of living that way and knowing no better, having ignorance reinforced by their own desires, family members, the media and the leaders of society, and not having the wisdom of the mysteries such as the Anunian Theurgy and the Tree of Life, it is hard to act any other way. So people lead themselves to many negative situations and worldly entanglements due to their ignorance and incapacity to live in accordance with a higher truth. They are caught in the matrix of their egoistic illusions, desires and fanciful notions about life and about the world, that is a life of blindness, of ignorance and suffering. That is the kind of life in which people can develop ideas of difference, separation, possessiveness, selfishness, fear, and the terrible things that people do to each other, the resentments, hatreds, grudges, and the conflicts, wars and atrocities they lead to are then possible because they have strayed far away from the higher truth that unites and binds all life and all Creation in fact.

So, as we continue our studies, we have already seen how we need to master the five lower principles that go to compose the human psyche, the human personality. And if we don't master those, we will not be able to reach up to the higher levels. That is to say, if we don't discover spiritual aspiration, if Heru is not born in our lives, we will not be able to discover the power or the strength to overcome the ego which is Set or the fear of death, which is Nebethet. And we will not be able to gain understanding of the mysteries of life through the study the wisdom philosophy that is Aset and realize the immortality of the soul, which is Asar.

And if the five lower principles that go to compose the psyche are not properly understood, then you will not be able to transcend those principles. You will not be able to go to the subtler levels of your own personality because you will be caught up in the complexes of life. You will be caught up in the problems and the toils and the trials and tribulations of human existence. And not that those trials and challenges should not be handled, but they should be handled from a position of mastery instead of slavery such that the higher power within may be used to confront and overcome them instead of them squashing the personality, limiting it and forming the basis for a miserable life; You will be running to fulfill desires because your ego holds sway. When your family members die, and they will one day, you will be distraught. In such a life, death and destruction is looming around every corner. Youth, instead of being a time of exuberance and promise becomes a time of depression, and escapism. You will have a midlife crisis because deep down you know that you are going to die too, and you haven't fulfilled what you want in this life. Or the things that you developed, you will have a fear of losing them, losing your family, losing your possessions since you have equated them with the worth and worthiness of your life, in other words, you have placed a value on your life which you trade and sell to the world like a prostitute. You have sold your soul to the world because you do not know that you have Asar within you. Your soul belongs to the mortgage company or to your job or to those who depend on you because you wanted children, a big house, cars, etc. and now you cannot be happy unless all bills are paid, unless you can buy presents for everyone during the holidays, unless you lose weight and look good, unless, unless, unless… And since you are so distraught and fearful and the cravings hold sway on you, your mind will never be clear enough, peaceful enough to lead a happy life, let alone understand the wisdom teaching. This predicament of life is of your own making since it is you who have created the only parameters by which you can be happy or at peace, the conditions in which happiness and peace can exist; you have constricted yourself, boxed yourself in and you have conditioned your mind and you have made happiness that much harder to achieve since it is firstly illusory and secondly it is also constricted and rarer. Happiness and peace are now tied to those occurrences that you have determined so it cannot be allowed unless those occurrences, which you have determined, come through. Thus you will never be truly happy or at peace because those objectives will never be achieved in an abiding way. So moving forward beyond this point will be difficult. You will not become the king of the world. You will not become a prince like Heru, rather you will be a slave to the senses, the desires, the dictates of the world and the conditions of the environment, like Set. Therefore, the upper movement will be veiled from you, it will be blocked.

The realm of such a person is the *Ta* realm. And Geb will keep them down in that realm as we saw a few lessons back, the Geb principle, the principle of physicality. The reason is that they have not understood that deep down they are not physical; so the misunderstanding will keep them down, it will hold them down. Using this idea of Anunian Tree of Life as a ladder, it is as if someone is holding your leg and you can't climb any further.

If you don't master these principles, you will not be able to climb up further, and go beyond. The human personality will be like an envelope that is holding you in, closing you off from higher knowledge, from higher experience. Geb will hold you down, and Nut will not be able to lift you up. You will not receive the divine food that she has. You will be sustained only on the physical plane, with physical sustenance, and that leads to a coagulated personality, a hard headed personality, a hard-hearted personality. It is said that man does not live by bread alone, but you will be one of those who will live by that bread alone, that concretized world without a window and without freedom. And this is what that represents. The offering, the food of the tree of Nut, is a beckoning for you to live on something higher than worldly desires and cravings and foods and so on and so forth. You do not see yourself as Asar, transcendental and immortal soul, but rather as a worldly personality and she cannot lift you up. She does not recognize you as her child. Geb does not recognize you as his child, so he does not allow you to go forth into the realm of the gods and goddesses.

But what if you were to master the lower principles through these meditations, through these philosophical reflections that we have discussed? What would happen if you were to practice the meditations that were discussed last time, the Nut meditation and the Geb meditation, which is to become as if like a mummy sleeping in a coffin, a coffin which is inside the earth, the coffin that Nut comes to raise you out of? And what if, in so doing, you became Asar? Aset would revive you. So at that point you have transcended Set and Nebethet having made Asar and Aset effective, and Geb allows you exit, opens the doors so that Nut can lift you up; Nut, which is expansion. If you can master these principles of expansion, then the parents of Geb and Nut, Shu and Tefnut, take notice. And then you can enter into a higher realm of the astral plane and live on higher food even than the Geb and Nut. So in this sense, Geb and Nut are the lower astral plane.

You should recall that we discussed that the principles of heaven (Nut) and earth (Geb) have a subtler and a grosser aspects, the subtler aspect of Nut, who is expansion, is infinity and the subtler aspect of Geb who is earth, is subtle matter and the concept of physicality itself. The gross is the physical world that we step on and the physical heavens that we see. There are subtle principles behind those. The subtle principle behind Geb is the principle of physicality. The gross principle of Geb is the physical earth. The subtle principle of goddess Nut is infinity, expansiveness and the physical, the gross manifestation of Nut are the stars, planets, and diffuse gasses, etc. in the vastness of outer space. What sustains the principle of expansiveness and infinity and the principle of physicality?

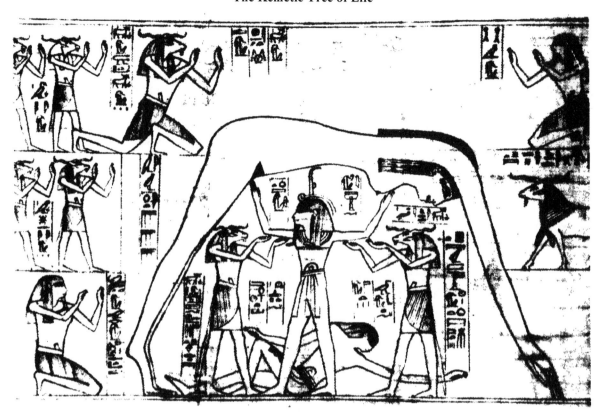

Figure 77: Shu Separating Geb and Nut [from papyrus Nesitanebashru]

In the story of the Creation that we went through earlier,[121] before this Tree of Life series, we discussed how Ra came into being. He emerged from the primeval ocean. That is the principle of demiurge consciousness in the form of the Creator, Khepri. The first principles he created were Shu and Tefnut. They came together and created Geb and Nut, who became locked in a sexual union, as we discussed earlier. Then he told Shu to come in between Geb and Nut to separate them. Nut was pregnant with the five principles of the personality who came into being: Asar, Aset, Set and Nebethet, and Heru Ur. Now we are at the level of the *Pet* realm and we are discussing how to raise ourselves to the higher level of that realm. Again, Ra told Shu to get in between Geb and Nut and that created space, created air. This is the space between our world and other stars; that is Shu.

Figure 78: Forms of the God Shu and Goddess Tefnut

---

[121] The Anunian Creation Myth: Series dates: 8/4/02 10015-10020, by Dr. Muata Ashby, See the Book *African Religion VOL. 1-ANUNIAN THEOLOGY THE MYSTERIES OF RA,* by Dr. Muata Ashby, ISBN: 1-884564-38-0

Shu has two aspects. *Shu* [hieroglyphs] has, again, the physical aspect, which is air, and the solar aspect, which is space, ether. And there is a form of sustenance or food that is in air but also in outer space or in a vacuum where there is no air. That sustenance comes from [hieroglyphs] *Tefnut.* Together, Shu and Tefnut are called [hieroglyphs] *Ruty* – or double lion. They are the two powers; the lion iconography and metaphor relates to power, strength. *"Tef"* means to spit or to pour out, and *"nut"* means heavens. This means that Tefnut is the higher power transcending Nut, from which Nut emanates. Tefnut is moisture, she is water, like a powerful tidal wave. She is a leonine life force energy, the Lion Power. Her principle iconography are the lion and the serpent. She is thus also the serpent power; the subtlest aspect of the serpent power is what Tefnut represents. And that subtle aspect of Life Force is poured into space, poured into air. It is the life force that enlivens all. So first Ra creates space [Shu] and then he pours into that space life force [Tefnut].

Figure 79: At left- Akher - the Two Horizons (Yesterday and Tomorrow).

Furthermore, Shu and Tefnut have much deep symbolism. As we said before, Ra came into being as one from the unitary and homogenous, undifferentiated Primeval Ocean, and then he becomes three [Ra-Shu-Tefnut]. This is the first major trinity that Ra becomes. This teaching is encapsulated in the formula:

Transliteration   *er i   m   chet   kheper   m   Neter   ua   Neter ḫámtaw*

Literal translation "As to myself transformed things became I form as   Divinity   one   Divinities three"

Contextual
Translation   **"As for myself, I transformed into things[122] from being one God to becoming three"**

This teaching is also symbolized in the *Aker* wisdom, the Aker symbolism. Aker is the two lions who sit back to back, and they support the sun disk. The sun disk is supported on their backs. The *Akerui* [Aker is one, *Akerui* is two], are the two lions, the Ruty. Shu and Tefnut are known as the same Ruty, the two lion god and goddess. The Akerui are known as *Sef & Duau,* and also *Bakau & Manu,* Sunset & Sunrise and Mountain of

---

[122] the objects of Creation

East & Mountain of West. Sef is yesterday and Duau is today the present and also the future, in other words, the before and the now and what will be. So the Akerui symbolizes time and space. Shu is space and Tefnut is time in this symbolism, since time requires movement and movement requires energy, energy to cause events, chemical reactions, etc. to occur in a sequence.[123] The same Akeru lions also represent *Manu & Bakau,* the mountains of the west and the east through which Ra sets in the evening and then emerges in the morning. The mountain of the morning is Bakau and the mountain of the evening is Manu. Bakau is a pun on the word pregnant. *Baka* means pregnant, pregnancy. So life begins with consciousness coming into time and space in the east, the before, and it comes to its conclusion in the west, the tomorrow. It comes to the beginning in the east, and comes to its ending in the west; and that duration of time in between the before and the after, the east and the west, that is the time of life on earth that a person is allotted. That time of life is controlled by Djehuti, the god of intellect, who holds in his hands a palm stem. On that palm stem are notches. Each notch represents a year that you are able to live in the world. Djehuti writes the number of years based on the divinities of his hands who are

Shai and *Renenutt,* fortune and destiny, which are based on a person's *ariu* [the *ariu-* {actions, deeds, unconscious mental impressions that impel the desires of the mind} accumulated over previous years and lifetimes]. These two are governed by Meskhent. Meskhent is the goddess who controls the result of your fortune and destiny, therefore, this dictates how long you will live on earth, as well as where a person will be born next time.

Figure 80: Khnum fashions a human body and Djehuti assigns it's years of life.

The God Khnum is the Ram headed man who is an aspect of Amun. In Khnum mythology Khnum is Creator of the bodies of human beings and he creates his creations on a potter's wheel. Mostly he fashions human beings out of clay, later the soul enlivens the clay. The god Djehuti stands behind him, counting notches in the spine of a palm frond. The notches signify the amount of years that the body is predestined to last.

This also should relate to your understanding of the concept of the Alpha and Omega, the beginning and the ending. Shu and Tefnut are the beginning and ending of all things. Nothing can exist outside of these, nothing in the world of time and space, that is. In order to come into being whatever is engendered by Ra must first go through the principles Shu and Tefnut before they go through Geb and Nut and so on. In order to end the existence in time and space they have to finally dissolve their Shu and Tefnut aspects and dissolve again to Ra.

If you were to transcend these principles, what would happen? If you were to transcend the concepts of today and yesterday? If your life was not based on what is going to happen today, what happened yesterday, what would things be like? Because these are what form your tomorrow! If you base your life on what you did yesterday, on your complexes, and say "Oh, I'm this terrible personality, and I can't learn the teaching" or "This crazy system is set up against me, I can't succeed..." "I can't do this, I can't do that", this is worldly thinking based on the past, which frames the mindset for the present in a limiting and degrading format. If your mind

---

[123] in reality there is no time, time does not exist; what we call time is the passage of one event to another in a sequence; in reality there is only eternity but events occur within segments of that eternity, and human beings with limited experience call that segment of eternity "time".

cogitates in the fashion, "I will be happy tomorrow, I will win the lottery and have a million dollars, or I will meet a new boyfriend and he will make me happy, or if I go shopping I will feel happy or if my boss gives me a good review I will be on top of the world or my neighbors are idiots so I will move to a good neighborhood and be happy," these are irrational hopes and dreams and desires for the future that can never fully and or abidingly provide comfort, peace or contentment; therefore they cannot lead to true happiness and they are thus mental delusions, imaginations based on egoistic desires that will not be fulfilled and will lead to frustration and unhappiness as well as anger and maybe even hatred.

Figure 81:- Shu holds up the sundisk

In the posture where Shu bears up the sundisk it is the symbol of *heh,* which means undetermined time, millions of years, etc. What all of this comes down to is this. In *Pyramid Texts* #796, #1014 and #1713 it is stated of the righteous soul: *the doors {gates} of Aker are opened for you.* The eternal present is the pathway between the physical plane and the astral plane. The past and the future do not exist. Only eternity (the present) is real. Therefore, once you have mastered the lower spheres, then the key at this level is through eternal present conscience and tapping into the power of air, which is the Life Force. This means putting aside the past or the future and being like the Aton [sundisk] of Ra, an Akhu [shining spirit], existing in the eternal present but also stretching out for millions of years into the past and millions of years into the future, encompassing the beginning and the end, Yesterday and Tomorrow, but existing in the eternal present. Shu presides over air and Tefnut over the life force in it. The study of this level of the Tree includes the research into the effect of the manipulation of air and life force. Certain breathing exercises can allow the manipulation and accumulation of life force as well as the cleansing of the personality; also they can allow the consciousness of the individual to merge with the consciousness of the universe. Through meditative practice [uaa "Meditation"] proper manipulation of air and life force can promote altered states of consciousness and meditative trance [Syh - Ecstasy, religious]. So air and life force through correct thought and breath promotes elevation here. The life force accumulation allows the personality to be filled with power that extends beyond the mortal body, empowering the mind and enlivening the astral body, enabling the personality to discover and discern that not only does the higher plane exist but that that is the higher reality, and not the mortal aspects. The emphasis on sustaining the sundisk through Shu is represented in the Shu posture wherein the God holds up the sundisk while in the Heh posture, with upraised arms. Heh means "indeterminate extent of time" –i.e., eternity. Thus eternity is achieved through holding up the sundisk [the eternal present] with the air and the life force present in it.

Translation of lines 796b:

doors of Aker are opened for you [the Asar], the doors of Geb are thrown open for you...

What does it mean to abide in the eternal present? It means achieving a state of peace and tranquility of mind wherein the thoughts of the past or future subside. That occurs when the mind is purified through ethical training and philosophical insight and through the practice of withdrawing the senses from the world of time and space realities including one's desires, hopes, aspirations, fears and ignorance. Goddess Aset teaches this kind of meditative practice, as a discipline of dwelling with her at the exclusion of all else.[124]

---

[124] See the books *INITIATION INTO EGYPTIAN YOGA AND NETERIAN RELIGION* by Dr. Muata Ashby, MEDITATION THE ANCIENT EGYPTIAN PATH TO ENLIGHTENMENT by Dr. Muata Ashby, *Mysteries of Isis* by Dr. Muata Ashby

Worldly thinking occurs in time and space. It is a circular kind of thinking process that leads you no where but back to itself, the ego and its desires, concepts and delusions, in a vicious circle. You must be able to learn how to transcend time, to go beyond space, and thereby realize that you are more than the air that you are breathing. You are more than this physical being, composed of an aggregate of elements, taking up a certain amount of space, a certain amount of volume in the physical universe. If you are to do that, while in that same meditative posture in your coffin, the mummy posture, the Asar posture, you are to be lifted up by Nut, then you would be able to live upon the food of Shu. Shu's food is the light of the sun rays of Ra. That is the same light that contains the life force of Tefnut, and this is what you must be able to live upon in your spiritual aspect. If you are to be able to live upon that light, you would not need the sustenance of the lower world for your mind and soul existence.

As we have said in the past, you may continue even to eat physical fruits and vegetables, but you will not be assigning these items the quality of life-sustaining as you know and experience a higher form of sustenance and in any case, the nutrient and life sustaining essence of even the physical fruits and vegetables is in fact that higher source anyway. But that form of sustenance, the higher form of sustenance, does not sustain your physical body as such. That is why it gets transformed into grosser physicality. So for your physical body, you need physical food. If you are going to live in the astral plane and in the causal plane in the Nun realm you have to learn how to live upon light. One should strive for *Ari em hetep* –[Work contentedly, with peace and contentment, without egoistic desire or expectations.] It is important to live a balanced {ma'at} life and avoid emotional exuberances and aberrant behaviors such as anger, hatred, loathing, passion, etc. and it is important to learn how to handle these when the control is lost, so that they do not squander the life force energy. Inordinate interest in the world which manifests as the pursuit of worldly desires is really a mentally straining problem. The mental impetus causes expenditure of energy in the world of time and space but it is the mental aspect of the personality that is most affected and most weakened, rendering the mind feeble and vulnerable to the effects of base emotions and feelings that prevent the intellect from being able to discern truth from untruth and leave personality open to the miseries of life. It is important to live a controlled sexual life as well for the same reason. Furthermore, it is important to refrain from gross foods and to emphasize subtle foods, also trying to make them as pure and organic as possible. The subtler foods are uncooked fruits and vegetables. Then the body and mind become more subtle and the need for gross foods is reduced and the sustenance drawn from the subtler foods becomes more sustainable to the body and mind. The cells of the body become lighter and do not need to rely so much on the plant's converting of sunlight into chlorophyll to be eaten as vegetables, but rather the cells can take more life force energy from the sun directly. A subtle body is less caught up in the illusions, dramas and sufferings of the world and is more able to fathom the depths of the mysteries of self.

And this teaching is called the 'realm of light'. This realm of light is already within you, you just don't know it. And it is by deeper and deeper levels of meditation that you discover the realm of light. In fact you are made up of spirit light, *Ra akh*. You are not a physical being. The sun rays, which produce the experience of gross physical warmth, have a solar aspect, a subtle astral aspect. If you were to elevate yourself through meditation you would experience the solar light of the astral plane, which is more powerful than the physical light of the sun that you experience. This becomes important, as you are going to see shortly.

First, before going into what is important you must discover and appreciate and understand the following. The god and goddess, Shu and Tefnut, who were created by Ra, are actually two halves of the same aspect. About Shu and Tefnut, the scripture says they share the same soul, in fact. By implication, all the other principles do as well. Geb and Nut share the same soul. Asar and Aset share the same soul. Set and Nebethet share the same soul. Why is it that Heru and Ra do not share souls with others (even though in some mythic teachings Heru has the counterpart Hetheru, and in Anunian Theurgy Ra has the counterpart Rat, but not in this particular teaching)? It is because they are realized oneness principles that mirror each other. In Ra and Heru-Ur, you discover that all is one. You discover non-duality. The male and female is there but merged, so they are androgynous. That is why Ra is called the Lord of Dualities. He contains the dualities within his oneness. So duality emanates from oneness just as anything that comes from something else causes a duality by its virtual presentation of itself as another beside the original. However, this presentation is of the nature of an illusion

238

because nothing comes from nothing, meaning that no thing has come forth besides a manifestation of the original even though it may appear as something separate, different or distinct. All the variations of Creations are aspects of Ra so therefore, philosophically and effectively the result has proceeded from a cause that is one with itself and never really separate. Therefore, there is no actual cause of Creation since nothing has been created. The Creation is Ra itself and therefore Ra has really done no-thing. The objects, the things of Creation are Ra.

So if you philosophically understand that you are one – that all is one – the earth is not separated from the heavens, and the havens are not separate from the rest of the universe you are on your way to Ra consciousness. The soul is not separated from wisdom, from intuition, intuitional knowledge of self except by obstruction of mind, due to ignorance caused by egoism and delusion. They are actually two sides of the same aspect, they are complementary principles. But if you transcend these obstructions then Heru consciousness is discovered and Heru is a reflection of Ra. Ra, at the top of the obelisk, is a master of the higher realms and Heru-Ur is an earthly reflection of Ra in time and space; the manifestation means master of the world, the physical world. Ra is a reflection of Heru in the highest plane, the highest time and space plane, the Duat; so upon reaching the level of Ra a person becomes the realized ruler, master of the higher realm and like Ra that person shines perennially, consciousness does not wane like the moon; people with moon conscience have flashes of insight and then they fall back into ignorance and limitation again. Also, as Ra they become golden; gold is the symbol of perfection and purity, a reflection of the sun on earth. Therefore, Ra and Heru represent "as above, so below." Further, the serpent encircling the sundisk, the fire spitting goddess Hetheru, represents eternal rebirth for just as a serpent sheds the slough, the dead skin, the old body and dons the new skin, so to Ra and all who become one with Ra, daily, annually, millennially, etc., etc. That is the teaching; mastery above and mastery below, knowledge of above and knowledge of below, on earth as it is in heaven.

If this concept, this teaching of oneness, is fully understood philosophically, then your meditations will become effective. If you leave behind fear of death, if you leave behind desire for worldly pleasures, if you realize that your true nature is Asar and not whatever name your parents called you when you were born, if you understand this wisdom, you understand that you are not a physical being even though you are manifesting as a physical being, that you are infinite and expansive, you go beyond the district of your home where you live, beyond your so-called race or your so-called country that you supposedly belong to, and your nationality, your culture, etc. If this is your form of understanding, then you can start living upon light itself.

And, therefore, the scripture says that Shu is the divinity that opens the mouth with the special iron instrument, the *Seba Ur* is the iron instrument that opens the mouth allowing the deceased {the initiate, you the spiritual aspirant practitioner of this teaching} to speak again, to think again, to awaken again.

Figure 82: Vignettes from the Opening of the Mouth Ceremonies from the Ancient Egyptian texts. Left- with Chepesh (Chpsh-foreleg), Right with the Seba (Sba) ur instruments.

"O Initiate, I have come in search of you, for I am Heru; I have struck your mouth for you, for I am your beloved son; I have split open your mouth for you... I have split open your eyes for you... with the Chepch (Chpsh) of the Eye of Heru- Chepesh (Foreleg). I have split open your mouth for you... I have split open your eyes for you... with the adze of Upuaut..... with the adze of iron . . . [PT 11-13]

Figure 83: The Mystical Constellation and Imperishable stars.

"Ursa Minor"

The opening of the mouth and eyes is a mystical teaching relating to expansion in consciousness expression (mouth) and awareness (open eyes). These factors (mouth and eyes), which are presided over by the gods *Hu* and *Saa*, are the signs of the existence of consciousness or its absence. The importance of *Hu*, divine taste, is the capacity to discern meaning which occurs when the knowledgeable mind recognizes be experiencing, and *Saa*, divine understanding, to be able to see things clearly, as the Ancient Egyptian saying goes: "understand things with the inner eye," is underscored by the presence of *Hu* and *Saa* at the birth of Heru Pa Khard. *Hu* and *Saa* were known to serve as bearers of the Eye of Heru (enlightened consciousness). They were also considered to be the tongue and heart of *Asar-Ptah* (the Self). Thus, they represent the vehicles through which human souls can experience and understand the teachings of moral and spiritual wisdom about the Self, i.e. the faculties of speech and intuitional understanding.

From the passages above we learn that the Priests and Priestesses "open" the mouth and eyes by touching them with the ritual instruments which symbolize the eternal, the absolute, in other words the expansion of consciousness, immortality and spiritual enlightenment. Also, we learn that the adze instrument (Ursa minor) is actually also the Eye of Heru, which is the greatest offering {arit *Heru* ⌒ | 𓅉 𓃀 𓏏𓏏𓏏 -Eucharist (Arit Heru Arat Hetep - Eye of Heru the divine offering)} of the Egyptian mysteries. The Eye symbolizes divine consciousness as it is one and the same with Heru, Asar and Ra. Therefore, being touched with these instruments means attaining god-consciousness.

Figure 84: Saa(A) and Uadjit(B), Djehuti(C), Aset with Heru pakhard(D), Amun(E), Nekhebit(F) and Hu(G) adoring the young divine child.

A   B   C   D   E   F   G

The *Seba Ur* is the higher, the highest teaching of initiatic science. This term "*sba*" {seba} is a pun with different layers of meaning. "Seba" means "illumination" and "teaching", and "Ur" means great. Also seba relates to the stars in the sky of the North Pole that do not move, because they are located in the center of the circle of the North Pole region of the sky. They are steady; they do not fluctuate, so their teaching is firm and not weak or speculative. The ones outside of the center circle, they move and they go up and out above the horizon and so on and so forth. That means that they come into existence, and they go out of existence. They reincarnate. They die and reincarnate. The *Sba Ur* stars do not die and reincarnate.[125]

Why should it be an iron instrument that Shu uses? In the opening of the mouth ceremony, this instrument is touched to the mouth and the mouth is opened. The mouth is where hekau, the creative word, comes

---

[125] See the Book **African Religion VOL. 1- ANUNIAN THEOLOGY THE MYSTERIES OF RA**, by Dr. Muata Ashby; and THE AFRICAN ORIGINS OF CIVILIZATION, RELIGION AND YOGA SPIRITUALITY AND ETHICS PHILOSOPHY by Dr. Muata Ashby

from. The Mouth is the instrument through which Ra created the universe, by sound. Sound reverberates through the Primeval Ocean and coagulates it into the forms of creation. Sound is the instrument of consciousness to engender Creation, therefore, opening the mouth means opening, expanding conscious awareness.

And referring to Shu, we talked about the northern pole of the sky in reference to the stars but also, from the same region, the North Pole, comes the northern wind. The northern wind is the same wind that Aset uses. She blows it with her wings to resurrect Asar. After her wisdom reconstituted his body parts, then the wings blow on the body to infuse it with life force that emanates from the northern, the cool northern region, from the place where there is immortality, from the place where the Seba Ur is located, from the realm of enlightenment. And what does this wind have in it that we have discussed previously? What is it within the air that is enlivening? The air is the vehicle for the life force, the life force of Tefnut.

But why should it be an iron instrument? If you go to the serpent power book,[126] you will recall that the *Sefech Ba Ra* – the seven souls of Ra, the seven energy centers of psycho-spiritual consciousness, have certain obstacles, certain elements that act as containers, as barriers between them and between the person who is trying to access them. These elements can be thought of as obstructions since a person has caused them to become dense, thick with egoistic notions and desires. In the myth of the Book of Djehuti,[127] these obstructions are explained as boxes enclosing the consciousness centers and thwarting the expansion. There are seven boxes, one for each of seven centers or spheres of consciousness.

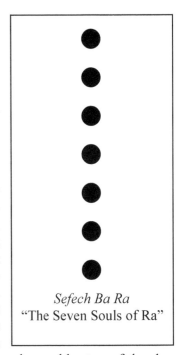

Sefech Ba Ra
"The Seven Souls of Ra"

The first box that must be opened in order to unlock the serpent power energy and move towards higher consciousness is made of iron. Iron, according to mythology of the Neterian Theurgy, is sacred because it is deemed to be a metal that falls from the sky as a meteor. Thus, iron is a solid, physical object that originates in the sky and becomes part of the physical earth. So an earthly object that originates in the sky is a perfect instrument to liberate a human being who exists on earth but whose real origin is in the sky. Like the human body, iron can rust and breaks down eventually. But if, before that breakdown was to occur, it is bent into the shape of the northern constellation that is enlightened, that is the bending of the personality not in a worldly shape, the shape of a person who becomes accustomed to worldly pleasures and desires, whose life is like that of the changeable stars of the sky, the non-polar region, but in accordance with the northern polar constellation, signifying enlightenment and perpetual wakefulness to the ultimate truth; this is the shape of sages and enlightened souls.

It is also said that Shu has power over the serpent. Again if you study the Serpent Power book and lectures, you will realize that this has already been discussed. There are certain breathing techniques that can manipulate and accumulate the life force energy. So Shu, the god of air and breath, has control over the life force within the air. Now, why should you control and accumulate the life force energy? The answer is that it has been discovered by mystics that if life force energy is accumulated in the personality, instead of being expended in the world of time and space exclusively, it will afford the personality the power to transcend the physical earth plane. The life force is also used to cleanse the gross and subtle nerve pathways of the body. There are certain techniques that are used to cleanse the *mettu*[128] - the conduits - the gross physical conduits of the body, meaning your blood vessels, your lymphatic vessels, and your gastrointestinal system, as well as the nervous conduits and the mental conduits, which are the thought pathways, that are blocked by complexes, the egoistic thoughts, desires, based on ignorance about the nature of the world and the self. The life force can be used to cleanse all of these, which is a necessary step on the spiritual path.

[126] see the book *The Serpent Power* by Dr. Muata Ashby
[127] see the book *The Serpent Power* by Dr. Muata Ashby
[128] see the book *The Kemetic Diet* by Dr. Muata Ashby and see the book *The Serpent Power* by Dr. Muata Ashby

If all of these conduits are cleansed and filled with life force, then in the thought process, the complex of the world cannot be entertained by the mind as a reality. In fact, the mind will come to a stop. Conscious awareness, in the human mind, depends on intermittent flashes of thought/idea forms held in the screen of mental awareness that can be compared, contemplated and desired or repudiated from the perspective of an individual egocentric personality. If the screen, the mind, were to be inundated with formless energies, undifferentiated thought matter, then the screen, or rather the field or matrix of mind, the mental field of awareness would become filled with indistinct energy consciousness that would eventually need to move from the confined mental field of individual ego conscience into expansion beyond the personality. Under these conditions the personality is energetically pushed out of exclusive individual awareness and into expanded awareness, in the manner of discovering, "I am this"; but the "this" now refers to the personality and what the expanded awareness now experiences beyond it. The previously egocentric (confined to the body and personality and relationships with others and the world as an individual limited and mortal being) awareness will be diverted – your consciousness will be introduced to higher planes of awareness. If that contact is practiced regularly the limited mind integrates the greater awareness and the greater awareness (beyond the ego and physical personality) becomes the higher perennial awareness; the personality is expanded, transformed and enlightened by that expanded awareness. And this is how the life force is raised – from the lower psycho-spiritual energy centers to the higher, thereby promoting higher consciousness awareness.

If a person is not ready, however, to experience higher consciousness, because they don't have an understanding of the philosophy since they are still basing their lives on lower principles, egocentrism, individuality, narcissism, pride, holding on to body consciousness, the degraded notions of life, and because they remain engaged in trials and tribulations, hatreds, fears, desires etc., if that remains in the personality, having experiences of higher consciousness can actually be a detrimental thing and can lead to mental instability as well as perhaps even a reverse spiritual movement, in other words, to spiritual contraction instead of expansion; the ego gets stronger and more concrete instead of subtle. And so, therefore, a person is prevented from doing that for their own good by having certain information kept from them until they are ready to understand what is to be experienced and how to go about inducing the experience.

This teaching is also known as the *Veil of Aset*. To the uninitiated and to the egocentric, the true nature of the world is veiled and the goddess's wisdom is restricted. This is the locking down, as it were, of Geb. Geb is like a jailer, if you will. He locks you down. And you can't do anything. You can't go anywhere. This is a miserable condition. And it is a condition that you have made yourself by your indulgence and ignorance, your indulgence in worldly thoughts, desires, actions, and feelings and believing those to be real and abiding instead of thinking about them as being illusory and temporary.

The god Shu and goddess Tefnut represent the space and energy of the outer universe as well as the space and energy of the inner universe, the mind. The god Shu has two aspects; on one level he is "Physical air". The other aspect is "Ethereal air", which is a subtler dimension. Shu is a key to opening up the subtle worlds beyond the physical plane. The gross physical air of the world is what all humans and animals breathe all the time to survive. That is the gross aspect of Shu. When working with the subtler aspect of Shu, the ether, a human being can learn to experience her/his ethereal nature which is space without content, dimension without volume or existence without form. The manipulation of the physical aspect through breathing exercises and special visualizations allows the subtler aspect to be revealed. The manipulation also allows the power of Tefnut, the subtle energy, *sekhem,* that resides within air, to be activated. That energy in turn stimulates and sets in motion the serpent power that awakens the psycho-spiritual consciousness centers of the subtle body, which in turn works to cleanse the personality and lead the soul to dismantle the physical world of illusory perceptions.

So when Shu and Tefnut are mastered, you have raised yourself totally above physicality. You have raised yourself above the concept of infinity and expansion. Now you are seeing yourself as time and space itself. You are just one step away from discovering non-duality, the ultimate "I" concept. Here we are not referring to the "I" that you have that is little, related to the life on earth, the "I" of the individual. With the little "I" you see yourself as this is your body and your personality and "that is what I am". You believe that you were born in a particular country and came from particular parents. Your true "I" that we're talking about now, the Ra "I", is the "I" that is all encompassing, the "I" that is universal, the "I" that makes you realize that you are one with all; that is your higher eye, the one in which your essential existence is discovered to be the same existence that everything is rooted in. At the level we are talking about now you would be one step away from that discovery. Through meditation on the serpent power, through manipulation of air and the life force contained in it; this is the pathway to raise from the Geb and Nut level to the Shu and Tefnut level. This discipline works for getting through the other spheres, but here at the top it becomes critical.

Next we will continue to close this series with a discussion with some words on the principle of Ra, though we have said much already throughout this lecture series. In the next lesson we will also explore the hieroglyphic symbols of the transcendental realm of consciousness. This concludes our lesson on the principles of Shu, Tefnut and Ra.

Lesson 13 Part 2: More on the Mysteries of Ra

Firstly, Ancient Egyptian Religion is not polytheism. In reality all the various divinities are emanations manifestations or projections of the Supreme Being. The following translations of original writings from Ancie Egypt attest to the wisdom, understanding and teaching of a single Supreme Being.

The following passages come from the Egyptian *Book of Coming Forth By Da*y (Chapter. clxxiii):

> "I praise thee, Lord of the Gods, God One, living in truth."

The following passage is taken from a hymn where princess Nesi-Khensu glorifies Amen-Ra:

> "August Soul which came into being in primeval time, the great god living in truth, the first Nine Gods who gave birth to the other two Nine Gods,[129] the being in whom every God existeth One One, the creator of the kings who appeared when the earth took form in the beginning, whose birth is hidden, whose forms are manifold, whose germination cannot be known."

UA _ or "One,"
UA NETER _ or "One God,"
"Only One" _ ,
"Only One Without a second" _
"One One" _

130

The reference to nine divinities may be taken to mean the divinities of the three realms (three of the physical, thre of the astral, three of the causal). The Kemetic sages wanted to leave no doubt as to the way in which the philosophy o Neter was to be understood. We have already seen designations for the Supreme Being as "God One" and "Only One but the sages went further and gave the following:

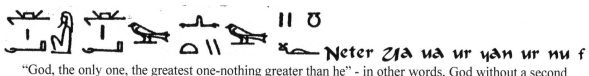

Neter *ʒʼa ua ur ʒʼaʼn ur nu f*

"God, the only one, the greatest one-nothing greater than he" - in other words, God without a second

Neter *ʒʼa ua ur*

"Only Divinity, one the ultimate"

Now, a few last words about Ra, the concept of demiurge and the concept of multiplicity. Ra is a demiurge meaning that he is the creator aspect of the transcendental divinity. The essence sustaining the demiurge is th transcendental Supreme Being.   As explained earlier, the demiurge divinity has a time and space name but ther

is also the 〰 〰 *an ren* – nameless name. That nameless name relates to a transcendental truth beyond th relative reality of time and space. This is in complement to the divinity referred to in the Pert M Heru text that i

---

[129] Ancient Egyptian mythology conceives of creation as an expression of God in which there are nine primordial cosmic principles or forces in the universe. These first nine may be seen as the cause from which all other qualities of nature *(the other two Nine Gods)* or creative forces in nature arise.

[130] Usage of the term "one one" and "only one" taken from various Ancient Egyptian scriptures.

described as having many names: *Nuk pa Neter aah Neter Uah asha ren*[131], **"I am that same God, the**

Supreme One, who has myriad of mysterious names." The ꟾ ꟾ ꟾ 〰 *asha ren,* "many names" concept relates the idea that the various forms of Creation, composed of the elements, are in reality manifestations of the same God. So the Supreme Being may be thought of as one and alone {referred to as monism} or one manifesting as many {referred to as henotheism}. But that god is none other than the nameless god. The named god has a name because it is in time and space but the nameless one cannot have a name because it does not exist in the realm of time and space, the realm of generation where the offsprings, the generated things, all get named. The nameless one cannot be named because it is beyond names, categories and nomenclatures of the time and space realm. This is because it encompasses and transcends the physicality as well as the conceptual bases of the Creation, that something has been created, that duality is an abiding reality.

The creation process that Ra used to bring Creation into being offers us insights into the nature of Creation and the nature of the mind's capacity to create a form of reality as well as what needs to be done in order for the mind to discover the higher truth beyond the relative reality of time and space. Ra emerged from the primeval Ocean {Nun} and made waves with his boat. Those movements from the boat of Ra condition part of the ocean into wave forms, a conditioned temporary reality, the Universe that subsides when Ra ends his journey. Consider that if you are asleep and having a dream, how would a person in your dream think of you if they could? How would they conceptualize you, who are beyond the dream world and to whom the dream world is an illusion? If you practice meditation successfully you can enter your dream world in a conscious way as opposed to in an unconscious way. You know how sometimes you are dreaming and you are aware that you are dreaming but most times you are caught in the dream believing it is real. If you enter consciously you can shape the dream world in accordance with your will. To a person in your dream witnessing that they would think it is a miracle because they have no idea that you are the owner, the creator of the dream world. If they were to meet you knowing that you are the Creator of the dream world and the performer of the great feats, what would they call you? In this metaphor you are God and the field of mind is your creation, the Universe and everything in it exists in and depends on you and in fact is you and what happens to that person in the dream when you wake up and you withdraw your conscience from that dream manifestation? That person of the dream never existed as an individual and separate entity from you the dreamer and when they cease to exist as a dream personality their essence becomes dissolved in your mind and goes back to its original nature, consciousness, your consciousness. So they never were born, never really died and it was all a temporary manifestation, of Spirit {Supreme Being, God, Goddess}, as you! But what if they were to realize it is a dream, before the dream world is withdrawn? In this case the person who is in the dream that wakes up within the dream is you when you go into your dream knowing you are dreaming, and in such a case what is the loss for that dream person? Should their dream family cry over them when they die in the dream? Have they really died? Was the person all "alive" to begin with?

And what did you, as the dreamer, the god of the dream world, get out of this dream process? What was the benefit of all of this for you the dreamer? Nothing! You are able to have experiences of manifesting in all the forms (objects and personalities) of the dream world but nothing changed; you dreamed a dream and withdrew the dream and you never changed, you just manifested a form of relative reality for a short while but you yourself were never changed by the process, you were always there sleeping on the bed. In reality, there is no philosophy that can circumscribe the true nature of the Higher Self, except to the extent of providing metaphors, thought models and mental indications about it for directing the mind to discover it directly, it is something that ultimately

requires experiencing it. The term *an ren* is also contrasted with ꟾ ꟾ ꟾ ꟾ *Asha Hrau,* the name of the serpent god of Creation, meaning "Many faced one". He (*Asha Hrau*) has 5 heads, but these heads represent "manifold," they represent multiplicity. Thus, the number "five" represents multiplicity and diversity. In the same way the divinities of the five upper spheres of the Tree of Life represent multiplicity of Creation, the universe, while the five lower represent the multiplicity of the desires, thoughts, concepts and feelings of the human personality.

---

[131] (Prt M Hru (Ancient Egyptian Book of the Dead) 9:4)

In the myth/legend of Ra and Aset we learned that Ra is not the absolute, the high Supreme Being; he is a demigod. The physical image and iconography are like the clothing he wears which in this sense is the time and space manifestation of the sun and its cosmic force, which include: life force, light, fire, perfection and immortality. The power and image of Ra is a dynamic manifestation but it is not an abiding existence, it is not the ultimate substratum, the true essential nature of the Supreme Divinity. Ra and his sundisk are merely a mask, a manifestation in time and space of a higher aspect, which has a hidden name. The name is hidden because it is not utterable and can only be known through experiencing it, that is, by becoming one with the essential transcendental nature which sustains it and all else.[132] The true essential nature is transcendental of that and is termed variously as, Neberdjer, Net, Ra-Harakty, or Nunu, etc.

Insights Into the Principle of Ra From the *Pert m Heru Text*

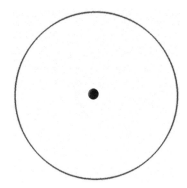

Figure 85: Above left- The Symbol of Ra, the Sundisk.

The following hymn is from the *Pert M Heru* or "Book of Enlightenment" from Ancient Egyptian Anunian Theurgy. Through it's verses we are able to discover key features of Anunian Theurgy as well as the nature of Ra which enlighten our practice of the Tree of Life spiritual path. Actually, as with other texts, it provides insights into the nature of several of the gods and goddesses that are related to Ra so we may glean much of their interrelationships and thus the reader will find much of what has been said about the gods and goddesses, in this present volume, contained and set forth in this Hymn, which is representative of the texts of the Pert M Heru. The text is written for a spiritual aspirant whose given name is preceded by the divine name, Asar. Therefore the passages are written for any aspirant and any person who adopts the teaching, who follows the teaching, and once initiated is referred to as an Asar.

A Hymn to Ra and Its Philosophical Principles

Hymn to Ra[133]

1.   Behold Asar_____[134] bringing divine offerings of all the gods and goddesses. Asar _____ speaks thus:

2.   Homage to thee, who comes in the form of Khepri[135], Khepri the Creator of the gods and goddesses. You rise and shine, illuminating your mother, goddess Nut, the sky, crowned as king of the gods and goddesses. Your mother Nut worships you with her two arms. The western

---

[132] See the book *THE MYSTERIES OF ISIS: **The Ancient Egyptian Philosophy of Self-Realization** by **Dr. Muata Ashby***

[133] From *The Ancient Egyptian Book of the Dead,* Muata Ashby, 2000

[134] Spaces are left so that the initiate for whom the text was written may enter his or her name.

[135] Morning sun, solar child-Nefertem.

horizon receives you in peace and Maat embraces you at the double season. Give Asar _____ Glorious Spirit being[136], and spiritual strength through righteous speaking. Grant the ability to come forth as a living soul so that Asar _____ may see Heru of the two Horizons.[137] Grant this to the Ka[138] of Asar _____ who is Righteous of Speech in the presence of Asar, the Divine Self. Asar _____ says: Hail to all the gods and goddesses, weighers of the house of the soul, in heaven and on earth by means of the scales of Maat, who are givers of Life Force sustenance.

3. Tatunen,[139] One, maker of men and women as well as the company of the gods and goddesses of the south, the north, the west and the east, in other words all the neteru[140], grant praises to Ra, the lord of heaven, sovereign of life, vitality and health, maker of the gods and goddesses. Adorations to thee in your form as all goodness, as you rise in your boat. The beings up high praise thee. Beings in the lower realms praise thee. Djehuti[141] and Maat[142] have written for thee, who are shining forth, every day. Your enemies are put to the fire. The fiends are put down, their arms and legs being bound securely for Ra. The children of weakness disrespect and insurrection shall not continue.

4. The great house[143] is in festival time. The voices of the participants are in the great temple. The gods and goddesses are rejoicing. They see Ra in his glorious rising, his beams of light piercing, inundating the lands. This exalted and venerable god journeys on and unites with the land of Manu, the western horizon, illuminating the land of his birth every day and at the same time he reaches the province where he was yesterday.

5. Be in peace with me! I see your beauties and I prosper upon the land; I smile and I defeat the ass fiend as well as the other fiends. Grant that I may defeat Apep[144] in his time of strength and to see the pilot fish of the Divine Boat of Ra, which is in its blessed pool.[145] I see Heru in the form as the guardian of the rudder. Djehuti and Maat are upon his two arms. Received am I in the prow[146] of the Mandet[147] Boat and in the stern of the Mesektet[148] Boat. Ra gives divine sight, to see the Aton[149], to view the moon god unceasingly, every day, and the ability of souls to come forth, to walk to every place they may desire. Proclaim my name! Find him in the wood board of offerings. There have been given to me offerings in the life-giving presence, like it is given to the followers of Heru[150]. It is done for me in the divine place in the boat on the day of the sailing, the journey of The God. I am received in the presence of Asar in the land of truth speaking[151] of the Ka of Asar _____.

---

other words allow the initiate to become an Akhu or Glorious Spirit.
e All-Encompassing Divine Self in the form of Heru.
iritual essence of the personality which holds a person's desires, impulses and impetus to incarnate; the Life Force which sustains the physical being.
eator -aspect of Ra, Atum, Asar, Khepri, Amun, Neberdjer, etc) who first arose on the primeval mound. Protector of the souls of Asar and Heru.
ds and goddesses
s headed deity, minister of Ra, originator of hieroglyphic writings and music.
ddess of righteousness, truth, regularity, and order.
yal family.
ader of the fiends, second only to Set.
e pool or lake is the symbol of the Primeval Ocean. In ancient times the temple complexes included a lake for ritually sailing the boat of Ra as well as for keeping fish, crocodiles and other animals as temple mascots.
nt section of a ship's hull, the bow.
e name of Ra's Divine boat when it is traveling from noon to midnight, in other words the evening boat.
e name of Ra's Divine boat when it is traveling from midnight to noon, in other words the morning boat.
e sundisk. Atonism dates to the New Kingdom era of Ancient Egyptian history {1800 B.C.E-1400 B.C.E.}
Kamitan Mystical Philosophy the principle of "Shemsu Heru" is very important. It may be likened to the disciples of Jesus in Christianity who were his "followers." It means living and acting like Heru, a life of truth and increasing spiritual enlightenment.
a-kheru.

Principles in the Hymn to Ra[152]

F irstly, let's look at the sundisk, which is the primary symbol of Ra. In the Ancient Egyptian religious tradition known as Atonism, which is a related solar religious tradition of Ancient Egypt, the wisdom of the use of the Aton as a focal meditative symbol was highlighted but there also it was recognized as a visible manifestation and not the actual essential nature of the divinity. The hieroglyphic sign above means "Aton," the sundisk. Atonism is the philosophy of devotional love to the Supreme Spirit by recognizing its dynamic aspect, the sun through which it sustains and enlivens all Creation, pervading and also manifesting as Creation. Therefore, Atonism is the art of discovering the Supreme Being everywhere and in all things. The main proponents of Atonism were the Sage king Akhenaton, his mother Queen *Ti* and the priest *Ai*. Atonism, like the other traditions within Neterianism, existed since the beginning of Kemetic history but was not emphasized until Akhenaton elevated it to the status of state religion. The Aton is the sundisk, the visible and dynamic object in the sky, but that is not the divinity itself, but rather its manifestation. The Aton is the sun, the ball of fire in the sky but it is also the boat, the vehicle through which the power of the Divine courses through the Creation. Aton is also the Sun – Right eye of Ra and Heru. So if the rays are followed to their source and if the sun were meditated upon that meditation would lead to the discovery of the power and consciousness behind the sundisk, which touches and sustains all.

The hymn to Ra is related to Aton since it was understood in Anunian Theurgy that Ra is the power behind the sundisk (verse 5 above). In the Hymn to Aton, the source of freedom from *"being [previously] restrained"* occurs through the *"movement in adoration to the Aton."* This movement in adoration allows the worshipper to be free from "worldly" restraints and allows the worshipper to attain unity with the Aton, the realization that we are all "millions of living beings within thee [the Aton] and that sustains life-breath in us." The invocatory hymn of any scripture is an important part of the overall feeling of the spiritual tradition. Ra, of course, symbolizes the Higher Self, the Supreme Being, The God. Thus, the invocation to God is a form of prayer, or devotional expression towards the Divine, but at the same time it is a form of propitiation. In essence, prayer can be understood as talking to God, but the hymn goes a step further. Most times in modern culture people pray in order to ask for something. Sometimes people want God to help them with a problem in their life. Sometimes the prayer is for good luck. Sometimes the prayer is asking for the right numbers to the lottery. At other times the prayer is for deliverance from some ordeal in life. But how often do people pray for deliverance from human life? How often do people ask God to show them the way to achieve spiritual enlightenment? This is the very objective of the Hymn to Ra. Note also, in contrast to most prayers where the devotee is asking for something from the Divine, the prayer above is primarily composed of descriptions and glorification of the beauties of the Divine.

The hymn opens with salutations and descriptive appellations of Ra, as he rises in the morning. This is not some distant God, but a familiar presence. Ra is a being who can be seen daily and who can be approached easily; he even touches people when they walk outside on a sunny day. He illumines all the earth and causes all life to be. Ra is the source from which all of the gods and goddesses, all life, all human beings, etc., emanate. He sustains Creation by establishing Maat (order) and Djehuti (reason) as he moves through Creation. It is especially acknowledged that Ra is not only the illuminer of the physical world, but also of the Netherworld, the Duat (kingdom of the dead). This signifies that Ra is not the sun itself. This is a very important point to understand.

If a person has acted with virtue and in accordance with the voice of their conscience, their soul will experience positive conditions in the astral realm. This condition is referred to as heaven. If a person acted according to their egoistic desires, selfishness and pride, they will experience pain and sorrow in the astral realm. This condition is referred to as hell. So the hymn goes on to invoke the grace of Ra. The astral realm is a subtle universe which is in a different plane than the physical. Ra passes through the astral realm just as he also passes through the physical. He passes through the physical realm in his Andetet Boat (day boat), and through the astral realm in the Sekhet (night) boat. However, when he passes through the Duat, there are certain ropes which hang

---

[152] Gloss On The Hymns to Ra: Its Meaning and Mystical Significance, *The Ancient Egyptian Book of the Dead,* Muata Ashby, 2000

from his boat. The desire of the spiritual aspirant reading the text is that {he/she} may be able to see and grab hold of the ropes which are hanging from the boat.

This is a beautiful hymn dedicated to the Divine, the Supreme Being, in the form of Ra. It also has several important additional teachings which are important to the study of *Pert Em Heru* philosophy.

The ropes, among other things, symbolize divine compassion and divine love. God, in this form as Ra, and following the theurgy of Anu, is extending his hand, as it were, to rescue the soul from the suffering that can occur outside of the boat, as if the boat is there to rescue people who are drowning after a naval disaster, to rescue them, as it were from drowning in the egoism and ignorance that lead to suffering in the realm of time and space. The boat itself is the abode of the God Ra just as the Aset {throne} is the abode of the God Asar. It is the place of contentment and peace, being closest to the Divine. All other realms are as if a separation from that divine perfection that is in the boat. They represent a distancing from God, a separation from what is Divine. The act of reaching out to grab the ropes and the capacity to pull oneself up are the act of spiritual aspiration and the willpower gained from living and practicing the teachings. It signifies the practice of the spiritual disciplines (of Sema Tawy {Egyptian Yoga[153]}) which enable a person to move towards their Higher Self as opposed to getting more deeply involved in the relative realms which are again, a separation from the Divine.

The idea of Ra emerging and "inundating the lands" with his life giving essence has special mystical significance. This teaching refers to the original creation when the entire universe and the forms of Creation were not yet in existence. The time prior to the dawn symbolizes the undifferentiated state of the universe as well as the human mind. In the beginning the universe was like a calm ocean and there was no differentiation in it. Everything looked the same. However, when Ra emerged from the ocean he caused waves, and these waves took on many different forms. These forms are what we refer to as elements or matter. Think of the time when you fall asleep. You lose consciousness of your waking personality and you are submerged in an ocean without forms. This is like the primeval ocean of creation. From it arises your dream world in which you are a character among other characters of your own creation. Thus, you are the Creator of your dream world and God is the creator of the dream of the universe.

God created the universe by thought, movement, breath and causing vibrations in that primordial ocean of his own consciousness by uttering sound. Sound is the medium by which God ordains what happens in Creation from its inception to its end. The word manifests through the power and faculty of speech. Therefore, speech is related to Cosmic Consciousness and the ability to create in the world of time and space as well as in the astral realm. In the same manner, a human being can create his or her world according to the desire of the heart.

Thus, just as a human being must breathe air in order to sustain life, this entire universe must receive the breath of life from the Divine in order to be sustained. However, ordinary human beings (ignorant masses) only know of the physical air that sustains the physical body. A spiritual aspirant seeks to breathe the air which sustains the elevated states of consciousness which are above the waking state of consciousness.

The hymn goes on to show that Ani praises the Divine at dawn and at eventide. This teaching relates to the necessity for devotional exercise such as prayers, chanting and recitation of the hekau or words of power which propitiate divine grace and promote spiritual knowledge and the kindling of spiritual feeling deep within the heart leading to purity and enlightenment. A person should not engage constantly in the world with its illusions without a respite and without practicing the disciplines. Thus, spiritual practice should be daily, encompassing every aspect of life, in order to overwhelm the worldly impressions produced by distraction, ignorance and the lower desires. The process of spiritual worship leads a human being to draw divine grace to {him/her} self. This is what is referred to as being one of the "favored ones" of God. This favored status is attained by becoming "one of those who worshipped thee upon earth" meaning while they were alive and in human form.

Many people mistakenly believe that the *Pert Em Heru* (Ancient Egyptian Book of the Dead) is a book of rituals only for people who have passed on to the next life, but in reality it is a fount of wisdom and is a guidebook of disciplines for those who are alive so that they may fare well during life and after death. The physical body is the best place to carry out a spiritual program, the practice of Egyptian Yoga and Mystical Religion. This is because it is the place where the soul can experience an extended period of waking consciousness in which to consciously work on purifying the heart. The dream and dreamless sleep states or

---

[153] see the books *Egyptian Yoga The Philosophy of Enlightenment* and *INITIATION INTO EGYPTIAN YOGA AND NETERIAN RELIGION* by Dr. Muata Ashby

subconscious and unconscious levels of the mind are inconstant and because of that minimal spiritual progress can be accomplished in these states.

There is one more thing. In reference to the question of eschatology, earlier we discussed about the possible fates of a personality after death. In the lesson on goddess Nut we discussed about the final resting place of the body as being in the trunk of a tree and the soul as being picked up by Nut and lifted to the sky and we also talked about the three possibilities for the soul. One is to suffer at the hands of the gods and goddesses, the second is to be admitted to the city of Asar to worship and do penance there to obtain purification or third, to become one with him. In the Pert m Heru it is customary to refer to the aspirant by his spiritual name and then the given name. Since the spiritual name is Asar the reference would be Asar Mike or Asar Imhotep. Thus, if the aspirant is named Asar and she goes to the netherworld after death to meet Asar what does that mean? It signifies that the aspirant is meeting herself; she and Asar are one, to the extent she is purified and aware of that reality. So in other words, she is the dream personality waking up and meeting her Creator who she already is essentially. To the extent she is not, to that extent she is separate and suffering other fates. This may be considered the lunar path, the path of Asar. In the path of Asar the body is buried. There is another viewpoint related to the Bennu. As the Bennu is a fire divinity and as it dies and is burnt in fire it throws off the ashes of the old body and revealing the new higher body, the path of fire is evident. This concept is also evident in the philosophy of the sloughing dead skin of the serpent and the serpent is a primary symbol of Ra, encircling his sundisk. In Anunian Religion, instead of being buried, the body can be cremated and the soul goes to the Duat, to live there and behold the majesty of Ra when he sails through that region with his night time boat. When a soul is ready it can climb on to the boat by means of tow ropes that hang down from it for those souls who are admitted. The ropes are not visible in the day time, that is to say, the physical world, the waking consciousness.[154] This concludes the lesson on the principle of Ra.

---

[154] For more on the teaching of the Bennu see the book *THE EGYPTIAN BOOK OF THE DEAD MYSTICISM OF THE PERT EM HERU "* by Dr. Muata Ashby

Questions and Answers:

Question:

You spoke about how many of the principles, like Shu and Tefnut, share a soul. I was wondering, as I'm looking at the Tree of Life of the Anunian Theurgy cosmiconomythograph, whether or not on the next level where the divinities Hetheru and Djehuti are, whether they share soul space there and then where does that leave goddess Ma'at? And does Ma'at share soul space with Djehuti?

Answer:

I believe this was primarily discussed in the Anunian Theurgy Creation Myth series a few months ago, which we did before this particular series relating to the other main divinities of Anunian Theurgy, Djehuti, Hetheru, Maat and Anpu. The divinities Djehuti, Hetheru, Maat and Anpu are also part of Anunian Theurgy. They represent subtler conceptual aspects of creation, like Nbthotep and Iusaasety. In fact, they may be thought of as aspects of the consciousness of Ra, in the form of conceptual principles governing the Creation, that are part of the Creation but from a structural basis instead of as an elemental basis. The main divinities of the Tree, which are pictured as being within the Obelisk, are elemental divinities; they compose the elements of Creation and the human physical and mental as well as spiritual constitution. For instance, Maat represents the principle of order, the principle of balance that you see throughout creation. A manifestation of this conceptual principle is when the sun courses through the sky but in a particular place, a prescribed course. It doesn't go haphazardly rising in the north and setting in the east. It's always moving from the east to west. And every day of the year you can know exactly where it is going to be. That is the principle of Maat, a conceptual principle of order. Djehuti represents the principle of mind, of intellect that Ra uses in order to reflect his conscience, thought and will in time and space. Hetheru means the eye through which he brings forth the power to time and space. So Hetheru is actually the sundisk, the eye of Ra, and she is related to all the other goddesses of the Tree. Anpu represents purified mind, right thinking, and right discernment.

While these divinities do not match up from the perspective of being considered spouses they are complementary in that they balance each other from a gender perspective and also complement each other from a philosophical, symbolic perspective as well; so we have two female divinities and two male divinities. Nevertheless, we may consider Djehuti as being complementary to Maat (A) and Hetheru as being complementary to Anpu (B), who is an aspect of Heru and in a mythic sense, according to the Asarian Resurrection tradition as well as the Predynastic history of ancient Kemet, Hetheru and Heru are mated divinities, a fact attested to by the correspondences of their respective temples in Egypt. The placement of Djehuti, Hetheru, and Maat in the Duat level signifies the subtlety of their conceptual basis even though they operate generally in the Duat, Pet and Ta realms. Now, Anpu is not in the Duat but that should not be necessarily taken to mean that he does not represent subtlety also because he does. As a divine principle, a cosmic force, Anpu is subtle, a principle that an aspirant can tap into to purify the mind, to attain the subtlety required for right thinking, wherein the rubbish of the mind is cleared so that a correct thinking process may occur. That rubbish is made up of gross impurities of the mind, ignorance of the knowledge of self, gross desires, fears, anxieties, etc. However, Anpu mostly operates in the Ta plane as he helps souls to elevate from that plane to the Pet and Duat realms, where he leads them to. Yet, the clarity of Anpu is of the nature of concentrated mind directed towards the higher goal of life and he is therefore an essential and important divinity.

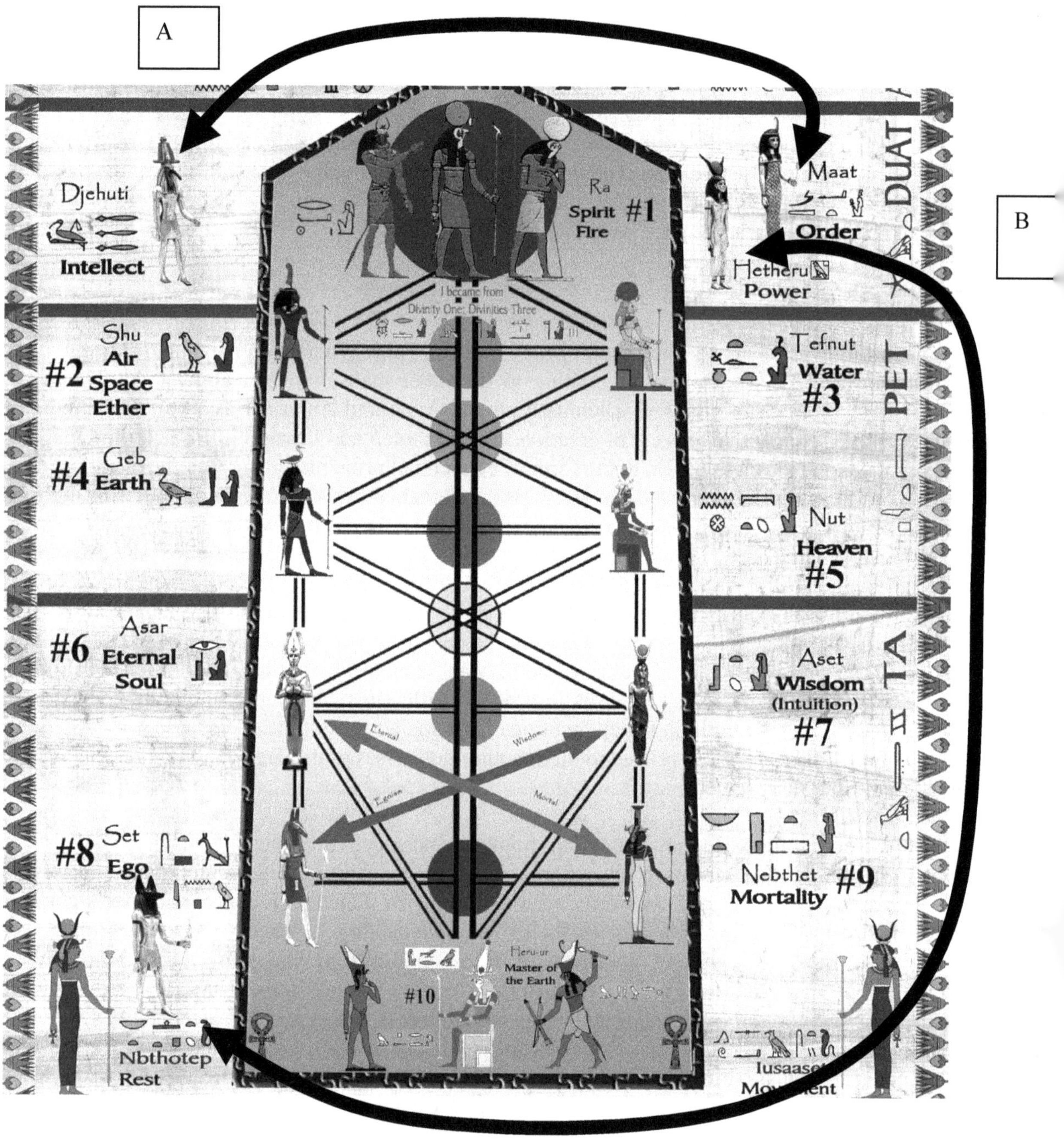

Figure 86: The Anunian Theurgy Cosmiconomythograph with focus on Djehuti, Hetheru, Maat and Anpu

This concludes the expanded teaching on Ra in the Anunian Tree of Life teaching. With this understanding we may discuss about the transcendental essence beyond the three realms of the Tree (Ta, Pet and Duat) by describing the most important aspects, symbols and descriptive hieroglyphic texts of the Supreme Being who gives rise to the Creation itself.

Reflection and Journal discipline:

1- **At the top of each page copy the following hieroglyphs to the best of your ability**

 [**_cht n ankh_** _" tree of life"_]

   After studying the Lesson proceed to answer the following question and write the answer in your journal. This exercise will require more than one reading and more than one journal entry, at least one page; write all you can find related to the subject of the question. Answer the questions first without referring to the text you just read. Then go back and see if you missed anything. This exercise is to be repeated until you become proficient with the principles of this sphere. The reflection exercise should be done after each reading or study session. Then you may practice meditation[155] on the wisdom you have learned. You may come back to add to your reflections even if you move on to other lessons.

REFLECTIONS: This air that I breathe and the energy in my personality are more than chemicals having a chemical reaction…they are gross manifestations of something so vast and so powerful that has been beyond my grasp. With these reflections and meditations I am going beyond the physical earth and sky to the very space and power behind them. With the air I breathe I will direct the energies of the cosmos to cleanse myself, to rejuvenate myself and to carry me forth to unknown realms that I will now know and I will abide there like the hawk of gold…

After studying the Lesson proceed to answer the following question and write the answer in your journal.

   Who came between Geb and Nut?

   What is(are) the main teaching(s) of this lesson and what do the principle(s) of the divinity(ies) discussed in this lesson mean in reference to my actions, feelings, thoughts and desires and understanding of the spiritual philosophy?

---

[155] Explained in more detail in Lesson 15

Lesson 14: The Substratum of Creation, Transcendental Plane, The Supreme Being and The Number Infinity ∞

Since the transcendental Supreme Being is the source of all Creation as well as the gods and goddesses, we will focus here on the conceptions of the supreme and transcendental all-encompassing divinity through a more detailed description of the four examples presented of the Supreme Being (*Neberdjer, Heru Akhuti, Mehturt, and Net*).

Creator Divinities

In Neterian spirituality it is recognized that there is an unnamable ∿∿∿ ∿∿ *an ren*, transcendental, androgynous and all-encompassing Supreme Being and that that Supreme Being may engender Creation directly or may operate through a High God or High Goddess, a demiurge, to engender Creation. In Anunian Theurgy relating to the Tree of Life, Ra is the High God and he engenders Creation by first emerging as a coagulated being from the Primeval Ocean and then bringing into being nine other divinities. Out of the formless and timeless Nun, the Primeval Ocean of energy, consciousness and eternity an all-encompassing Creator divinity arises, taking on a form in time and space, and causes parts of the Nun to take on shapes and forms and movement of composition and decomposition through chemical reactions that occur in time and space, which we call Creation. These divinities contain within themselves the entire matrix that becomes Creation. Therefore they are essentially androgynous, containing within themselves the capacity to produce opposites. It must be understood that there is only one Creator, but it can be named differently in different myths and theurgical contexts. However, we know that there is only one because the scriptures themselves tell us so, as we demonstrated previously. Therefore, the Creator divinities of the different Neterian traditions are actually manifestations of the same creative principle but described in different ways in order to highlight particular teachings. The main Creator Divinities are *Mehturt, Net, Neberdjer, Ra-Harakty-Herumakhet, Amun-Ra, Asar, Ptah and Khepri*. Each divinity is endowed with a particular form, name and myth in order to convey the teaching of divine and human origins in a particular way. So, again, it is important to understand however that all of these divinities are related to each other and they all emanate from the same substratum, the primeval ocean, and thus their teaching is not contradictory but rather complementary.

The Creator God/Goddess created the universe by willing that the raw materials that already existed, in the form of Nun, should take on the forms and nature of the neteru. A human being can create in the same way to a limited extent. For example, the thoughts in the mind are composed of subtle matter, raw materials of existence, energies that coagulate and coalesce into thought forms and concepts. If given enough power, through continuous reflection, meditation, concentration and emphasis as well as working on them "creatively" they can become realities in people's lives, their physical reality. If a group of people focus on the same ideas they can accomplish vast manifestations in the physical world, and all of that started with an idea, a subtle mental thought. And this is how God also created the universe, from a subtle thought that caused the undifferentiated raw material of existence, to take shape in the form of the world and universe that we now see.

Here we will present background information about the essential and transcendental Supreme Being who is behind the divinities of the Tree of Life and which is the ultimate and absolute goal of all the philosophy and disciplines of the Tree of Life metaphysical technology and philosophy. It is presented here so that you the spiritual aspirant may know what the goal is and that the divinities of time and space are mere masks for a mystical essence of being that is to be discovered. The aspirant is to "re-create" the true state of identity as a higher being instead of as a weak and mortal human being. This discipline is designed to promote a mystical movement, the discovery of higher planes of being, and not just a spiritual movement, religious practice or even exploration of unknown realms beyond the physical. A mystical movement leading to a mystical experience is when a human being not only discovers higher planes of being but discovers and unites with the ultimate source and essence behind all manifestations, the infinite, in other words the Supreme Being.

Neberdjer and Khepri

Now in the center of the T.O.L cosmiconomythograph just below the Nun picture, we have the Khepri Asha Hrau, the creator becoming the many, or specifically as the iconography gives us, from one to three to five (multiplicity). If you look at Khepri he represents the one. And at his feet are three symbols, ᕽᕽᕽ. Those three symbols mean "flesh", so Khepri became flesh; he becomes the trinity of Khepri, Ra and Tem. He is actually lying on that primeval ocean, and in the Primeval Ocean there is a giant serpent. This is another version of that same creation myth. That serpent has five heads. But the name of the serpent is Asha Hrau. Asha means "many" and Hrau means "face". Thus, Asha Hrau means "the one of many faces." So the five (heads) really means many and mystically, the many symbolizes "manifold in number." Another name that is given for this serpent is

Mehen. Recall the term *Meh* which means "fullness".

Figure 87: Image of the god Mehen

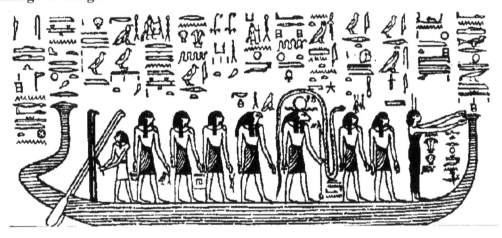

The God Amun-Ra, as a Ram-headed man, traverses through the Duat ream on his boat. The serpent god Mehen covers him as a canopy and as protector. God is accompanied on the journey by *Aset, Saa, Heka, Heru Hekenu, Ka-Ma'at, Nehes* (the lookout), and Hu, who acts as steersman –From the Ancient Egyptian Book of Gates

Mehen means the serpent of fullness, and he is the one who lives in the Primeval Ocean. Khepri does the work of creation by stirring him up, by having him move his coils, and when he moves he churns the ocean, and when the ocean churns, waves form and the ocean takes the forms of creation. That is the concept behind it. You will find the same exact teaching, that occurs later elsewhere in African religion and Indian religion[156] as well...this concept of the Serpent with thousands of coils, etc. There is an image of Neberdjer (see below) depicting him/her standing over a serpent that is eating his own tail. That serpent encompasses (circumscribes) even natural forces, symbolized by seven animals. The use of animals to metaphorically reference the mode, power, feeling and instinctual character of a natural force, a neteru, is an ancient and well documented format of Neterian religion. As the all-encompassing divinity, *Neberdjer* is also in control of the seven energy forms, the seven powers that course through the universe and manifest variously as the seven colors of the rainbow, the seven musical notes, and also the seven psycho-spiritual consciousness centers of the subtle body known as *arat sekhem,* the Serpent Power.

---

[156] *THE AFRICAN ORIGINS OF CIVILIZATION, RELIGION AND YOGA SPIRITUALITY AND ETHICS PHILOSOPHY* by Dr. Muata Ashby

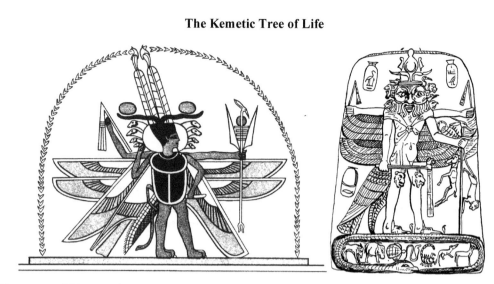

Figure 88: Images of Neberdjer, the All-encompassing Divinity

So *Khepri-Asha Hrau* represents the concept of one going to the trinity and then to multiplicity. These are the main teachings related to the spirit in Anunian Theurgy in the TREE OF LIFE. And this is the substratum, the Spirit that gives rise to the *Ben Ben*, or the first point of creation. Actually you should understand this *Ben Ben* as the first physical aspect of creation (Khepri); From this *Ben Ben* point all of the divinities of creation, all of the physical creation emerges, as you see here in the form of the elements. Now we will look at the *Duat* section.

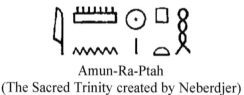

Amun-Ra-Ptah
(The Sacred Trinity created by Neberdjer)

There are several Trinities in Ancient Egyptian myths, each conveying a special message through the symbolic references and relationships of the symbols. The Trinity of Ra-Nut-Geb, representing the three basic principles of physical existence: Spirit (God-Supreme Being), Heaven and Earth, is one of the oldest forms of this concept to be found in the Dynastic period of Ancient Egyptian history. As the evolution of the exposition of the Supreme Being progressed, its elucidation through the medium of theurgy and mystical philosophy was refined. This refinement, which occurred over a period of 5,000 to 10,000 years, led to the teachings of the Asarian Trinity of Asar, Aset and Heru, and those of Neberdjer: Amun-Ra-Ptah.

In the early history there were no iconographical depictions of Neberdjer. He-She was considered as being transcendent of form and concept. In the late period of Kemetic history the image as encompassing all of the attributes of the other gods and goddesses appeared in the form of a composite all-encompassing divine image containing all attributes of divinity.

As stated earlier, the TREE OF LIFE teaching of Anunian Theology as depicted in the Anunian Tree of Life Cosmiconomythograph is based on the creation myth of Anu and the pyramid texts of Anunian Theurgy. Anunian Theurgy is one of the main theurgies of Kemetic (Kemetic) religion, of Neterianism. Neterianism is the theurgy of Neter. All of the Kemetic divinities are called Neteru. They are aspects of Divinity, of the one Divine Self. The one Divine Self differentiates Itself out of the primeval, undifferentiated matter, the Nun. It creates aspects or forms of itself that carry out several different tasks or functions in order to sustain creation. So the theology breaks down the Supreme Divinity into parts that can be easily understood, but these are always understood to be aspects of the one supreme Divinity. Therefore, Neterianism is not only a monotheistic religion that expresses in a polytheistic iconography, it is actually a monistic or non-dual philosophy.

"Nondual" means that it states and shows unequivocally that since all manifestation is an aspect of the Divine, therefore there is no existence outside of the divine. There is one existence. That is what monism means…non-duality. Thus, even though the world manifests as duality, there is no duality and we are going to expand on that as we go along.

First of all, at the center of the picture we have a boat, and in that boat there is a scarab, and that scarab is sustaining or pushing a red circle, and that is the sundisk, that is the god Khepri (the scarab), the Creator. He is emerging from the horizon of the ocean into the sky/heavens, and Nun is lifting him up. With him he has a group of divinities, and these divinities are the main divinities of the Tree of Life of Anunian Theurgy.

The order in which they emerge and the principles and relationships they represent give us the keys to understand the mysteries of the tree. And of course, the purpose of giving this tree is to provide a ladder so people can lift themselves up, again, to discover the source of creation. Why do you want to discover the source of creation? Because this earth realm is finite… It is imperfect; It is the realm of pain and sorrow, and death. And so naturally people want to escape that. So think of it as an escape ladder if you want to!

Death and finiteness come from immortality and infiniteness. Death and finiteness are actually pieces of immortality and the infinite that have extended into the earth realm temporarily. Those who do not climb this ladder before the time of their death, they will experience pain and sorrow. Those who discover the mysteries, those who master the principles given by this ladder in this tree, they transcend and escape pain and sorrow.

That Khepri is the first phase of Creation He is the creator of the world, of the universe. He is the first phase or first main aspect of the divinity Ra. But actually you should understand that Khepri comes out of the Nun. The Nun is Khepri's body, as it were. Khepri is like a focal point of the consciousness of the Nun, and Nun is the undifferentiated, unformed substratum, the all encompassing essence of creation that interpenetrates and permeates all creation. It is explained as an ocean, however remember it should not be thought of as a physical ocean, like when you go to the beach, but like outer space can be thought of as an ocean, it is an expanse of existence. And as has been explained by even modern physicists, outer space actually is not empty space. The void is not actually a void. Space is actually physical matter, and we have shown the truth of this. Modern astronomers and physicists have shown that gravitational forces bend space. If a space that had all the air vacuumed out of it or if outer space was empty, if it was nothing, it could not be bent, could it? Something that is void, that is nothing, can't have anything done to it. And yet gravitation bends space. Space therefore is an object. And that is substratum that is in all space is the Nun, and from that substratum comes the physical universe, the planets and the stars and everything you can see and touch and feel and so on and so forth, as well as everything that is not.

Now physicists and astronomers are seeing that there is more activity in outer space than can be accounted for by the matter that they can detect in outer space. Now they are saying that they are theorizing about some more subtle kind of matter that is operating in space and now they are calling this "dark matter." And I would say that with this dark matter concept they are getting closer to the essence of Nun, however even this dark matter is a physical manifestation of the Nun. The Nun is even much subtler than that.

And Nun or Nunu means that, subtle essence, the primeval essence. The hieroglyphs on the left side mean *Sheta* which means secret or mysteries and the ones on the right mean Anu, so we have the mysteries of the teachings of Anu. On the left we have Neberdjer, which means all encompassing divinity. Now these are the four main aspects of this creator essence…if you will. Again, this Nun manifests as Kehpri, the Creator, when the work of creation is to be done.

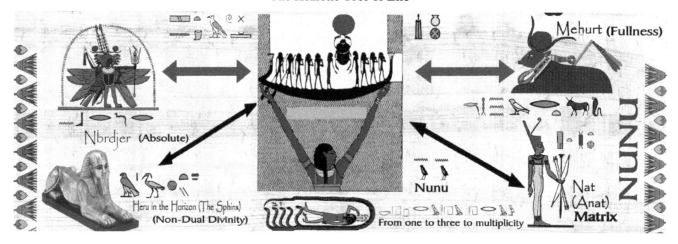

On both sides of the Anunian Theurgy cosmiconomythograph, you will see that there are male and female divinities, male on the left and female on the right and in the center you see the divinities that transcend gender, that encompass gender. Khepri is genderless, he has male and female…the Nun also, the Ra also, the Heru Ur at the bottom also. The male and female divinities counter each other, balance each other.

Neberdjer encompasses all the attributes of all the other divinities. So right there, in the mystical meaning of this icon, we are faced with non-duality, we are faced with monism, not polytheism or monotheism. What this iconography, of Neberdjer, with many arms, objects, scepters, etc. is telling us is that all of the attributes of the divinities, roll up into one essential being. And remember, this is a late period symbolism for Neberdjer. In earlier times Neberdjer was never depicted, because how can you depict something that is all encompassing? This iconographic interpretation of Neberdjer is just a symbol that gives you an idea of all-encompassingness, because the depiction implies he has all of the attributes, including all of the scepters, all of the wings, all of the plumes, all of the headdresses, and so on an so forth (actually he does not display all in the image, but he has most of them and that implies the rest, since no other divinity is depicted in this manner except *Sekhemit Bas Ra*). This idea of gathering all the attributes, in itself is a transcendental concept since there is no end to that possibility but conceptually, it is therefore a metaphor of infinity.

We are here speaking of these four main manifestations, and there are others, but these are the main ones, what we are giving here are the four main principles, from Neterian Religion, of this primeval essence as it manifests in creation, and as it exists transcending creation. We discussed the primeval essence, the ocean itself, the Nun, first of all. Now we are talking about Neberdjer which means absolute existence, transcendental consciousness. And juxtaposed with that from a female perspective, we have Mehturt. Neberdjer manifests the transcendental concept with male tendency, although it encompasses both male and female.

The Ancient Egyptian Trinity composed of Amun, Ra and Ptah was formally known as:

"Neberdjer, Everything is Amun-Ra-Ptah, three in one."

The statement above is another example of a Neterian *Correlative Theological Statement*, a statement that links theological traditions that outwardly appear to be different and separate. These are statements that correlate the main divinities and unequivocally show them to be manifestations of other divinities within the same tradition and within the other main traditions of Neterian religion. In the passages above we not only learn that the three main theological traditions are linked and the organizations of their connection but also that the gods of the Egyptian Trinity of Amun-Ra-Ptah, arise from the nameless Supreme Being known as Neberdjer or Neter Neteru. Therefore, the Trinity is in reality describing one Divinity which expresses in three aspects.

Figure 89: The Gods, Amun (left), Ra (center) and Ptah (right)

In the creation story involving the Asarian Mysteries, Asar assumes the role of Khepera and Tem, while at the same time giving insight into the nature of Neberdjer:

"Neb-er-djer saith, I am the creator of what hath come into being, and I myself came into being under the form of the god Khepera, and I came into being in primeval time. I had union with my hand, and I embraced my shadow in a love embrace; I poured seed into my own mouth, and I sent forth from myself issue in the form of the gods Shu and Tefnut." "I came into being in the form of Khepera, and I was the creator of what came into being, I formed myself out of the primeval matter, and I formed myself in the primeval matter. My name is Asar."

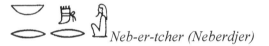 *Neb-er-tcher (Neberdjer)*

In the creation story involving the Asarian Mysteries,[157] the All-God assumes the role of Khepera and Tem:

"I was alone, for the Gods and Goddesses were not yet born, and I had emitted from myself neither Shu nor Tefnut. I brought into my own mouth, hekau, and I forthwith came into being under the form of things which were created under the form of Khepera."

These passages above all point to the fact that while the name of the Supreme Being under the different priesthoods appears to be different, these are merely names for different expressions of the same principles and teachings which present additional complementary wisdom about the Divine; therefore, there is no separation, discontinuity or confusion within the theurgies. These are again, *Correlative Theological Statements*, here also linking Neberdjer to Asar. More importantly, the last passage reminds us that all of the names and forms are merely outward expressions of the same Supreme Being, *Neb-er-djer,* in its physical manifestation. Neberdjer, as previously discussed, is a name which signifies the all-encompassing meaning of the collective members of the Trinity, which along with their theistic importance in their own traditions also conceptually represent the triune nature of time and space awareness requiring a subject, a witness, an abject to be aware of, Ptah, and the medium of interaction between the two, which is Ra the power of mind. Neberdjer includes all male and female aspects of the Trinity, and is therefore to be understood as the androgynous and primordial being from which arose all names and forms, all gods and goddesses, all creation and all opposites in Creation (male and female, hot-cold, etc.) the passages above from the Anunian Theurgy may be termed *Correlative Theological Statements*. So, *Correlative Theological Statements* are found in the four main Neterian Traditions (Anunian, Wasetian, Meneferian, Asarian) and they correlate the main divinities of the traditions to each other.

---

[7] See the book *African Religion Vol. 4 Asarian Theology* by Dr. Muata Ashby.

(Papyrus 10,018 –British Museum)

The important passage and iconography above explain and illustrate the majestic vision of tantric philosophy in Neterian spirituality. Far from sexual vulgarity, the teaching reveals secrets about the nature of the Divine Self. In the previous passage we had *I had union with my hand, and I embraced my shadow in a love embrace; I poured seed into my own mouth,* and in the last one we have *I brought into my own mouth, hekau.* This textual and iconographical juxtaposition of seed and hekau with semen is a profound understanding of the creative potential of word, thought and consciousness (*Paut* the stuff or matter or substance) out of which Creation is created. It means that Neberdjer impregnated "him/herself," with word, that is, vibration; at once making him an androgynous being as well as the source matter of "her" own creation. So from the All comes the All. Everything comes from God and is composed of God, so too all is Divine, all exists in the Divine and all is rooted in the Divine.

Neberdjer has a female aspect called *Neberdjert.* Neberdjert may be thought of as a goddess but in reality Neberdjert and Neberdjer are one all-encompassing divinity. This is also a name of the eye of Heru.

Heru-akhuti

In the graphic, under the image of Neberdjer we have the divinity Herukhuti, Herakhuti or Harakti, means Heru, the shining spirit of the two horizons. Heru of the two horizons encompasses the Supreme divinity in all three forms. The horizon of the morning is Kehpri, the horizon of the evening is Tem, therefore Herukhuti encompasses from beginning to end…infinity…transcendental existence. "Heru-akhuti or Herukhuti" (Heru spirit of the two horizons – Sphinx) (Khepri and Tem combined – beginning to end)

The two horizons represent the beginning and the end. This concept is similar to the idea of the Alpha and Omega (Gr. "το Άλφα και το Ω") of Christianity. This is an appellation of God relating to the fact that Alpha (A) and Omega (Ω) are respectively the first and last letters of the Greek alphabet. This is like calling something "the A to Z" in English. Thus, "the Beginning and the End" symbolizes all-encompassing of time, being the beginning of it and the end of it. Heru-akhuti also signifies the completion of the journey of human and animal to higher consciousness and God/Goddesshood.

The opening verses of the Hymn to Aton by Akhnaton (Amenhotep IV {Greek- Amenophis}) provide insight into the ancient nature of Aton worship and how it is tied to the divinity Ra as well as the oldest form of worship known in Kemet, that of *Heru-Akhuti (Herumakhet* - the Great Sphinx). Note that adorations are made to the *living Heru-Akhuti* (verse 1) and Akhnaton refers to being one with Ra (verse 3) through living by Maat (righteousness) – (verse 3 and 4). Thus, Aton worship is, in the New Kingdom Period (1580-1075 B.C.E.), a form of renaissance of Ra worship (5,500 B.C.E.), who is a form of *Heru-Akhuti* worship that goes back to the inception of Ancient Egyptian culture and spirituality (10,000 B.C.E.). Therefore, the concept of one God was present in Neterian spirituality from the earliest times.

Hymn To Aton by Akhenaton[158]

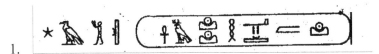

1.

1.1. Dua Ankh Herakhuti Hai m Akhet

1.2. Adorations to the living Heru Akhuti whose body manifests through the horizon as the sundisk (Aton)

GLOSS: Right from the start the verse informs us that the Supreme Being (under the name Heru Akhuti) is not the Aton but manifests as it, as a High God, a demiurge.

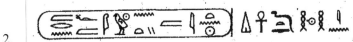

2.

2.1. m ren f m shu nty m Aton rdy Ankh djeta heh in

2.2. through the name his through Shu who is in the Aton. Giving life forever and eternity by

GLOSS: Now this verse introduces the idea that that same Heru Akhuti, who is manifesting as the Aton also contains the divinity Shu.

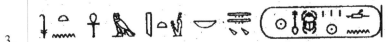

3.

3.1. suten ankh m Maat neb tawi nefer kheperu Ra wa n Ra

3.2. the king living through Maat, lord of the two lands, beautiful creations of Ra, One with Ra

GLOSS: Now we are informed that that supreme divinity gives life to the king, Akhenaton, who is representative of a model devotee, who is the head of Egypt, which is a creation of Ra; further, this is afforded to Akhenaton because he lives by ma'at. Also, he is one with Ra.

4.

4.1. sa ankh m Maat neb Kau Akhen Aton Maakheru

4.2. son living through Maat, lord of risings Akh-n-Aton, true of speech

GLOSS: Akhenaton lives through Ma'at as son of the supreme, under the name Akh-n-Aton, the purified (righteous, virtuous {due to the practice of ma'at}).

5.

5.1. aha-f rdy ankh djeta heh chaa k nefer pa Aton

5.2. standing (raising) up giving living forever and eternal risings, beauteous this Aton

GLOSS: Akhenaton now says that the divinity rises giving life as the beautiful sundisk; so the power of the divine to give life operates through the sundisk; it is not the sundisk itself. Therefore, this is not sun worship but a deep metaphysical understanding that the sun is a dynamic manifestation of a power that spans time { djeta } and is also eternal { heh }.

---

[158] Original translation by Dr. Muata Ashby {Sebai MAA}

Herumakhet - the Great Sphinx

Figure 90: (A)The Great Sphinx of Ancient Egypt-showing the classical headdress popularized in the later Pharaonic Dynastic period. (B)Also, the water damage can be seen in the form of vertical indentations in the sides of the monument.

The dating of the establishment of the *Herumakhet* - the Great Sphinx has been estimated as c. 10,500 B.C.E.-7,000 B.C.E. The term *Sphinx* is a western interpretation of the Ancient Egyptian which means Hor-m-akhet or Heru (Heru) in the horizon. The *Herumakhet* is composed of the body of a lion and the head of a man. This means that the King is one with the Spirit, Ra as an enlightened person possessing an animal aspect (lion body) and illuminated intellect (human head). In other words, the person who attains this has mastered the forces of nature (symbolized by the lion iconography) as well as the knowledge of the mysteries (symbolized by the human head iconography). Of course this also means that such a person has mastered that which is below (lion) and that which is above (intuition). Also, this iconography means that the intellect, knowledge, intuition are to command the life forces, the sekhem, that those forces are a vehicle for the mind and that God is all of that in a macrocosmic way while humans are that microcosmically. The Great *Herumakhet* looks out towards the east. At certain special astronomical times he looks on directly at the sun which rises exactly in front of him. At those special times he is looking at himself in the form of the celestial constellation of the lion. Thus, in the same way an aspirant may assume the *Herumakhet* posture and look out at the sun at dawn to discover herself, to recognize herself and in so doing realize the greater essential nature of self as being *wa n Ra*, One with Ra.

The idea of the Primeval Ocean (Nun) and the original primeval spirit which engendered life in it occurs in several world myths. The earliest occurrence of the idea of the primeval waters is found in the Egyptian religion which predates all other known developed religions of the world in human history. This pre-dynastic (10,000-5,500 B.C.E.), myth speaks of a God who was unborn and undying, and who was the origin of all things. This deity was un-namable, unfathomable, transcendental, gender-less and without form, although encompassing all forms. This being was the God of Light which illumines all things, and thus was associated with the sun, the forms of *Ra* or *Tem,* and with *Heru* who represents *that which is up there,* in other words, the Divine. Tum, Atum, Tem or Temu is an Ancient Egyptian name for the deep and boundless abyss of consciousness from which the phenomenal universe was born. *Khepera (or Khepri),* the dung beetle, represents the morning sun which is becoming, creating. This form is also associated with the young Heru, *Heru in the Horizon,* also known as *The Sphinx.*

One striking form of symbolism that is seen from the beginning to the end of the Ancient Egyptian history is the Sphinx/Pharaonic Leonine headdress.

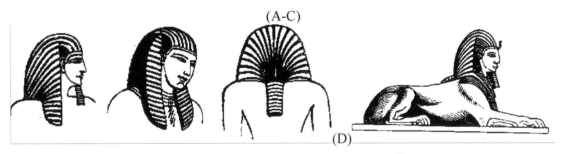

(A-C)

(D)

Above (A-C) - The Heru-m-akhet (Sphinx) Pharaonic headdress.[159]

Above (D)- Drawing of the Sphinx from a sculpture in Egypt

The Great Sphinx of Ancient Egypt-shows the predynastic Pharaonic headdress popularized in later classical Dynastic times. It imitates the leonine mane and the lion power of Herukhuti (Ra as Heru of the two horizons).

Figure 91: Below-images of the feline aspects of the Ancient Egyptian Goddess, from left to right: Sekhmit relief, Sekhmit sculpture, Sekhmit ritual mask, Tefnut, Bast

An important element of the Goddess is the feline aspect. Most prominent is the leonine concept, which is the foundation of the Great Sphinx. In nature, cats have an inimical relationship with serpents. In Ancient Egyptian mythology, the *Serpent of Darkness* is seen as the embodiment of ignorance and evil which threatens the movement of the Boat of Ra and which prevents the spiritual aspirant from attaining enlightenment. Therefore, the Goddess in the form of a cat (Bast), and a lioness (Tefnut-Sekhmet-Hetheru), is seen as the warrior and champion of the gods (Asar and Heru) as well as the aspirant. She is the one who paves the way for spiritual evolution by destroying the evil of ignorance and sinfulness in the human heart. Herukhuti, being also a form of the *Hu* (Great Sphinx), makes use of the leonine aspect and should therefore be considered as a combination of the female element supporting, empowering and completing the male essence. Furthermore, the leonine power is the strength of the Peraah (Pharaoh).

Again, the term "two Horizons" within the name *Herukhuti* refers to Heru's two important forms: completer). In this capacity he may be seen as the culmination of the form of Heru called *Heru Behudet*. While Heru Behudet

---

these illustrations appeared in the book *The Ancient Egyptians: Their Life and Customs*-Sir J. Garner Wilkinson 1854 A.C.E.

263

defeated Set, *Herukhuti* is the quintessence of Heru as victor. Therefore, *Herukhuti* is the direct link in the Tree of Life from the *Ta* Realm to the *Duat* Realm, directly linking Heru to Ra and this is represented by the vertical shaft in the center of the Tree of Life cosmiconomythograph.

Figure 92: Herukhuti: Heru of the two Horizons, the all encompassing one. Heru is the defender.

He represents spiritual aspiration and will power to back up that aspiration to overcome unrighteousness, ignorance and even death. He assisted in the resurrection of his father and through his warrior skills defeated Set, the agent of ignorance and freed the land from injustice. Herukhuti is also a form of the *Hu* (Great Sphinx). The term "two Horizons" refers to Heru's two important forms: Khepri (morning sun, the Creator - beginner) and *Tem* (Atum, Temu), the setting sun (dissolver –completer).

The sword is a wielded instrument for cutting and striking an enemy. It can also be manipulated to thrust at an enemy from a distance. The idea is to engage in slashing motions, keeping the opponent at bay until an opportunity opens to engage a decisive cutting blow or thrust.

In the same way, in battling the demons of life an aspirant should use the sword of intellect which cuts away at illusions and unrighteousness and ignorance in order to establish understanding and truth. However, remember that the sword has two edges. So it cuts both ways. A true practitioner of the mysteries cannot cut away at some ignorance and then leave others untouched. Sometimes aspirants want to deal with things that they are comfortable with but not deal with those things that are more difficult. Wisdom cuts both ways and this also means that if an aspirant is ready to slash away at the external world of illusion he/she should prepare also to slice away the internal illusions, closely held beliefs and ignorant notions. Spirituality is a battle that is internal but which reflects externally as well.[160]

1- the god Amun holds a sickle shaped knife-sword {scimitar} with which he assists the King, again in the form of the god Heru, to slay the enemies of the state.

When used for warfare knives are fearsome instruments that are used for close-in fighting, stealthiness and swift attack. They are regarded as weapons for battles on to death. The gods and goddesses use these to cut off the heads of evil serpents, the demons which are slithery and slippery, stealthy and smooth. In like manner the ego is slithery, and stealthy. It hides in the shadows of the unconscious mind until ready to strike and when it does the personality is filled with the poison of desire. The knives cut off the head, which delivers that venom and with it the desire that leads to worldly entanglements and delusions. Aspirants should develop these qualities so as to

---

[160] See also the lecture series *Travels of Asar and His Spiritual Message: Class 4: Mysteries of War and violence.*

hold in the hands the knives of good intellect, agreeable nature and right discernment, which cut away at the errors that lead to strife and unrest in life.

Scimitar
Source: L.Casson, *Ancient Egypt*

Mehturt and Net

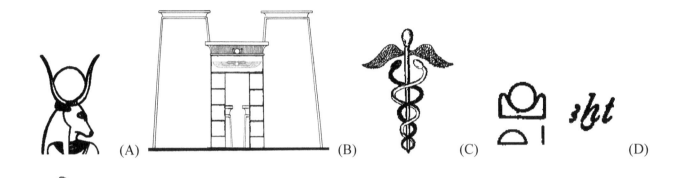

(A) (B) (C) (D)

Mehturt, who is depicted on the female (right) side of the Anunian Theurgy cosmiconomythograph, also encompasses the male gender. **Mehturt** means "The Mighty Full One". She is depicted as a cow with horns and the sundisk between the horns(A) . This gives you and idea also of the Trinity of existence, the two horns and the one solar disk. This symbolism is actually the same symbolism that you find on the iconography of the new kingdom temples (B) with the two pylons and the single door. It is the symbolism that runs through Neterianism, which is the caduceus (C), as well as the Akhet symbol (D), the horizon, and the two mountains on either side, the Manu mountains of the west and the valley through which the sundisk, , sets. We have in that concept, duality, as well as non-duality that goes through the center. We have the opposites. The opposites are duality which has appeared out of the non-duality of oneness. In this iconography the opposites are the finite, worldly aspect of creation, and the sun itself represents the infinite. When the opposites are balanced, the male and female essence, the infinite manifests. If you were to transcend your maleness and your femaleness, the opposites within yourself, or for example, if you were to balance your male **or female** aspects within yourself,[161] your male hormones shall we say, and your female hormones, which influence your self-concept as a gender being (thinking of yourself as a male or female personality) and you were able to discover your androgynousness, you would also begin to discover your infinite nature through your androgynous nature, your non-generated aspect of self-identity.

---

[161] all human beings have male and female elements, what we call maleness or femaleness is in reality just a tendency. There is no one who is all male or all female.

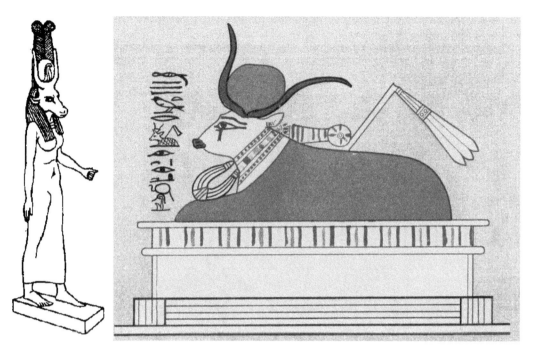

Figure 93: Left-Goddess Mehturt as a composite goddess with bovine head (zoomorphic) and female body (anthropomorphic). Right-Mehturt as Cow goddess (zoomorphic) with the Menat necklace and the Flail

Figure 94: Below: The goddess administering the Menat

We have an image of the goddess Hetheru, who is an aspect, a manifestation of Mehturt; she has a *Menat* necklace 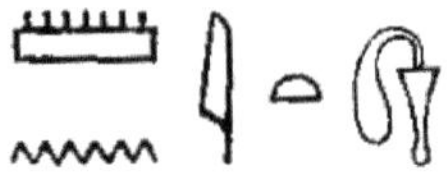 , which means the power of female creation; she is lifting it up and offering it to the king, the Pharaoh. Goddess Mehturt also has the male *nekaku* scepter, the flail.

Figure 95: Mysticism of the Flail

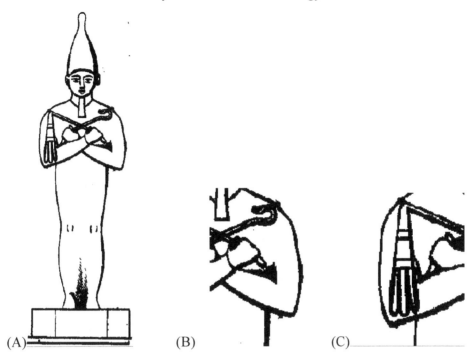

(A)   (B)   (C)

The god Asar (Above left-(A)) of Ancient Egypt is in possession of the crook(B) staff and the flail(C) staff. The crook is the symbol of leadership. This refers to the ability to lead oneself as well as others to what is righteous and good, just as a shepherd leads a flock to what is good. The flail is the instrument used for separating the chaff from the seed. In modern times machines do this work. The thresher is an agricultural machine used to separate grain from chaff and straw. The first threshers were the feet of humans and animals or flails. The mystical implication is that spiritual aspirants must separate themselves from egoism and ignorance in order to move from what is untruth to truth, from un-reality to reality and from mortality to immortality. This process is accomplished as a person studies, practices and realizes the mystical teachings being imparted.

The flail has three sections, which represent the three worlds, so Hetheru and Asar are masters of the three worlds, the Duat, the Pet and the Ta, meaning the netherworld, the heavenly realm, and the earth realm; so she is the master of all that. Again, *Meh* means fullness and *urt* means mighty, and she is that same fullness of the Nun which permeates all creation. She is like a glass that is full of water that is full to the brim. You put one more drop in it and it overflows. And this world is just like that full glass of water. You can't put one more drop in it because it is completely full with spirit, that is, full of Mehturt.

Mehturt is also said to be the cow goddess who gives birth to the sundisk, gives birth to Ra, *Mesu Ra*. In the scripture she is actually equated with Ra. So all of these divinities have a male or female tendency but they are also acknowledged as being androgynous as well (encompassing both genders). So, the depictions of the Supreme Being can never be wholly male or wholly female, but only use certain gender features to the extent that they help the mind to grasp the concepts. So the concepts of God the father and God the mother are merely that, concepts, and not absolute realities (transcendental truths), because the divinities transcend gender. But limited minds need assistance, and so therefore the sages have invented these symbolisms.

Net (Anet) [The Weaver]

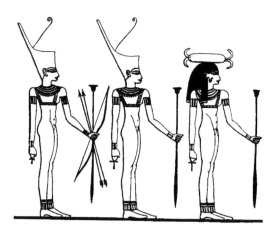

Looking at the T.O.L. Cosmiconomythograph, on the top right side: Juxtaposed with Herukhuti is Goddess *Nat* or *Net* or *Anat*. She represents the matrix of Creation. Net is one of the most important divinities of Neterian theurgy. The seat of her worship in ancient times was the Ancient Egyptian city named *Zau* (Greek or Arabic= Sais). She is the goddess of creation and war, as well as protection, honor and decisive action. Her attributes are the bow, shield and arrows as well as the weaving spool. She is androgynous (neither male nor female), and was known to watch over Asar's ceremonial bed when he lay dead, along with Aset and Nebthet. She assisted Djehuti in bringing justice for Heru in the Asarian myth. The goddess Net is the primordial Supreme Divinity with female aspect. She is the ancient form of the goddesses Aset and Hetheru, and her worship extended to the far reaches of antiquity, into the Pre-Dynastic period of Ancient Egyptian history. There are records from both priests and priestesses who served the temples of goddess Net. These show that worship of her was popular, and expressed generally throughout the land of Egypt in ancient times. As we will see, the teachings related to goddess Net are profound and in every way as elevated as those of the Supreme Divinities of Ancient Egypt which portray the male aspect.

In *Pyramid Text* line 606, Net, together with Aset, Nebethet and Serqet, watched over the funerary bed of Asar. Goddess Net gives the bandages and shrouds used for the mummy of the deceased and through these she imparts her protection as well as her blessings in the form of spiritual power.

Sebek

In *Pyramid Text* line 620-627, it is explained that the initiate is Sebek {Sebek or Sobek is the son of Net), and that the initiate rises like the son of Net. In the city of Net, Sebek is recognized as a form of Heru. Thus, the statement above is a *Correlative Theological Statement*, in which the tradition of Net is associated with that o Heru, and Asar. Therefore, there is no conflict in finding that the goddess Aset was ascribed her attributes in th later dynastic period. The veil of Net became also the veil of Aset. The following speech of the goddess is also used by goddess Aset.

> *"I am everything which has been, and which is, and which shall be and there has never been any mortal person who has uncovered my veil."*

Of the goddess it is said that she:

> *"Created the seed of the gods and goddesses and men and women."*

Net is the Goddess of Light, and thus her festival is characterized by the practice of lighting torches and lamps, and in modern times: candles. As light she gave birth to Ra, the sun divinity, who lights up the world. So Net is the:

> *"Divine Cow who gave birth to Ra."*

The statement above is a *Correlative Theological Statement*, in which the tradition of Net is associated with that of Ra (Anunian Theurgy). Thus, Net is *Mehturt* (Creator cow goddess), the primeval waters from which creation arose.

Her androgynous nature is related in the following epithet:

> *"Father of all fathers and mother of all mothers."*

> *"Net-Menhit, the Great Lady, Lady of the south, the great cow who gave birth to the sun, who made the seed of the gods and goddesses and men and women, the mother of Ra, the one who raised up Tem in the primeval time,[162] who existed when nothing else had existence and who created that which exists after she came into existence."*

The goddess gave birth to the gods and goddesses and to human beings, but she herself was not given birth. She brought herself into existence and gave birth without being impregnated. She was the primeval ocean and she emerged as herself out of herself and all has come forth through and from her. She is self-existent, and her nature is secret, a *shetat* or mystery to all.

shetat – (deep mysterious nature of the goddess Net)

Net is also referred to as:

"Ua-Netert"
"Divinity {Goddess} One"

Thus, Net encompasses the non-dual, absolute, all-encompassing divinity, in other words, she is Neberdjer. This teaching is further illustrated through the hieroglyphic symbols of her name.

Her symbols are the bow, ⌣, two arrows, ⇐ the shield, ⬥, and the knitting spool, ⧓ .

At the time of Creation.

The name *Net*, ⌂ 𓏥, or *Anet*, is a play on the word *nt*, ⌂, or *ntet*, ⌂ ⌂, meaning "that which is," "that which exists," in other words that which is real, true, and abiding. The Kemetic word *nt* - is linked to the root of the Egyptian word for 'weave' - *ntt*. The goddess provides *saa,* 𓎼, or protection for the spiritual aspirant. She uses a bow and arrow to shoot down the enemies of the righteous (lies, unrighteousness, anger, hatred, greed, jealousy, envy, lust, etc.). That is to say, her attributes, solar fire consciousness (rays), all-encompassing divinity,

inscrutability, determination, etc. are the arrows she shoots. In her name of *Net hetep,* ✕⎯, the goddess is the abiding supreme peace. The shield represents protection from injury and crossed arrows are neutralization of duality. The shield and arrows are used to put evil spirits to sleep.

Net is also known as *Amentet*, the hidden goddess and consort of the god Amen as well as *Rat*, the consort of the god Ra. Thus we are to understand that all the goddess forms are in reality aspects of Net. So, the epithets of Net constitute *Correlative Theological Statements*, in which the tradition of Net is associated with that of Amun, Aset and Hetheru.

Net is also known as *Mehenyt,* 𓈖𓇋𓇋⌂𓂋, the weaving goddess. The reference to goddess Net as *Mehenyt* holds deep mystical implications. *Mehenyt* also means goddess of fullness. As such she is a

manifestation of ⌂ ⌂ 𓃒 *Mehturt*, who is the ultimate fullness manifestation. *Mehenyt,* Net, weaves a garment, a matrix of Creation that is all-encompassing, all-pervading of the Creation.

The material woven by the goddess is used for wrapping the mummy, but she also weaves her own clothing. This clothing is the outer appearance of the physical universe. The objective of spiritual movement within the

Het-Net, 𓉐⌂𓏥⌂⊗, the house of Net (temple of Net, Creation), is to propitiate the goddess to remove her clothing, to unveil herself, so that the initiate may see her true form...absolute existence.

Being the Goddess of Light and having the power to weave the intricate web of Creation wherein all is connected, the goddess allows herself to be disrobed by those who follow the path to her discovery. This path was given in the teaching and hieroglyphs of Net and in the Temple of Aset, who is a later form of goddess Net.

(above: the god Nun)

The Garment of Nun

The Kemetic teaching, *"Weaving the garment of Nun,"* is an allusion to the Ancient Egyptian goddess Net, the progenitor of goddess Aset, with whom the teaching "no mortal man hath ever unveiled me" is also associated. This phrase appears as one of the descriptions of the goddess. She is known as the "weaver" who brought Ra, the light, into being. The garment of Creation is also to be understood as the patchworks, which compose the day-to-day reality of life, that in turn deludes the mind. In fact, Creation is composed of atoms and molecules, which interact and come together to compose elements. However, these atoms are in themselves composed of energy, but the limited mind and senses do not perceive this ocean of energy, which is an aspect of the Nun, the Primeval Ocean. The goddess establishes projections of light that interlace and appear as a patchwork that holds the Nun in particular forms but also, as clothing, give it a certain appearance. Nun wears the garment created for him by Net but Nun is not changed by the garment in the same way that the Atlantic Ocean is not changed by the waves on it's surface.

This effect of not perceiving the most subtle essence of Creation, the Nun, and only being aware of the garment, the outer appearance, is the veil of the goddess, and therefore, it is the goal of every aspirant to unveil her, that is, to see her true form, the pure light of consciousness devoid of the ignorance. The existence of this veil however, is not the fault of or an effect created by the Goddess. It is the fault of ignorance and the reliance exclusively upon gross perception through the mind and senses, which has deluded the mind of the individual. This is true because upon attaining enlightenment, a human being discovers the underlying essence of Creation, beyond the illusions they had made for themselves. This essence is there even now, but the deluded mind cannot perceive it because it is besieged by ignorance that is reinforced with desires, passions, mental agitations (anger, hatred, greed, lust, etc.) and egoism. The various paths of Neterian Theurgy act to tear asunder the veil of illusion about the world. Here below you will see the actual Ancient Egyptian hieroglyphic text which speaks of the goddess's clothes and propitiation so that she may become naked so that her true essence may be beheld.

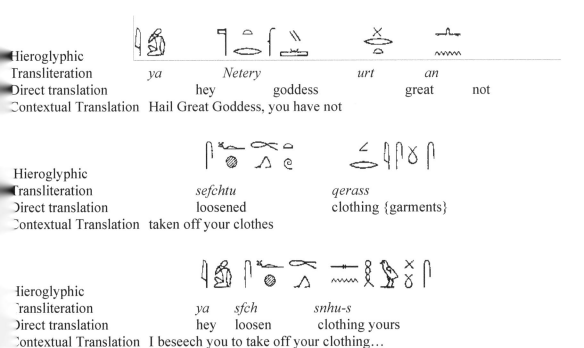

Hieroglyphic					
Transliteration	*ya*	*Netery*		*urt*	*an*
Direct translation		hey	goddess		great	not
Contextual Translation	Hail Great Goddess, you have not

Hieroglyphic		
Transliteration	*sefchtu*	*qerass*
Direct translation	loosened	clothing {garments}
Contextual Translation	taken off your clothes

Hieroglyphic			
Transliteration	*ya*	*sfch*	*snhu-s*
Direct translation	hey	loosen	clothing yours
Contextual Translation	I beseech you to take off your clothing…

It is fascinating and also crucial to the metaphysical understanding of this teaching to discover the use of the Ancient Egyptian hieroglyph, ✗, which is a Determinative[163] meaning "break," "divide", "over load," "cross," or "meet" and the like. It signifies separation and duality. Notice that the symbol is used in one of the goddess's epithets, ⟨glyphs⟩ *shetat* – (deep mysterious, hidden goddess: Net). So the cross is something that creates a separation and the separation hides or causes something to be hidden, as in the true nature of the goddess. Conversely, the opposite of separation, the union, the sema, takes away the mystery. Thus, uniting with the goddess through the process of ⟨glyphs⟩ *Shedy* and the disciplines of *smai-tawy* ⟨glyphs⟩ "Egyptian Yoga."

Now, notice that in the text above this glyph is used also in the words related to the goddess's clothing. Let us recall one of the primary symbols of the goddess Net, the ✗ crossed arrows. In the context of the word ✗ *Net hetep,* Goddess of peace, and ⟨glyph⟩ protection, the arrows of Net symbolize the neutralization of the effect of the cross; so while the cross ✗ causes separation and duality, the crossed arrows cause peace which is borne of the unity of opposites. We know this because the Hetep slab ⟨glyph⟩ is a ritual artifact meaning union of opposites.[164] Therefore, the arrows which the goddess shoots, the rays that illumine, reveal the truth by uniting the opposites and bringing an end to duality {ignorance}.

The name Net actually means web, and she is a weaver. She weaves the web of creation, and everything exists in and through that web. Remember that we previously gave an example of bumper cars in a state fair. The bumper car touches the ground which is electrified, but does not shock you because there is no circuit. The car runs when there is a circuit of electricity and that happens because it has this pole that goes up to a mesh on the top also, and if that pole touches that mesh anywhere, that electrical connection will be made, and creation is like that mesh. The spirit is everywhere in that mesh, and therefore your body can travel anywhere in that mesh and still be connected to spirit. So it is not your soul that is traveling around hither and thither; actually it is your body that is traveling around, and your body gives your soul as if a window into creation through the physical mind and senses. But the soul is everywhere, wherever your body may go. The soul and the Spirit are one. The soul is an aspect or a small focal portion of that Spirit, just like Khepri is a focal point of the Nun, and there by, you are a microcosm of that creation. It is very important to understand the concept of this matrix of Creation. It is the foundation upon which creation exists…that is, all the physical aspects of creation. You cannot get out of creation. Creation exists on a foundation or substratum of spirit. And you cannot as if go to the edge of creation and then jump out and continue to exist. Your physical existence is dependent on creation, and your spiritual existence is dependent upon the sustaining spirit. So you can get out of Creation if you leave the body behind, since your body is part of Creation, and you can exist as a spirit being, a soul, but you cannot get out of Spirit since you are Spirit and you cannot not be yourself. As a matter of fact you have no existence outside of spirit. Think about it…All your egoism, all your self-centered mentality, and all your ideas of independence are illusions.

---

[163] Symbol used to determine a particular meaning of a word. See the book *Ancient Egyptian Hieroglyphs for Beginners* by Dr. Muata Ashby

[164] see the book *THE AFRICAN ORIGINS OF CIVILIZATION, RELIGION AND YOGA SPIRITUALITY AND ETHICS PHILOSOPHY* by Dr. Muata Ashby

Reflection and Journal discipline:

1- At the top of each page copy the following hieroglyphs to the best of your ability

[***cht n ankh*** *" tree of life"*]

After studying the Lesson proceed to answer the following question and write the answer in your journal. This exercise will require more than one reading and more than one journal entry, at least one page; write all you can find related to the subject of the question. Answer the questions first without referring to the text you just read. Then go back and see if you missed anything. This exercise is to be repeated until you become proficient with the principles of this sphere. The reflection exercise should be done after each reading or study session. Then you may practice meditation[165] on the wisdom you have learned. You may come back to add to your reflections even if you move on to other lessons.

What is All composed of and rooted in?

What is(are) the main teaching(s) of this lesson and what do the principle(s) of the divinity(ies) discussed in this lesson mean in reference to my actions, feelings, thoughts and desires and understanding of the spiritual philosophy?

---

[165] Explained in more detail in Lesson 15

Lesson 15: The Disciplines for the Anunian Theurgy Neterian Tree of Life Spiritual Evolution System

Throughout the lessons of this series we have described in detail the mental disciplines to be practiced in relation to each of the spheres of the Anunian Tree of Life. Those disciplines include several mental exercises and thought practices and reflections to understand the metaphysical teaching and reshape the mind for greater expansion through the wisdom presented in each subsequent lesson. We will now describe a meditative discipline to be practiced by those following the Anunian Theurgy Tree Of Life (T.O.L..) spiritual evolution system. It is a practice that is heavily based in metaphysical disciplines involving philosophical insight, metaphysical visualization, breathwork and subtle life force energy manipulations. This practice will combine elements of breath and philosophy and mental disciplines in order to achieve the goal of promoting higher consciousness awareness as prescribed in the T.O.L. teaching.

Now, you are to understand that this practice means eventually going beyond the subtlety in the Nut and Geb, and Shu and Tefnut levels that we discussed last time. What you want to do now is not just to visualize or feel yourself as subtle air, but as the subtle principle within air. This physical air is around our globe, around the world. But this same space, that same ether, extends beyond the atmosphere of the earth, where air is found. In outer space, there are particles too. It is not a true vacuum. All of outer space is not a true vacuum. There are sun rays from different stars that are coursing through space. It is full of stuff. But you cannot go out there with your physical body. Your physical body belongs with a sustainable biosphere composed of the elements that it, itself is made of. Yet, beyond the particles, even if we had a complete vacuum the space itself is alive just as the space that is created by the human mind when it is asleep but the mind is not dreaming. The point is that Shu represents space, ether itself, beyond air. But there is a way to experience that vastness and accessing that vastness can also provide insights about the universe.

How do you think that, before the development of modern astronomy, the Dogon people of West Africa discovered that the star *Digitaria*, Sirius is one of the densest stars? Digitaria is a binary star system but with the naked eye it looks like one star. How do you think that the Dogon discovered that there was a second star there, first of all and secondly, that it was an extremely dense star? This is something that western culture did not discover until 1970 A.C. When the Dogon people of ancient Africa, discovered this 700 years ago, did they have telescopes? Did they have Apollo rocket ships? Did they have space shuttles? Did they have warp speed like on Star Trek? Or star drive? Or super radio or optical telescopes? The answer is no. The trip can be made with astral bodies, and the journey is faster than the speed of light. They could make the journey with the speed of mind. And with the speed of mind, you can go anywhere and witness anything instantly. But if you are hampered because of your egoism, because of your ignorance, your fears, your delusions that limit you, you can't go anywhere. You can't do anything outside of the limited domain of the physical body and its limitations within time and space. You are stuck with the little ego, the little "I" and you are a slave to time and space reality.

Furthermore, mental travel is a safer form of travel. You don't have to worry about rocket ships blowing up on you. But if you are a fearful personality, it actually can be scarier because it is like an unknown abyss, with no rocket ship around you. How would you like to step out of your body and there is no place for your foot to step? It is like an endless abyss that you can fall into; that's scary. At least in your physical body, in your rocket ship, you know that you may blow up, but at least you'll be in some place that you know, that you feel, touch, etc. right? You will be dead, but at least you know where you are going to be.

The expansion of consciousness is that abyss; Nut, the vastness of the heavens, is something that can only be known intuitively. You can't know the end of infinity, can you? Can you know the end of infinite expansion? Jump from a high air plane or go to the Grand Canyon and look over the edge of the Grand Canyon and see what happens to your personality; it starts to shutter due to the depth of space beneath but just think, that is just the space around the planet. Now imagine how the vastness of outer space would affect the mind and senses. The depth of the human mind is fathomable but the depth of consciousness is unfathomable. You could be falling in there forever, potentially. But, of course, if you realize that you pervade the vastness of endless expansion, the issues of fear have no concern for you because wherever you go, there you are and that vastness is recognized as of part of the greater "I"; and how can one get lost in one's own body? Using our analogy of falling, where are you to fall if it is all you? Do you understand this? If you do not, then you have to study more. If you can understand this, then you can proceed with the practice.

How Does Philosophy and Meditation Work to Promote Higher Consciousness?

Table 2: How Mind Vibrates in the different Realms of Existence

Mind in the Three Realms of Existence		
Realms	Operations of mind	
Ta	Form	Lower vibration
Pet	Thought	Average vibration
Duat	Concept	Higher vibration

Mental operations are in reality manipulations of subtle matter that reflect in the lighte of Spirit, focused through individuality [soul] so as to create a temporary idea of objects, situations and events related to itself as a personality. To accomplish this the mind arranges subtle matter and energy into forms, thoughts and concepts it can shuffle in the mind in relation to itself. This process is called thinking. The feelings about the thought process motivate the personality to take actions that in turn determine events and new thoughts and feelings, in a seemingly endless cycle all based in an illusory concept of self as individual and of objects as realities that relate to the individual and can cause pleasure or pain, happiness or sorrow, fulfillment or frustration. Form operates in the mind as the arrangements of atoms and molecules into recognizable gross shapes and appearances with distinct outlines. Thoughts operate in the mind as the manipulation of the forms and the meanings assigned to them, the meanings in relation to other forms and in relation to the self. The thoughts dictate the actions the personality will perform and therefore define its behaviors. Concept operates in the mind as the belief system (ethics, morals, standards, etc.) that develops in the mind.

In the context of this teaching it should be understood that mind is composed of the same elements of Creation (air, water, fire, earth, ether, energy) that the rest of the physical universe is composed of. As a manipulation of subtle matter (subtle aspect of the physical elements) mind exists in three realms, the Ta or physical dimension, the Pet or astral dimension and the Duat or cosmic dimension. The matter in the Ta realm vibrates at a lower rate while the matter in the Duat realm vibrates on a higher level. So the mind of a person that is very worldly is vibrating at a low rate. The mind of a person that has discovered higher realms of consciousness is vibrating at a higher level. Therefore it is important to promote those ways of thinking, feeling, acting and understanding that lead to higher vibrational awareness. The disciplines of this teaching [T.O.L.] cause the personality to vibrate on higher and higher levels until the higher realms are discovered and eventually transcended; this transcendence occurs when the vibration of mind is subtle enough so as to allow the awareness of the Higher Self to be perceived, as when the waters of a lake become clear and it is possible to see through to the bottom, when the waters become calm. If a person's awareness transcends the vibrations (higher and lower) of the mind altogether and along with the transcendence of the vibrations also transcendence of the gross elements of mind (groupings of subtle elements into heavier mental operations based on ignorance, that go to form desires, illusions, and feelings based on these) that reflect in such a mind (like sediments in an agitated lake that make the waters murky), it (mind) has dissolved the gross mental elements reducing opacity in the mind, producing clarity and only the awareness of the Higher Self remains without the need for reflecting awareness in the prism of subtle or gross mental elements, which were acting as a screen upon which awareness reflected to produce the illusory appearance of ego conscience (individuality in the midst of distinct physical objects and physical reality (Garment of Nun). This last level of conscious awareness of mind is subtle enough so as to allow the awareness of the Higher Self to be perceived. So if the awareness transcends the vibrations of the mind altogether it has dissolved and only the awareness of the Self beyond the mind remains. This last level of conscious awareness is called *yanrutef.*

Table 3: Realms of mental operation and their level of Subtlety or Grossness

Ta	Pet	Duat	Yanrutef
Gross	Subtle	Subtlest	Transcendental

The garment of Nun is actually the perception of polarized objectified Nun matter that appears as such due to the nature of polarized mind due to egoism and spiritual ignorance. So the egoistic ignorant mind itself is the cause of the existence of the garment; in other words it is given reality by the ignorant mind but conversely, it is not sustained in the enlightened mind. The garment exists in the three realms, from gross to subtle. The grossest aspect is found the Ta realm. The subtler is the Duat.

When the spiritual journey is conducted properly, meaning that the wisdom teaching of the philosophy and metaphysics have been understood and the disciplines have been practiced sufficiently the garment of Nun, that was created by goddess Net, is dissolved; this is a deconstruction of the illusory matrix the mind that had been created through the ignorant adoption of egoistic views of the world which were arrived at through ignorant notions of self due to the absence of the knowledge of the expanded aspects of the personality.

NOTE > This section presents a meditation and spiritual discipline protocol specifically for the T.O.L. practice. For more details on the themes presented here see the books *Meditation The Ancient Egyptian Path to Enlightenment* and *The Serpent Power,* both by Muata Ashby

Meditation may be thought of or defined as the practice of mental exercises and disciplines to enable the meditator to achieve control over the mind, specifically, to stop the vibrations of the mind due to unwanted thoughts, imaginations, etc. Consciousness refers to the awareness of being alive and of having an identity, or existing and knowing existence. It is this characteristic which separates humans from the animal kingdom. Animals cannot become aware of their own existence and ponder the questions such as *Who am I?, Where am I going in life?, Where do I come from?,* etc. They cannot write books on history and create elaborate systems of social history based on ancestry, etc. Consciousness expresses itself in three modes. These are: Waking, Dream Sleep and Dreamless-Deep-Sleep.

However, ordinary human life is only partially conscious. When you are driving or walking, you sometimes lose track of the present moment. All of a sudden you arrive at your destination without having conscious awareness of the road which you have just traveled. Your mind went into an "automatic" mode of consciousness. This automatic mode of consciousness represents a temporary withdrawal from the waking world. This state is similar to a day dream (a dreamlike musing or fantasy). This form of existence is what most people consider as "normal" everyday waking consciousness. It is what people consider to be the extent of the human capacity to experience or be conscious.

What most people consider to be the "awake" state of mind in which life is lived is in reality only a fraction of the total potential consciousness which a human being can experience. The "normal" state of human consciousness cannot be considered as "whole" or complete because if it was there would be no experience of lapses or gaps in consciousness. In other words, every instant of consciousness would be accounted for. There would be no awareness lapse states wherein one loses track of time or awareness of one's own activities, sometimes even as they are being performed. In the times of lapse, full awareness or consciousness is not present, otherwise it would be impossible to not be aware of the passage of time while engaged in various activities. Trance is a similar state of mind wherein people can enter into an altered state of mind due to an ecstatic feeling or concentration on a particular perspective like getting lost in thoughts of a loved one or a religious possession by spirits or losing oneself in the religious ritual experience. As used above, it refers to the condition of being so lost in solitary thought as to be unaware of one's surroundings. People can experience trances due to ignorance or dull thinking or recreational drug usage and may further be characterized as a stunned or bewildered condition, a fog, stupor, befuddlement, daze, muddled state of mind. Most everyone has experienced this condition at some point or another. Trance here should be differentiated from the mystical form of trance like state induced through study of mystical philosophy {such as is presented in this book} and conscious meditation.

First we will look at a schematic depiction of the states of mind and how they relate to the planes of existence and to Universal consciousness. This will allow your mind to understand a different concept of existence as well as the relative location and relationship of the human spiritual elements in relation to the cosmic spiritual elements.

The Kemetic Tree of Life
Understanding the process of meditation.

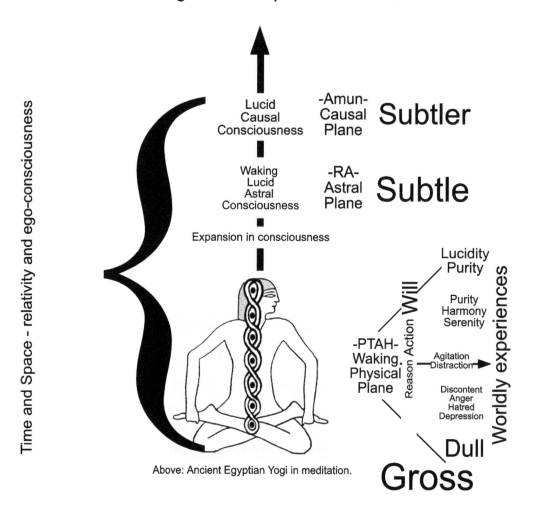

Eternity

Pa-Neter
-Nebertcher-
The Self

Infinity

Universal Consciousness

Subtlest

Transcending time and space - The absolute

Lucid
Causal
Consciousness

-Amun-
Causal
Plane

Subtler

Waking
Lucid
Astral
Consciousness

-RA-
Astral
Plane

Subtle

Expansion in consciousness

Time and Space - relativity and ego-consciousness

Lucidity
Purity

Purity
Harmony
Serenity

-PTAH-
Waking.
Physical
Plane

Reason Action Will

Agitation
Distraction

Discontent
Anger
Hatred
Depression

Worldly experiences

Dull

Gross

Above: Ancient Egyptian Yogi in meditation.

Above: The relative states of consciousness and the path of meditation. A figure from Ancient Egypt is sitting in the yoga lotus posture. Superimposed on him are the seven rings symbolizing the seven centers of psycho-spiritual energy consciousness known as Arat in Ancient Egyptian Yoga mystical philosophy. Through the process of meditation a meditator lifts him/her self up beyond ordinary consciousness and discovers the transcendental realms and finally the Absolute Self. The meditation practice occurs within the realm of time and space. Working through the dull, agitated mind the meditator produces a lucid mind that is unencumbered by egoistic thoughts and desires; this is purity of mind. Then the meditator can move beyond the physical plane, to discover the Astral and Causal planes and finally the transcendental realm of universal consciousness, the Absolute.

Stage 1:

In the Temple of Aset the process of spiritual practice is described as a three step program including Listening to the teachings, then reflecting upon them and finally meditating upon them. Throughout this volume you have been listening (reading) and then reflecting on the teaching that has been presented. Now you can proceed to the formal practice of meditation which we are enjoining here.

The purpose of the first stage of the practice of the meditation discipline is to cleanse the *Mettus*. Mettu means "conduits", the vascular systems, the nervous systems, the gastrointestinal system, etc. This can be done by introducing air into the body by inhaling and visualizing the life force within that air going through all the cells of your body and cleansing them, breaking down blockages, the emotional, physical obstacles as discussed earlier. Here also the purpose is to promote health and vitality which will be needed for the day to day activities in ordinary life and also to sustain the spiritual studies and practices. At this stage there should be a focus on rhythmic breathing.

Posture

When entering a temple or when approaching the altar you have set up, in your designated area for practicing the disciplines enjoined in this volume, you should make the preliminary obeisance. First raise both arms with palms facing towards the altar and the divinity. This is the dua posture, a posture of humility and adorations. Next kneel down in front of the altar and touch your fore head to the ground. This is a posture signifying greater humility and it is also known as the scarab posture, a posture of consolidating power and creative energy (see the book *Egyptian Yoga Postures of the Gods and Goddesses* by Muata Ashby). It is useful in this discipline (given in the lessons about each divinity) to practice the postures of the gods and goddesses as this heightened the connection with their principles and facilitates the cultivation of their energies as well as understanding their wisdom teaching. (see the book *Egyptian Yoga Postures of the Gods and Goddesses* by Muata Ashby

For the purposes of formal practice with this TOL system, the practitioner should sit or lie down comfortably either in a cross legged posture or in a chair with both feet on the gorund and hands on the thighs.

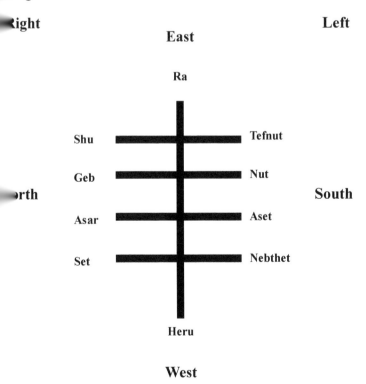

Right

East

Ra

Shu — Tefnut

Geb — Nut

North

Asar — Aset

Set — Nebthet

Heru

West

Left

South

The altar should face east and the propitiations for commencement and ending the exercises should be facing the altar. However, the practitioner should face in the direction of the divinity preciding over the principle being studied in accordance with the following diagram. You will notice that the male divinitied are of the north and the female divinities are of the south. Ra and Heru are between them at east and west respectively. When facing the Cosmiconomythograph its left side is one's right side and its right side is one's left side.

MEDITATION POSTURES

OBEISANCE POSTRES

Dua Posture

left:
e Lotus
sture

At left:
The seated
position with
arms resting
on the thighs.

Scarab Posture

Below:
the Corpse
pose.

Proper Breathing

Most people in the modern world do not know how to breathe properly. Most people (especially males) have learned to breathe by pushing out the chest in a "manly" or "macho" fashion. This mode of breathing is harmful for many reasons. The amount of air taken in is less and vital cosmic energy is reduced and becomes stagnant in the subtle vital energy channels, resulting in physical and mental diseases. The stagnation of the flow of energy through the body has the effect of grounding one's consciousness to the physical realities rather than allowing the mind and body to operate with lightness and subtlety.

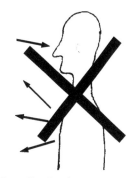

Above: Chest breathing.
Below: Abdominal breathing.

"Belly breathing" or abdominal breathing massages the internal organs and develops Life Force energy (Ra, Chi or Kundalini). It will be noticed that it is our natural breathing pattern when we lie down on our back. Instruction is as follows:

Diagram 11: Proper Breathing Diagram

A- Breathe in and push the stomach out. B- Breathe out and pull the stomach in. This form of breathing is to be practiced at all times, not just during meditation. It allows the natural Life Force in the air to be rhythmically supplied to the body and nervous system. This process is indispensable in the achievement of physical health and mental-spiritual power to control the mind (meditation).

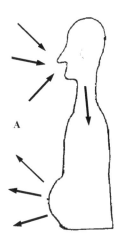
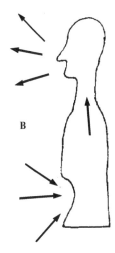

A   B

Stage 2:

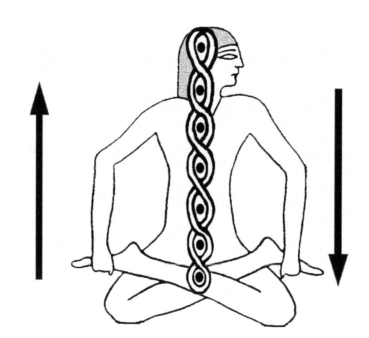

Breathe Out	Breathe In
Visualize life force moving up from the base of the spine through the other souls of Ra, to the crown of the head and then out through the nostrils	Visualize life force moving through lungs and down to the base of the spine

Cleansing breath for the psycho-spiritual energy centers {Sefech Ba Ra}. Moving forward, a cleansing technique is to bring the life force to the root of your spine, which is the first psycho-spiritual consciousness center of the *uaa Sefech Ba Ra*, the first soul of Ra, bringing it up to the crown of your head and then back down again as you exhale and then breathing in again. If this technique is practiced it will eventually lead to the advanced practices automatically.

Stage 3:

After some time practicing the cleansing stage (weeks or months as needed), there are more advanced techniques that I will not give here because those who may read this, they may not be ready to hear that. They may not be qualified to practice those techniques. Those are given to practitioners that achieve the level of temple initiation. So those desiring to practice the more advanced metaphysical meditative disciplines should inquire with their instructors who have been certified in this system. Nevertheless, they are hinted at in the book Serpent Power, but they are not discussed directly. As I said, the manipulation of air and life forces is a deep mystery and a very effective and powerful spiritual technique of dissolution that can also be detrimental if one is not ready, if one is not purified. Also, if the philosophical understanding is faulty that will affect the practice detrimentally when certain inner experiences are achieved without the proper insights.

Now we will proceed to the parameters of the disciplines that are to be practiced in order to advance on the path of the Kemetic Tree of Life.

Parameters of the Discipline of the T.O.L.

When you engage in the study of the TOL you will work with each Sphere or principle, at a time. As you begin your study/practice session you will follow the program outlined below.

PART 1: ITEMS REQUIRED

Altar: For this practice you will need to set up an altar. The altar is to face to the east and it will contain an offering:

Offering: maintain the following items as part of the altar where the discipline is to be maintained. [preferably there should be a special room where these items are kept and where the disciplines of offering, chant, reflection and meditation will be carried out.]

1) Candle – to be lit during the practice time
2) Incense – to be lit during the practice time
3) Food – fresh food item
4) Libation offering Hotep slab or offering bowl
5) Amulet of each divinity[166] – to be added as the sphere of that divinity is studied.
6) Icon of each divinity – to be placed in the altar as the sphere of that divinity is studied. [The icon may be a statue or an image such as those presented in this book] {see plates section} [the Anunian Theurgy Tree of Life Poster is useful for this purpose]
7) Meditation mat

PART 2: STARTING THE SESSION – OPENING CHANT

Hekau [Chant] General: Use the following chant to open the practice for the day.

Adorations to Ra When he rises[167]

Dua Ra Cheft Uben F is a direct translation of the first section of the Hymn to Ra contained in the Pert Em Hru or Book of Coming Forth By Day of Any. It is a reference to and propitiation to Ra for his illumination and influence over the other Neteru to cause them to promote their cooperation in the study and meditative process. It is translated:

1) *Dua Ra Cheft Uben F em aket abdet ent Pet*	1) Adorations to Ra When he rises in horizon eastern
2) *Anetej Ra-k iti em Khepera*	2) Homage to Ra, coming forth as Khepera
3) *Khepera qemam neteru*	3) Khepera, Creator of the gods and goddesses
4) *Cha – k uben – k pesd Mut – k*	4) Rising thee, shinning thee, lighting up thy mother
5) *Cha ti em suten neteru*	5) Rising as Lord, king of the gods and goddesses
	6) Your mother Nut does an act of worship to you with both arms
6) *Iri – nek mut Nut aiui – em iri nini*	7) Manu (Western Horizon) receives thee in peace, Maat embraces thee at the double season (perennially)
7) *Manu em hetep hept-tu Maat er tra*	

---

[166] **Amulets** – you may acquire amulets, such as jewelry, for this practice and purify them by soaking in pure water for 7 days or use the images contained in this book, making a copy of the page and placing it at the altar.
[167] Translation by Dr. Muata Ashby

PART 3: SPHERE CHANT

Sphere Chant: As you study of the TOL you are to concentrate on each Sphere which is presided over by a particular divinity. Use one of the following chants for each of the spheres when that sphere is being concentrated upon. For example, if you are studying Sphere 1, the teaching of Heru, then use chant #1 while you are working with this sphere. When using the chant it is to be uttered 10 times.

Sphere	*Chant in Kemetic language*	**Translation**
1) Sphere of Heru [Audible chant]	1) Dua Heru Hotep di si neter iri rech ab m Maakheru	1) Adorations to Heru with this offering being made to cause him to provide self knowledge and spiritual perfection
2) Sphere of Set [Audible chant]	2) Dua Set Hotep di si neter iri rech ab m Maakheru	2) Adorations to Set with this offering being made to cause him to provide self knowledge and spiritual perfection
3) Sphere of Nebthet [Audible chant]	3) Dua Nebethet Hotep di si neter iri rech ab m Maakheru	3) Adorations to Nebethet with this offering being made to cause her to provide self knowledge and spiritual perfection
4) Sphere of Aset [Audible chant]	4) Dua Aset Hotep di si neter iri rech ab m Maakheru	4) Adorations to Aset with this offering being made to cause him to provide self knowledge and spiritual perfectio
5) Sphere of Asar [Audible chant]	5) Dua Asar Hotep di si neter iri rech ab m Maakheru	5) Adorations to Asar with this offering being made to cause her to provide self knowledge and spiritual perfection
6) Sphere of Geb [Silent chant]	6) Dua Geb Hotep di si neter iri rech ab m Maakheru	6) Adorations to Geb with this offering being made to cause him to provide self knowledge and spiritual perfection
7) Sphere of Nut [Silent chant]	7) Dua Nut Hotep di si neter iri rech ab m Maakheru	7) Adorations to Nut with this offering being made to cause her to provide self knowledge and spiritual perfection
8) Sphere of Tefnut [Silent chant]	8) Dua Tefnut Hotep di si neter iri rech ab m Maakheru	8) Adorations to Tefnut with this offering being made to cause him to provide self knowledge and spiritual perfection
9) Sphere of Shu [Silent chant]	9) Dua Shu Hotep di si neter iri rech ab m Maakheru	9) Adorations to Shu with this offering being made to cause her to provide self knowledge and spiritual perfection
10) Sphere of Ra [Silent chant]	10) Dua Ra Hotep di si neter iri rech ab m Maakheru	10) Adorations to Ra with this offering being made to cause him to provide sel knowledge and spiritual perfection

PROGRAM OUTLINE

Daily spiritual practice and Meditation protocol

Daily practice – find a convenient time to practice regular meditation – preferably in accordance with Anunian tradition, the worship and meditation is to be practiced at dawn, noon and dusk.[168]

1) Uncover altar
2) Light candle
3) Light incense
4) Pour water as libation
5) Invocatory chant – utter once:

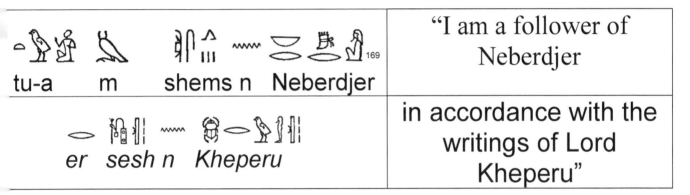

tu-a m shems n Neberdjer [169]	"I am a follower of Neberdjer
er sesh n Kheperu	in accordance with the writings of Lord Kheperu"

6) Opening chant {*Dua Ra Cheft Uben F* }–utter 10 times

7) Sphere chant –utter 10 times –cumulatively up to the sphere that is being studied [for example, if you are studying sphere number 3 {Nebthet} then utter the chants of spheres 1, 2 and 3.

8) Journaling- see the instructions at the end of the lesson you are currently working on and write in your journal as instructed

---

[168] see the book *The Devotional Worship Manual of Shetaut Neter* by Dr. Muata Ashby
[169] "I am follower of Neberdjer…" *Pert M Heru* Chap 4 (commonly 17)

9) <u>Meditation Period</u>

<u>MEDITATION PRACTICE: FOR SPHERES 1-5</u>

A. Close your journal. Find a comfortable posture with the back straight. This meditative discipline can be enjoined in different postures. Sitting in a chair, or on a cushion with legs crossed or in the mummy posture, resting comfortably on your back, on a soft but firm surface proceed as follows.

B. Allow yourself to breathe in air rhythmically and deeply concentrated the attention from sphere 1 to 7 of the *Sefech Ba Ra.*

C. Focus on the breath – breathe in and out deeply and rhythmically. Visualize that you are breathing in the energetic principle of the divinity that you are studying right now. Visualize that you are embodying the principle divinity that you are studying, that you are manifesting those principles within yourself.

D. Focus awareness on the sphere being studied, visualize a golden pure light at that region, cleansing and purifying it.

E. Audible Chant: utter the following: <u>Dua Ra, Dua Ra, Dua Ra, with each inhalation, without pause</u>
<u>Dua Ra, Dua Ra, Dua Ra, with each exhalation without pause</u>

F. Conclude the meditation with 10-20 rounds of the cleansing breath (see <u>Stage 2</u> above).

G. Time for meditation: Minimum 15 minutes-maximum 1 hour

MEDITATION PRACTICE: FOR SPHERES 6-10

A. Close your journal. Find a comfortable posture with the back straight.

B. Focus on the breath – breathe in and out deeply and rhythmically. Visualize that you are breathing in the energetic principle of the divinity that you are studying right now. Visualize that you are embodying the principle divinity that you are studying, that you are manifesting those principles within yourself.

C. Focus awareness on the sphere being studied, visualize a golden pure light at that region, cleansing and purifying it.

D. Silent Chant: utter the following: Dua Ra, Dua Ra, Dua Ra, with each inhalation, pause briefly (silence) Dua Ra, Dua Ra, Dua Ra, with each exhalation, pause briefly (silence)

E. Conclude the meditation with 10-20 rounds of the cleansing breath (see Stage 2 above).

F. Time: Minimum 1 hour-maximum 3 hours

10) <u>Reflection period:</u> complete Journal assignment

<u>Reflection and Journal discipline:</u>

<u>1-</u> **At the top of each page, that you write on in your journal, copy the following hieroglyphs to the best of your ability**

[***cht n ankh*** *" tree of life"*]

After meditation practice proceed to answer the following question and write the answer in your journal. This reflection exercise does not need to be done every meditation period. You may feel free to skip this section and go directly to the meditation practice. The reflection exercise should be done with meditation practice at least once per week.

> *Describe your feeling at this moment.*
> *Describe your mental state at this time.*
> *Describe any insights you may have.*

11) **Closing chant for meditation session:** {*Dua Ra Cheft Uben F* }–utter 1 time

Adorations to Ra When he rises[170]

    Dua Ra Cheft Uben F is a direct translation of the first section of the Hymn to Ra contained in the Pert Em Hru or Book of Coming Forth By Day of Any. It is a reference to and propitiation to Ra for his illumination and influence over the other Neteru to cause them to promote their cooperation in the study and meditative process. It is translated:

1) *Dua Ra Cheft Uben F em aket abdet ent Pet*	1) Adorations to Ra When he rises in horizon eastern
2) *Anetej Ra-k iti em Khepera*	2) Homage to Ra, coming forth as Khepera
3) *Khepera qemam neteru*	3) Khepera, Creator of the gods and goddesses
4) *Cha – k uben – k pesd Mut – k*	4) Rising thee, shinning thee, lighting up thy mother
5) *Cha ti em suten neteru*	5) Rising as Lord, king of the gods and goddesses
6) *Iri – nek mut Nut aiui – em iri nini*	6) Your mother Nut does an act of worship to you with both arms
7) *Manu em hetep hept-tu Maat er tra*	7) Manu (Western Horizon) receives thee in peace, Maat embraces thee at the double season (perennially)

---

[170] Translation by Dr. Muata Ashby

INDEX

SEMA INSTITUTE

Cruzian Mystic P.O.Box 570459, Miami, Florida. 33257 (305) 378-6253, Fax. (305) 378-6253

www.Egyptianyoga.com

Other Books From C M Books

P.O.Box 570459
Miami, Florida, 33257
(305) 378-6253 Fax: (305) 378-6253

This book is part of a series on the study and practice of Ancient Egyptian Yoga and Mystical Spirituality based on the writings of Dr. Muata Abhaya Ashby. They are also part of the Egyptian Yoga Course provided by the Sema Institute of Yoga. Below you will find a listing of the other books in this series. For more information send for the Egyptian Yoga Book-Audio-Video Catalog or the Egyptian Yoga Course Catalog.

Now you can study the teachings of Egyptian and Indian Yoga wisdom and Spirituality with the Egyptian Yoga Mystical Spirituality Series. The Egyptian Yoga Series takes you through the Initiation process and lead you to understand the mysteries of the soul and the Divine and to attain the highest goal of life: ENLIGHTENMENT. The *Egyptian Yoga Series*, takes you on an in depth study of Ancient Egyptian mythology and their inner mystical meaning. Each Book is prepared for the serious student of the mystical sciences and provides a study of the teachings along with exercises, assignments and projects to make the teachings understood and effective in real life. The Series is part of the Egyptian Yoga course but may be purchased even if you are not taking the course. The series is ideal for study groups.

Prices subject to change.

1. *EGYPTIAN YOGA: THE PHILOSOPHY OF ENLIGHTENMENT* An original, fully illustrated work, including hieroglyphs, detailing the meaning of the Egyptian mysteries, tantric yoga, psycho-spiritual and physical exercises. Egyptian Yoga is a guide to the practice of the highest spiritual philosophy which leads to absolute freedom from human misery and to immortality. It is well known by scholars that Egyptian philosophy is the basis of Western and Middle Eastern religious philosophies such as *Christianity, Islam, Judaism,* the *Kabala*, and Greek philosophy, but what about Indian philosophy, Yoga and Taoism? What were the original teachings? How can they be practiced today? What is the source of pain and suffering in the world and what is the solution? Discover the deepest mysteries of the mind and universe within and outside of your self. 8.5" X 11" ISBN: 1-884564-01-1 Soft $19.95

2. *EGYPTIAN YOGA: African Religion Volume 2-* Theban Theology U.S. In this long awaited sequel to *Egyptian Yoga: The Philosophy of Enlightenment* you will take a fascinating and enlightening journey back in time and discover the teachings which constituted the epitome of Ancient Egyptian spiritual wisdom. What are the disciplines which lead to the fulfillment of all desires? Delve into the three states of consciousness (waking, dream and deep sleep) and the fourth state which transcends them all, Neberdjer, "The Absolute." These teachings of the city of Waset (Thebes) were the crowning achievement of the Sages of Ancient Egypt. They establish the standard mystical keys for understanding the profound mystical symbolism of the Triad of human consciousness. ISBN 1-884564-39-9 $23.95

3. *THE KEMETIC DIET: GUIDE TO HEALTH, DIET AND FASTING* Health issues have always been important to human beings since the beginning of time. The earliest records of history show that the art of healing was held in high esteem since the time of Ancient Egypt. In the early 20th century, medical doctors had almost attained the status of sainthood by the promotion of the idea that they alone were "scientists" while other healing modalities and traditional healers who did not follow the "scientific method' were nothing but superstitious, ignorant charlatans who at best would take the money of their clients and at worst kill them with the unscientific "snake oils" and "irrational theories". In the late 20th century, the failure of the modern medical establishment's ability to lead the general public to good health, promoted the move by many in society towards "alternative medicine". Alternative medicine disciplines are those healing modalities which do not adhere to the philosophy of allopathic medicine. Allopathic medicine is what medical doctors practice by an large. It is the theory that disease is caused by agencies outside the body such as bacteria, viruses or physical means which affect the body. These can therefore be treated by medicines and therapies The natural healing method began in the absence of extensive technologies with the idea that all the answers for health may be found in nature or rather, the deviation from nature. Therefore, the health of the body can be restored by correcting the aberration and thereby restoring balance. This is the area that will be covered in this volume. Allopathic techniques have their place in the art of healing. However, we should not forget that the body is a grand achievement of the spirit and built into it is the capacity to maintain itself and heal itself. Ashby, Muata ISBN: 1-884564-49-6 $28.95

4. INITIATION INTO EGYPTIAN YOGA Shedy: Spiritual discipline or program, to go deeply into the mysteries, to study the mystery teachings and literature profoundly, to penetrate the mysteries. You will learn about the mysteries of

initiation into the teachings and practice of Yoga and how to become an Initiate of the mystical sciences. This insightful manual is the first in a series which introduces you to the goals of daily spiritual and yoga practices: Meditation, Diet, Words of Power and the ancient wisdom teachings. 8.5" X 11" ISBN 1-884564-02-X   Soft Cover $24.95 U.S.

5.   *THE AFRICAN ORIGINS OF CIVILIZATION, RELIGION AND YOGA SPIRITUALITY AND ETHICS PHILOSOPHY* HARD COVER EDITION Part 1, Part 2, Part 3 in one volume 683 Pages Hard Cover First Edition Three volumes in one. Over the past several years I have been asked to put together in one volume the most important evidences showing the correlations and common teachings between Kamitan (Ancient Egyptian) culture and religion and that of India. The questions of the history of Ancient Egypt, and the latest archeological evidences showing civilization and culture in Ancient Egypt and its spread to other countries, has intrigued many scholars as well as mystics over the years. Also, the possibility that Ancient Egyptian Priests and Priestesses migrated to Greece, India and other countries to carry on the traditions of the Ancient Egyptian Mysteries, has been speculated over the years as well. In chapter 1 of the book *Egyptian Yoga The Philosophy of Enlightenment,* 1995, I first introduced the deepest comparison between Ancient Egypt and India that had been brought forth up to that time. Now, in the year 2001 this new book, *THE AFRICAN ORIGINS OF CIVILIZATION, MYSTICAL RELIGION AND YOGA PHILOSOPHY,* more fully explores the motifs, symbols and philosophical correlations between Ancient Egyptian and Indian mysticism and clearly shows not only that Ancient Egypt and India were connected culturally but also spiritually. How does this knowledge help the spiritual aspirant? This discovery has great importance for the Yogis and mystics who follow the philosophy of Ancient Egypt and the mysticism of India. It means that India has a longer history and heritage than was previously understood. It shows that the mysteries of Ancient Egypt were essentially a yoga tradition which did not die but rather developed into the modern day systems of Yoga technology of India. It further shows that African culture developed Yoga Mysticism earlier than any other civilization in history. All of this expands our understanding of the unity of culture and the deep legacy of Yoga, which stretches into the distant past, beyond the Indus Valley civilization, the earliest known high culture in India as well as the Vedic tradition of Aryan culture. Therefore, Yoga culture and mysticism is the oldest known tradition of spiritual development and Indian mysticism is an extension of the Ancient Egyptian mysticism. By understanding the legacy which Ancient Egypt gave to India the mysticism of India is better understood and by comprehending the heritage of Indian Yoga, which is rooted in Ancient Egypt the Mysticism of Ancient Egypt is also better understood. This expanded understanding allows us to prove the underlying kinship of humanity, through the common symbols, motifs and philosophies which are not disparate and confusing teachings but in reality expressions of the same study of truth through metaphysics and mystical realization of Self. (HARD COVER) ISBN: 1-884564-50-X $45.00 U.S.   81/2" X 11"

6.   *AFRICAN ORIGINS BOOK 1 PART 1* African Origins of African Civilization, Religion, Yoga Mysticism and Ethics Philosophy-Soft Cover $24.95 ISBN: 1-884564-55-0

7.   *AFRICAN ORIGINS BOOK 2 PART 2* African Origins of Western Civilization, Religion and Philosophy (Soft) -Soft Cover $24.95 ISBN: 1-884564-56-9

8.   *EGYPT AND INDIA AFRICAN ORIGINS OF Eastern Civilization, Religion, Yoga Mysticism and Philosophy*-Soft Cover In chapter 1 of the book *Egyptian Yoga The Philosophy of Enlightenment,* 1995, I first introduced the comparison between spiritual teachings and symbols of Ancient Egypt and India that had been brought forth up to that time. Now, this book, *EGYPT AND INDIA,* more fully explores the motifs, symbols and philosophical correlations between Ancient Egyptian and Indian mysticism and clearly shows not only that Ancient Egypt and India were connected culturally but also spiritually. This book presents evidences like the discovery of the "OM" symbol in Ancient Egyptian texts. How does this knowledge help the spiritual aspirant? This discovery has great importance for the Yogis and mystics who follow the philosophy of Ancient Egypt and the mysticism of India. It means that India has a longer history and heritage than was previously understood. It shows that the mysteries of Ancient Egypt were essentially a yoga tradition which did not die but rather developed into the modern day systems of Yoga technology of India. It further shows that African culture developed Yoga Mysticism earlier than any other civilization in history. All of this expands our understanding of the unity of culture and the deep legacy of Yoga, which stretches into the distant past, beyond the Indus Valley civilization, the earliest known high culture in India as well as the Vedic tradition of Aryan culture. Therefore, Yoga culture and mysticism is the oldest known tradition of spiritual development and Indian mysticism is an extension of the Ancient Egyptian mysticism. By understanding the legacy which Ancient Egypt gave to India the mysticism of India is better understood and by comprehending the heritage of Indian Yoga, which is rooted in Ancient Egypt the Mysticism of Ancient Egypt is also better understood. This expanded understanding allows us to prove the underlying kinship of humanity, through the common symbols, motifs and philosophies which are not disparate and confusing teachings but in reality expressions of the same study of truth through metaphysics and mystical realization of Self. **$29.95 (Soft) ISBN: 1-884564-57-7**

9.   *THE MYSTERIES OF ISIS: **The Ancient Egyptian Philosophy of Self-Realization*** - There are several paths to discover the Divine and the mysteries of the higher Self. This volume details the mystery teachings of the goddess Aset (Isis) from Ancient Egypt- the path of wisdom. It includes the teachings of her temple and the disciplines that are enjoined for the initiates of the temple of Aset as they were given in ancient times. Also, this book includes the teachings of the main myths of Aset that lead a human being to spiritual enlightenment and immortality. Through the study of ancient myth and the illumination of initiatic understanding the idea of God is expanded from the mythological comprehension to the metaphysical. Then this metaphysical understanding is related to you, the student, so as to begin understanding your true divine nature. ISBN 1-884564-24-0 $22.99

10. *EGYPTIAN PROVERBS:* collection of —Ancient Egyptian Proverbs and Wisdom Teachings -How to live according to MAAT Philosophy. Beginning Meditation. All proverbs are indexed for easy searches. For the first time in one volume, ——Ancient Egyptian Proverbs, wisdom teachings and meditations, fully illustrated with hieroglyphic text and symbols. EGYPTIAN PROVERBS is a unique collection of knowledge and wisdom which you can put into practice today and transform your life. $14.95 U.S   ISBN: 1-884564-00-3

11. *GOD OF LOVE: THE PATH OF DIVINE LOVE The Process of Mystical Transformation and The Path of Divine Love* This Volume focuses on the ancient wisdom teachings of "Neter Merri" –the Ancient Egyptian philosophy of Divine Love and how to use them in a scientific process for self-transformation. Love is one of the most powerful human emotions. It is also the source of Divine feeling that unifies God and the individual human being. When love is fragmented and diminished by egoism the Divine connection is lost. The Ancient tradition of Neter Merri leads human beings back to their Divine connection, allowing them to discover their innate glorious self that is actually Divine and immortal. This volume will detail the process of transformation from ordinary consciousness to cosmic consciousness through the integrated practice of the teachings and the path of Devotional Love toward the Divine. 5.5"x 8.5" ISBN 1-884564-11-9 $22.95

12. *INTRODUCTION TO MAAT PHILOSOPHY: Spiritual Enlightenment Through the Path of Virtue* Known commonly as Karma in India, the teachings of MAAT contain an extensive philosophy based on ariu (deeds) and their fructification in the form of shai and renenet (fortune and destiny, leading to Meskhenet (fate in a future birth) for living virtuously and with orderly wisdom are explained and the student is to begin practicing the precepts of Maat in daily life so as to promote the process of purification of the heart in preparation for the judgment of the soul. This judgment will be understood not as an event that will occur at the time of death but as an event that occurs continuously, at every moment in the life of the individual. The student will learn how to become allied with the forces of the Higher Self and to thereby begin cleansing the mind (heart) of impurities so as to attain a higher vision of reality. ISBN 1-884564-20-8 $22.99

13. *MEDITATION The Ancient Egyptian Path to Enlightenment* Many people do not know about the rich history of meditation practice in Ancient Egypt. This volume outlines the theory of meditation and presents the Ancient Egyptian Hieroglyphic text which give instruction as to the nature of the mind and its three modes of expression. It also presents the texts which give instruction on the practice of meditation for spiritual Enlightenment and unity with the Divine. This volume allows the reader to begin practicing meditation by explaining, in easy to understand terms, the simplest form of meditation and working up to the most advanced form which was practiced in ancient times and which is still practiced by yogis around the world in modern times. ISBN 1-884564-27-7 $22.99

14. *THE GLORIOUS LIGHT MEDITATION* Technique of Ancient Egypt New for the year 2000. This volume is based on the earliest known instruction in history given for the practice of formal meditation. Discovered by Dr. Muata Ashby, it is inscribed on the walls of the Tomb of Seti I in Thebes Egypt. This volume details the philosophy and practice of this unique system of meditation originated in Ancient Egypt and the earliest practice of meditation known in the world which occurred in the most advanced African Culture. ISBN: 1-884564-15-1 $16.95 (PB)

5. *THE SERPENT POWER: The Ancient Egyptian Mystical Wisdom of the Inner Life Force.* This Volume specifically deals with the latent life Force energy of the universe and in the human body, its control and sublimation. How to develop the Life Force energy of the subtle body. This Volume will introduce the esoteric wisdom of the science of how virtuous living acts in a subtle and mysterious way to cleanse the latent psychic energy conduits and vortices of the spiritual body. ISBN 1-884564-19-4 $22.95

6. *EGYPTIAN YOGA The Postures of The Gods and Goddesses* Discover the physical postures and exercises practiced thousands of years ago in Ancient Egypt which are today known as Yoga exercises. Discover the history of the postures and how they were transferred from Ancient Egypt in Africa to India through Buddhist Tantrism. Then practice the postures as you discover the mythic teaching that originally gave birth to the postures and was practiced by the Ancient Egyptian priests and priestesses. This work is based on the pictures and teachings from the Creation story of Ra, The Asarian Resurrection Myth and the carvings and reliefs from various Temples in Ancient Egypt 8.5" X 11" ISBN 1-884564-10-0 Soft Cover $21.95   Exercise video $20

7. *SACRED SEXUALITY: EGYPTIAN TANTRA YOGA: The Art of Sex* Sublimation and Universal Consciousness This Volume will expand on the male and female principles within the human body and in the universe and further detail the sublimation of sexual energy into spiritual energy. The student will study the deities Min and Hathor, Asar and Aset, Geb and Nut and discover the mystical implications for a practical spiritual discipline. This Volume will also focus on the Tantric aspects of Ancient Egyptian and Indian mysticism, the purpose of sex and the mystical teachings of sexual sublimation which lead to self-knowledge and Enlightenment. 5.5"x 8.5" ISBN 1-884564-03-8 $24.95

8. *AFRICAN RELIGION Volume 4: ASARIAN THEOLOGY: RESURRECTING OSIRIS* The path of Mystical Awakening and the Keys to Immortality NEW REVISED AND EXPANDED EDITION! The Ancient Sages created stories based on human and superhuman beings whose struggles, aspirations, needs and desires ultimately lead them to discover their true Self. The myth of Aset, Asar and Heru is no exception in this area. While there is no one source where the entire story may be found, pieces of it are inscribed in various ancient Temples walls, tombs, steles and papyri. For

the first time available, the complete myth of Asar, Aset and Heru has been compiled from original Ancient Egyptian, Greek and Coptic Texts. This epic myth has been richly illustrated with reliefs from the Temple of Heru at Edfu, the Temple of Aset at Philae, the Temple of Asar at Abydos, the Temple of Hathor at Denderah and various papyri, inscriptions and reliefs. Discover the myth which inspired the teachings of the *Shetaut Neter* (Egyptian Mystery System - Egyptian Yoga) and the Egyptian Book of Coming Forth By Day. Also, discover the three levels of Ancient Egyptian Religion, how to understand the mysteries of the Duat or Astral World and how to discover the abode of the Supreme in the Amenta, *The Other World* The ancient religion of Asar, Aset and Heru, if properly understood, contains all of the elements necessary to lead the sincere aspirant to attain immortality through inner self-discovery. This volume presents the entire myth and explores the main mystical themes and rituals associated with the myth for understating human existence, creation and the way to achieve spiritual emancipation - *Resurrection.* The Asarian myth is so powerful that it influenced and is still having an effect on the major world religions. Discover the origins and mystical meaning of the Christian Trinity, the Eucharist ritual and the ancient origin of the birthday of Jesus Christ. Soft Cover ISBN: 1-884564-27-5 $24.95

19.   *THE EGYPTIAN BOOK OF THE DEAD MYSTICISM OF THE PERT EM HERU* " I Know myself, I know myself, I am One With God!–From the Pert Em Heru "The Ru Pert em Heru" or "Ancient Egyptian Book of The Dead," or "Book of Coming Forth By Day" as it is more popularly known, has fascinated the world since the successful translation of Ancient Egyptian hieroglyphic scripture over 150 years ago. The astonishing writings in it reveal that the Ancient Egyptians believed in life after death and in an ultimate destiny to discover the Divine. The elegance and aesthetic beauty of the hieroglyphic text itself has inspired many see it as an art form in and of itself. But is there more to it than that? Did the Ancient Egyptian wisdom contain more than just aphorisms and hopes of eternal life beyond death? In this volume Dr. Muata Ashby, the author of over 25 books on Ancient Egyptian Yoga Philosophy has produced a new translation of the original texts which uncovers a mystical teaching underlying the sayings and rituals instituted by the Ancient Egyptian Sages and Saints. "Once the philosophy of Ancient Egypt is understood as a mystical tradition instead of as a religion or primitive mythology, it reveals its secrets which if practiced today will lead anyone to discover the glory of spiritual self-discovery. The Pert em Heru is in every way comparable to the Indian Upanishads or the Tibetan Book of the Dead." □ $28.95   ISBN# 1-884564-28-3 Size: 8½" X 11

20.   *African Religion VOL. 1- ANUNIAN THEOLOGY THE MYSTERIES OF RA* The Philosophy of Anu and The Mystical Teachings of The Ancient Egyptian Creation Myth Discover the mystical teachings contained in the Creation Myth and the gods and goddesses who brought creation and human beings into existence. The Creation myth of Anu is the source of Anunian Theology but also of the other main theological systems of Ancient Egypt that also influenced other world religions including Christianity, Hinduism and Buddhism. The Creation Myth holds the key to understanding the universe and for attaining spiritual Enlightenment. ISBN: 1-884564-38-0 $19.95

21.   *African Religion VOL 3: Memphite Theology: MYSTERIES OF MIND* Mystical Psychology & Mental Health for Enlightenment and Immortality based on the Ancient Egyptian Philosophy of Menefer -Mysticism of Ptah, Egyptian Physics and Yoga Metaphysics and the Hidden properties of Matter.   This volume uncovers the mystical psychology of the Ancient Egyptian wisdom teachings centering on the philosophy of the Ancient Egyptian city of Menefer (Memphite Theology). How to understand the mind and how to control the senses and lead the mind to health, clarity and mystical self-discovery. This Volume will also go deeper into the philosophy of God as creation and will explore the concepts of modern science and how they correlate with ancient teachings. This Volume will lay the ground work for the understanding of the philosophy of universal consciousness and the initiatic/yogic insight into who or what is God? ISBN 1-884564-07-0 $22.95

22.   *AFRICAN RELIGION VOLUME 5: THE GODDESS AND THE EGYPTIAN MYSTERIESTHE PATH OF THE GODDESS THE GODDESS PATH* The Secret Forms of the Goddess and the Rituals of Resurrection The Supreme Being may be worshipped as father or as mother. *Ushet Rekhat* or *Mother Worship*, is the spiritual process of worshiping the Divine in the form of the Divine Goddess. It celebrates the most important forms of the Goddess including *Nathor, Maat, Aset, Arat, Amentet and Hathor* and explores their mystical meaning as well as the rising of *Sirius,* the star of Aset (Aset) and the new birth of Hor (Heru). The end of the year is a time of reckoning, reflection and engendering a new or renewed positive movement toward attaining spiritual Enlightenment. The Mother Worship devotional meditation ritual, performed on five days during the month of December and on New Year's Eve, is based on the Ushet Rekhit. During the ceremony, the cosmic forces, symbolized by Sirius - and the constellation of Orion --, are harnessed through the understanding and devotional attitude of the participant. This propitiation draws the light of wisdom and health to all those who share in the ritual, leading to prosperity and wisdom. $14.95 ISBN 1-884564 18-6

23.   *THE MYSTICAL JOURNEY FROM JESUS TO CHRIST* Discover the ancient Egyptian origins of Christianity before the Catholic Church and learn the mystical teachings given by Jesus to assist all humanity in becoming Christlike. Discover the secret meaning of the Gospels that were discovered in Egypt. Also discover how and why so many Christian churches came into being. Discover that the Bible still holds the keys to mystical realization even though its original writings were changed by the church. Discover how to practice the original teachings of Christianity which leads to the Kingdom of Heaven. $24.95   ISBN# 1-884564-05-4 size: 8½" X 11"

24. *THE STORY OF ASAR, ASET AND HERU:* An Ancient Egyptian Legend (For Children)　Now for the first time, the most ancient myth of Ancient Egypt comes alive for children. Inspired by the books *The Asarian Resurrection: The Ancient Egyptian Bible* and *The Mystical Teachings of The Asarian Resurrection, The Story of Asar, Aset and Heru* is an easy to understand and thrilling tale which inspired the children of Ancient Egypt to aspire to greatness and righteousness.　If you and your child have enjoyed stories like *The Lion King* and *Star Wars you will love The Story of Asar, Aset and Heru.* Also, if you know the story of Jesus and Krishna you will discover than Ancient Egypt had a similar myth and that this myth carries important spiritual teachings for living a fruitful and fulfilling life.　This book may be used along with *The Parents Guide To The Asarian Resurrection Myth: How to Teach Yourself and Your Child the Principles of Universal Mystical Religion.* The guide provides some background to the Asarian Resurrection myth and it also gives insight into the mystical teachings contained in it which you may introduce to your child. It is designed for parents who wish to grow spiritually with their children and it serves as an introduction for those who would like to study the Asarian Resurrection Myth in depth and to practice its teachings. 8.5" X 11"　ISBN: 1-884564-31-3 $12.95

25. *THE PARENTS GUIDE TO THE AUSARIAN RESURRECTION MYTH:* How to Teach Yourself and Your Child the Principles of Universal Mystical Religion.　This insightful manual brings for the timeless wisdom of the ancient through the Ancient Egyptian myth of Asar, Aset and Heru and the mystical teachings contained in it for parents who want to guide their children to understand and practice the teachings of mystical spirituality. This manual may be used with the children's storybook *The Story of Asar, Aset and Heru* by Dr. Muata Abhaya Ashby.　ISBN: 1-884564-30-5　$16.95

26. *HEALING THE CRIMINAL HEART.* Introduction to Maat Philosophy, Yoga and Spiritual Redemption Through the Path of Virtue　Who is a criminal? Is there such a thing as a criminal heart? What is the source of evil and sinfulness and is there any way to rise above it? Is there redemption for those who have committed sins, even the worst crimes? Ancient Egyptian mystical psychology holds important answers to these questions. Over ten thousand years ago mystical psychologists, the Sages of Ancient Egypt, studied and charted the human mind and spirit and laid out a path which will lead to spiritual redemption, prosperity and Enlightenment.　This introductory volume brings forth the teachings of the Asarian Resurrection, the most important myth of Ancient Egypt, with relation to the faults of human existence: anger, hatred, greed, lust, animosity, discontent, ignorance, egoism jealousy, bitterness, and a myriad of psycho-spiritual ailments which keep a human being in a state of negativity and adversity　ISBN: 1-884564-17-8 $15.95

27. *TEMPLE RITUAL OF THE ANCIENT EGYPTIAN MYSTERIES--THEATER & DRAMA OF THE ANCIENT EGYPTIAN MYSTERIES*: Details the practice of the mysteries and ritual program of the temple and the philosophy an practice of the ritual of the mysteries, its purpose and execution. Featuring the Ancient Egyptian stage play-"The Enlightenment of Hathor' Based on an Ancient Egyptian Drama, The original Theater -Mysticism of the Temple of Hetheru 1-884564-14-3 $19.95　By Dr. Muata Ashby

28.　GUIDE TO PRINT ON DEMAND: SELF-PUBLISH FOR PROFIT, SPIRITUAL FULFILLMENT AND SERVICE TO HUMANITY Everyone asks us how we produced so many books in such a short time. Here are the secrets to writing and producing books that uplift humanity and how to get them printed for a fraction of the regular cost. Anyone can become an author even if they have limited funds. All that is necessary is the willingness to learn how the printing and book business work and the desire to follow the special instructions given here for preparing your manuscript format. Then you take your work directly to the non-traditional companies who can produce your books for less than the traditional book printer can. ISBN: 1-884564-40-2　$16.95 U. S.

29. *Egyptian Mysteries: Vol. 1,* Shetaut Neter What are the Mysteries? For thousands of years the spiritual tradition of Ancient Egypt, S*hetaut Neter,* "The Egyptian Mysteries," "The Secret Teachings," have fascinated, tantalized and amazed the world. At one time exalted and recognized as the highest culture of the world, by Africans, Europeans, Asiatics, Hindus, Buddhists and other cultures of the ancient world, in time it was shunned by the emerging orthodox world religions. Its temples desecrated, its philosophy maligned, its tradition spurned, its philosophy dormant in the mystical *Medu Neter*, the mysterious hieroglyphic texts which hold the secret symbolic meaning that has scarcely been discerned up to now.　What are the secrets of *Nehast* {spiritual awakening and emancipation, resurrection}. More than just a literal translation, this volume is for awakening to the secret code *Shetitu* of the teaching which was not deciphered by Egyptologists, nor could be understood by ordinary spiritualists. This book is a reinstatement of the original science made available for our times, to the reincarnated followers of Ancient Egyptian culture and the prospect of spiritual freedom to break the bonds of *Khemn,* "ignorance," and slavery to evil forces: *Såaa* . ISBN: 1-884564-41-0　$19.99

30. *EGYPTIAN MYSTERIES VOL 2:* Dictionary of Gods and Goddesses This book is about the mystery of neteru, the gods and goddesses of Ancient Egypt (Kamit, Kemet). Neteru means "Gods and Goddesses." But the Neterian teaching of Neteru represents more than the usual limited modern day concept of "divinities" or "spirits." The Neteru of Kamit are also metaphors, cosmic principles and vehicles for the enlightening teachings of Shetaut Neter (Ancient Egyptian-African Religion). Actually they are the elements for one of the most advanced systems of spirituality ever conceived in human history. Understanding the concept of neteru provides a firm basis for spiritual evolution and the

pathway for viable culture, peace on earth and a healthy human society.   Why is it important to have gods and goddesses in our lives? In order for spiritual evolution to be possible, once a human being has accepted that there is existence after death and there is a transcendental being who exists beyond time and space knowledge, human beings need a connection to that which transcends the ordinary experience of human life in time and space and a means to understand the transcendental reality beyond the mundane reality. ISBN: 1-884564-23-2 $21.95

31. *EGYPTIAN MYSTERIES VOL. 3* The Priests and Priestesses of Ancient Egypt This volume details the path of Neterian priesthood, the joys, challenges and rewards of advanced Neterian life, the teachings that allowed the priests and priestesses to manage the most long lived civilization in human history and how that path can be adopted today; for those who want to tread the path of the Clergy of Shetaut Neter. ISBN: 1-884564-53-4 $24.95

32. *The War of Heru and Set:* The Struggle of Good and Evil for Control of the World and The Human Soul This volume contains a novelized version of the Asarian Resurrection myth that is based on the actual scriptures presented in the Book Asarian Religion (old name –Resurrecting Osiris). This volume is prepared in the form of a screenplay and can be easily adapted to be used as a stage play. Spiritual seeking is a mythic journey that has many emotional highs and lows, ecstasies and depressions, victories and frustrations. This is the War of Life that is played out in the myth as the struggle of Heru and Set and those are mythic characters that represent the human Higher and Lower self. How to understand the war and emerge victorious in the journey o life? The ultimate victory and fulfillment can be experienced, which is not changeable or lost in time. The purpose of myth is to convey the wisdom of life through the story of divinities who show the way to overcome the challenges and foibles of life. In this volume the feelings and emotions of the characters of the myth have been highlighted to show the deeply rich texture of the Ancient Egyptian myth. This myth contains deep spiritual teachings and insights into the nature of self, of God and the mysteries of life and the means to discover the true meaning of life and thereby achieve the true purpose of life. To become victorious in the battle of life means to become the King (or Queen) of Egypt.Have you seen movies like The Lion King, Hamlet, The Odyssey, or The Little Buddha? These have been some of the most popular movies in modern times. The Sema Institute of Yoga is dedicated to researching and presenting the wisdom and culture of ancient Africa. The Script is designed to be produced as a motion picture but may be addapted for the theater as well. $21.95   copyright 1998 By Dr. Muata Ashby ISBN 1-8840564-44-5

33. *AFRICAN DIONYSUS: FROM EGYPT TO GREECE:* The Kamitan Origins of Greek Culture and Religion ISBN: 1-884564-47-X   From Egypt to Greece   This insightful manual is a reference to Ancient Egyptian mythology and philosophy and its correlation to what later became known as Greek and Rome mythology and philosophy. It outlines the basic tenets of the mythologies and shoes the ancient origins of Greek culture in Ancient Egypt. This volume also documents the origins of the Greek alphabet in Egypt as well as Greek religion, myth and philosophy of the gods and goddesses from Egypt from the myth of Atlantis and archaic period with the Minoans to the Classical period. This volume also acts as a resource for Colleges students who would like to set up fraternities and sororities based on the original Ancient Egyptian principles of Sheti and Maat philosophy. ISBN: 1-884564-47-X $22.95 U.S.

34. *THE FORTY TWO PRECEPTS OF MAAT, THE PHILOSOPHY OF RIGHTEOUS ACTION AND THE ANCIENT EGYPTIAN WISDOM TEXTS* <u>ADVANCED STUDIES</u> This manual is designed for use with the 1998 Maat Philosophy Class conducted by Dr. Muata Ashby. This is a detailed study of Maat Philosophy. It contains a compilation of the 42 laws or precepts of Maat and the corresponding principles which they represent along with the teachings of the ancient Egyptian Sages relating to each. Maat philosophy was the basis of Ancient Egyptian society and government as well as the heart of Ancient Egyptian myth and spirituality. Maat is at once a goddess, a cosmic force and a living social doctrine, which promotes social harmony and thereby paves the way for spiritual evolution in all levels of society. ISBN: 1-884564-48-8 $16.95 U.S.

35.   THE SECRET LOTUS: *Poetry of Enlightenment*
Discover the mystical sentiment of the Kemetic teaching as expressed through the poetry of Sebai Muata Ashby. The teaching of spiritual awakening is uniquely experienced when the poetic sensibility is present. This first volume contains the poems written between 1996 and 2003. **1-884564--16 -X $16.99**

36. The Ancient Egyptian Buddha: The Ancient Egyptian Origins of Buddhism

This book is a compilation of several sections of a larger work, a book by the name of African Origins of Civilization, Religion, Yoga Mysticism and Ethics Philosophy. It also contains some additional evidences not contained in the larger work that demonstrate the correlation between Ancient Egyptian Religion and Buddhism. This book is one of several compiled short volumes that has been compiled so as to facilitate access to specific subjects contained in the larger work which is over 680 pages long. These short and small volumes have been specifically designed to cover one subject in a brief and low cost format. This present volume, The Ancient Egyptian Buddha: The Ancient Egyptian Origins of Buddhism, formed one subject in the larger work; actually it was one chapter of the larger work. However, this volume has some new additional evidences and comparisons of Buddhist and Neterian (Ancient Egyptian) philosophies not previously discussed. It was felt that this subject needed to be discussed because even in the early 21st century, the idea persists that Buddhism originated only in India independently. Yet there is ample evidence from ancient writings and perhaps more importantly, iconographical evidences from the Ancient Egyptians and early Buddhists themselves that prove otherwise. This handy volume has been designed to be accessible to young adults and all others who would like to have an easy reference with documentation on this important subject. This is an important subject because the frame of reference with which we look at a culture depends strongly on our conceptions about its origins. in this case, if we look at the Buddhism as an Asiatic religion we would treat it and it's culture in one way. If we id as African [Ancient Egyptian] we not only would see it in a different light but we also must ascribe Africa with a glorious legacy that matches any other culture in human history and gave rise to one of the present day most important religious philosophies. We would also look at the culture and philosophies of the Ancient Egyptians as having African insights that offer us greater depth into the Buddhist philosophies. Those insights inform our knowledge about other African traditions and we can also begin to understand in a deeper way the effect of Ancient Egyptian culture on African culture and also on the Asiatic as well. We would also be able to discover the glorious and wondrous teaching of mystical philosophy that Ancient Egyptian Shetaut Neter religion offers, that is as powerful as any other mystic system of spiritual philosophy in the world today. ISBN: 1-884564-61-5 $28.95

37. The Death of American Empire: Neo-conservatism, Theocracy, Economic Imperialism, Environmental Disaster and the Collapse of Civilization

This work is a collection of essays relating to social and economic, leadership, and ethics, ecological and religious issues that are facing the world today in order to understand the course of history that has led humanity to its present condition and then arrive at positive solutions that will lead to better outcomes for all humanity. It surveys the development and decline of major empires throughout history and focuses on the creation of American Empire along with the social, political and economic policies that led to the prominence of the United States of America as a Superpower including the rise of the political control of the neo-con political philosophy including militarism and the military industrial complex in American politics and the rise of the religious right into and American Theocracy movement. This volume details, through historical and current events, the psychology behind the dominance of western culture in world politics through the "Superpower Syndrome Mandatory Conflict Complex" that drives the Superpower culture to establish itself above all others and then act hubristically to dominate world culture through legitimate influences as well as coercion, media censorship and misinformation leading to international hegemony and world conflict. This volume also details the financial policies that gave rise to American prominence in the global economy, especially after World War II, and promoted American preeminence over the world economy through Globalization as well as the environmental policies, including the oil economy, that are promoting degradation of the world ecology and contribute to the decline of America as an Empire culture. This volume finally explores the factors pointing to the decline of the American Empire economy and imperial power and what to expect in the aftermath of American prominence and how to survive the decline while at the same time promoting policies and social-economic-religious-political changes that are needed in order to promote the emergence of a beneficial and sustainable culture. **$25.95soft** 1-884564-25-9, Hard Cover **$29.95soft** 1-884564-45-3

38. The African Origins of Hatha Yoga: And its Ancient Mystical Teaching

The subject of this present volume, The Ancient Egyptian Origins of Yoga Postures, formed one subject in the larger works, African Origins of Civilization Religion, Yoga Mysticism and Ethics Philosophy and the Book Egypt and India is the section of the book African Origins of Civilization. Those works contain the collection of all correlations between Ancient Egypt and India. This volume also contains some additional information not contained in the previous work. It was felt that this subject needed to be discussed more directly, being treated in one volume, as opposed to being contained in the larger work along with other subjects, because even in the early 21st century, the idea persists that the Yoga and specifically, Yoga Postures, were invented and developed only in India. The Ancient Egyptians were peoples originally from Africa who were, in ancient times, colonists in India. Therefore it is no surprise that many Indian traditions including religious and Yogic, would be found earlier in Ancient Egypt. Yet there is ample evidence from ancient writings and perhaps more importantly, iconographical evidences from the Ancient Egyptians themselves and the Indians themselves that prove the connection between Ancient Egypt and India as well as the existence of a discipline of Yoga Postures in Ancient Egypt long before its practice in India. This handy volume has been designed to be accessible to young adults and all others who would like to have an easy reference with documentation on this important subject. This is an important subject because the frame of reference with which we look at a culture depends strongly on our conceptions about its origins. In this case, if we look at the Ancient Egyptians as Asiatic peoples we would treat them and their culture in one way. If we see them as Africans we not only see them in a different light but we also must ascribe Africa with a glorious legacy that matches any other culture in human history. We would also look at the culture and philosophies of the Ancient Egyptians as having African insights instead of Asiatic ones. Those insights inform our knowledge bout other African traditions and we can also begin to understand in a deeper way the effect of Ancient Egyptian culture on African culture and also on the Asiatic as well. When we discover the deeper and more ancient practice of the postures system in Ancient Egypt that was called "Hatha Yoga" in India, we are able to find a new and expanded understanding of the practice that constitutes a discipline of spiritual practice that informs and revitalizes the Indian practices as well as all spiritual disciplines. $19.99 ISBN 1-884564-60-7

39. The Black Ancient Egyptians

This present volume, The Black Ancient Egyptians: The Black African Ancestry of the Ancient Egyptians, formed one subject in the larger work: The African Origins of Civilization, Religion, Yoga Mysticism and Ethics Philosophy. It was felt that this subject needed to be discussed because even in the early 21st century, the idea persists that the Ancient Egyptians were peoples originally from Asia Minor who came into North-East Africa. Yet there is ample evidence from ancient writings and perhaps more importantly, iconographical evidences from the Ancient Egyptians themselves that proves otherwise. This handy volume has been designed to be accessible to young adults and all others who would like to have an easy reference with documentation on this important subject. This is an important subject because the frame of reference with which we look at a culture depends strongly on our conceptions about its origins. in this case, if we look at the Ancient Egyptians as Asiatic peoples we would treat them and their culture in one way. If we see them as Africans we not only see them in a different light but we also must ascribe Africa with a glorious legacy that matches any other culture in human history. We would also look at the culture and philosophies of the Ancient Egyptians as having African insights instead of Asiatic ones. Those insights inform our knowledge bout other African traditions and we can also begin to understand in a deeper way the effect of Ancient Egyptian culture on African culture and also on the Asiatic as well. ISBN 1-884564-21-6 $19.99

40. The Limits of Faith: The Failure of Faith-based Religions and the Solution to the Meaning of Life

faith belief in something without proof? And if so is there never to be any proof or discovery? If so what is the need of intellect? If faith trust in something that is real is that reality historical, literal or metaphorical or philosophical? If knowledge is an essential element in ath why should there by so much emphasis on believing and not on understanding in the modern practice of religion? This volume is a mpilation of essays related to the nature of religious faith in the context of its inception in human history as well as its meaning for religious practice and relations between religions in modern times. Faith has come to be regarded as a virtuous goal in life. However, many people have asked how can it be that an endeavor that is supposed to be dedicated to spiritual upliftment has led to more conflict in human history than any other social factor? ISBN 1884564631 SOFT COVER - $19.99, ISBN 1884564623 HARD COVER -$28.95

41. Redemption of The Criminal Heart Through Kemetic Spirituality and Maat Philosophy

Special book dedicated to inmates, their families and members of the Law Enforcement community to promote understanding of the cause of transgressions and how to resolve those issues so that a human being may rediscover their humanity and come back to the family of humanity and also regain the capacity to fully engage in positive spiritual evolution. ISBN: 1-884564-70-4

42. COMPARATIVE MYTHOLOGY

What are Myth and Culture and what is their importance for understanding the development of societies, human evolution and the search for meaning? What is the purpose of culture and how do cultures evolve? What are the elements of a culture and how can those elements be broken down and the constituent parts of a culture understood and compared? How do cultures interact? How does enculturation occur and how do people interact with other cultures? How do the processes of acculturation and cooptation occur and what does this mean for the development of a society? How can the study of myths and the elements of culture help in understanding the meaning of life and the means to promote understanding and peace in the world of human activity? This volume is the exposition of a method for studying and comparing cultures, myths and other social aspects of a society. It is an expansion on the Cultural Category Factor Correlation method for studying and comparing myths, cultures, religions and other aspects of human culture. It was originally introduced in the year 2002. This volume contains an expanded treatment as well as several refinements along with examples of the application of the method. the apparent. I hope you enjoy these art renditions as serene reflections of the mysteries of life. ISBN: 1-884564-72-0
Book price $21.95

43. CONVERSATION WITH GOD: Revelations of the Important Questions of Life
$24.99 U.S.

This volume contains a grouping of some of the questions that have been submitted to Sebai Dr. Muata Ashby. They are efforts by many aspirants to better understand and practice the teachings of mystical spirituality. It is said that when sages are asked spiritual questions they are relaying the wisdom of God, the Goddess, the Higher Self, etc. There is a very special quality about the Q & A process that does not occur during a regular lecture session. Certain points come out that would not come out otherwise due to the nature of the process which ideally occurs after a lecture. Having been to a certain degree enlightened by a lecture certain new questions arise and the answers to these have the effect of elevating the teaching of the lecture to even higher levels. Therefore, enjoy these exchanges and may they lead you to enlightenment, peace and prosperity. ISBN: 1-884564-68-2

44. MYSTIC ART PAINTINGS

(with Full Color images) This book contains a collection of the small number of paintings that I have created over the years. Some were used as early book covers and others were done simply to express certain spiritual feelings; some were created for no purpose except to express the joy of color and the feeling of relaxed freedom. All are to elicit mystical awakening in the viewer. Writing a book or philosophy is like sculpture, the more the work is rewritten the reflections and ideas become honed and take form and become clearer and imbued with intellectual beauty. Mystic music is like meditation, a world of its own that exists about 1 inch above ground wherein the musician does not touch the ground. Mystic Graphic Art is meditation in form, color, image and reflected image which opens the door to the reality behind the apparent. I hope you enjoy these art renditions and my reflections on them as serene reflections of the mysteries of life, as visual renditions of the philosophy I have written about over the years. ISBN 1-884564-69-0 $19.95

45. ANCIENT EGYPTIAN HIEROGLYPHS FOR BEGINNERS

This brief guide was prepared for those inquiring about how to enter into Hieroglyphic studies on their own at home or in study groups. First of all you should know that there are a few institutions around the world which teach how to read the Hieroglyphic text but due to the nature of the study there are perhaps only a handful of people who can read fluently. It is possible for anyone with average intelligence to achieve a high level of proficiency in reading inscriptions on temples and artifacts; however, reading extensive texts is another issue entirely. However, this introduction will give you entry into those texts if assisted by dictionaries and other aids. Most Egyptologists have a basic knowledge and keep dictionaries and notes handy when it comes to dealing with more difficult texts. Medtu Neter or the Ancient Egyptian hieroglyphic language has been considered as a "Dead Language." However, dead languages have always been studied by individuals who for the most part have taught themselves through various means. This book will discuss those means and how to use them most efficiently. ISBN 1884564429 **$28.95**

46. ON THE MYSTERIES: Wisdom of An Ancient Egyptian Sage -with Foreword by Muata Ashby

This volume, On the Mysteries, by Iamblichus (Abamun) is a unique form or scripture out of the Ancient Egyptian religious tradition. It is written in a form that is not usual or which is not usually found in the remnants of Ancient Egyptian scriptures. It is in the form of teacher and disciple, much like the Eastern scriptures such as Bhagavad Gita or the Upanishads. This form of writing may not have been necessary in Ancient times, because the format of teaching in Egypt was different prior to the conquest period by the Persians, Assyrians, Greeks and later the Romans. The question and answer format can be found but such extensive discourses and corrections of misunderstandings within the context of a teacher - disciple relationship is not usual. It therefore provides extensive insights into the times when it was written and the state of practice of Ancient Egyptian and other mystery religions. This has important implications for our times because we are today, as in the Greco-Roman period, also besieged with varied religions and new age philosophies as well as social strife and war. How can we understand our times and also make sense of the forest of spiritual traditions? How can we cut through the cacophony of religious fanaticism, and ignorance as well as misconceptions about the mysteries on the other in order to discover the true purpose of religion and the secret teachings that open up the mysteries of life and the way to enlightenment and immortality? This book, which comes to us from long ago, offers us transcendental wisdom that applied to the world two thousand years ago as well as our world today. ISBN 1-884564-64-X $25.95

47. The Ancient Egyptian Wisdom Texts -Compiled by Muata Ashby
The Ancient Egyptian Wisdom Texts are a genre of writings from the ancient culture that have survived to the present and provide a vibrant record of the practice of spiritual evolution otherwise known as religion or yoga philosophy in Ancient Egypt. The principle focus of the Wisdom Texts is the cultivation of understanding, peace, harmony, selfless service, self-control, Inner fulfillment and spiritual realization. When these factors are cultivated in human life, the virtuous qualities in a human being begin to manifest and sinfulness, ignorance and negativity diminish until a person is able to enter into higher consciousness, the coveted goal of all civilizations. It is this virtuous mode of life which opens the door to self-discovery and spiritual enlightenment. Therefore, the Wisdom Texts are important scriptures on the subject of human nature, spiritual psychology and mystical philosophy. The teachings presented in the Wisdom Texts form the foundation of religion as well as the guidelines for conducting the affairs of every area of social interaction including commerce, education, the army, marriage, and especially the legal system. These texts were sources for the famous 42 Precepts of Maat of the Pert M Heru (Book of the Dead), essential regulations of good conduct to develop virtue and purity in order to attain higher consciousness and immortality after death. ISBN1-884564-65-8 $18.95

48. THE KEMETIC TREE OF LIFE
THE KEMETIC TREE OF LIFE: Newly Revealed Ancient Egyptian Cosmology and Metaphysics for Higher Consciousness The Tree of Life is a roadmap of a journey which explains how Creation came into being and how it will end. It also explains what Creation is composed of and also what human beings are and what they are composed of. It also explains the process of Creation, how Creation develops, as well as who created Creation and where that entity may be found. It also explains how a human being may discover that entity and in so doing also discover the secrets of Creation, the meaning of life and the means to break free from the pathetic condition of human limitation and mortality in order to discover the higher realms of being by discovering the principles, the levels of existence that are beyond the simple physical and material aspects of life. This book contains color plates **ISBN: 1-884564-74-7**
$27.95 U.S.

49. APPLIED ETHICS FOR MODERN AFRICAN SOCIETY: Based on African Proverbial Wisdom Teachings by Muata Ashby

This volume sets out the fundamental principles of African ethics and their practical application for use by an organization or society that seeks to model its ethical/spiritual policies using the Traditional African values and concepts of ethical human behavior for the proper sustenance and management of society. Furthermore, this outline will provide guidance as to how the Traditional African Ethics may be viewed and applied taking into consideration the technological and social advancements to the present. This volume also presents the principles of ethical culture and their relation to the metaphysical evolution of a society. It also references each ethical principle to specific injunctions from Traditional African Proverbial Wisdom teachings from varied Precolonial African societies from Yoruba to Ashanti, Kemet to Malawi, Nigeria to Ethiopia, Galla to Ghana and many more… ISBN: 1-884564-77-1 $16.95 u.s.

50. "Little Book of Neter" a summary of the most important teachings of Shetaut Neter (Ancient Egyptian religion) for all aspirants to have for easy reference **guide to the basic practices and fundamental teachings $5.00 (Soft) ISBN: 1-884564-58-5**

51. Dollar Crisis: The Collapse of Society and Redemption Through Ancient Egyptian Monetary Policy (Paperback) by Muata Ashby   This book is about the problems of the US economy and the imminent collapse of the U.S. Dollar and its dire consequences for the US economy and the world. It is also about the corruption in government, economics and social order that led to this point. Also it is about survival, how to make it through this perhaps most trying period in the history of the United States. Also it is about the ancient wisdom of life that allowed an ancient civilization to grow beyond the destructive corruptions of ignorance and power so that the people of today may gain insight into the nature of their condition, how they got there and what needs to be done in order to salvage what is left and rebuild a society that is sustainable, beneficial and an example for all humanity. $18.99 u.s.
- **ISBN-10:** 1884564763
- **ISBN-13:** 978-1884564765

Music Based on the Prt M Hru and other Kemetic Texts
Available on Compact Disc $14.99 and Audio Cassette $9.99

Adorations to the Goddess

Music for Worship of the Goddess

NEW Egyptian Yoga Music CD
by Sehu Maa
Ancient Egyptian Music CD
Instrumental Music played on reproductions of Ancient Egyptian Instruments– Ideal for <u>meditation</u> and reflection on the Divine and for the practice of spiritual programs and <u>Yoga exercise sessions.</u>

©1999 By Muata Ashby
CD $14.99 –

MERIT'S INSPIRATION
NEW Egyptian Yoga Music CD
by Sehu Maa
Ancient Egyptian Music CD
Instrumental Music played on
reproductions of Ancient Egyptian Instruments– Ideal for <u>meditation</u> and
reflection on the Divine and for the practice of spiritual programs and <u>Yoga exercise sessions.</u>
©1999 By
Muata Ashby
CD $14.99 –
UPC# 761527100429

ANORATIONS TO RA AND HETHERU
NEW Egyptian Yoga Music CD
By Sehu Maa (Muata Ashby)
Based on the Words of Power of Ra and Hetheru
played on reproductions of Ancient Egyptian Instruments **Ancient Egyptian Instruments used: Voice, Clapping, Nefer Lute, Tar Drum, Sistrums, Cymbals** – The Chants, Devotions, Rhythms and Festive Songs Of the Neteru – Ideal for meditation, and devotional singing and dancing.
©1999 By Muata Ashby
CD $14.99 –
UPC# 761527100221

SONGS TO ASAR ASET AND HERU
NEW
Egyptian Yoga Music CD
By Sehu Maa
played on reproductions of Ancient Egyptian Instruments– The Chants, Devotions, Rhythms and Festive Songs Of the Neteru - Ideal for meditation, and devotional singing and dancing.
ased on the Words of Power of Asar (Asar), Aset (Aset) and Heru (Heru) Om Asar Aset Heru is the third in a series of usical explorations of the Kemetic (Ancient Egyptian) tradition of music. Its ideas are based on the Ancient gyptian Religion of Asar, Aset and Heru and it is designed for listening, meditation and worship. ©1999 By uata Ashby

CD $14.99 –
UPC# 761527100122

HAARI OM: ANCIENT EGYPT MEETS INDIA IN MUSIC
NEW Music CD
By Sehu Maa

The Chants, Devotions, Rhythms and
Festive Songs Of the Ancient Egypt and India, harmonized and played on reproductions of ancient instruments along with modern instruments and beats. Ideal for meditation, and devotional singing and dancing.
Haari Om is the fourth in a series of musical explorations of the Kemetic (Ancient Egyptian) and Indian traditions of music, chanting and devotional spiritual practice. Its ideas are based on the Ancient Egyptian Yoga spirituality and Indian Yoga spirituality.

©1999 By Muata Ashby
CD $14.99 –
UPC# 761527100528

RA AKHU: THE GLORIOUS LIGHT
NEW
Egyptian Yoga Music CD
By Sehu Maa

The fifth collection of original music compositions based on the Teachings and Words of The Trinity, the God Asar and the Goddess Nebethet, the Divinity Aten, the God Heru, and the Special Meditation Hekau or Words of Power of Ra from the Ancient Egyptian Tomb of Seti I and more...
played on reproductions of Ancient Egyptian Instruments and modern instruments - Ancient Egyptian Instruments used: Voice, Clapping, Nefer Lute, Tar Drum, Sistrums, Cymbals
– The Chants, Devotions, Rhythms and Festive Songs Of the Neteru – Ideal for meditation, and devotional singing and dancing.
©1999 By Muata Ashby
CD $14.99 –
UPC# 761527100825

GLORIES OF THE DIVINE MOTHER
Based on the hieroglyphic text of the worship of Goddess Net.
The Glories of The Great Mother
©2000 Muata Ashby
CD $14.99 UPC# 761527101129`

Online Book Store

www.Egyptianyoga.com

Order Form

Telephone orders: Call Toll Free: 1(305) 378-6253. Have your AMEX, Optima, Visa or MasterCard ready.

    Fax orders: 1-(305) 378-6253   E-MAIL ADDRESS: Semayoga@aol.com

Postal Orders: Sema Institute of Yoga, P.O. Box 570459, Miami, Fl. 33257. USA.

Please send the following books and / or tapes.

ITEM

_____Cost $_____

_____Cost $_____

_____Cost $_____

_____Cost $_____

_____Cost $_____

                                                              Total $_____

Name:_____

Physical Address:_____

City:_____ State:_____ Zip:_____

Sales tax: Please add 6.5% for books shipped to Florida addresses

_____Shipping: $6.50 for first book and .50¢ for each additional

_____Shipping: Outside US $5.00 for first book and $3.00 for each additional

_____Payment:_____

_____Check -Include Driver License #:

        _____

_____Credit card: _____ Visa, _____ MasterCard, _____ Optima,

_____ AMEX.

Card number:_____

Name on card:_____ Exp. date:_____/_____

Copyright 1995-2005 Dr. R. Muata Abhaya Ashby
Sema Institute of Yoga
P.O.Box 570459, Miami, Florida, 33257
(305) 378-6253 Fax: (305) 378-6253

CPSIA information can be obtained
at www.ICGtesting.com
Printed in the USA
LVHW012250261221
707024LV00006B/47